Birds of Yosemite and the East Slope

Keith Hansen 1986

Birds of Yosemite

and the East Slope

DAVID GAINES

Illustrated by Keith F. Hansen

ARTEMISIA PRESS

Lee Vining, California

Cover painting: California Towhee and Williamson's Sapsucker, by Keith F. Hansen
Spine painting: Great Gray Owl, by Keith F. Hansen
Back cover painting: Eared Grebes on Mono Lake, by Keith F. Hansen

ISBN 0-932347-05-3
Design and layout by David Gaines.
Printed in the United States of America.

ARTEMISIA PRESS
P.O. Box 119
Lee Vining, CA 93541

To Ma Nature for Yosemite and her birds.

One touch of nature makes the whole world kin;
and it is truly wonderful how love-telling the small voices of
these birds are, and how far they reach through the woods
into one another's hearts and into ours...

John Muir

It is the province of this work to appreciate
and, so far as it is possible, to express, not alone the conceptual
entities of science called species, but the very persons and lives
of those hundreds of millions of our fellow travelers and
sojourners, called birds..

William Leon Dawson

Go and ask...
the birds of the air to inform you,
or tell the creatures that crawl to teach you,
and the fishes of the sea to give you instruction...

Job 12:7-8.

Introduction to the 1992 edition

The first edition of this book was in press when Dave died in an auto accident; he never saw the finished product.

Since 1988 a lot of birdwatching has gone on, especially on the east side. When it came time to reprint I wanted to add in the new species, and to update with new statuses and extreme dates. I have drawn from the accessible reports sent to the American Birds editors. I plan on keeping this book current with updates, so send in your exceptional sightings to the American Birds editors. If you are in the Mono Basin stop by the Mono Lake Committee headquarters to check or add to the rare bird record board.

I collected significant birdwatching records from areas just east of the book's stated boundaries. I have included canyons and lakes to the east of Glass and Granite mountains. Since they are not on the endpiece maps, I refer to these sites as "just east of our area". I have also broken with Dave's style and common usage by deleting the misnomer "lake" to any major reservoir.

There have been some changes in the past five years to the Mono Basin. In 1989, due to a temporary court order, three creeks resumed their flows to Mono Lake. The creeks continue to be worked on by restoration specialists. Some riparian vegetation has become reestablished attracting birds back after a fifty year hiatus.

In 1991, Mono Lake was designated a reserve in the Western Hemisphere Shorebird Reserve Network. The network is a voluntary collaboration of government and private organizations committed to the protection of invaluable shorebird migratory and breeding sites. Annual spring and fall lake censuses have expanded our knowledge of what shorebird species use Mono Lake in these seasons.

Thanks to everyone who helped, especially Lauren Davis, Dave DeSante, Helen Green, Peter Metropulos, Michael Patten, Dave Shuford, and Emilie Strauss. And of course to my two kids who wondered when mom was ever going to be done with "the bird book".

Let the rain and snow fall and the creeks flow!

Sally Gaines
Mono Lake
Spring Equinox, 1992

Preface

The Yosemite Sierra is a powerful place. The source of that power is not just falling water, granite walls, giant trees, desert lakes and Great Gray Owls. It is the organic wholeness of a land still free, or almost free, of human disturbance. Not just a great national park, but a great *natural* park.

Unlike humans, birds are not tourists in the Yosemite Sierra. In ways as varied as the 343 species, they sustain themselves and make their homes in the region's forests, woodlands, meadows, marshes, scrub and other diverse habitats.

For over 20 years I have pilgrimaged to the Yosemite Sierra to befriend its birds. In this book, I detail their distribution, abundance and habitat requirements.

The project of reviewing and synthesizing a century of published and unpublished bird records grew from conversations with Yosemite Park naturalists Michael Sutton and Clyde Morris and biologists Stephen Granholm and Ted Beedy during the summer of 1976. We felt that detailed descriptions of the status and haunts of Yosemite's birds would be welcomed by birdwatchers and ornithologists alike. Moreover we believed that such descriptions could serve as baselines for monitoring future trends in avian populations and, in a larger sense, the quality and health of the natural environment.

During the following year, I summarized a wealth of information in my book, *Birds of the Yosemite Sierra*, which was published in 1977. I included, not just Yosemite National Park, but the east slope, Mono Lake and other, adjacent areas as well.

In the decade since that book appeared, many skilled, perceptive birdwatchers have amassed an enormous amount of new information on the Yosemite Sierra's avifauna. Moreover my own knowledge has matured and deepened. As a result, what began as an update metamorphosed into a thorough revision. I expanded and rewrote virtually every page, added thousands of new citations, redrew the bar graphs and spiced the text with Keith Hansen's drawings and a few photographs of rarae aves.

While I have strived to be careful and thorough, this book is not a scientific treatise. I also try to convey, with the help of naturalists like John Muir, William Leon Dawson and Charles Michael, some of the essence of these fellow living beings we know as birds. Though I hope the book earns the approbation of ornithologists, I will be well pleased if it speaks to the hearts of bird lovers.

Last July, I interrupted my writing to guide a tired television crew around Mono Lake. They had spent a hot morning touring the Los Angeles Aqueduct with Department of Water and Power officials. As dutiful reporters, they thought they should hear "the other side" of the Mono Lake controversy. But I knew they were looking forward to beers back at the motel.

Ten thousand phalaropes welcomed us to Mono's dominion. As the cameraman filmed, the birds exploded into flight, veering and diving as a Prairie Falcon cut through their midst.

That burst of wings and talons immersed us in a drama more vivid and real than anything on television or in a book. In some ineluctable way, the grace of those shorebirds, the power of that falcon, overpowered our preoccupied brains. No longer merely observers, we were swept by the flow of this living planet.

As I write, the phalaropes—minus the few that foddered falcons—are 3,000 miles away in South America, where they are cavorting with flamingos on saline lakes high in the Andes. Yet somehow the paths they travel, while beyond human design, are parallel with our own. They have as much right to be here as we do—not because they are useful or beautiful, but because they are kin.

The birds and animals, trees and grasses, rocks, water and wind are our allies. We need to see them with our hearts as well as our minds, to let them speak to us of where we have come and where we are going, of three-and-a-half billion years of shared evolutionary travel, of our place on this planet.

David Gaines
Mono Lake
Autumn Equinox, 1987

Contents

Illustrations

Photographs

Acknowledgments

While many people contributed to this book, I am especially indebted to David DeSante, David Shuford and Jon Winter for critically reviewing the manuscript, directing my attention to flaws and omissions, and offering innumerable helpful suggestions. Their complementary expertise—David DeSante on the high country, David Shuford on Mono Lake and the Great Basin and Jon Winter on the west slope coniferous forests—pervades every page.

Mary Vocelka of the Yosemite Research Library could not have been more helpful. She not only loaned or copied rare materials from the archives, but carefully read the entire manuscript. Her comments were always on target. She spared me the embarassment of several pervasive mispellings.

My workload was lightened by Ken Croy and Terry Hart, who at different times in the past decade, sorted and recorded vast numbers of bird records.

Many ornithologists and birdwatchers placed their field notes at my disposal and offered valuable advice and encouragement. I am especially indebted to Don Banta, Ted Beedy, Jefferson Birch, Erica Buhrmann, Mark Chichester, Mark Chappell, Ken Croy, Dean Cutter, Gayle Dana, David DeSante, Jon Dunn, Brett Engstrom, Dick Erickson, Gary Fugle, Stephen Granholm, Russell Greenberg, Helen Green, Keith Hansen, Tina Hargis, John Harris, Terry Hart, Rob Hayden, Sallie Hejl, Joan Humphreys, Michael Jeneid, Stuart Johnson, Paul Johnson, Joseph R. Jehl Jr., Mary Kozak, John Lovio, Cliff Lyons, Ilene Mandelbaum, Marie Mans, Clint McCarthy, Len McKenzie, Jon Miller, Clyde Morris, Marilyn Muse, Virginia Norris, Michael Ohlwyler, Gary Page, Jim and Debby Parker, Diane Payne, Michael Praether, Peter Pyle, Michael Ross, David Shuford, Paul Springer, Richard Stallcup, Dale Steele, Bob Stewart, Emilie Strauss, Paul Super, Michael Sutton, Chris Swarth, Jarred Verner, Richard Webster, Christine Weigen, Larry White, David Wimpfheimer, David Winkler, Jon Winter and John Zablackis.

For the photographs I am grateful to Michael R. Dressler, Jon Dunn, Joseph R. Jehl Jr., Linda LaPierre, Marie Mans, Michael Wihler and the Yosemite Museum.

Throughout the two and a half years I spent on this project, my colleagues on the Mono Lake Committee and especially my wife Sally were always supportive and encouraging.

Finally I thank my young children, Vireo and Sage, for many joyful distractions.

How To Use This Book—And A Few "Headlines"

This is primarily a reference book. I expect readers to pick around in it like sparrows at a feeder.

If you are interested in a particular bird, turn first to the appropriate species account. Then peruse the locality lists on pages 28 - 55. Finally, consult the cross-references listed in the index.

The introduction, necessarily a little dry, defines and discusses terminology, codes, bar graphs, species accounts and sources. It is followed by lively essays on local ornithological history, the avifauna during the changing seasons and birdwatching in the Yosemite Sierra.

While proofing the manuscript, I was struck repeatedly by newsworthy information. If there were avian newspapers, some of these birds would have made headlines. In hopes of enticing readers to peruse more thoroughly the pages that follow, I list a few examples:

White Pelican Lays Egg In Gull Colony

Bittern Lost in Snowstorm

Asian Murrelets Reach Mono Lake

Hundreds of Lewis' Woodpeckers Cross Sierran Pass

Chestnut-backed Chickadees Invade Yosemite

Dippers Colonize Resurrected Stream

Mountain Bluebirds Scout Snow Conditions

Northern Shrike Kills Hairy Woodpecker

Yellow Warblers Nesting in Montane Chaparral

Bullfrog Swallows Tanager

Meadowlark on Half Dome

Crossbills Singing on New Year's Eve

Introduction

Goals and Objectives

For each species of bird that occurs in the Yosemite Sierra, I have strived to answer the following questions: What is its status? How numerous is it? Where and when does it occur? What are its habitat requirements? Where does it forage?

This book does not address identification. Nor does it delve into food habits, behavior, nesting ecology and other aspects of birds' life histories. This information is available elsewhere, as in the National Geographic Society's *Field Guide to North American Birds* (1987), Edward Beedy and Stephen Granholm's *Discovering Sierran Birds* (1985) and John K. Terres *The Audubon Society Encyclopedia of North American Birds* (1980).

In contrast, this book is provincial, focusing on the relationships between birds and the Yosemite Sierra environment. I have spiced the text, however, with tidbits of regional bird-lore, such as bullfrogs dining on tanagers, and nuthatches stashing nuts in Yosemite's vertical walls (p. 285 and p. 223).

Besides prose species accounts, I employ coded lists, bar graphs and prose. The lists on pp. 28-55 code the status and abundance of every species on the west slope, east of the Sierran crest, in Yosemite National Park and at eight specific, representative localities. The graphs, which accompany the species accounts, depict seasonal abundance, general habitat preferences, status and elevational range. The text provides details, discussions, sources and a modicum of encomiastic prose.

Region Covered

This book focuses on the birds which occur in the vicinity of Yosemite National Park from the western foothills east across the Sierran crest to Mono Lake and other Great Basin valleys. To bound this area, which is much larger than the park itself, I have arbitrarily elected to utilize the United States Geological Survey's map, *Yosemite National Park and Vicinity*, and extend it eastwards 17' to longitude 118°43', and northwards 7' to latitude 38°20' in order to include most of Long and Bridgeport valleys.

On the west, the region is bounded by the town of Mariposa (2000') on the south and the Middle Fork Stanislaus River below Donnell's Dam (4000') on the north, and includes the Tuolumne River above 2000' and the Merced River above 1200' (near Briceburg). On the east, it is bounded by the Hilton Creek drainage on the south and by Powell Mountain (9580') on the north, and includes Mt. Hicks (9143'), Granite Mountain (8920') and Glass Mountain (11,123'). Also within the region, in addition to all of Yosemite National Park, are El Portal, Fish Camp, the San Joaquin River above 4000' (near Squaw Dome), the Ritter Range, Devil's Postpile National Monument, Mammoth Lakes, June Lake, the Mono Basin National Forest Scenic Area, Mono Lake, Twin Lakes (west of Bridgeport), Bridgeport Lake Reservoir, Crowley Lake Reservoir, the Bodie Hills and Red Slate Mountain southeast of Mammoth Lakes (13,163'). On the front and back endpapers are maps of the region which include all the localities mentioned in the text.

While I focus on the Yosemite Sierra, the information on status, abundance and habitat is usually applicable to birds throughout the central and southern Sierra Nevada. Where it is not, I have mentioned the major exceptions. For this reason, this book will be useful throughout most of the "Range of Light."

Nomenclature and Subspecies

I have followed the nomenclature and order of the Sixth Edition of the American Ornithologists' Union *Check-list of North American Birds* (1983) as modified by its 1985, 1987 and 1989 supplements (*Auk* 102:680-686; *Auk* 104:591-596; *Auk* 106:532-538). Where the vernacular differs from field guide usage, I retain the familiar common names in parentheses. I treat subspecies when they are identifiable in the field.

Criteria for Acceptance of Records and Confirmation of Nesting

In general I have accepted records that are congruent with a bird's pattern of occurrence elsewhere in California and especially the Sierra Nevada. I have been more critical in accepting extremely rare and unseasonal sightings, relying on a combination of written and verbal descriptions, photographs and observer expertise. If a record has been reviewed by the California Bird Records Committee, I have deferred to their judgement.

Under the heading "representative nesting localities," I list both positive and highly probable sites. Positive records, which are not in parentheses, are based on observations of (1) nests with eggs or young, (2) nest-building, (3) food being carried repeatedly to a likely nest site, or (4) locally hatched fledglings being fed by adults. Probable records, shown in parentheses, are based on the continual presence during the nesting season of singing or territorial birds.

Status Terminology and Codes

I have adapted the following terminology and codes from DeSante and Pyle (1986). I employ the codes in the lists on pp. 28-55, and the terminology throughout the book:

R = Year-round resident and confirmed breeder. I use this term for species, such as Hairy Woodpecker and Mountain Chickadee, that occur in given localities throughout the year in numbers that are so consistent they belong in the same abundance category.

R* = Non-breeding year-round resident. I use this term for species, such as Great Blue Heron, which occur throughout the year in similar numbers, but are not known to nest.

S = Summer resident and confirmed breeder. I use this term for species, such as California Gull, Western Wood Pewee and White-crowned Sparrow, whose numbers in summer are substantially different from their numbers in winter or during migrations.

S* = Summer visitor. I use this term for species, such as Eared Grebes, Ruddy Ducks and, at higher elevations, Orange-crowned Warblers and Lesser

Goldfinches, which summer in given localities, but are not known to nest. In contrast to *transients*, which are en route from northern breeding to southern wintering areas or vice versa, "non-breeding summer residents" are loitering throughout the summer, or drifting upslope after having nested or fledged at lower elevations.

T = Transient. I use this term for birds during their migrations. In the matrices, I employ it for species, such as Western Sandpiper and Townsend's Warbler, whose numbers during migration are substantially greater than at other times of year. In the species accounts, but not in the matrices, I distinguish between *spring transients*—birds on their northward migration—and *fall transients*—birds on their southward migration. In fact, while spring transients pass through predominantly in spring, most fall transients pass through from mid- to late summer.

V = Vagrant. I use this term in place of transient for species, such as Marbled Murrelets and Cerulean Warblers, whose established migration routes lie outside the Yosemite Sierra.

W = Winter resident or visitor. I use this term for species, such as Rough-legged Hawks and Golden-crowned Sparrows, whose numbers in winter are substantially different than their numbers in summer or during migrations. In the species accounts, I use *resident* to describe species which winter in a specific area. In contrast, I employ *visitor* for species, such as Common Ravens above 5000', which visit irregularly during the winter.

? = Probable but uncertain. In the locality lists, I add the suffix "?" to indicate that a given status is probable but uncertain.

e = Extirpated. In the locality lists, I add the suffix "e" to the status codes "R" and "S" to indicate that a bird has been extirpated or no longer occurs as a nesting species.

Abundance Terminology and Codes

I have modified the following abundance codes and terminology from DeSante and Pyle (1986). I employ the codes in the locality lists on pp. 28-55, and the terminology in the bar graphs and species accounts.

These terms reflect, not absolute densities, but detectability, i.e., the number of individuals an experienced observer can see or hear within a bird's range and preferred habitat at a given time of year. They indicate average detectability; in specific localities, a bird may be more or less numerous. Band-tailed Pigeons, for example, are usually "common" in the vicinity of the stables behind the Yosemite Valley Visitor Center, but are "uncommon" overall. Except for "extremely rare," the terms are based on careful but subjective judgments of myself and other birdwatchers; in the future, given hourly tallies by habitat, these judgments could be refined quantitatively.

c = ▇▇▇▇ = Common or abundant. Always or almost always encountered, usually in relatively large numbers, without special searching. Numbers vary from a few (on more than 90 percent of one's hours afield) to many (on more than 50 percent of one's hours afield).

f = ▇▇▇ = Fairly common. Usually encountered in small numbers, sometimes in relatively large numbers, but may require searching. Numbers vary from a few (on 50 to 90 percent of one's hours afield) to many (on 10 to 50 percent of one's hours afield).

u = ▬▬▬▬▬ = Uncommon. Usually missed unless a special search is made. Numbers vary from a few (on 10 to 50 percent of one's days afield) to many (on less than 10 percent of one's days afield).

r = ———————— = Rare. Cannot be expected on any given day or even every year. Usually no more than a few are found on less than 10 percent of one's days afield.

x = Extremely rare. Less than five records of different flocks or individuals in a given season during the past 50 years.

In addition, I employ the following prefixes to modify abundance codes:

i = ▒▒▒▒▒ = Irregular. I use this prefix for species, such as Red Crossbills, whose numbers fluctuate markedly from year to year. The abundance code, or the width of the bar on the bar graphs, is indicative of numbers during a flight year; the species may be much less numerous, or lacking entirely, during other years. I employ the phrase "irregularly rare" to describe a species that has occurred more than five times in a season, but is not found every year.

l = Local. I use this prefix for species, such as Willow Flycatcher and Bank Swallow, which are found in but a few, discrete localities or are absent from many areas of apparently suitable habitat.

Most Sierran birds are "irregular and local" to some extent, especially during winter when food resources are least dependable. I reserve these terms, however, for species that exemplify these tendencies.

Geographic Terminology

As used in this book, the following geographic terms carry specific meanings:

WEST SLOPE = the west slope of the Sierra Nevada.

EAST SLOPE = the east slope of the Sierra Nevada.

CREST = the crest of the Sierra Nevada.

EAST OF CREST = the entire region east of the crest of the Sierra Nevada, i.e., not just the east slope.

EAST OF THE ESCARPMENT = east of the base of the Sierra Nevada mountains, i.e., Bridgeport Valley, Bodie Hills, Mono Basin, Mono Craters, Deadman Summit, Long Valley, Glass Mountain and adjacent areas.

GLASS MOUNTAIN REGION = the forested region east of the Sierran escarpment stretching from the Mono Craters on the north to Glass Mountain on the south.

Habitat Codes

On the bar graphs, "HAB" denotes "habitat." I have employed the following letter symbols to convey, in a general way, the habitat(s) in which a species usually occurs (in rough order of preference):

A — Aerial, i.e., soars or flies in the open air over a wide range of habitats

B — Buildings and bridges

C — Cliffs, rocks and talus slopes

D — Dumps, stables, campgrounds and picnic areas

G — Grasslands, meadows and other open terrain with, at most, scattered trees

L — Freshwater lakes, ponds and reservoirs

Ma — Marshes

Mo — Mono Lake

Mu — Mudflats and muddy shores

O — Forests or woodlands dominated by oaks, maples and other hardwoods

P Forests or woodlands dominated by pines, firs or other conifers

R — Rivers and streams

S — Scrub, including chaparral, montane chaparral and sagebrush scrub

W — Willows, cottonwoods and other riparian hardwoods

Interpreting the Bar Graphs

I have graphed the seasonal abundance of all birds which are "uncommon," "fairly common" or "common" either west or east of the Sierran crest during some part of the year. I have excluded "rare" and "extremely rare" species, since their occurrence is detailed in the text.

Each graph is divided into "west" and "east." This refers to west and east of the Sierran crest, i.e., the Pacific Coast and Great Basin drainages.

The letters "J, F, M, etc." across the top of the graphs denote months of the year. I have strived to graph abundance to the nearest half a month. A dot indicates that a species, though "extremely rare" at that season, has been recorded at least once.

"ELEV" refers to the elevational range in which a bird regularly occurs as a nesting (n), transient (t) or wintering (w) species. I have rounded elevations to the nearest thousand feet. "F" refers to foothills.

The graphs should be interpreted cautiously. The arrivals, departures and numbers of virtually all Sierran birds vary with elevation and weather conditions. Dark-eyed Juncos, for example, arrive at 4000' several weeks before they arrive at 8000'. At higher elevations, a lingering snowpack can delay the return of many species, especially those that forage or nest on the ground (AFN 21:600, AFN 23:619).

The elevations can also be misleading. A species graphed as "common," for example, may not be plentiful in the higher parts of its range. Moreover, birds respond, not to elevation per se, but to vegetation, topographical relief, proximity of water and similar factors. At any given altitude, these vary enormously.

The graphs, in sum, are schemata designed to quickly convey status, seasonal abundance, general habitat preferences and elevational range. They are fleshed out by the text and records that follow.

Species Accounts

The first paragraph of the species accounts, set off in italics, describes the bird's status and abundance by elevation.

If a bird is "extremely rare," whether throughout the year, seasonally or at particular elevations, I cite all the records I have been able to locate in chronological order. If a bird is "rare," "uncommon," "fairly common" or "common," I discuss its haunts, habitat requirements, foraging places and seasonal movements.

To avoid burdening the text with latin names for trees, shrubs and other plants, I borrow vernacular names from Weeden's (1986) *A Sierra Nevada Flora* and Munz and Keck's (1970) *A California Flora.*

Following the prose, if not mentioned in the text, I cite the "high elevation" record or records for most species. Under "extreme dates," I enumerate the earliest and latest seasonal records. If there are no other reports within a week of these records, I give penultimate "extreme dates" as well. Under "representative nesting localities," I list known and probable nesting sites, the latter in parentheses (see p. 4 for criteria); I have ordered them geographically from west to east.

Sources

So that others can follow my trail, I have strived to cite sources for most of my information. When the source is a book or major article, I usually cite the author and date in parenthesis; the full citation is listed in the "literature cited" section at the back of the book (pp. 341-346). When the source is an individual or brief report from a book or journal, I have used the following abbreviations. Individuals are sources of information, but not necessarily the parties responsible for the original observations:

AB = *American Birds*

ABR = Unpublished records kept by editors of *American Birds*

AFN = *Audubon Field Notes*

AUK = *The Auk*

B = Bent, Arthur Cleveland, 1923-1966, *Life histories of North American Birds.*

BE = Brett Engstrom

BG = Bruce Gerow

BS = Bob Stewart

C = *Condor*

CC = Chris Corben

CFG = *California Fish and Game*

CH = Charlotte Harbeson
CL = Cliff Lyons
CM = Clyde Morris
CMc = Clint McCarthy
CS = Chris Swarth
D = Dawson (1923)
DB = Don Banta
DC = Dean Cutter
DDeS = David DeSante
DE = Dick Erickson
DFG = California Department of Fish and Game, Bishop, California
DG = David Gaines
DP = Diane Payne
DS = David Shuford
DSt = Dale Steele
DT = Dean Taylor
DW = David Winkler
DWi = David Wimpfheimer
D&SJ = Dean and Sally Jue
EB = Erica Buhrmann
EM = Enid Michael (1927)
ES = Winkler et al. (1977)
ESt = Emilie Strauss
GD = Gayle Dana
GF = Gary Fugle
GM = Grinnell and Miller (1944)
GP = Gary Page
GS = Grinnell and Storer (1924)
GSt = George Stroud
HG = Helen Green
IM = Ilene Mandelbaum
JB = Jefferson Birch
JD = Jon Dunn
JH = John Harris
JHu = Joan Humphreys
JL = John Lovio
JJ = Joseph R. Jehl Jr.
JM = Jon Miller
JP = Jim Parker
JS = Jean Saulbury
JV = Jarred Verner
JW = Jon Winter
JZ = John Zablackis
KC = Ken Croy

KH = Keith Hansen
LF = Larry Ford
LH = Lisa Hug
LMcK = Len McKenzie
LW = Larry White
MC = Mark Chappell
MCh = Mark Chichester
MJ = Michael Jeneid
MK = Mary Kozak
MLTSR = Mono Lake Tufa State Reserve
MM = Marie Mans
MO = Michael Ohlwyler
MMu = Marilyn Muse
MP = Michael Prather
MR = Michael Ross
MRD = Michael R. Dressler
MS = Michael Sutton
MVZ = Museum of Vertebrate Zoology, Berkeley
PJ = Paul Johnson
PL = Parson's Lodge (Sierra Club) bird list
PM = Peter Metropulos
PP = Peter Pyle
PS = Paul Springer
PSu = Paul Super
RG = Russell Greenberg
RH = Rob Hayden
RS = Richard Stallcup
RT = Ron Thorne
RW = Richard Webster
SG = Stephen Granholm
SGu = Stephen Gustafsen
SH = Sallie Hejl
SJ = Stuart Johnson
T&JH = Tom and Jo Heindel
TB = Ted Beedy
TH = Tina Hargis
THa = Terry Hart
VN = Virginia Norris
WB = *Western Birds*
WC = Wanda Conway
YM = Yosemite Museum, unpublished records
YNN = *Yosemite Nature Notes*

The Data Base:
A Brief History from Muir to the Present

Since 1878, when John Muir published his winsome portrait of American Dippers in *Scribner's Monthly*, there has been a constant stream of popular articles on the birds of the Yosemite Sierra. Of the batch, Muir's are among the finest. Though a flawed ornithologist (he mistook Great Blue Herons for Sandhill Cranes), he knew the birds as friends. I have quoted from his writings throughout the book.

Until the 1920s, however, Yosemite's ornithological literature consisted, to paraphrase the title of W. O. Emerson's 1893 article, of "random bird notes." Pieces by Keeler (1908), Grinnell (1911) and Mailliard (1918) appeared in *Sierra Club Bulletins* and *The Condor*, but were anecdotal travelogues or popular introductions.

In 1914, however, a University of California professor decided to embark on a thorough study, not only of Yosemite's birds, but of its amphibians, reptiles and mammals as well. For six years, Joseph Grinnell and his colleagues made numerous trips to the Yosemite Sierra and Mono Lake. They censused birds, collected thousands of specimens and filled journal after journal with meticulous field notes which still reside in Berkeley's Museum of Vertebrate Zoology. In 1924, the university published their 751-page tome, *Animal Life in the Yosemite*, which documented, among other things, the discovery of a new species of salamander and the nesting of Great Gray Owls in the continental United States. I cite their work throughout this book.

About this same time, a more romantic ornithologist was exploring the mountains and valleys east of the crest. William Leon Dawson combined Grinnell's scientific perspicacity with Muir's impassioned lyricism. His magnum opus, the four-volume *Birds of California,* has been undeservedly forgotten by all but a few cognoscenti. I've spiced this book with excerpts from his writings.

In 1919, while Grinnell was still busily collecting data, Charles and Enid Michael celebrated their marriage among the valley's caroling robins and grosbeaks. The following year, Charles moved to Yosemite to assume the duties of assistant postmaster. "He knew the slightest sound of every bird," Enid wrote after his death, "and could identify every species from their movements in the sky." She was equally adept, and also knew animals and especially plants.

For at least eleven years, Charles and Enid Michael kept meticulous daily records of every bird they saw in Yosemite Valley (Linsdale 1932, YNN 12:55). Their monthly "reports," which reside in the Yosemite Museum archives, are filled with sparkling descriptions of storms, flower blooms, bird migrations and countless other natural events.

Charles was a climber as well as a birdwatcher, and made the first ascent of the spire-like Minaret in the Ritter Range that now bears his name. His prowess enabled him to carry camera gear into precipitous Tenaya Canyon, and obtain some of the few photographs ever taken of nesting Black Swifts (p. 166-167). Reminiscing about this remarkable naturalist, Walter Fitzpatrick (1943) called their years together "indescribably rich in companionship and the attempt to attain...the inward harmony of one who is at home with Mother Earth."

Since Michael's death in 1941, many others have advanced our knowledge of Yosemite's birds. In 1943, Russell Grater organized 25 years of observations into usable form; his meticulous summaries, housed in the Yosemite Library's archives, have been of inestimable value in writing this book. Walter Fitzpatrick, who succeeded Michael in the Yosemite post office, continued to report unusual birds and organize Christmas Counts until the 1960s.

In recent years, there has been a revival of scientific interest in Yosemite's avifauna. In the 1980s, for example, biologists working on the west slope completed Ph.D theses on "the effects of surface fires on birds," "bird community structure" and "bird assemblages in true fir forests" (Granholm 1982, Beedy 1982, Hejl 1987).

Among active researchers, Jon Winter has greatly advanced our understanding of the avifauna of mid-elevation forests and meadows. While studying Great Gray Owls, he has kept detailed records of all the birds in Ackerson Meadow (4600'), rivalling the Michaels' legacy from Yosemite Valley.

Near treeline, David DeSante and a host of volunteers have expanded our knowledge of the high country avifauna. Since 1977, the Carnegie Institution of Washington and Inyo National Forest have permitted DeSante and his colleagues to summer in the Harvey Monroe Hall Natural Area north of Tioga Pass. Under the auspices of the Point Reyes Bird Observatory, they have monitored and studied breeding, transient and, to a lesser extent, wintering bird populations at elevations ranging from approximately 9800' to 12,000'. Their work, which is being prepared for publication, is cited throughout this book (DeSante and Engstrom MS; DeSante MS).

East of the Sierran escarpment, during the past decade, researchers have altered our understanding of virtually every water bird, and many land-dwelling fowl as well. In particular, David Shuford, Gary Page, David Winkler and Joseph Jehl Jr., though focusing on Mono Lake's California Gulls, Snowy Plovers, Eared Grebes and Wilson's and Red-necked phalaropes, have added to our knowledge of many other species.

But most of the information has come, not from professional scientists, but from avid amateurs like Charles Michael. Their observations, reported to the Yosemite Museum, published in *American Birds* or shared with me directly, are the bedrock of this book.

LIFE IN A SEASONAL ENVIRONMENT:
The Avifauna During the Changing Seasons

The lives of birds cycle with the seasons. Singing, egg-laying, molt, migration, flocking and other phenomena coincide with favorable conditions in a changing environment. In this section, I follow birds through the year, sketching their responses to the Yosemite Sierra's seasonal fluctuations. My intent is not to be exhaustive, but to touch on major motifs. For more details, the reader is referred to individual species accounts.

A Migratory Avifauna

Most Sierran birds could not survive the winter, at least at high elevations. Flycatchers, swallows, vireos, warblers and other insectivores, for example, would find little to eat when the mercury dipped below freezing. Quail, flickers, robins, sparrows and other ground-foraging species would starve when their dining tables were covered by snow. Ducks and shorebirds would perish when lakes and mudflats froze.

Most of these birds follow the sun south in late summer and fall to winter in balmier climes or at lower elevations. Of 84 species that regularly nest in Yosemite Valley (4000'), for example, 54 percent are rare or absent in winter. In the colder climates of higher elevations, as at Crane Flat (6200'), Tuolumne Meadows (8600') and Tioga Pass (9800'), the proportion increases to approximately 75 percent.

Sierran birds may be conveniently classified as long-distance migrants, short-distance migrants and residents. Though there are many exceptions, birds which dine on active or aerial insects are usually long-distance migrants, crossing the deserts to winter in subtropical or tropical Mexico and Middle America; a few, such as Common Nighthawks, Olive-sided Flycatchers and Barn Swallows, journey as far as South America. Birds which feed on the ground, sap or fruit tend to be short-distance migrants, wintering in the lowlands of California, the Southwest and northern Mexico (though they may come from as far away as Alaska). Those able to eke out livings among the ice and snow, such as chickadees, nuthatches and woodpeckers, are usually residents, even at high elevations, throughout the year.

WINTER:
Searching for Sustenance

During winter, above 4000' on the west slope and 7000' east of the crest, the mixed conifer, fir and lodgepole forests often seem bereft of birds. I've searched for hours before encountering mixed flocks of chickadees, nuthatches and kinglets, frequently with a creeper or woodpecker, seeking out the eggs, pupae and adults of quiescent, over-wintering insects. These winter flocks, which usually number 10 to 40 individuals, gypsy through the forests in search of sustenance. By joining in flocks, the birds probably increase their foraging success, and are able to warn one another of the presence of predators.

Other hardy residents, such as Clark's Nutcrackers, Pine Grosbeaks and Red Crossbills, survive the winter on buds and pine nuts. Townsend's Solitaires rely on juniper berries, while Blue Grouse subsist on monotonous diets of pine needles.

Not all these birds winter at high elevations every year. The failure of pines to produce nuts, for example, may force Clark's Nutcrackers, Pinyon Jays, Red Crossbills and Red-breasted Nuthatches to lower elevations. On the west slope, a dearth of acorns may compel Band-tailed Pigeons, Acorn Woodpeckers and Steller's Jays to scrounge the lowlands for sustenance. Even insectivorous residents, such as Brown Creepers and Golden-crowned Kinglets, sometimes desert the mountains en masse.

In the high, cold valleys east of the crest, the winter avifauna is even more variable. So long as there is open water, ducks linger in large numbers. Hawks, eagles, larks, pipits and other ground-foraging birds remain until valleybottoms are buried in snow. If junipers are fruitful, flocks of robins compete with Townsend's Solitaires for the bitter berries. In willow thickets, Bushtits, Bewick's Wrens and Song Sparrows try to hide from Northern Shrikes. In pinyon woodlands, Cassin's Finches mingle with jays, nutcrackers, chickadees and nuthatches.

On the west slope, many more species winter below snowline in oak woodlands and chaparral. Residents, such at Nuttall's Woodpeckers, Scrub Jays, Canyon Wrens, Western Bluebirds, California Thrashers and Brown and Rufous-sided towhees, are joined by short-distance migrants, such as flickers, Hermit Thrushes, American Robins, Cedar Waxwings, Ruby-crowned Kinglets, Yellow-rumped Warblers, Fox Sparrows and Golden-crowned Sparrows. Robins, waxwings and many others are lured by foothill berry crops, especially toyon and madrone; their numbers vary from year to year in response to the abundance of fruit.

One would think the short-distance migrants which nest in the Yosemite Sierra would move downslope to winter in the nearby foothills and lowlands. With the exception of Mountain Quail, however, most spend the winter, not in our foothills, but hundreds or even thousands of miles away in the American Southwest or northern Mexico. Wintering Hermit Thrushes, Fox Sparrows and White-crowned Sparrows, for example, are not Sierran natives, but northern-nesting subspecies.

To explain this anomaly, we need to envision the Sierra 13,000 years ago. At the close of the last ice age, retreating glaciers opened up nesting habitat in the higher mountains. Young thrushes, sparrows and other short-distance migrants colonized in the glaciers' wake. When they retreated for the winter, they found the foothills and lowlands already occupied by others of their kind. As a result, they had to "leap-frog" into new wintering areas further south.

SPRING:
The Return of the Migrants

The first premonitions of Spring appear in February. By the end of the month, Cinnamon Teal, Say's Phoebes, Mountain Bluebirds, Sage Thrashers and Red-winged Blackbirds have returned to valleys east of the Sierran escarpment, and robins and Red-winged Blackbirds have begun to sing. Even in the snowbound higher mountains, Great Horned Owls resume their hooting.

By March, wintering flocks of small, resident birds have broken up into vociferous, feisty territorial pairs. Short-distance migrants, such as flickers, Mountain Bluebirds, American Robins, sparrows and juncos, usually arrive at nesting haunts in March and April. Long-distance migrants arrive later, not because they have farther to travel, but because the active insects on which they prey emerge later in spring. Above 4000', vireos, warblers, orioles and Black-headed Grosbeaks, which glean caterpillars and other larval insects from foliage, generally appear in April. Nighthawks, flycatchers and tanagers, which prey largely or entirely on flying insects, usually wait until May or early June when more larvae have metamorphosed into flying adults. Birds arrive at lower elevations, of course, earlier than in the higher mountains.

There are also exceptions. Swallows, which are insectivorous, long-distance migrants, have been known to materialize in February snowstorms, though they do not become numerous until April.

At the same time migrants are returning to Yosemite Sierran nesting haunts, others are passing north. Small waves of peregrinating passerines descend upon the western foothills, which are green and rich in insects after the winter rains. Flycatchers, warblers, tanagers and others feed and fatten east of the crest as well, especially in deciduous groves along the base of the Sierran escarpment.

As transient landbirds gather in woods and thickets, ducks, shorebirds and other water birds flock to lakes, ponds and mudflats east of the Sierran escarpment. Most are bound for nesting sites further north, some as far away as the Arctic circle.

LATE SPRING THROUGH EARLY SUMMER: Familial Responsibilities

Long before the last northbound travelers have departed, most of the Yosemite Sierra's breeding birds are building nests, incubating eggs or feeding young. They nest in spring and early summer when food is most plentiful. The alchemy of long, warm days and moist conditions produces, not just blooms of flowers, but blooms of insects as well. While we grouse about mosquitoes, birds are feeding them and other insects to hungry young. Insect-rich diets stimulate the chicks' growth rates, shortening the time when they are flightless and vulnerable to predators. Even sparrows and juncos, which feed largely on seeds during most of the year, raise their chicks on insect-rich diets.

All things considered, conditions must be exceptionally propitious for raising and fledging young birds. Why else would so many species brave the dangers of long migrations to rear young in the Yosemite Sierra? Compared to the tropics, there is not only plenty of food, but longer days, fewer nest predators and less competition with other birds and animals. In stark contrast to winter, this is a bountiful time when finding enough food—at least for oneself—is rarely if ever a problem.

The tide of nuptial energy, which begins in late February, crests in May and early June. The woods, scrub and marshes of the Yosemite Sierra resound with birdsong, especially at dawn, when the myriad voices of males declaiming their territories blend into rich, vibrant choruses.

With the onset of incubation and familial cares, singing begins to wane. As the year progresses, the importunate demands of hungry youth take precedence over virtually all else. Everywhere one looks, birds are winging purposefully through the air with moths, caterpillars and other prey protruding from their bills. Anxious calls betray the presence, usually well-concealed, of nearby nests or troops of bob-tailed fledglings. Fat youngsters pursue their parents everywhere, whining piteously for meals until, at last, tired adults force them to fend for themselves. At lower elevations, as in Yosemite Valley, many nesting birds raise second broods; at higher elevations, where the season is shorter, most rear only one.

Not all birds feed their young. Within hours after hatching, quail and grouse chicks are able to follow their mothers and feed themselves. Unlike songbirds, which are naked, blind and helpless at birth, these "precocial" chicks are feathered and mobile. They freeze at the first sign of danger, trusting to camouflaging plumage to escape detection. East of the Sierran crest, many grebes, ducks and shorebirds rear precocial chicks in marshes and wetlands.

While nesting birds are caring for young or beginning to molt, some lowland species follow spring into the higher mountains. After nesting in the foothills, for example, Orange-crowned Warblers wander all the way to treeline, appearing above their nesting range as early as June. Red-tailed Hawks, American Kestrels, Mourning Doves, Anna's Hummingbirds, Belted Kingfishers, Bushtits, House Wrens, Nashville Warblers, MacGillivray's Warblers, Lazuli Buntings, California Towhees, Western Meadowlarks, Brewer's Blackbirds, Lesser Goldfinches and many other birds also drift upslope after nesting or fledging in the valleys or foothills. Some mountain species, such as American Dippers, Chipping Sparrows and juncos, also wander above their natal elevations.

The extent of up-mountain drift varies from year to year. Droughts force more birds to seek refuge, or even nest, at higher elevations. Juveniles are especially prone to upslope wandering; youthful wanderlust is prevalent in birds as well as humans.

MID-SUMMER THROUGH AUTUMN: Molt and Farewell

By mid-summer, the woods and scrub are nearly silent. Most nesting birds are molting last year's feathers and growing new ones. Even fledglings shed their body feathers, molting from juvenile into basic (winter) plumage. Juvenile American Robins, for example, trade breast spots for the orange vests of adults.

Growing new feathers, like raising young, requires more energy than simply staying alive. In mid-summer, insects are still abundant, and fruits and seeds are beginning to ripen. They provide the extra food birds need while changing clothes.

Beginning in mid-summer, ripening fruits and berries afford many Sierran birds a change in diet. American Robins, Western Bluebirds, Hermit Thrushes, Western Tanagers, Black-headed Grosbeaks, Northern Flickers and even Pileated Woodpeckers feast on the fleshy fruits of dogwoods, cherries, elderberries and currants. East of the crest, Sage Thrashers and House Finches flock to buffalo-berries and currants. By fall, juniper and mistletoe berries ripen as well, luring solitaires, bluebirds and robins.

Prior to migrating, birds gorge themselves on food. If they waited for hunger to prompt their departures, they would be unable to accumulate stores of fat to fuel their journeys. While they migrate to avoid starvation, they leave while food is still plentiful.

For this reason, long-distance migrants like flycatchers, vireos, warblers, tanagers, Black-headed Grosbeaks, Lazuli Buntings and Northern Orioles complete their post-breeding molts and leave, by and large, by the end of August. Short-distance migrants like robins, sparrows and juncos undergo more leisurely molts, lingering at higher elevations through September.

In general, long-distance migrants are the last to arrive and the first to depart. Because they are dependent on active or flying insects, they cannot risk September cold spells, which can devastate insect populations almost overnight. Short-distance migrants leave the higher mountains before October storms blanket them in snow.

Before nesting birds have fledged the last of their young, the first southbound migrants have already arrived. It's strange to speak of "fall" migration around the summer solstice, yet southbound female Wilson's Phalaropes arrive at Mono Lake, and southbound male Rufous Hummingbirds invade mountain meadows, by late June. Both female phalaropes and male hummingbirds take no part in raising young, leaving their mates behind before their chicks have fledged.

In fact, the fall songbird migration is largely a summer affair. By August, mid-elevation meadows, such as Crane Flat (6200'), are swarming with hummingbirds, warblers, tanagers and other long-distance migrants. Most are probably northerners pausing to rest and refuel on their journeys south. In contrast to spring, they shun the dry, sun-baked foothills in favor of the higher mountains, which are still green and buzzing with insects.

At the same time landbirds are using the mountains as southward migration routes, grebes, egrets, dabbling ducks, shorebirds, gulls, terns and other water birds are congregating on lakes and mudflats east of the Sierran escarpment. By the end of September, most shorebirds depart for wintering areas as far away as southern South America. Dabbling ducks linger into late autumn, and are joined in October by Common Loons and diving ducks. Three-quarters of a million Eared Grebes amass on Mono Lake, departing by Thanksgiving or early December.

In late summer and early autumn, after completing molts and prior to migrating, many birds bid adieu with snatches of song. Ruby-crowned Kinglets, American Robins, Solitary Vireos, Song Sparrows and many others occasionally break the silence to reminisce of spring. Resident species, too, such as Pygmy Owls, Brown Creepers and especially Townsend's Solitaires, vocalize during the weeks before and after the equinox.

Compared to spring's cacophany, autumnal singing is poignant and subdued. Scientists say it is triggered by decreasing daylength and consequent changes in birds' hormonal levels. But it still speaks to me of transience, the cycling seasons and the coming of winter.

Human Impacts

Compared to other parts of California, humans have not yet had substantial impacts on most of the birds of the Yosemite Sierra. With the exception of Barrow's Goldeneyes (p. 88), American Bitterns (p. 67) and possibly Harlequin Ducks (p. 85), Yellow Rails (p. 115) and Short-eared Owls (p. 161), no nesting species have been entirely extirpated.

Yet human activities have affected birds, and threaten to becloud the not-too-distant future. In this brief survey, I discuss the effects of grazing and logging, non-native species, roads, stables and tourism, and dams and water diversions. In the individual species accounts, I give additional details.

Grazing and Logging

Though not permitted in Yosemite National Park, grazing and logging on other lands have affected some of our scarcest birds. Willow Flycatchers, for example, do not nest in willows whose lowermost foliage has been denuded by livestock (p. 192). Great Gray Owls rarely forage in grazed meadows; for this reason, they are rarely stray outside the park boundaries (p. 159).

East of the crest, grazing by cattle and especially sheep has favored sagebrush over grassland birds. Despite their name, Sage Grouse have suffered as much as any species, for they depend on grasses and forbs as much as scrub (p. 111). Vesper Sparrows have declined as well (p. 297).

Logging may favor some meadow and woodland birds, but it's disastrous for old-growth species, which are often found nowhere else. Spotted and Great Gray owls and Pileated Woodpeckers, for example, are particularly vulnerable to selective- as well as clear-cutting (pp. 157, 159 and 188).

Plans to turn much of the Sierra's forests into tree farms could be disasterous for virtually all woodland birds. "Even-aged management," as its euphemistically called, is a prescription for biological sterility. It means clear-cutting virtually all old-growth timber that is not on steep slopes or in wilderness areas. It means stripping away understory vegetation and planting pines bred or genetically-engineered to produce the most wood in the shortest amount of time. It means chemical warfare against other trees, shrubs, insects, porcupines and other native species which are suddenly perceived as "pests."

These even-aged tree farms would have as much biotic diversity as corn-fields—next to nothing. Even in spring, they would not be living forests, but silent sepulchers, bereft of birds and other animals. For birds need more than even-aged trees; they need fecund forests rich in insects, undergrowth, saplings, logs and snags.

Non-native Species

Five non-native species—Chuckars, Rock Doves, White-tailed Ptarmigans, European Starlings and House Sparrows—have become established in the Yosemite Sierra. Only two are widespread—European Starlings at lower elevations, and White-tailed Ptarmigan above treeline. Starlings compete with native species for nest holes, and have reduced populations of Violet-green Swallows, House Wrens and Mountain Bluebirds in places like Lee Vining Canyon (p. 261). Ptarmigan are altering the alpine ecosystem, and may be threatening some of the native flora (p. 111).

Roads, Stables and Tourism

Many birds have followed in our footsteps. Black Phoebes and Cliff and Barn swallows avail themselves of nest sites on building, barns and bridges (pp. 197, 208 and 209). Common Ravens patrol highways, fattening on road-kills (p. 217). Steller's Jays scrounge campgrounds and picnic areas (p. 211). Gulls and blackbirds dine at dumps (pp. 142, 313, 316). These and other species have benefitted from industrialized tourism and the annual influx of millions of visitors.

One beneficiary, however, has been deleterious to its fellow birds. Brown-headed Cowbirds have followed livestock and pack animals from the foothills to treeline. They lay their eggs in nests of small songbirds, such as vireos and warblers, who raise the cowbird young, usually at the expense of their own. Near stables and campgrounds, cowbirds have probably reduced the nesting populations of some of their hosts (p. 318).

Human disturbance has probably driven some of the more reclusive birds from bustling habitats. Common Mergansers, for example, have not bred in Yosemite Valley for decades, and Canada Geese no longer nest in the June Lake loop (pp. 89 and 75).

Dams and Water Diversions

The thirst of distant metropoli have taken tolls both west and east of the Sierran crest. In 1923, the City of San Francisco completed O'Shaughnessy Dam, turning Hetch Hetchy Valley into a reservoir. In 1941, the City of Los Angeles tapped the upper Owens River and Mono Basin streams, flooding marshes, destroying riparian forests and threatening Mono Lake's ecosystem.

On the west slope, O'Shaugnessy Dam was built at the cost of habitat that may have been unique in Yosemite National Park. We will never know what birds dwelt on the floor of Hetch Hetchy Valley (3700'), for no one birded its boggy meadows before they were flooded. Pied-billed Grebes, Cinnamon Teal, Virginia Rails and other wetland species may have bred in considerable numbers.

On the other hand, Hetch Hetchy and especially its sister reservoirs, Cherry Lake (4700') and Lake Eleanor (4700'), attract small numbers of Great Blue Herons, diving ducks, coots, gulls and Bald Eagles.

East of the crest, the Los Angeles Department of Water and Power has shunted most of Rush, Lee Vining, Parker and Walker creeks into the Los Angeles Aqueduct, turning forested streams into cobbled washes. Between Grant Lake dam and Mono Lake, for example, Rush Creek's banks were formerly green with aspens, cottonwoods, willows and pines interspersed with lush meadows, backwater sloughs, ponds and cattail marshes. John Muir (1894) wrote glowingly of following the stream "through gentian meadows and groves of rustling aspen to Lake Mono." Joseph Grinnell suspected that

Least Bitterns were nesting in marshes near its mouth (Grinnell and Storer 1924). But without water, its forests and marshes withered and died (Stine, Gaines and Vorster 1981).

Grant, Crowley, Bridgeport and other reservoirs created additional habitat for loons, diving ducks, Bald Eagles, coots, shorebirds and other water birds at the expense of stream, marsh, meadow and forest species. Crowley inundated the nesting haunts of at least three species—American Bitterns, Short-eared Owls and Yellow Rails—that are no longer known to nest in the region; in California, Yellow Rails have been found breeding at only one other locality.

If Los Angeles proceeds with plans to enlarge Crowley Lake Reservoir, it would flood nesting habitat for ducks, rails and other wetland species, and endanger the region's colony of Bank Swallows (p. 207).

Mono Lake

Los Angeles also holds the fate of Mono Lake and its vast flocks of nesting and migratory birds. The insatiable thirst of this distant metropolis has conspired with engineering skill to deprive this ancient sea of water. As a result, the lake has fallen approximately 40 vertical feet, its volume has decreased by half and its salinity has doubled. Unless diversions are curtailed, increasing salinity will poison its ecosystem. Our children will inherit a birdless, chemical sump (Gaines 1981, Patten 1987).

Leading the fight to save the lake is the non-profit Mono Lake Committee, which I helped organize in 1978. At stake are some of the largest bird concentrations on the continent, including tens of thousands of gulls and phalaropes and hundreds of thousands of grebes. For more on this embattled avian oasis, refer to the species accounts for Eared Grebe (p. 60), Wilson's and Red-necked phalaropes (pp. 134 and 136) and California Gull (p. 142).

Conservation Organizations

We must speak for the birds of the Yosemite Sierra, and defend their rights to diverse and healthy habitats. The following non-profit groups deserve your support:

MONO LAKE COMMITTEE, P.O. Box 29, Lee Vining CA 93541
NATIONAL AUDUBON SOCIETY, 555 Audubon Pl., Sacramento, CA 95825
THE NATURE CONSERVANCY, 785 Market St., San Francisco, CA 94103
SIERRA CLUB, 730 Polk St., San Francisco, CA 94109
YOSEMITE ASSOCIATION, P.O. Box 230, El Portal, CA 95318
CALIFORNIA WILDERNESS COALTION, 2655 Portage Bay, suite 5, Davis, CA 95616

Birdwatching in the Yosemite Sierra

Be patient.

Even the most furtive species reveal themselves to those who learn their habits and haunts. If you hurry through the mountains, your acquaintance with birds will be fleeting and brief. Take your time and they will become your friends.

Be attentive.

A rustling of leaves, a movement in the trees, or a speck on the horizon may alert your attention to birds.

Listen.

Many birds are more easily heard than seen. Learning to recognize songs and calls will increase your success and tune your sense.

Get away from roads.

Only when you leave your car behind will you hear the mountains sing.

Explore.

Birds live everywhere, not just in localities mentioned in this book. Take the time to search forests, marshes and meadows off the beaten path.

Take notes.

Observations which are not written down fade from memory. Most birdwatchers at least keep "trip lists" of species heard and seen. The more detailed your notes, the more you will remember.

Help improve this book.

Send copies of your observations on the west slope to the Yosemite Museum, Yosemite National Park, California 95389. Send observations east of the crest to the Mono Lake Committee Research Library, P.O. Box 29, Lee Vining, California 93541. They will be added to permanent files available to future researchers.

Dark-eyed Junco, courtesy Discovering Sierra Birds

Locality Lists with Status and Abundance Codes

These lists, presented in the form of matrices, summarize the status and abundance of every bird known to occur on the west slope, east of the crest, in Yosemite National Park and in eight representative localities. They code a wealth of information while facilitating comparisons between localities and elevations.

At first glance, the matrices may look like hieroglyphic spreadsheets. But the codes, defined on pp. 4 - 7, are quickly memorized. Small letters code abundance, capitalized ones seasonal status. For example, "xV" means Red-throated Loons are "extremely rare vagrants"; "uSrW" means Mallards are "uncommon summer residents and rare winter residents"; "fScT" means MacGillivray's Warblers are fairly common summer residents and common transients."

At the bottom of the lists, I total the number of species as well as the numbers that regularly nest or winter.

The eight localities are representative of elevation and habitat. With the exception of El Portal, their avifaunas are relatively well known.

El Portal (1200'-3000')

Merced River Canyon below 3000' from Briceburg (1200') east to the Arch Rock Entrance Station (2800').

Birdwatchers, eager to reach higher elevations, have neglected the chaparral, oak woodlands and grass-covered slopes of the foothills. And no wonder. Most of its species, widespread throughout the lowlands, are backyard birds to Californians. Here, however, they are nesting on elevational frontiers.

El Portal is the only locality where the number of wintering species (71) exceeds the number of breeding ones (61). This is hardly surprising, for the winters are relatively balmy, with rain rather than snow. The low overall species total (126) reflects sparse coverage; many other birds undoubtedly occur, but have yet to be recorded.

Yosemite Valley (3800'-5000')

Yosemite Valley below 5000' from the junction of Highways 140 and 120 (3800') east to Snow Creek (4200') and Vernal Falls (4400').

Yosemite's vertical walls cradle diverse habitats: open, dry woodlands, dense, humid forests, riparian thickets, shrubby hillsides, boggy meadows and talus slopes, just to name a few. Within a few minutes of the Visitor Center, for example, one may walk through black oaks, canyon oaks, ponderosa and lodgepole pines, douglas firs, incense cedars, cottonwoods, willows, alders and azaleas.

Because of varied habitat and extensive coverage, Yosemite Valley has the highest overall species total (210) of any west slope locality, and the highest breeding bird total

(89) of any locality. These sums include many rare species. The high winter total (68) is misleading, as over two-thirds are irregular or rare.

Ackerson Meadow (4600')

Ackerson Meadow system and surrounding forest along Ackerson Creek on the unglaciated divide between the south and middle forks of the Tuolumne River.

This large, varied mid-elevation meadow system is margined by forests of ponderosa and sugar pines, white firs, incense cedars and black oaks. Dense willow thickets line most of the slowly meandering creek. Regrettably, most of the area lies outside Yosemite National Park, and is subject to logging and grazing.

Ackerson Meadow supports a highly seasonal avifauna. Unlike El Portal and Yosemite Valley, the number of breeding species (74) far exceeds the number of wintering ones (32). In this respect, it resembles higher elevation localities. The overall species total (153), which includes many rarities, reflects extensive coverage.

Crane Flat (6200'-6600')

Crane Flat meadow system, Crane Flat Lookout and surrounding forest along Hwy. 120 on the unglaciated divide between the Tuolumne and Merced Rivers.

Like Ackerson, Crane Flat is an extensive meadow system, but 1,500 feet higher. Its deep, unglaciated soils nurture verdant, flowery meadows and magnificent forests, its steeper slopes black oaks and montane chaparral. Towering red firs and sugar pines, adorned with chartreuse staghorn liches, rise nearly 200 feet in height.

At this elevation, winter brings heavy snow. Crane Flat's wintering total (14) is less than half that at Ackerson Meadow and one-fourth that in Yosemite Valley and El Portal. The number of breeding species (46) is lower as well. Its low overall species total (106) is due to spotty coverage rather a lack of birds; many of the rarities recorded at Tuolumne Meadows and Tioga Pass will eventually be found here as well.

Tuolumne Meadows (8600'-9400')

Tuolumne Meadow system, Lembert (9400') and Pothole (9000') domes and surrounding forests.

At this elevation, one leaves oaks and firs behind. Vast meadows, the largest in the Sierra, are margined by lodgepole pines. In a few places, there are mountain hemlocks and Sierran junipers. Willows grow in scattered thickets along the river.

The ratio of nesting to wintering species at Tuolumne Meadows (42:16) is similar to those at Crane Flat (46:14) and Tioga Pass (37:12), which are also highly seasonal environments. Because of extensive coverage, Tuolumne has a high species total (142) that includes many rarities.

Tioga Pass (10,000'-13,100')

Tioga Pass region above 10,000' from Mt. Dana (13,053') north to Mt. Conness (12,590'), including the Hall Natural Area.

Here one meets avian mountaineers. Lodgepole pines, mixed with meadows and lakes, grow on glacial till. Whitebark pines and low, shrubby willows mountaineer to approximately 11,000'. Above the trees are meadows, fell-fields, talus and cliffs.

The high overall species total (140) reflects extensive coverage, especially in the Hall Natural Area.

Lee Vining Canyon (7200'-9000')

Lee Vining Canyon below 9000' from the Forest Service Ranger Station (7200') to the Poole Hydroelectric Plant (8000').

East of Tioga Pass, glaciers have carved Lee Vining Creek's steep-sided, level-floored canyon. Among diverse habitats are aspen groves, willow thickets, meadows, mixed conifer forests, pinyon pine woodlands, sagebrush scrub and rock outcroppings.

Compared to Crane Flat, Tuolumne Meadows and Tioga Pass, Lee Vining Canyon supports many more breeding (73) and wintering (37) species. These totals are comparable to Ackerson Meadow. Its overall species total (130), however, is surpassed by Tuolumne and Tioga—not because they harbor more birds, but because they have been more extensively birded.

Mono Lake (6400'-6500')

Mono Lake, islands, exposed lakebottom and adjacent meadows, scrub, thickets and trees.

Twice the size of San Francisco, Mono Lake dominates the landscape east of the Sierran escarpment. Streams flow into it, but none flow out. Over hundreds of thousands of years, evaporation—abetted since 1941 by water diversions—has concentrated its water to twice the salinity and one thousand times the alkalinity of seawater. Though too saline for fish, the lake is nutrient-rich and ultra-productive. During the summer, its shores swarm with astronomical numbers of brine flies, while its waters teem with endemic brine shrimp (*Artemia monica*).

Grebes, phalaropes, gulls and other birds come for easy meals. In freshwater lakes, fish predation keep numbers of invertebrates to relatively low levels. At Mono, in contrast, the absence of fish renders the lake an "all you can eat" restaurant, albeit with a limited menu. For more on the lake's importance to birds, turn to the species accounts on Eared Grebe (p. 60), Snowy Plover (p. 121), Wilson's Phalarope (p. 134), Red-necked Phalarope (p. 136) and California Gull (p. 142). For more on its biology and ecosystem, I can recommend my own *Mono Lake Guidebook* (1981).

Because it includes terrestrial as well as aquatic habitats, and has been thoroughly birded, Mono Lake has the highest total species count (288) of any locality. It lags just behind Yosemite Valley in nesting species (82), and just ahead in wintering ones (69).

	West Slope	East of Crest	Yosemite Park	El Portal
Red-throated Loon	-	xV	-	-
Pacific Loon	xV	rV	xV	-
Common Loon	xT	rS*lfT	xT	-
Pied-billed Grebe	rTxW	uScTrW	rTxW	rT
Horned Grebe	xT	xS*uT	xT	-
Eared Grebe	rT	cSluW	rT	-
Western Grebe	xT	lcSrW	xT	-
Clark's Grebe	xT	uS	xT	-
White Pelican	xS*rT	lcS*uT	xS*rT	-
Brown Pelican	-	xV	-	-
Double-crested Cormorant	xT	lfS*	xT	-
Pelagic Cormorant	-xV	-	-	-
Magnificent Frigatebird	-	xV	-	-
American Bittern	xT	eSrT	xT	-
Least Bittern	-	xT	-	-
Great Blue Heron	uR*	lcR*	uS*rW	uR*
Great Egret	xT	luS*lfT	xT	-
Snowy Egret	xT	rSuT	xT	-
Cattle Egret	-	rT	-	-
Green-backed Heron	xT	rTrS*	xT	-
Black-crowned Night Heron	xT	uSxW	-	-
White-faced Ibis	-	rS*	-	-
Tundra Swan	xT	luTrW	-	-
Trumpeter Swan	-	xT	-	-
Greater White-fronted Goose	-	rT	-	-
Snow Goose	xT	rT	xT	-

Yosemite Valley	Ackerson Meadow	Crane Flat	Tuolumne Meadow	Tioga Pass	Lee Vining	Mono Lake
-	-	-	-	-	-	xV
xV	-	-	-	-	-	xV
-	-	-	-	-	-	rT
rTxW	-	-	-	-	-	rT
-	-	-	-	-	-	xS*uT
xT	-	-	-	-	-	cS*luW
-	-	-	-	-	-	uT
-	-	-	-	-	-	xT
xT	-	-	-	-	-	rT
-	-	-	-	-	-	xV
xT	-	-	-	-	-	uS*
-	-	-	-	-	-	-
-	-	-	-	-	-	xV
xT	-	-	xT	-	-	xT
-	-	-	-	-	-	xT
uS*rW	xT	xT	rS*	rS*	rS*	rR*
xT	-	-	xT	-	-	rT
xT	-	-	xT	-	-	rSrT
-	-	-	-	-	-	rT
xT	-	-	-	-	-	rT
-	-	-	xT	xT	-	uS
-	-	-	-	-	-	rS*
-	-	-	-	-	-	rT
-	-	-	-	-	-	xT
-	-	-	-	-	-	rT
-	-	xT	xT	-	-	rT

	West Slope	East of Crest	Yosemite Park	El Portal
Ross' Goose	-	S*irT	-	-
Brant	-	xS*rV	-	-
Canada Goose	rT	lcR	rT	xT
Wood Duck	rR	xSirT	eSxT	-
Green-winged Teal	rT	uScTlcW	rT	rT
Mallard	uSrW	cSlfW	uSrW	rT
Northern Pintail	xT	uScTirW	xT	-
Blue-winged Teal	xT	rT	xT	-
Cinnamon Teal	rT	cS	rT	-
Northern Shoveler	xT	rS*cTirW	xT	-
Gadwall	xT	fScTfW	xT	-
Eurasian Wigeon	-	xV	-	
American Wigeon	xT	uScTfW	xT	-
Canvasback	xT	xS*rT	xT	-
Redhead	-	uSlcT	-	-
Ring-necked Duck	xW	uTxS	xW	-
Greater Scaup	-	rT	-	-
Lesser Scaup	xT	uT	xT	-
Harlequin Duck	rS	-	rS	-
Oldsquaw	-	xV	-	-
Black Scoter	-	xV	-	-
Surf Scoter	-	rV	-	-
White-winged Scoter	-	rV	-	-
Common Goldeneye	xW	uT	xT	-
Barrow's Goldeneye	eS	-	eS	-
Bufflehead	xT	S*lcTuW	xT	-

Yosemite Valley	Ackerson Meadow	Crane Flat	Tuolumne Meadow	Tioga Pass	Lee Vining	Mono Lake
-	-	-	-	-	-	S*irT
-	-	-	-	-	-	xS*rV
rT	-	xT	xT	-	-	uSfW
eSxR	-	-	-	-	-	irT
rT	-	-	xT	-	-	uScTfW
uSrW	uS	-	uS	uS	uS	uScTuW
xT	-	-	-	xT	-	uScTirW
xT	-	-	-	-	-	rT
rT	xT	-	xT	-	-	fS
xT	-	-	-	-	-	rS*cTirW
-	-	-	-	-	-	fSrW
-	-	-	-	-	-	-
xT	-	-	xT	-	-	fTrW
xT	-	-	-	-	-	xT
-	-	-	-	-	-	rSuT
xW	-	-	-	-	-	xS*uT
-	-	-	-	-	-	xT
xT	-	-	-	-	-	rT
xS	-	-	-	-	-	-
-	-	-	-	-	-	xV
-	-	-	-	-	-	xV
-	-	-	-	-	-	xV
-	-	-	-	-	-	xV
xT	-	-	-	-	-	rT
-	-	-	-	-	-	-
xT	-	-	-	-	-	rTxW

	West Slope	East of Crest	Yosemite Park	El Portal
Hooded Merganser	xW	xT	xW	-
Common Merganser	rR	rSlfTuW	rR	rR*
Red-breasted Merganser	-	irT	-	-
Ruddy Duck	rT	uS*cTlcW	rT	-
Turkey Vulture	rT	uS*fT	rT	rT
Osprey	xSrT	rS	xSrT	?
Black-shouldered Kite	lrS	xT	xT	-
Mississippi Kite	-	xV	-	-
Bald Eagle	xS*luW	xS*lfTuW	xS*luW	rW
Northern Harrier	rTxW	uSfTifW	rTxW	-
Sharp-shinned Hawk	rRuT	rRuT	rRuT	uTrW
Cooper's Hawk	rRuT	rRuT	rRuT	uTrW
Northern Goshawk	rR	rR	rR	irW
Red-shouldered Hawk	xT	xS*rT	xT	-
Swainson's Hawk	irT	rS	irT	-
Red-tailed Hawk	fR	fRlcT	fR	fR
Ferruginous Hawk	liuW	xT	-	-
Rough-legged Hawk	xW	ifW	xW	-
Golden Eagle	uR	uR	uR	uR
American Kestrel	uR	fSiuW	uR	uR
Merlin	rW	rW	rT	rW
Peregrine Falcon	rSirW	rSirW	rSirW	xT
Prairie Falcon	uS*	uR	uS*	-
Chuckar	-	uR	-	-
Blue Grouse	uR	uR	uR	-
White-tailed Ptarmigan	uR	uR	uR	-

Yosemite Valley	Ackerson Meadow	Crane Flat	Tuolumne Meadow	Tioga Pass	Lee Vining	Mono Lake
xW	-	-	-	-	-	xT
rR*	-	-	xT	-	-	-
-	-	-	-	-	-	irT
rT	-	-	-	-	-	rS*cTfW
rT	rT	xT	-	xT	rT	rS*fT
rT	xT	-	rT	rT	rT	rS
xT	-	xT	-	-	-	-
-	-	-	-	-	-	xV
rW	-	-	xT	-	rW	uW
rTxW	rT	-	rT	rT	rT	uSfTifW
rSuT	uT	rS?uT	uT	uT	uT	uT
rRuT	rRuT	uT	uT	uT	rRuT	uT
rR?	rR	-	rS	rS*	rR	rW
-	xT	-	xT	xT	-	xS*rT
-	-	-	?	irT	-	rT
fR	fR	uS*	fS*	fS*	fR	fR
-	xT	-	-	-	-	-
-	-	-	xW	-	-	ifW
rR	xT	-	uS*	uS	uR	uR*
uR	uS*	-	uS*	uS*	uS	fSiuW
rT	rT	-	-	rT	rW	rW
rSirW	-	-	rS*	rT	rS	rT
-	xT	-	uS*	uS*	uS	uR*
-	-	-	-	-	-	-
rR*	-	-	uR	rS*	uR	-
-	-	-	-	uR	-	-

	West Slope	East of Crest	Yosemite Park	El Portal
Sage Grouse	xT	luR	xT	-
California Quail	iuR	rR?	irR	iuR
Mountain Quail	fR	uSrW	fR	uR
Yellow Rail	xT	xT	xT	-
Virginia Rail	rS	uSrW	rS	-
Sora	xT	uS	xT	-
Common Moorhen	lrT	xS*rT	-	-
American Coot	xS*rTlrW	lcRcT	xS*rT	-
Sandhill Crane	-	xT	-	-
Black-bellied Plover	-	uT	-	-
Lesser Golden Plover	-	xT	-	-
Snowy Plover	-	lcS	-	-
Semipalmated Plover	-	fT	-	-
Killdeer	luSrW	cSifW	luSrW	rW
Mountain Plover	-	xT	-	-
Black-necked Stilt	xT	rSuT	xT	-
American Avocet	xT	lcScT	xT	-
Greater Yellowlegs	xT	uT	xT	-
Lesser Yellowlegs	-	uT	-	-
Solitary Sandpiper	xT	rT	xT	-
Willet	xT	lfS	xT	-
Wandering Tattler	-	irV	-	-
Spotted Sandpiper	luSxW	lfSxW	luSxW	uS
Whimbrel	-	rT	-	-
Long-billed Curlew	-	rS*	-	-
Marbled Godwit	-	rT	-	-

Yosemite Valley	Ackerson Meadow	Crane Flat	Tuolumne Meadow	Tioga Pass	Lee Vining	Mono Lake
-	-	-	-	-	-	xT
xT	xT	-	-	-	-	rR?
uR	fR	uS	rS	rS*	uS	rW
-	-	-	xT	-	-	xT
rS	-	-	-	-	-	uSrW
xT	-	-	-	-	-	uS
-	-	-	-	-	-	rT
rT	-	-	xT	xT	-	uSfT
-	-	-	-	-	-	xT
-	-	-	-	-	-	uT
-	-	-	-	-	-	xT
-	-	-	-	-	-	cS
-	-	-	-	-	-	fT
rR*	rS	xS	uS	-	rS	cSiuW
-	-	-	-	-	-	xT
xT	-	-	-	-	-	rSuT
-	-	-	-	-	-	fScT
-	-	-	xT	-	-	uT
-	-	-	-	-	-	uT
-	-	-	xT	-	-	rT
xT	-	-	-	-	-	uT
-	-	-	-	-	-	irV
uSxW	-	-	uS	uS	rS	fSxW
-	-	-	-	-	-	rT
-	-	-	-	-	-	rS*
-	-	-	-	-	-	rT

	West Slope	East of Crest	Yosemite Park	El Portal
Ruddy Turnstone	-	rT	-	-
Red Knot	-	rT	-	-
Sanderling	-	rT	-	-
Semipalmated Sandpiper	-	rV	-	-
Western Sandpiper	-	cT	-	-
Least Sandpiper	xT	cT	xT	-
White-rumped Sandpiper	-	xV	-	-
Baird's Sandpiper	-	uT	-	-
Pectoral Sandpiper	-	uT	-	-
Stilt Sandpiper	-	xV	-	-
Dunlin	-	fT	-	-
Ruff	-	xV	-	-
Short-billed Dowitcher	-	fT	-	-
Long-billed Dowitcher	-	fT	-	-
Common Snipe	rTxW	fSifW	rTxW	-
Wilson's Phalarope	xT	fScT	xT	-
Red-necked Phalarope	xT	rS*cT	xT	-
Red Phalarope	xV	rV	xV	-
Pomarine Jaeger	-	xV	-	-
Parasitic Jaeger	-	rV	-	-
Long-tailed Jaeger	-	xV	-	-
Jaeger species?	*xV*	-	*xV*	-
Little Gull	-	xV	-	-
Franklin's Gull	xT	-	-	-
Bonaparte's Gull	-	rS*icT	-	-
Heerman's Gull	-	-	-	-

Yosemite Valley	Ackerson Meadow	Crane Flat	Tuolumne Meadow	Tioga Pass	Lee Vining	Mono Lake
-	-	-	-	-	-	rT
-	-	-	-	-	-	rT
-	-	-	-	-	-	rT
-	-	-	-	-	-	rV
-	-	-	-	-	-	cT
-	-	-	xT	-	-	cT
-	-	-	-	-	-	xV
-	-	-	-	-	-	uT
-	-	-	-	-	-	uT
-	-	-	-	-	-	xV
-	-	-	-	-	-	fT
-	-	-	-	-	-	-
-	-	-	-	-	-	fT
-	-	-	-	-	-	fT
rTxW	rTxW	rT	rT	-	uS	fSifW
xT	-	-	xT	-	-	fScT
xT	-	-	-	xT	-	rS*cT
xV	-	-	-	-	-	rV
-	-	-	-	-	-	xV
-	-	-	-	-	-	rV
-	-	-	-	-	-	xV
-	-	-	*xV*	-	-	-
-	-	-	-	-	-	-
-	-	-	-	-	-	xT
-	-	-	-	-	-	rS*icT
-	-	-	-	-	-	xV

	West Slope	East of Crest	Yosemite Park	El Portal
Ring-billed Gull	xT	rS*fTrW	xT	-
California Gull	lfS*	cSrW	lfS*	rT
Herring Gull	-	xS*rW	-	-
Yellow-footed Gull	-	xV	-	-
Glaucous-winged Gull	-	xV	-	-
Sabine's Gull	-	rV	-	-
Caspian Tern	xT	uS	xT	-
Common Tern	-	rT	-	-
Arctic Tern	-	xV	-	-
Forster's Tern	-	luS*uT	-	-
Forster's or Common Tern	*xT*	-	*xT*	-
Least Tern	-	xV	-	-
Black Tern	-	rS*	-	-
Marbled Murrelet	-	xV	-	-
Ancient Murrelet	-	xV	-	-
Rock Dove	rT	rT	rT	rT
Band-tailed Pigeon	uSicW	rS	uSicW	uSicW
White-winged Dove	-	xV	-	-
Ground Dove	-	xV	-	-
Mourning Dove	uSrW	fS	uSrW	uSrW
Black-billed Cuckoo	-	xV	-	-
Yellow-billed Cuckoo	-	xT	-	-
Greater Roadrunner	rR	xT	xT	-
Barn Owl	lfR	rT	xT	-
Flammulated Owl	uS	xT	uS	-
Western Screech-Owl	lfR	xT	rT	fR

Yosemite Valley	Ackerson Meadow	Crane Flat	Tuolumne Meadow	Tioga Pass	Lee Vining	Mono Lake
xT	-	-	-	-	-	rS*uTrW
uS*	rT	rT	fS*	fS*	cS*	cSrW
-	-	-	-	-	-	xS*rW
-	-	-	-	-	-	-
-	-	-	-	-	-	-
-	-	-	-	-	-	rV
-	-	-	xT	xT	-	uS
-	-	-	-	-	-	rT
-	-	-	-	-	-	xV
-	-	-	-	-	-	rT
-	-	-	-	-	-	-
-	-	-	-	-	-	-
-	-	-	-	-	-	rT
-	-	-	-	-	-	xV
-	-	-	-	-	-	xV
rT	rT	-		-	xT	rTrT
uSicW	rS*	rS*	rS*	rS*	rS*	rS*
-	-	-	-	-	-	xV
-	-	-	-	-	-	-
rSirW	uSirW	rT	rT	rT	uT	fS
-	-	-	-	-	-	xV
-	-	-	-	-	-	xT
xT	-	-	-	-	-	xT
xT	irT	xT	-	-	-	rT
?	uS	-	-	-	?	-
rT	xT	-	xT	xT	-	-

	West Slope	East of Crest	Yosemite Park	El Portal
Great Horned Owl	fR	fR	fR	fR
Northern Pygmy-Owl	uR	rR	uR	uR
Burrowing Owl	xT	rT	xT	-
Spotted Owl	uR	xS*	rR	-
Great Gray Owl	rR	xT	rR	-
Long-eared Owl	rR?	uSrW	rR?	?
Short-eared Owl	-	eSrT	-	-
Northern Saw-whet Owl	rR	rR	rR	xT
Common Nighthawk	rTxS?	cS	rT	?
Common Poor-will	fS	fS	lfS	fS
Black Swift	fS	rT	fS	?
Chimney Swift	-	xV	-	-
Vaux's Swift	rS	rT	rS	?
White-throated Swift	cSuW	luS	cS	cSuW
Black-chinned Hummingbird	rS	rS	rS	rS
Anna's Hummingbird	lfR	rT	uS*	fR
Costa's Hummingbird	xT	-	xT	-
Calliope Hummingbird	fS	fS	fS	rT
Broad-tailed Hummingbird	xT	lrS	xT	-
Rufous Hummingbird	cT	cT	cT	fT
Allen's Hummingbird	xT?	-	xT?	-
Belted Kingfisher	uR	rR	uR	uR
Lewis' Woodpecker	irT	uS	irT	irT
Acorn Woodpecker	cR	xT	cR	cR
Red-naped Sapsucker	xS*rW	xSrT	xS*rW	-
Red-breasted Sapsucker	fSuW	cSxW	fSrW	uW

Yosemite Valley	Ackerson Meadow	Crane Flat	Tuolumne Meadow	Tioga Pass	Lee Vining	Mono Lake
fR	fR	rR*	uR	uR	fR	fR
uR	uR	rR	xT	-	rR	-
-	-	-	-	-	-	rT
rR	rR	-	-	-	-	-
xW	rR	rS	-	-	-	-
rR?	irR	rT	xT	rT	rS	uSrW
-	-	-	-	-	-	rT
rR	rR	rS?	-	-	?	-
rT	rT	rT	xT	-	rT	cS
uS	rT	rT	-	rT	fS	fS
fS	rS*	rS*	?	rS*	-	xT
-	-	-	-	-	-	xV
rT	rS*	rS	-	xT	-	rT
cS	uS*	rS*	rS*	rS*	uS	rS*
rS	xT	-	-	xT	-	rS
uS*	rS*	rT	rT	rT	rT	rT
-	-	-	-	-	-	-
uS	fS	uS	rS*	rS	fS	uS
-	-	-	-	-	-	-
fT	cT	cT	cT	cT	cT	fT
xT?	-	-	-	-	-	-
uR	rT	-	rT	rT	rR	rT
irT	irT	-	irT	irT	irT	rT
cR	-	-	xT	xT	-	-
rW	-	-	-	-	xSrT	rT
rSfTrW	fS	fS	uS	uS	cS	fS

	West Slope	East of Crest	Yosemite Park	El Portal
Williamson's Sapsucker	uR	uSxW	uR	-
Nuttall's Woodpecker	lfR	rT	lrR	fR
Downey Woodpecker	uR	luR	uR	uR
Hairy Woodpecker	fR	fR	fR	?
White-headed Woodpecker	fR	rR	fR	-
Black-backed Woodpecker	rR	xT	rR	-
"Red-sh." Northern Flicker	fSifW	fSifW	fSifW	uSfW
"Yellow-shafted" N. Flicker	xV	xV	-	xV
Pileated Woodpecker	uR	-	uR	-
Olive-sided Flycatcher	fS	uS	fS	uT
Western Wood Pewee	cS	cS	cS	rT
Willow Flycatcher	lrS	lrS	lrS	?
Least Flycatcher	-	xV	-	-
Hammond's Flycatcher	cS	rT	cS	uT
Dusky Flycatcher	fS	fS	fS	uT
Gray Flycatcher	xT	lfS	xT	-
Western Flycatcher Complex	luS	rS	luS	uS
Black Phoebe	lfR	rT	luSiuW	fR
Eastern Phoebe	-	-	-	-
Say's Phoebe	rTxW	uSfTxW	rT	xW
Vermilion Flycatcher	-	xV	-	-
Ash-throated Flycatcher	fS	rT	lfS	fS
Tropical Kingbird	-	xT	-	-
Western Kingbird	luS	uTrS*	rS*	uS
Eastern Kingbird	-	xV	-	-
Scissor-tailed Flywatcher	-	-	-	-

Yosemite Valley	Ackerson Meadow	Crane Flat	Tuolumne Meadow	Tioga Pass	Lee Vining	Mono Lake
uW	rW	rT	uS	rS*	rTxW	rT
rW	irR*	-	-	-	-	rT
uR	uR	rT	xT	-	rR	uR
fR	rR	fR	fR	uR	fR	fR
uR	fR	fR	-	xT	-	-
xS*	xS*	xR	rR	xW	-	-
fSifW	fSifW	fS	fS	fS	fSifW	fSifW
-	xV	-	-	xV	-	-
uR	uR	uR	-	-	-	-
uS	fS	fS	uS	rS	uS	uT
cS	cS	cS	cS	rS*	cS	fS
eSrT	lrS	rT	-	xT	rS	rT
-	-	-	-	-	-	xV
uT	fS	cS	rT	rT	rT	rT
uT	uS	uS	fS	cS	fS	uT
-	xT	-	-	xT	-	fS
uS	rS	rT	rT	rT	rS*	rT
uSiuW	uS	xT	-	xT	xT	rT
-	-	-	-	-	-	xV
rT	rT	xT	xT	xT	-	uSfTxW
-	-	-	-	-	-	xV
rT	rT	xT	xT	-	-	rT
-	-	-	-	-	-	-
rT	rT	-	xT	-	-	uT
-	-	-	-	-	-	xV
-	-	-	-	-	-	xV

	West Slope	East of Crest	Yosemite Park	El Portal
Horned Lark	lfSxW	cSiuW	lfSxW	-
Purple Martin	luS	xT	-	-
Tree Swallow	uS	uSfT	uS	uS
Violet-green Swallow	cS	cS	cS	uS
N. Rough-winged Swallow	uS	rSuT	uS	uS
Bank Swallow	xT	lcS	xT	-
Cliff Swallow	lcS	lcS	iuS	lcS
Barn Swallow	lcS	uSfT	lcS	uS
Steller's Jay	cR	cSicW	cR	fR
Scrub Jay	lcR	uR	rR	cR
Pinyon Jay	irT	lcSicW	irT	-
Clark's Nutcracker	cSicW	cSicW	cSicW	-
Black-billed Magpie	xV	lcR	xV	-
Yellow-billed Magpie	-	xT	xT	-
American Crow	rT	rT	rT	?
Common Raven	lfR	lcR	fSrW	fR
Mountain Chickadee	cR	cR	cR	uW
Chestnut-backed Chickadee	luR	-	luR	-
Plain Titmouse	lcR	rSuW	rR	cR
Bushtit	lcR	rSfW	uR	cR
Red-breasted Nuthatch	cR	lfR	cR	icW
White-breasted Nuthatch	lfR	uR	uR	uR
Pygmy Nuthatch	luR	fR	luR	-
Brown Creeper	fSifW	fSiuW	fSifW	ifW
Rock Wren	luR	uS	uS	uR
Canyon Wren	fR	uR	fR	fR

Yosemite Valley	Ackerson Meadow	Crane Flat	Tuolumne Meadow	Tioga Pass	Lee Vining	Mono Lake
rT	rTxW	-	xT	fS	-	cSiuW
-	-	-	-	-	-	-
uS	uS	rT	rS	xT	uS	uSfT
cS	cS	fS	fS	rS*	cS	cS
uS	uS	-	xT	xT	-	rSuT
xT	-	-	-	-	-	rT
iuS	iuS	xT	xT	xT	?	uT
uS	cS	-	xT	-	-	uSfT
cR	cR	cSuW	fSrW	uS	cSicW	fSicW
rR*	rT	-	rS*	rS*	rW	rS*uW
irT	-	-	irT	irT	irT	uS*
rW	rW	rT	cSicW	cSifW	cSicW	fSicW
xV	-	-	-	-	-	cR
xT	-	-	-	-	-	-
rT	xT	xT	xT	-	-	rT
uSrW	fSrR	fSrW	fS*rW	rS*	fSrW	cSuW
fR	cR	cR	cR	cR	cR	uSfW
luR	xR	-	-	-	-	-
rR	-	-	-	-	rW	rSuW
uR	uS*	uS*	rS*	rS*	rW	rSfW
fSicW	cSifW	uSifW	iuS	icT	ifR	rW
rR	rT	-	uR	uR	uR	uR
iuR	iuR	-	xS*	xT	fR	-
fSifW	fSifW	fSifW	iuS	iuW		fSiuWuW
rS	xT	-	rS	uS	uS	uS
fR	-	-	-	xT	uR	rW

	West Slope	East of Crest	Yosemite Park	El Portal
Bewick's Wren	lfR	rSuW	rS	fR
House Wren	lcS	cS	uSfT	cS
Winter Wren	luR	rW	luR	-
Marsh Wren	rTxW	rSfTrW	rT	-
American Dipper	fR	fR	fR	fR
Golden-crowned Kinglet	cSicW	uSiuW	cSicW	icW
Ruby-crowned Kinglet	uScW	rScT	uSuW	cW
Blue-gray Gnatcatcher	uS	uSxW	rS	uS
Western Bluebird	fR	uSxT	lfSiuW	fR
Mountain Bluebird	uSrW	uSfTrW	uSxW	rTxW
Townsend's Solitaire	uSluW	uSfW	uSluW	rW
Swainson's Thrush	rS	rS	rS	-
Hermit Thrush	fSrW	fSrW	fSrW	uW
American Robin	cSicW	cSicW	cSicW	cSicW
Varied Thrush	ifW	irTxW	ifW	ifW
Wrentit	lcR	-	lfR	cR
Gray Catbird	-	xV	-	-
Northern Mockingbird	rS*xW	rS*xW	-	rS*
Sage Thrasher	xT	cSxW	-	-
Brown Thrasher	-	xV	-	-
California Thrasher	lfR	-	xT	fR
Water Pipit	luSrTxW	luScTiuW	luSrTxW	-
Bohemian Waxwing	xT	xT	xT	-
Cedar Waxwing	rTifW	uTrW	rT	ifW
Phainopepla	xT	xT	xT	-
Northern Shrike	xW	rW	xW	-

Yosemite Valley	Ackerson Meadow	Crane Flat	Tuolumne Meadow	Tioga Pass	Lee Vining	Mono Lake
rS	rTxW	-	-	-	rW	rSuW
uSfT	uS	fT	fT	fT	cS	cS
uR	uR	rSxW	xT	xT	rW	rW
rTxW	xT	-	xT	-	-	rSuTrW
fR	xT	-	uSirW	uSifW	fR	-
uSicW	cSicW	cSicW	rS	rS	uSiuW	iuW
uTrW	uW	uT	uS	rSuT	fT	cT
rS	-	-	xT	-	uS	uSxW
uSiuW	fSiuW	rT	xT	-	-	-
eSrTxW	rT	rT	uS	uS	uS	uSfTrW
rT	rS	rT	uSrW	iuS	uSfW	rW
eS	-	-	-	-	rS	-
uTrW	uT	fS	fS	fS	fS	uTrW
cSirW	cS	cS	cSirW	cS	cSicW	cSicW
ifW	irT	-	xT	xT	irTxW	irT
-	-	-	-	-	-	-
-	-	-	-	-	-	-
xW	rS*xW	-	-	xT	-	xTrS*
xT	xT	-	-	-	-	cSxW
-	-	-	-	-	-	-
-	-	-	-	-	-	-
rT	rTxW	rT	rT	uS	rT	cTiuW
xT	-	-	-	-	xT	-
rT	rT	-	-	xT	uTrW	uTrW
xT	xT	-	-	-	xT	xT
-	xW	-	-	xT	rW	rW

	West Slope	East of Crest	Yosemite Park	El Portal
Loggerhead Shrike	rT	uSrW	irT	?
European Starling	lcSuW	cSlcW	lcSrW	cR
White-eyed Vireo	-	xV	-	-
"Cassin's" Solitary Vireo	fS	uT	fS	uT
"Plumbeous" Solitary Vireo	-	rS	-	-
Yellow-throated Vireo	-	xV	-	-
Warbling Vireo	cS	cS	cS	uT
Red-eyed Vireo	-	xV	-	-
Blue-winged Warbler	-	xV	-	-
Golden-winged Warbler	-	xV	-	-
Tennessee Warbler	xV	irV	xV	-
Orange-crowned Warbler	cS	cS*	uScS*	cS
Nashville Warbler	cS	rSuT	cS	uT
Virginia Warbler	xV	irS	xT	-
Northern Parula	xV	irV	xV	-
Yellow Warbler	cS	cS	cS	cS
Chesnut-sided Warbler	-	xV	-	-
Magnolia Warbler	xV	xV	xV	-
Black-throated Blue Warbler	-	xV	-	-
"Aud." Yellow-rumped Warb.	cSuW	cSrW	cSrW	cTuW
"Myrtle" Yellow-rumped Warb.	xT	rT	xT	-
Black-throated Gray Warbler	cSxW	luS	cSxW	uTxW
Townsend's Warbler	uTrW	uT	uTrW	uTrW
Hermit Warbler	cS	lrT	cS	rT
Grace's Warbler	-	xV	-	-
Prairie Warbler	-	xV	-	-

Yosemite Valley	Ackerson Meadow	Crane Flat	Tuolumne Meadow	Tioga Pass	Lee Vining	Mono Lake
irT	xT	-	irT	xT	-	uSrW
uS	cS	-	-	-	cS	cR
-	-	-	-	-	-	-
fS	fS	uS	rT	rT	uT	uT
-	-	-	-	-	-	-
-	-	-	-	-	-	xV
cS	cS	cS	uS	rT	cS	fS
-	-	-	-	-	-	xV
-	-	-	-	-	-	-
-	-	-	-	-	-	-
	xV	-	-	-	xV	xV
fS*	fS*	cS*	cS*	cS*	fS*	fS*cT
cS	fS	uSfT	uT	uT	rSuT	uT
xT	xT	xT	-	xT	rS	xT
xV	-	-	-	-	xV	irV
cS	cS	rT	-	xT	cS	cS
-	-	-	-	-	-	-
xV	-	-	-	-	-	-
-	-	-	-	-	xV	-
uScTrW	cS	cS	cS	cS	fScT	cTrW
xT	xT	-	-	-	rT	rT
cS	uS	fT	rT	rT	rT	rT
uTrW	-	uT	uT	uT	uT	uT
uS	fS	cS	rT	rT	xT	xT
-	-	-	-	-	-	-
-	-	-	-	xT	-	-

	West Slope	East of Crest	Yosemite Park	El Portal
Palm Warbler	-	xV	-	-
Blackpoll Warbler	xV	xV	xV	-
Cerulean Warbler	xV	-	xV	-
Black-and-White Warbler	xV	xV	xV	-
American Redstart	-	rT	-	-
Prothonotary Warbler	-	xV	-	-
Ovenbird	xV	xV	xV	-
Northern Waterthrush	-	xT	-	-
Kentucky Warbler -		xV	-	-
MacGillivray's Warbler	fSicT	fS	fSicT	uT
Common Yellowthroat	rTxS*	fTrS*	rTxS*	rT
Hooded Warbler	-	xV	-	-
Wilson's Warbler	uScT	uScT	uScT	uT
Canada Warbler	-	xV	-	-
Yellow-breasted Chat	xT	rTirS*	xT	-
Summer Tanager	-	xV	-	-
Western Tanager	fS	fS	fS	uT
Rose-breasted Grosbeak	xV	irV	xV	-
Black-headed Grosbeak	cSxW	uS	cSxW	uT
Blue Grosbeak	xS	-	xT	xS
Lazuli Bunting	lfS	lfS	lfS	rS
Indigo Bunting	-	xT	-	-
California Towhee	rSxW	cSxW	rS	xW
Rufous-sided Towhee	cR	lfR	lfR	cR
Brown Towhee	lcR	-	luR	cR
Cassin's Sparrow	-	xV	-	-

Yosemite Valley	Ackerson Meadow	Crane Flat	Tuolumne Meadow	Tioga Pass	Lee Vining	Mono Lake
-	-	-	-	xV	-	--
xV	-	-	-	-	-	xV
xV	-	-	-	-	-	-
xV	-	-	-	-	-	xV
-	-	-	-	xT	rT	xT
-	-	-	-	-	-	xV
xV	-	-	-	-	-	-
-	-	-	-	-	xT	-
-	-	-	-	-	-	xV
fS	fS	fSicT	icT	icT	fS	fT
rTxS*	rT	xT	-	xS*	-	rS*fT
-	-	-	-	-	-	xV
rScT	uS	rScT	uSfT	uSfT	uScT	cT
-	-	-	-	-	-	-
xT	-	-	-	-	-	irS*rT
-	-	-	-	-	-	xV
fS	fS	fS	rT	rT	fS	uT
xV	-	-	-	-	xV	irV
cSxW	cS	uS	rT	rT	uS	uT
xT	-	-	-	-	-	-
rS	fS	uS	uT	uT	uT	fS
-	-	-	-	-	-	xT
rT	rT	rT	xT	rT	cS	cS
rR	rT	rT	rT	rT	uR	rSuW
-	-	-	-	-	-	-
-	-	-	-	-	-	xV

	West Slope	East of Crest	Yosemite Park	El Portal
Rufous-crowned Sparrow	luR	-	xT	luR
American Tree Sparrow	-	irW	-	-
Chipping Sparrow	cS	fS	cS	uT
Brewer's Sparrow	rT	cS	rT	-
Black-chinned Sparrow	lrS	irS?	rS	-
Vesper Sparrow	rT	uS	rT	-
Lark Sparrow	rTlrW	rT	rT	rW
Black-throated Sparrow	xT	iuS	xT	-
Sage Sparrow	rR	lcSxW	xT	rT
Lark Bunting	-	xT	-	-
Savannah Sparrow	luS	cSrW	luS	rT
Grasshopper Sparrow	irS	-	xS*	-
Fox Sparrow	cSuW	cSxW	cSrW	uW
Song Sparrow	cSrW	cSlfW	cSrW	cSrW
Lincoln's Sparrow	fSrW	rSuTrW	rSuT	uTrW
Swamp Sparrow	-	irW	-	-
White-throated Sparrow	xW	rT	xT	-
Golden-crowned Sparrow	xS*lcW	uT	uW	cW
"Mtn." White-crowned Sparrow	cS	cS	cS	-
"Gambel's" White-cr. Sparrow	uTrW	cTrW	uTrW	uTrW
Harris' Sparrow	xT	-	xT	-
"Oregon" Dark-eyed Junco	cR	cSicW	cSuW	icW
"Slate-colored" Junco	rW	rW	rW	rW
"Gray-headed" Junco	xW	xW	xW	-
McCown's Longspur	-	xV	-	-
Chestnut-collared Longspur	xT	rT	xT	-

Yosemite Valley	Ackerson Meadow	Crane Flat	Tuolumne Meadow	Tioga Pass	Lee Vining	Mono Lake
xT	-	-	-	-	-	-
-	-	-	-	-	-	irW
uS	cS	cS	cS	ifS	fS	fT
xT	rT	-	xT	rT	cS	cS
-	-	-	-	-	-	-
rT	rT	-	rT	rT	rT	uS
rT	rT	rT	xT	xT	xT	rT
-	xT	-	-	xT	-	iuS?
xT	-	xT	-	xT	-	uS
-	-	-	-	-	-	xT
rT	rT	rT	uS	rT	fS	cSrW
-	irS	-	-	-	-	-
uT	uT	cS	rT	rT	cS	uT
cSrW	cS	rS*	rS*	rS*	cS	cSfW
uSrW	uS	fS	uS	uT	uT	uTrW
-	-	-	-	-	-	irW
xT	-	-	-	-	-	rT
rT	rT	rT	xS*rT	rT	uT	rT
eS	xT	rT	cS	cS	rSfT	cT
uTrW	uT	uT	fT	fT	cT	cTrW
xT	-	-	-	xT	-	-
uSifW	fS	cS	cS	cS	cSifW	uTifW
rW	-	-	-	xT	rW	rW
xW	-	-	-	-	-	-
-	-	-	-	-	-	xV
-	xT	-	-	-	-	rT

	West Slope	East of Crest	Yosemite Park	El Portal
Bobolink	xV	xV	xV	-
Red-winged Blackbird	cSrW	cSrW	cSxW	uSrW
Western Meadowlark	uSrW	fSxW	uSrW	uSrW
Yellow-headed Blackbird	rT	lcS	rT	-
Rusty Blackbird	-	xVxW	-	-
Brewer's Blackbird	lcSrW	cSrW	lcSrW	cSrW
Great-tailed Grackle	xV	xV	xV	-
Common Grackle	-	xV	-	-
Brown-headed Cowbird	lcS	lcS	lcS	fS
Orchard Oriole	-	xV	-	-
Hooded Oriole	-	irT	-	-
"Bullock's" Northern Oriole	cS	fS	uS	cS
"Baltimore" Northern Oriole	-	xV	-	-
Rosy Finch	fSirW	fSilcW	fSrW	-
Pine Grosbeak	ifR	iuR	ifR	-
Purple Finch	cR	xT	cR	icW
Cassin's Finch	cSrW	cSifW	cSrW	-
House Finch	rS*	lcS	rS*	rS*
Red Crossbill	ifR	ifR	ifR	iuW
Pine Siskin	cSifW	icSrW	cSifW	ifW
Lesser Goldfinch	fSifW	uS	-	fSifW
Lawrence's Goldfinch	iuS	xT	iuS	iuS
American Goldfinch	rTxW	fTrW	rTxW	rT
Evening Grosbeak	icR	rSicW	icR	ifW
House Sparrow	lcR	cR	luR	cR
TOTAL SPECIES	252	337	242	126

Yosemite Valley	Ackerson Meadow	Crane Flat	Tuolumne Meadow	Tioga Pass	Lee Vining	Mono Lake
-	-	-	-	-	-	xV
cSxW	cS	-	fS	xT	cS	cSrW
rS	uS	rT	rT	rT	uT	fS
rT	rT	-	xT	-	-	lcS
-	-	-	-	-	-	xV
cSrW	cS	cS	cS*	ifS*	cS	cSrW
xV	-	-	-	-	-	-
-	-	-	-	-	-	-
cS	fS	fS	cS	uS	cS	cS
-	-	-	-	-	-	xV
	-	-	-	-	-	irT
uS	rT	rT	-	xT	fS	fS
-	-	-	-	-	-	-
xW	-	-	-	fSirW	ifW	rW
xT	xT	rT	ifR	iuR	-	-
uR	cR	fS	-	xT	-	-
rW	fSrW	rS	cS	cS	cSrW	cSifW
rS*	rS*	-	-	xT	rT	lcScT
ifR	ifR	ifR	ifR	ifR	ifR	rT
ifR	ifR	ifR	cSifW	iuS	icSrW	ifTrW
uSxW	cS	iuS*	iuS*	iuS*	uS*	uS
xT	iuS	xT	-	-	-	xT
rTxW	rT	-	xT	-	-	fTrW
icR	icR	icR	iuS*	xS*	rSicW	rT
uR	xT	-	-	-	-	rT
210	153	106	142	140	130	288

Eared Grebe

Order GAVIIFORMES: LOONS

Family GAVIIDAE: LOONS

Loons dive for fish on large, deep freshwater lakes and reservoirs. Of our three species, only Commons are regular transients. None remain to nest.

The alkali-coated carcasses of loons are washed up regularly on Mono Lake's shores. These ill-fated birds alight on the lake's alkaline, fishless waters after exhausting migratory journeys. Finding little if anything that they can eat, and lacking the fat reserves to fly elsewhere, they leave their bones at this salty, inland sea.

RED-THROATED LOON (*Gavia stellata*)

Rare vagrant east of crest.

Six records. 6500' Bridgeport Reservoir 6/12-8/21/89 (AB 43:1362, PM); 6400' Mono Lake 6/11/76 (AB 30:997) and 11/7/81 (DG); 7600' June Lake 11/21/76 (AB 31:367)and 11/26/88 (JJ); 6900' Grant Reservoir 12/6/85 (DG).

PACIFIC (ARCTIC) LOON (*Gavia pacifica*)

Extremely rare vagrant on west slope; irregularly rare fall vagrant below 8000' east of crest.

While Pacific Loons usually migrate and winter along the coast, they occasionally stray to large, inland lakes and reservoirs. Of two records at Mono Lake (6400'), one was found dead on the summery date of 7/25/82; as this bird had been dead at least several months (JJ), it was probably an errant spring migrant.

West slope records: 8100' Tenaya Lake 9/1/64 (DDeS); 4000' Merced River, Yosemite Valley, 12/6-12/10/29 (GM 36; YNN 15:79); (I have rejected an April record from Lake Eleanor because of the lack of details—YM).

Extreme dates east excluding July record, eight records since 1975: 9/13/89 6900' Crowley Reservoir (PM); 10/31/86 6500' Bridgeport Lake Reservoir (DS, SJ) - 12/8/76 7600' June Lake (AB 31:367).

Additional references: AB 34:195; AB 30:118.

COMMON LOON (*Gavia immer*)

	J	F	M	A	M	J	J	A	S	O	N	D	HABITAT	ELEVATIONS		
														N	T	W
WEST				•	•					•					4-8	
EAST													LMo		6-8	

Extremely rare transient on west slope; extremely rare transient above 7500' on east slope; locally fairly common transient and rare summer resident below 7500' east of crest.

East of the crest, Common Loons can usually be found on Bridgeport Lake (6500'), Crowley Lake (6800') and Grant Lake (7100') reservoirs. Less frequently, they visit other deep, freshwater lakes, and even Mono Lake's alkaline, fishless waters, as well. Unlike grebes and ducks, they usually fish alone or in pairs. They linger in autumn as long as open water remains extensive, but are not known to overwinter.

Common Loons are usually dressed in drab winter or immature plumage, but spring birds sometimes sport brilliant breeding finery. In April and May, I've heard their long, quavering cries and maniacal laughter, though the closest breeding haunts are 300 miles north. They sometimes summer, but are not known to nest.

Peak counts: 27, Crowley Reservoir 4/17/90 (AB 44:491); 25, 11/7/90 Grant Reservoir (AB 44:145).

West slope records: 3700' Hetch Hetchy Reservoir 4/12-15/87 (YM); 6400' Laurel Lake 5/1-2/76 (YM); 8100' Tenaya Lake, 2, 5/29/77 (YM), 6/15-9/9/77 (YM, TB) and, 2, 10/19/85 (MC); 4700' Lake Eleanor Reservoir 10/28-11/?/86 (YM).

East slope records above 8000': 9700' Tioga Lake, 2, 5/28/77 (YM), 7/6-10/27/77 (YM, DeSante and Engstrom MS) and 11/3/87 (DG).

Extreme dates: 3/25/80 Mono Lake (DW) - 12/20/80, 2, Crowley Lake Reservoir (AB 35:715).

Additional reference: AFN 6:35.

Order PODICIPEDIFORMES: GREBES

Family PODICIPEDIDAE: GREBES

These duck-like diving birds frequent lakes, ponds and occasionally the languid portions of streams, especially east of the Sierran escarpment. They prey primarily on fish and aquatic invertebrates. In winter, when lakes freeze over, most migrate to balmier climes. Of our five species, four raise young on east-side waters. The Pied-billed conceals its nest in the marshy margins of lakes and ponds, while the others utilize mats of algae floating out in open water.

PIED-BILLED GREBE (*Podilymbus podiceps*)

	J	F	M	A	M	J	J	A	S	O	N	D	HABITAT	ELEVATIONS		
														N	T	W
WEST	•											•	LR		F-6	
EAST													LMo	6-8	6-8	6-7

Rare summer resident in Mariposa region (2000'—CL); rare transient below 5000', extremely rare transient at higher elevations and extremely rare winter visitor below 4000' elsewhere on west slope; uncommon spring transient and summer resident, common fall transient and rare winter resident on fresh water below 8000' and extremely rare transient at higher elevations east of crest; rare transient on Mono Lake (6400').

Pied-billed Grebes are inconspicuous visitors to freshwater ponds, lakes and languid streams. These drab, diminutive birds prefer the lower elevations, where they are often overlooked among rafts of coots and waterfowl. They appear on large, deep lakes as well as small, shallow ponds. Partial to fresh water, they rarely tarry on Mono Lake's brine; of Mono's myriad grebes, they are the scarcest, outnumbered even by Horneds.

Pied-bills nest on quiet waters margined by cattails or other dense marsh vegetation. Their numbers swell in fall, when as many as 70 have been tallied on Crowley Lake Reservoir (6800'—DG). Most leave before large lakes freeze, but some brave mild winters.

On the west slope, transient Pied-billed Grebes appear on rivers, lakes, ponds and reservoirs. They are more frequent in fall than spring, and summer near Mariposa (CL). A few may nest on marshy lakes and ponds.

Record above 5000' west slope: 6400' Laurel Lake 9/27/76 (DG).

Record above 8000' east of crest: 8900' Lake Mary 12/7/76 (DG).

Winter records west slope: Yosemite Valley 1948-49 (YM); 12/17-26/52 (AFN 7:232).

Extreme dates west slope excluding Mariposa region and winter records: 3/7/25 Yosemite Valley (YM) - 4/13/29 Yosemite Valley (YM); 9/25/27 Yosemite Valley (YM) - 11/30/15 below Cascade Falls (GS 248).

Nesting localities: 7000' ponds near junction of U.S. 395 and Hwy. 203 (DG); 7600' June Lake (DS)—this may be California's highest nesting locality.

HORNED GREBE (*Podiceps auritus*)

	J	F	M	A	M	J	J	A	S	O	N	D	HABITAT	ELEVATIONS		
														N	T	W
WEST										•					5	
EAST										—	—	—	LMo		6-8	

Extremely rare transient on west slope; extremely rare spring transient and summer visitor, and uncommon fall transient below 8000' east of crest.

Because their winter plumages are so similar, Horned Grebes are often overlooked among multitudes of Eareds. Yet, in the fall, up to 20 have been tallied along the west shore of Mono Lake (6400'—AB 38:240), and they can usually be found at Crowley Lake Reservoir (6800'), Grant Lake Reservoir (7100'), June Lake (7600') and other large, deep bodies of water. In spring, when they are dressed in nuptial finery, the vast majority must travel along the coast.

West slope record: 9/21-11/1/86 4700' Lake Eleanor Reservoir (YM).

Spring and summer records, all Mono Lake (6400'): 5/28/82 (DB); 6/6/87 (HG, DG); 6/24-28/76 (RS, ES:97); 7/21/76 (DW); 8/14/76 (AB 39:997).

Extreme dates excluding above records: 9/14/74 6400' Dechambeau Ponds (ABR) - 12/19/81 Crowley Lake Reservoir (DG, AB 36:745).

EARED GREBE (*Podiceps nigricollis*)

	J	F	M	A	M	J	J	A	S	O	N	D	HABITAT	ELEVATIONS		
														N	T	W
WEST			•	•	•	•	•	•	—	—	—		LR		4-12	
EAST	—	—	—	■	■	■	■	■	■	■	■	—	MoL	6-7	6-8	6

Extremely rare spring transient and rare fall transient below 12,000' on west slope; rare fall transient above from 8,000' to 11,000' on east slope; fairly common spring transient, rare summer resident, common fall transient and rare winter resident on fresh water below 8000' east of crest; common transient and summer visitor and uncommon winter resident on Mono Lake (6400').

Eared Grebes may materialize on almost any type of open water from the foothills to the highest peaks. They have even appeared on swimming pools in Yosemite Valley (4000'—YNN 26:48) and at Wawona (4000'—YM). Near the Lyell Glacier, they have twice been seen on tarns at 12,000' (YNN 12:25; AFN 10:50). They frequent large, deep lakes as well as small, shallow ponds.

While Eared Grebes visit fresh water, they are partial to Mono Lake's salty, alkaline brine. There they embody the term "abundant." For much of the year they are the most numerous bird. Spring transients pass through from mid-March to at least late May; estimates of peak numbers range from 15,000-20,000 (Jehl 1985) to 45,000 (AB 32:1051). Twenty thousand to 35,000 non-breeders summer on the lake (Jehl 1985). Then, beginning in late July, tens of thousands arrive from breeding areas across western Canada and the United States, swelling the ranks to 500,000-1,000,000 in late October and early November (Jehl 1985; ES:95-100; AB 28:98). Most depart by the end of November or early December, leaving only about 100 to brave the winter (Jehl 1985; DG). In exceptional years large numbers may remain through December as documented by the Mono Lake Christmas Bird Counts. For example, on the 12/16/89 count, 75,000 were seen and on 1990's event a rough estimate of 500,000 were tallied (AB 45:315).

Especially in autumn, Eared Grebes pepper much of Mono Lake's surface. I've imagined walking across 13 miles of water stepping from the back of one bird to the back of the next. In fact the birds are not evenly distributed, but concentrate in different areas at different times. On the west side, for example, I've seen hundreds of thousands one day, then a fraction that many the next.

The abundance of Eared Grebes, exceeded in North America only at Utah's Great Salt Lake, reflects Mono Lake's fecundity. The birds feast on the lake's brine shrimp, using their relatively large tongues to squeeze out the salty water. During their stay, they never leave the lake, obtaining fresh water entirely from the bodies of the shrimp (Mahoney and Jehl 1985). The superabundant food also provides the energy they need to molt worn feathers and grow new ones, and to fatten in preparation for the next leg of their migration (Storer and Jehl 1985). Some become so fat they cannot fly, and have to diet back into shape before departing for Salton Sea and Gulf of California wintering areas (JJ).

In years to come, however, Eared Grebes may find little if anything to eat at Mono Lake. Unless the Los Angeles Department of Water and Power curtails water diversions from the lake's tributary streams, increasing salinity will poison the brine shrimp on which the grebes depend for sustenance (p. 21).

Eared Grebes apparently migrate at night, for, despite their numbers, no one has observed their arrivals or departures. After rainy nights, flocks have landed on rain-soaked highways and parking lots in Lee Vining and Mammoth Lakes. They mistake the wet pavement for water, and cannot take off from dry land (DB). Albino and partially albino Eared Grebes are regular at Mono Lake, especially among the non-breeding and probably youthful summer population. Some of these striking birds are nearly pure white (Jehl 1985).

Breeding colonies were established in 1990 and 1991 at Bridgeport and Crowley reservoirs (AB 45:146, PM). On 8/19/91 371 nests and a minimum of fourteen broods were reported at Owens River mouth, Crowley Reservoir (DS).

Eared Grebes are the last of Mono's common birds to depart. One November day I trod through foot-deep snow to the lake's south shore. Wisps of icy fog veiled the tufa towers. Out of the silence rose the voices of grebes, a quiet, lilting chorus that seemed to sparkle like crystals on a frozen lake.

Spring and summer records west slope and above 8000' east slope: 4000' Yosemite Valley 4/10/74 (YM), 5/2/29 (YM) and 5/9/55 (AFN 9:353); 4700' Lake Eleanor 3/29/87 (YM) and 6/5/83 (YM); 8200' Tenaya Lake 6/4/77 (YM); 8000' Siesta Lake 7/10/74 (YM); 11,000' near Summit Lake 7/24/75 (AFN 29:1025); 8100' Harden Lake 8/6/49 (YM).

Extreme dates west slope excluding above records: 8/21/17 4000' Mirror Lake (YM) - 12/20/32 Yosemite Valley (YM).

Extreme dates above 8000': 7/10/74 8000' Siesta Lake (YM) - 9/29/55 Mt. Lyell (AFN 10:50).

Additional references: AFN 7:33; AB 27:113; AB 28:98; AB 31:217; YNN 14:28.

WESTERN GREBE (*Aechmophorus occidentalis*)

	J	F	M	A	M	J	J	A	S	O	N	D	HABITAT	ELEVATIONS		
														N	T	W
WEST				•		•				•					4-8	
EAST														6-7		6-7

Extremely rare transient on west slope; extremely rare transient above 8000' on east slope; locally common summer resident and rare winter resident on fresh water below 7500' east of crest; uncommon transient on Mono Lake (6400').

Western Grebes are vocal, conspicuous denizens of Crowley Lake (6800') and Bridgeport Lake (6500') reservoirs, where they fledge their young from floating nests anchored to tules or rushes. These graceful piscivores also visit other deep, freshwater lakes, such as Grant Reservoir (6900') and June Lake (7600'), and occasionally small ponds and languid streams. They are surprisingly regular on Mono Lake's fishless brine as well, where a peak of 24 were tallied on 4/18/77 (AB 32:1051); like loons, their encrusted carcasses occasionally adorn Mono's lonely shores.

In spring and early summer, Crowley and Bridgeport reservoirs host the Western Grebe's dashing courtship displays and water dances. Their rasping calls sound all day and most of the night, dominating the lakes' bird choirs. In 1985, 118 nests were tallied at Bridgeport (RS); and on 7/21/91 117 active nests were espied at Crowley Reservoir (PM).

West slope records: 4300', found dead, Big Oak Flat Entrance Station 4/14/73 (YM); 8200' Tenaya Lake 6/4/61 (ABR), 6/4/77 (SG, TB) and 10/28/86 (DS, SJ).

East slope records above 8000': 9700' Garnet Lake 9/28/85 (JZ); 9700' Tioga Lake 10/25/59 (AFN 14:68), 10/28/77 (DeSante and Engstrom MS) and 11/3/87 (DG); 10,100', 3, Saddlebag Lake 10/23/78 (AB 33:209, DeSante and Enstrom MS).

CLARK'S GREBE (*Aechmophorus clarkii*)

Status uncertain; extremely rare transient on west slope; probably rare to uncommon summer and rare winter resident below 7500' east of crest.

Based on limited data, Clark's Grebes seem to visit most of the same lakes as Westerns, including Mono Lake (DS, JJ, DG). In this region, approximately one out of every 200 *Aechmophorus* grebes appear to belong to this species, which until 1985 was considered a light color phase of the Western (see WB 12:41-46). They breed at Bridgeport Reservoir (6500'), four nests in 1985 (RS), and Crowley Reservoir (6900'), 26 nests in 1991 (DS).

Record west slope: 8200' Tenaya Lake 6/6/87 (Roger Marlowe and Terry Colborn).

Order PELECANIFORMES: Pelicans and Cormorants

Family PELECANIDAE: PELICANS

AMERICAN WHITE PELICAN (*Pelecanus erythrorhynchos*)

	J	F	M	A	M	J	J	A	S	O	N	D	HABITAT	ELEVATIONS		
														N	T	W
WEST							•						A		F-10	
EAST													LA		6-7	

Rare spring transient and extremely rare summer visiter on west slope and on east slope; uncommon transient and locally common summer visitor below 7000' east of Sierran escarpment.

In spring, flocks of American White Pelicans travel east from coastal and Central Valley wintering areas to Great Basin nesting sites. On the west slope, they have been seen over foothills as well as lofty peaks. With one exception, they have always been overhead, never on lakes or streams; that exception is also the only summer record. Flocks have numbered from 25 to 57 individuals (AFN 8:327; GSt). In 1961, a pelican's bones were discovered at 12,000' on the moraine at the eastern lobe of the Lyell Glacier (YM).

East of the Sierran escarpment, American White Pelicans summer on Crowley Lake (6900') and Bridgeport Lake (6500') reservoirs, where distant lines of large, white birds are usually this species. They are rare on Grant Lake reservoir (7100'), Mono Lake (6400') and other lakes and ponds. Migrating flocks wing over all types of habitat. Most arrive in April, and depart before the weather chills in October.

In September 1989, 300 were found dead at Crowley Reservoir (AB 44:156). California Department of Fish and Game personnel autopsied many specimens, but came to no definitive conclusion as to cause of mortality (AB 44:156).

During June and July flocks of American White Pelicans sometimes depart northwards from Crowley Lake and Bridgeport Lake reservoirs. Do these strong, graceful fliers commute to nesting areas on Pyramid Lake's Anaho Island, 150 miles to the north (RS)?

While American White Pelicans have not nested at Mono Lake in historical times, an egg did appear in the gull colonies on May 28, 1981 (DW). The pelican who laid it must have made a hasty departure, for it was never seen by the resident researchers. The gigantic egg, about twice the size of a California Gull's, was incubated by gulls, but never hatched.

Summer records west and east slopes: 6/19/89 13,000' flying southward over Koip Crest, 8 (Sally Miller) 7/22/87 8200' Tenaya Lake (YM); 8/26/78 approx. 10,500' flying southeast over Saddlebag Lake, 38 (DeSante and Engstrom MS).

Peak counts: 200+ Dechambeau Ponds 5/27/84 (IM, PSu); 500+ Crowley Lake Reservoir 9/7/87 (DS).

Extreme dates west: 3/3/81 Yosemite Valley (GSt) - 6/30/33 7200' Glacier Point, 21 (YM).

Extreme dates east: 3/18/86 9200'+ Mono Craters, approx. 100 - 12/15/79 Crowley Lake Reservoir (AB 34:651; DG).

Additional references: AFN 8:327; AFN 9:354; AB 32:1051; YNN 29:45.

BROWN PELICAN (*Pelecanus occidentalis*)

Extremely rare vagrant east of Sierran Escarpment.

Four records: 7/3-5/89 6400 Negits Islets; 7/16/88 found weak on Lundy Lake road (7800') and brought to ranger station (AB 43:1363); 7/23/88 6400' Mono Lake (MBTSR); 7/25-8/21/89 6500' Bridgeport Reservoir (AB 43:2363, AB 44:156).

This species is rare inland in Southern California and has been recorded in the Great Basin of Nevada and Utah (Ryser 1985). Birds likely wander north from the Gulf of California via the Salton Sea.

Family PHALACROCORACIDAE: CORMORANTS

DOUBLE-CRESTED CORMORANT (*Phalacrocorax auritus*)

	J	F	M	A	M	J	J	A	S	O	N	D	HABITAT	ELEVATIONS		
														N	T	W
WEST					•	•	•	•							4-7	
EAST				▬	■	■	■	■	■	■	▬	–	LMoA		6-9	

Extremely rare transient on west slope; extremely rare transient above 8000' on east slope; locally fairly common summer visitor below 8000' east of crest.

While Double-crested Cormorants may appear on any large body of water, they generally shun the mountains in favor of lakes and reservoirs east of the Sierran escarpment. From spring until fall, these fish-eating fowl are fairly common on Crowley Lake (6800') and Bridgeport Lake (6500') reservoirs; flocks of up to 30 have been tallied in April (DG, JD), and up to 120 in September and early October (DG). They are uncommon on other large lakes, including Mono (6400'), which they regularly visit despite the lack of fish. Most depart before the weather chills in November, but a few linger until the lakes freeze, and perhaps brave mild winters.

Six pair of Double-crested Cormorant nested at Bridgeport Lake Reservoir in 1974 (AB 28:944), but have not returned in recent years (DG). The closest active colony I know of is on Pyramid Lake's Anaho Island 150 miles northeast, where over one thousand raise their young (Ryser 1985). But I would not be surprised if they also bred 50 miles to the northeast at Walker Lake in Nevada.

West slope records: 3700' Hetch Hetchy Reservoir 5/20/50 (YM); 4000' Yosemite Valley 6/21-7/20/32 (YM); 7200' Merced Lake 8/26/82 (MR).

East slope records above 8000': 9500' Ellery Lake, 2, 9/1-12/79 (AB 34:195, DeSante and Engstrom MS); 9000' Green Lake 8/26-28/82 (AB 37:119).

Extreme dates: 3/24/86 - 12/22/85 Crowley Lake Reservoir (DG).

PELAGIC CORMORANT (*Phalacrocorax pelagicus*)

Extremely rare vagrant east of Sierran escarpment.

The Pelagic Cormorant that visited Silver Lake (7200') on 12/8/76 is arguably the most unusual bird ever found in this region (AB 31:368). Frigatebirds, murrelets and other waifs may be more exotic, but regularly wander inland. This, however, is the only interior record for a strictly coastal species.

Family FREGATIDAE: FRIGATEBIRDS

MAGNIFICENT FRIGATEBIRD (*Fregata magnificens)*

Extremely rare vagrant east of Sierran escarpment.

No one saw the Magnificent Frigatebird gliding above Mono Lake's tufa towers on eight-foot wings. But its bleached remains were discovered on 7/28/85 on Java Islet northeast of Negit Island (6400'—JP, DS). While I know of no other records in the Great Basin, frigatebirds have wandered into the Southern California mountains (Garrett and Dunn 1981).

Order CICONIIFORMES: Herons, Ibises and Allies

Family ARDEIDAE: BITTERNS AND HERONS

Eight species visit our region, three nest. Only Great Blue Herons are frequent mountaineers. Most of the others are scarce transients on mudflats, lake margins, marshes and wet meadows east of the Sierran escarpment.

AMERICAN BITTERN (*Botaurus lentiginosus*)

Extremely rare on west slope; formerly summer resident east of Sierran escarpment, but now nearly extirpated; no records since 1982.

American Bitterns formerly nested in marshes east of the Sierran escarpment (C 36:36), but have been recorded only six times since 1975, and not at all from 1982 to 1990. Water diversions, reservoirs and recreational developments have obliterated much of the dense, marsh vegetation these birds require, and what remains is heavily grazed. A few miles east of our region, they still breed in marshes in Adobe Valley (6500'--PM).

This said, I must mention one American Bittern who dared to be different. No marshes for this bird. On 1/6/82, after a severe snowstorm, it surprised Larry White on a cross-country ski trail near Mammoth Lakes (8000'). He writes: "It flew to a young Jeffrey pine, where it assumed its classic 'tule freeze position' with head pointed skyward...I'm convinced, given enough time, one may see just about any bird in any habitat, from frigatebirds over the desert to warblers over the ocean."

Records west slope: 8600' Tuolumne Meadows 5/24/87 (YM); 9/14/87 4000' Yosemite Valley (Michael Frye).

Recent records excluding above: 7000' Long Valley 12/21/75 (AB 30:592); 6400' near Mono Lake 4/16/78 (GP) 4/28/91 (AB 45: 492); 6400' Dechambeau Ponds 6/24-7/2/76 (DW, BE); 7000' Owens River marshes, "few each spring" in mid '70s (John Derby).

LEAST BITTERN (*Ixobrychus exilis*)

Status uncertain; probably a rare transient east of the Sierran escarpment.

Despite only two recent records, Least Bitterns are probably regular but secretive visitors to cattail and tule marshes east of the Sierran escarpment, and formerly may have bred. In June, 1916, Grinnell flushed a bird from the marshes along lower Rush Creek, and thought it might be nesting (GS 256); subsequently, the diversion of Rush Creek's water into the Los Angeles Aqueduct destroyed this habitat.

Recent records: 6400' Dechambeau Ponds 6/13/81 (DG); 7600' June Lake 6/3/85 (AB 39:957).

GREAT BLUE HERON (*Ardea herodias*)

	J	F	M	A	M	J	J	A	S	O	N	D	HABITAT	ELEVATIONS		
														N	T	W
WEST													LRGA		F-10	F-5
EAST													LRGA		6-8	6-7

Uncommon visitor below 5000' and rare summer visitor to treeline on west slope; uncommon summer visitor below 8000' and extremely rare summer visitor to treeline on east slope; locally common visitor below 7500' in valleys east of Sierran escarpment.

Great Blue Herons stalk fish, frogs and even mice along the margins of ponds, lakes and reservoirs, and in fields and boggy meadows. They roost both on the ground and in large, stout trees. En route to feeding or roosting areas, they may fly over any type of habitat.

On the west slope, Great Blue Herons are most numerous at lower elevations, as along the Merced River between Briceburg (1200') and Yosemite Valley (4000'). During summer and early autumn, a few wander to treeline. Even during frigid winters, they have lingered as high as Yosemite Valley (YNN 26:48, EM 2, YM) and Lake Eleanor (4700'--YM); one at Red's Meadow was at 7800' on 12/30/77 (DG).

East of the Sierran escarpment, Great Blue Herons congregate along the margins of Crowley Lake and Bridgeport Lake reservoirs, and in nearby fields and pastures. I tallied 63, for example, near the Hot Creek Fish Hatchery on 12/19/82, many roosting on a rocky, sagebrush-covered hill; this hatchery is a fine heron feeder! They brave all but the harshest winters.

On other eastside lakes, streams and marshes, including Mono Lake, Great Blues are uncommon visitors. In recent years, one has lingered on Lundy Lake (7800') as long as there was any open water; in December and January, I've watched it hunt from the edge of the ice.

Though Great Blue Herons have nested in similar habitat in the northern Sierra Nevada (AFN 18:483), they are not known to breed in our region.

Record above 8000' east slope: 10,100' Hall Natural Area 8/4-7/87 (DeSante and Engstrom MS).

High elevation record: 10,500' Lower McCabe Lake 8\1\39 (YM); (11,200' Center Basin, Kings Canyon National Park 6/13/47—C 50:133).

Extreme dates over 5000' west slope and 8000' east of crest: 8/1/39 Lower McCabe Lake (YM) - 10/26/39 6000' Little Yosemite Valley (YM).

GREAT EGRET (*Casmerodius albus*)

	J	F	M	A	M	J	J	A	S	O	N	D	HABITAT	ELEVATIONS		
														N	T	W
WEST				•				•							4-9	
EAST													LMaGMo		6-7	

Extremely rare transient on west slope; uncommon spring transient, uncommon summer visitor and fairly common fall transient on Crowley Lake (6900') and probably Bridgeport Lake (6500') reservoirs; rare transient below 7000' elsewhere east of Sierran escarpment.

Great Egrets usually frequent the margins of lakes, ponds or languid streams, or boggy meadows or fields, often in the company of Great Blue Herons. While most are loners, fivegraced Mono Lake's shores on 4/27-28/91 (Pacific Flyway Census) and 10 flocked there on 9/20/81 (JJ). One strayed to Mono's Paoha Islets on 5/12/83 (DS).

West slope records: 4000' Yosemite Valley 4/29/83 (YM) and 8/7-14/43 (YNN 22:79); 8600' Tuolumne Meadows 8/30/53 (YM) and 10/2/85 (YM).

Extreme dates: 4/7/78 Mono Lake (AB 32:1051) - 10/25/87 7000' Alkali Ponds (DG).

SNOWY EGRET (*Egretta thula*)

	J	F	M	A	M	J	J	A	S	O	N	D	HABITAT	ELEVATIONS		
														N	T	W
WEST				•											4	
EAST													LMaMo	6	6-7	

Extremely rare spring transient on west slope; uncommon transient and rare summer visitor at Crowley Lake (6900') and probably Bridgeport Lake (6500') reservoirs; rare transient and summer visitor or resident below 7000' elsewhere east of Sierran escarpment.

Snowy Egrets visit the muddy margins of ponds and lakes. In April and May, Snowys usually outnumber greats; in autumn the opposite is true. Even on the west slope, all four records cluster in April.

In 1991 a pair fledged two young on Twain Islet in Mono Lake (DS) providing the east side's first nesting record.

While Snowy Egrets are usually loners, flocks of six have twice visited Dechambeau Ponds (6400'—BE, DG). On 7/30/76, 20 flew over Mono Lake (6400'—ES:97).

West slope records: 4000' 4/3/81 (YM), 2, 4/13/77 (YM), 8, 4/23/46 (YNN 25:95) and 4/30/80 (YM); 8600' Tuolumne Meadows 5/26/87 (YM).

Extreme dates east of crest: 4/11/82 Mono Lake (HG) - 9/30/82 Mono Lake (PS); 12/2/83 6400' Simon's Spring (MK).

CATTLE EGRET (*Bubulcus ibis*)

Irregularly rare spring and extremely rare fall transient east of Sierran escarpment.

A Cattle Egret was first observed near Mono Lake (6400') in 1978 (AB 32:1051), and has been seen there seven times since, all but once in spring. This African immigrant usually visits meadows and pastures, where it often consorts with horses, sheep and other livestock. On 4/24/85, however, one mingled with gulls on Mono's barren Paoha islets (JJ).

Fall record: 6, nw. Mono Lake, 11/16-18/83 (DG).
Extreme dates excluding fall record: 3/21/82 6900' Goat Ranch (DW) - 5/23/78 Mono Lake (AB 32:1051).

GREEN-BACKED (GREEN) HERON (*Butorides striatus*)

Extremely rare transient on west slope; rare transient and summer visitor below 8000' east of crest.

On the east side, Green-backed Herons skulk along the margins of languid streams, ponds and lakes as well as marshes and wet meadows. They visit both Great Basin valleys and deep Sierran canyons, as along the June Lake Loop (7100'-7600') and near Lundy Lake (7800'). Twice I've found them perched incongruously on Mono Lake's tufa towers (6400'). At Hot Creek, they regularly raid the fish hatchery (7100').

On the west slope, though Green-backed Herons nest along the lower Merced and Tuolumne rivers (GS 258), they rarely wander upriver. They have never been recorded, for instance, along the Merced between Briceburg and El Portal.

High elevation record: approx. 8000' near Mammoth Lakes 5/26/86 (AB 40:519).
West slope records: 4000' Yosemite Valley 8/18/34 (YNN 13:76); 7200' Merced Lake 8/?/19 (YNN 13:76) and 8/5/87 (Peggy Smith).
Extreme dates: 4/5/78 Mono Lake (AB 32:1091) - 11/2/75 6500' Bridgeport Lake Reservoir (DE).

BLACK-CROWNED NIGHT-HERON (*Nycticorax nycticorax*)

	J	F	M	A	M	J	J	A	S	O	N	D	HABITAT	ELEVATIONS		
														N	T	W
WEST							•	•							9	
EAST				—	▬	▬	▬	▬	—				LMaMo	6	6-12	7

Extremely rare transient on west and east slopes; uncommon summer resident or visitor and extremely rare winter resident below 7000' east of the Sierran escarpment.

East of the Sierran escarpment, Black-crowned Night-Herons usually outnumber egrets and Green-backed Herons, but are not nearly as numerous as Great Blues. They dwell in marshes, wet meadows, ponds, mudflats and their wooded margins, frequently

Cattle Egret with California Gulls on one of the Paoha Islets in Mono Lake, April 24, 1985 (see p. 70). Photograph by Joseph R. Jehl Jr.

roosting in willows or other trees. Often they raid the Hot Creek Fish Hatchery (7100'), where a high count of 26 was tallied on 4/13/86 (DG). In 1986 and 1987, up to 13 birds wintered at this fish hatchery, lulled into lingering by easy pickings (DG; AB 40:994); there are no other winter records.

Previous to 1987, immature herons had been seen regularly on Mono's bleak islets in June and July (DS). In 1987 nesting was confirmed on Twain Islet in Mono Lake (ESt). From 1988 to 1991 the number of nests on the islets increased from roughly 2 to 20. (AB 43:532, 1363, Jan Dierks).

Black-crowned Night-Herons may also nest near Bridgeport Lake Reservoir (6500') and the Owens River marshes (7000'), but there are no positive records.

Yosemite's only Black-crowned Night-Herons wandered to Tuolumne Meadows (8600') on 7/11/84 (Bruce Maxwell) and 8/5/87 (MR). But others have mountaineered to even higher elevations. Just east of the crest, I surprised a juvenile near Ellery Lake (9600') on 9/9/85; it was huddled in a lodgepole during a snowstorm, and looked very cold. The Mallory of the species, however, was found dead in the snow at 11,700' near McGee Pass on 7/14/80 (AB 34:925); may he (or she) rest in peace among the Rosy Finches!

Extreme dates excluding winter records: 4/11/82 6400' Mono Lake, 5 (HG) - 9/26/87 6500' Dechambeau Ponds, 9 (DG).

Family THRESKIORNITHIDAE: Ibises and Spoonbills

WHITE-FACED IBIS (*Plegadis chihi*)

Rare transient and summer visitor below 7000' east of the Sierran escarpment.

White-faced Ibis frequent the muddy margins of ponds and lakes as well as wet meadows and marshes. While usually seen alone or in small groups, a gang of 30 convened 9/22/90 at Bridgeport Reservoir (AB 45:146). Reported sightings have increased since 1987 with a half dozen sightings each year.

Extreme dates: 4/13/76 6900' Long Valley (DG) - 9/24/87 6500' Dechambeau Ponds (PP).

Order ANSERIFORMES: SWANS, GEESE AND DUCKS

Family ANATIDAE: SWANS, GEESE AND DUCKS

Waterfowl are numerous on marshes, lakes and reservoirs east of the Sierran escarpment, and scarce in the mountains proper. Of 33 species, eleven regularly breed. Most occur as transients, passing through in late summer and fall, and returning with the thaw in late February or March. Diving ducks, in general, arrive later in fall than dabblers. Many linger until Crowley Lake Reservoir, Bridgeport Lake Reservoir and other large bodies of water freeze over; some brave all but the harshest winters on the open water remaining near the mouths of streams. In 1982, for example, mild weather kept waters open, and 2,039 ducks and geese were tallied on the Mammoth Lakes Christmas Bird Count; in 1977, frigid conditions froze the lakes in early December, and only three individuals could be found (AB 32:868; AB 37:758).

Two species—Harlequin Duck and Barrow's Goldeneye—have nearly or entirely disappeared from Sierran nesting haunts.

TUNDRA (WHISTLING) SWAN (*Cygnus columbianus*)

	J	F	M	A	M	J	J	A	S	O	N	D	HABITAT	ELEVATIONS		
														N	T	W
WEST		•										•			5	
EAST	—	—	—							•	•	▬	LMoA		6-7	6-7

Extremely rare transient on west slope; locally uncommon fall transient and rare winter resident below 7000' east of Sierran escarpment.

Except for the four early birds seen 10/29/89 along the north shore of Mono Lake (ESt), most wait until after Thanksgiving to materialize on lakes, ponds, reservoirs and stream deltas east of the Sierran escarpment. On dark, snowy nights, I've lain awake listening to their calls. On foggy days, I've glimpsed their graceful forms dissolving in the white air.

Peak count: 175, 6900' Crowley Lake Reservoir 11/28/76 (T&JH).
West slope records, both Eleanor Lake Reservoir (4700'): 2/?/37 and 12/?/39 (YNN 19:27).
Extreme dates, both Crowley Lake Reservoir: 11/28/76 - 3/28/76 (T&JH).

TRUMPETER SWAN (*Cygnus buccinator*)

Extremely rare transient east of Sierran escarpment.

Record: 6400' Mono Lake, 4, 11/27/77 (AB 32:251); record accepted by California Bird Records Committee.

GREATER WHITE-FRONTED GOOSE (*Anser albifrons*)

Irregularly rare spring and probably rare fall transient and extremely rare summer visitor below 7000' east of Sierran escarpment.

While White-fronted Geese generally visit large meadows or the muddy margins of lakes, one strayed to Mono's bleak Negit islets (6400') on 4/19-23/81 (DW). They are among our scarcest waterfowl; birdwatchers have reported them but six times in spring and once in fall, though hunters bag a few most autumns (DB, DFG). The few that wander to our region are usually loners; on 10/8/78, however, 24 were pasturing on Mono's southeastern shore (BE).

Summer record: w. shore Mono Lake 5/22-8/15/83 (DS).

Extreme dates excluding summer and fall records (I do not have specific extreme dates for fall, though I know they have been taken as late as early December (DB): 2/21/82 6400' Mono Lake County Park (PJ) - Mono Lake 4/23/81 (DW).

SNOW GOOSE (*Chen caerulescens*)

Extremely rare transient on west slope; rare fall transient below 7000' east of Sierran escarpment.

Snow Geese occasionally visit large meadows or the margins of lakes, including Mono Lake (6400'), alone or in small flocks.

West slope records, all flying overhead: 4400' Big Meadow, 10, 11/24/83 (YM); 6200' Crane Flat, approx. 60, 3/1/77 (YM); approx. 7500' Badger Pass, approx. 50 (YM); 8600' Tuolumne Meadows, 11, 3/19/83 (MMu); (I have rejected an undocumented June record from Lower Ottoway Lake [9700'—YM], an unlikely date and location).

Extreme dates east of crest, both Mono Lake (6400'): 11/19/83 (MK) - 1/1/84, 25 (AB 38:793).

ROSS' GOOSE (*Chen rossii*)

Probably irregularly rare fall transient east of Sierran escarpment.

Ross' Geese probably occur more frequently than the four records imply, for they are easily confused with Snows.

Records: 7100' Grant Lake Reservoir, 2, 11/27/77 (DG, DW); 6400' Mono Lake, juvenile found dead 12/9/85 (JJ); 6400' Simon's Spring) 12/15/83 (MK); Mono Lake, shot by hunter 1/1/84 (DG, AB 38:793).

BRANT (*Branta bernicla*)

Irregularly rare spring vagrant (0-5/year) and rare summer visitor and fall vagrant east of Sierran escarpment; all records but three from Mono Lake (6400').

Though primarily maritime, Brant regularly stray to Mono Lake, where they usually linger near the mouths of creeks. While most are loners, flocks of up to five have been encountered on several occasions.

Peak count: 10, 6900' Crowley Reservoir, 6/11/91 (AB 45:1156).
Extreme dates: 4/21/78 Mono Lake (DW) - 11/19/86 Crowley Reservoir (DP).

CANADA GOOSE (*Branta canadensis*)

	J	F	M	A	M	J	J	A	S	O	N	D	HABITAT	ELEVATIONS		
														N	T	W
WEST											•	•	ALM		F-7	
EAST													GLMoA	6-7	6-7	6-7

Locally fairly common winter resident in Mariposa area (2000'—CL); rare spring transient below 5000', extremely rare spring transient at higher elevations and extremely rare fall transient elsewhere on west slope; locally common resident below 7000' east of Sierran escarpment.

East of the Sierran escarpment, especially in Bridgeport and Long valleys, one may encounter herds of Canada Geese grazing with cattle in meadows and pastures. These large, hardy waterfowl loaf and sleep on large lakes and reservoirs, where they are safe from mainland predators. Flocks of honking commuters fly over all types of habitat.

On the west slope, except near Mariposa, Canada Geese are usually seen on the wing, sometimes in sizable flocks. Small groups or lone individuals occasionally rest on or near lakes, ponds, slow-moving rivers and large meadows. Near Mariposa, wintering birds frequent pastures and farm ponds (CL).

Canada Geese may sometimes blunder into the mountains on their spring migration. All the Yosemite records for large flocks (35-100 individuals) cluster in February. One hundred, for example, flew over Badger Pass (7200') on the wintry date of 2/14/78 (YM), and approximately 60 passed over Crane Flat (6200') on 2/9/77 (YM). Not only are geese on the move at this time, but their Central Valley haunts are frequently cloaked in dense tule fog.

Canada Geese nest around Mono Lake (6400'—3-4 pairs—DG, JJ, DB), Bridgeport Lake Reservoir (6500'—about 50 pairs—AB 29:1026) and Crowley Lake Reservoir (6800'—about 15 pairs—DB, CFG). They have even bred on one of the small islets northeast of Mono's Negit Island (DS). These geese, which belong to the large subspecies *B. c. moffitti*, formerly bred near June Lake (C 36:36, DB), and probably in other marshes and wet meadows as well; their habitat has been reduced, however, by dams, water diversions and resort and residential development.

In late autumn, the eastside nesting population is augmented by an influx of migrants. I know of peak counts of 372 Canada Geese at Mono Lake on 12/30/90 (AB 44:979), 450 near Bridgeport Reservoir on 11/29/77 (DG), and 571 near Crowley Lake Reservoir on 12/31/83 (DG, AB 38:792). They usually leave the Bridgeport Valley when the reservoir freezes, but linger near Crowley through all but the harshest winters (T&JH). The February thaw brings another pulse of northbound travelers.

High elevation record: 8600' Tuolumne Meadows, 2, 5/15/75 (TH).

Fall records west slope excluding Mariposa: 4000' Yosemite Valley 11/27/73 (YM); 7200' Badger Pass, 11, 12/10/72 (YM); ? Yosemite Christmas Bird Count 12/23/73 (AB 28:544).

Extreme dates west slope excluding fall records: 2/6/80 4400' Big Meadow (GSt) - 4/26/80 Big Meadow (GSt); 5/15/75 Tuolumne Meadows (TH).

Additional references: AFN 8:327; AFN 13:59.

WOOD DUCK (*Aix sponsa*)

Rare resident below 4000' on west slope; irregularly rare fall (0-2/year) and extremely rare summer visitor below 7500' east of Sierran escarpment.

In the western foothills, on quiet ponds, languid streams and backwater sloughs, one may chance upon pairs or small flocks of Wood Ducks. These bejeweled waterfowl nest on quiet waters margined by large cottonwoods, oaks and other trees with commodious cavities. In the safety of these cavities, high above the ground, the hens hatch their chicks, whose first step is a downward tumble. In 1941 and 1943, they nested in Yosemite Valley (4000'—YNN 21:31; YNN 22:74), but, as far as I know, have not returned in subsequent decades.

During migration, Wood Ducks are not restricted to wooded waters, but also visit ponds and even lakes and reservoirs far from trees. East of the Sierran crest, they are among the scarcest of waterfowl; no more than two have ever been seen together, and they are not encountered every year.

Summer record east of crest: 6500' Bridgeport Lake Reservoir 6/18/85 (AB 39:957).

Extreme dates east of crest excluding summer record: seven records since 1982: 9/4-5/90 Lundy Canyon (ESt) - 12/31/82 6400' nw. Mono Lake, 2 (DW).

Additional representative nesting localities: 2000' near Mariposa (CL); (3500' Skelton Creek—DG).

GREEN-WINGED TEAL (*Anas crecca*)

	J	F	M	A	M	J	J	A	S	O	N	D	HABITAT	ELEVATIONS		
														N	T	W
WEST													RL		F-5	
EAST													LMaMuMo	6-8	6-7	6-7

Rare winter resident near Mariposa (2000'); rare spring transient below 5000', rare fall transient below 8000' and extremely rare transient at higher elevations elsewhere on west slope; rare summer resident below 8000' on east slope; common transient, uncommon summer resident and locally common winter resident below 7000' east of Sierran escarpment.

During autumn, hundreds of Green-winged Teal erupt from shallow ponds and muddy stream deltas east of the Sierran escarpment, and flee in frenzied flight. These diminutive dabblers forage in shallow water, on mudflats and occasionally on slow-moving streams, but resort to large lakes and reservoirs to loaf and sleep in safety from predators.

On the west slope, Green-winged Teal appear on rivers and streams as well as ponds. While usually alone or in small flocks, 24 strayed to Yosemite Valley on 2/9/55 (AFN 9:280).

East of the Sierran escarpment, Green-winged Teal frequently outnumber all other ducks. Particularly in late autumn, they and Ruddys dominate the waterfowl scene. For example, 580 were tallied on the north shore of Mono Lake (6400') on 1/1/84 (DB, AB 38:793), and 702 on Crowley Lake Reservoir (6800') on 12/19/82 (DG, AB 37:758). They are also exceptionally hardy, braving all but the most unforgiving winters. The February thaw brings northbound travelers, but not as many as fall; they are usually outnumbered by northbound Cinnamon Teal.

Though a common transient, Green-winged Teal are among our scarcest breeding ducks. The first nesting pair was discovered, not in the wetlands east of the Sierran escarpment, but at 8200' on a heavily wooded beaver pond in Lundy Canyon (1980 and subsequent years--MM, DG). They are also known to breed near Simons Spring (6400'—JJ) and in the Owens River marshes (6900'—DG).

Records above 8000': 8200' Tenaya Lake 10/14/87 (DG); 8600' Tuolumne Meadows, 2, 5/12/87 (MR).

Additional fall records exclusive of Mariposa area west slope, both Yosemite Valley: 10/6/30 (YNN 13:117); 10/10/39 (YM).

Extreme dates west slope excluding Mariposa area: 2/19/40 4000' Yosemite Valley (YM) - 5/25/77 Yosemite Valley (YM); 10/1/77 6400' Laurel Lake, 3 (D&SJ) - 10/14/87 8000' Siesta Lake, 5 (DG) and 8200' Tenaya Lake (DG).

Additional reference: YNN 13:117.

MALLARD (*Anas platyrhynchos*)

	J	F	M	A	M	J	J	A	S	O	N	D	HABITAT	ELEVATIONS		
														N	T	W
WEST													LMaR	F-10		F-4
EAST													LMoMaR	6-10	6-7	6-7

Uncommon summer resident below 8000', locally rare summer resident or visitor to 10,000' and rare winter resident below 4000' on west slope; uncommon summer resident below 8000' and locally rare summer resident or visitor to 10,000' on east slope; common summer resident and locally fairly common winter resident below 7000' east of Sierran escarpment.

Of all our waterfowl, Mallards take mountaineering laurels, nesting higher than any other duck. In fact, they are the only member of their family to breed, albeit sparingly, from the western foothills to the eastside valleys.

In the mountains, nesting Mallards favor ponds, lakes or quiet backwaters bordered by marsh or dense herbaceous vegetation. Suitable habitat—and hence nesting birds—are widely scattered. Transients are not so discriminating, and may appear in small numbers on quiet waters almost anywhere. In winter they have lingered as high as Yosemite Valley (YM).

East of the Sierran escarpment, nesting Mallards are more numerous, and migratory flocks may number in the thousands. At least 3,000, for example, crowded into Simons Spring (6400') on 11/17/82 (DG). They prefer shallow ponds bordered by marsh vegetation, but also raft with other ducks on large lakes and reservoirs. They are hardy fowl, and brave most winters near deltas, hot springs and wherever else there is open water. The March thaw brings an influx of northbound migrants and nesters, but instead of flocks they are mostly in scattered pairs.

While Mallards usually conceal nests in moist marsh or meadow vegetation, they occasionally use nearby sagebrush scrub as well (CMc).

High altitude record: 10,000' Tioga Pass, many records.

Earliest date Tuolumne Meadows (8600'): 4/19/84 (YM).

Representative nesting localities: 4000' Yosemite Valley (YNN 10:32, 13:117, 18:113-114); 5200' Swamp Lake (YNN 18:113-114); 7200' Merced Lake (YM); 8600' Tuolumne Meadows (YM); 10,000' Tioga Pass (AFN 8:359, WB 4:112); 6900' Owens River marshes (DG); 6400' Dechambeau Ponds (DG).

Additional reference: YNN 10:22.

(N.Pintail X Mallard Hybrid)

On 4/23/90 a drake Northern Pintail X Mallard hybrid was observed at Bridgeport Reservoir 6500' (AB 44:492).

NORTHERN PINTAIL (*Anas acuta*)

	J	F	M	A	M	J	J	A	S	O	N	D	HABITAT	ELEVATIONS		
														N	T	W
WEST						•			•	•	•				4-9	
EAST													LMoMa	6-7	6-7	6-7

Extremely rare transient on west slope; extremely rare transient on east slope; fairly common spring and common fall transient, uncommon summer resident and irregularly rare winter resident below 7000' east of Sierran escarpment.

Like most dabblers, Northern Pintail are much more numerous during migrations than they are during the nesting season. These slender-necked waterfowl feed on shallow ponds and in adjacent meadows, retreating to large bodies of water for safety.

East of the Sierran escarpment, Northern Pintail breed at Dechambeau Ponds and the Sulfur Ponds near Mono Lake (6500'—AB 38:1057; KC, DS, DG) and in the Owens River marshes (6900'), where nests may be concealed in sagebrush scrub over a mile from water (CMc). Probably they breed in the Bridgeport Valley as well.

In late summer and early fall, hundreds of Northern Pintail gather near stream deltas at Mono Lake and Crowley Lake and Bridgeport Lake reservoirs; 764, for example, were at Mono Lake on 8/30/76 (ES:97). They are usually outnumbered, however, by Green-winged Teal, Mallards and Northern Shovelers. They are not as hardy as Green-wingeds, Mallards, American Wigeon and Ruddy Ducks, and mostly depart by early December. On the northbound journey, they generally arrive in March about a month after Green-winged and Cinnamon teal.

West slope records: 8600' Tuolumne Meadows, pair, 6/4/77 (TB, SG), 3 drakes, 8/18/79 (YM) and 9/18/86 (ESt); 4000' Yosemite Valley 10/4/47 (YNN 26:123); 8600' Tenaya Lake 11/11/59 (ABR).

East slope and high elevation record: 10,000' Hall Natural Area, 27 overhead, 10/7/79 (DeSante and Engstrom MS).

BLUE-WINGED TEAL (*Anas discors*)

Extremely rare transient on west slope; rare spring transient and summer visitor below 7000' east of Sierran escarpment—breeding probable; fall status uncertain.

Blue-winged Teal consort with much more numerous Cinnamons east of the Sierran escarpment. In 1938, a nest was reported near the Owens River, but the incubating hen may have been a female Cinnamon; the identification was based on her association with a Blue-winged drake (6900'—C 36:35); in recent years, pairs have been seen in June and July at Dechambeau Ponds (6400'—KC, DS), Simon's Spring (DG), and Rush Creek (Steve Clifton).

In late summer and autumn, eclipse-plumaged drakes and hen Blue-winged Teal are probably overlooked among similar Cinnamons. There are four records, ranging from Bridgeport to Crowley reservoirs (AB 44:156, PM, ESt, HG, DDeS) . More on this problem in the following account.

West slope record: 4000' Yosemite Valley, drake, 3/14/47 (YNN 26:71).
Earliest date east of crest: 3/28/82 s. Mono Lake (BE).

CINNAMON TEAL (*Anas cyanoptera*)

	J	F	M	A	M	J	J	A	S	O	N	D	HABITAT	ELEVATIONS		
														N	T	W
WEST			—	—	—		•	•		•			LR		F-5	
EAST		—	■	■	■	■	■	■	■	—			MaLMo	6-7	6-7	

Rare spring and extremely rare summer visitor and fall transient below 5000' and extremely rare transient at higher elevations on west slope; common summer resident below 7000' in valleys east of Sierran escarpment.

To begin with, I confess to the assumption, reflected in the graphs, that virtually all late summer and autumn "blue-winged type" teal are Cinnamons. They're the common spring and summer species, so this surmise is reasonable. But it could be wrong. In Arizona, Alan Phillips suggests that Blue-winged Teal actually outnumber Cinnamons in the fall (WB 6:71).

Why the problem? Cinnamon and Blue-winged drakes are unmistakable in handsome nuptial dress, but by late summer have molted into drab eclipse plumages that closely resemble the very similar hens. At this season the two species can only be separated by slight differences in plumage color, facial pattern and bill length and shape (for details, see the National Geographic Society's *Field Guide*, p. 74). Here is a challenge for the seasoned birder! In the following account, I call these autumn birds "blue-winged types."

Cinnamon Teal frequent ponds, marshes, mudflats, languid streams and stream deltas. Unlike most ducks, they rarely venture out on large lakes. Breeding birds favor quiet waters bordered by marsh vegetation or grass. While most nests are concealed in bank vegetation, they may also be hidden in sagebrush scrub some distance away (CMc).

East of the Sierran escarpment, the arrival of Cinnamon Teal is a harbinger of spring. I've seen as many as 60 smartly-attired drakes crowd the small Dechambeau Ponds (6400') in late February. Smaller numbers remain to nest; they are, with Mallards and Gadwall, our commonest breeding ducks.

August brings an influx of southbound "blue-winged type" teal, but by the end of September most have already departed for Mexico. This first duck to arrive is also the first to depart. I don't know of a single November or positive winter record, though one was reported without details on the Mammoth Lakes Christmas Bird Count on 12/21/75 (AB 30:592); in light of December records in Lassen County, this sighting is plausible. A January record from Yosemite Valley (YM) is also unsupported.

Records above 5000' west slope, all Tuolumne Meadows (8600'): 7/14/79, 3 (YM); 7/16/87 (MR); 8/26/79 (YM); 9/8/77 (TB).

Additional summer and fall records on west slope, all Yosemite Valley (4000'): 8/28/28 (YNN 13:117); 5, 10/11/47 (YNN 26:123).

Extreme dates west slope excluding above records: 2/20/86 Yosemite Valley (YM) - 5/3/87, 6, 3700' Hetch Hetchy Reservoir (YM).

Extreme dates east excluding hypothetical winter record: 2/11/89, 6400' Mono Lake County Park (ESt) - 10/15/86, 2, Crowley Lake Reservoir (DG).

Representative nesting localities: 6500' Dechambeau Ponds (DG); 6500' Bridgeport sewage ponds (DG); 6900' Owens River marshes (CMc, DG).

(BLUE-WINGED X CINNAMON TEAL)

Sometime in the early 1970s, a drake Blue-winged X Cinnamon Teal hybrid was observed at the Bridgeport Sewage Ponds (6500'—RS).

NORTHERN SHOVELER (*Anas clypeata*)

	J	F	M	A	M	J	J	A	S	O	N	D	HABITAT	ELEVATIONS		
														N	T	W
WEST					•	•						•			4	
EAST													LMaMuMo		6-7	6-7

Extremely rare transient on west slope; uncommon spring transient, rare summer visitor, common fall transient and rare winter resident below 7000' east of Sierran escarpment.

In late summer and early autumn, Northern Shovelers are often the most numerous duck on shallow ponds and muddy stream deltas east of the Sierran escarpment. On 9/14/76, for example, 2,230 were tallied at Mono Lake (6400'—ES:97). They also feed on mudflats, but retreat to large bodies of water for safety, where they raft with other dabblers. By the end of October, most have departed for balmier climes. Unlike most dabblers, spoonbills are scarce in spring, passing north in small flocks or as scattered individuals.

West slope records: 4000' Yosemite Valley, "flock," 12/26/14 (GS 254); 3500' below O'-Shaughnessy Dam, three pair, 5/3/87 (YM); 9500' May Lake, 5, 6/2/87 (YM); (I have rejected a report of a hen with young at Ostrander Lake [8500'] on 7/5/54 [YM], as it was probably a misidentified Mallard).

GADWALL (*Anas strepera*)

	J	F	M	A	M	J	J	A	S	O	N	D	HABITAT	ELEVATIONS		
														N	T	W
WEST							•		•	•					4-5	
EAST													LMaMo	6-7	6-7	6-7

Extremely rare transient on west slope; locally common transient, fairly common summer resident and locally fairly common winter resident below 7000' east of Sierran escarpment.

Though not as flashy as Cinnamon Teal and Mallards, Gadwalls are a debonairly dressed denizen of shallow ponds, stream deltas and slow-moving streams east of the Sierran escarpment. When replete with food, they retreat to large lakes and reservoirs for safety, where they raft with other dabblers.

Of the ducks nesting in eastside valleys, Gadwall may be the most numerous. Breeding birds favor quiet water margined by marsh or herbaceous vegetation, though nests may be hidden in sagebrush scrub some distance away (CMc). A clutch of nine eggs, for example, was discovered near the center of Mono Lake's waterless Negit Island on 7/4/76 (ES:97); to survive, these ducklings would have had to paddle at least a mile to the mainland, for they would not be able to live on the lake's alkaline water (JJ).

While common transients east of the Sierran escarpment, Gadwall are usually outnumbered by Mallards, Northern Pintail, Green-winged Teal, Northern Shovelers and Ruddy Ducks. Many linger until large lakes freeze, and some overwinter near deltas, hot springs and other open water.

Peak counts, both Crowley Lake Reservoir (6800'): 260, 4/12/86 (DG); 403, 12/20/80 (AB 35:715; DG).

West slope records: 3700' Hetch Hetchy Reservoir, 2, 7/4/78 (YM); 4900' Lake Eleanor Reservoir 9/26/76 (AB 31:217); 8200' Tenaya Lake, pair, 10/14/87 (DG; I suspect this demurely dressed dabbler is overlooked.

Additional representative nesting localities: 6400' Dechambeau Ponds (DS); 6400' near Mono Lake (ES:97); 7000' Owens River marshes (CMc, ABR); 7000' Hot Creek (DG); Crowley Reservoir (ESt); 7100' Laurel Ponds near Mammoth Lakes (DS).

EURASIAN WIGEON (*Anas penelope*)

Extremely rare vagrant east of Sierran escarpment.

Records, both 6500 Bridgeport Reservoir: 4/28/90, 1 male, (JHu et al); 4/20/91, 1 male, (JHu).

AMERICAN WIGEON (*Anas americana*)

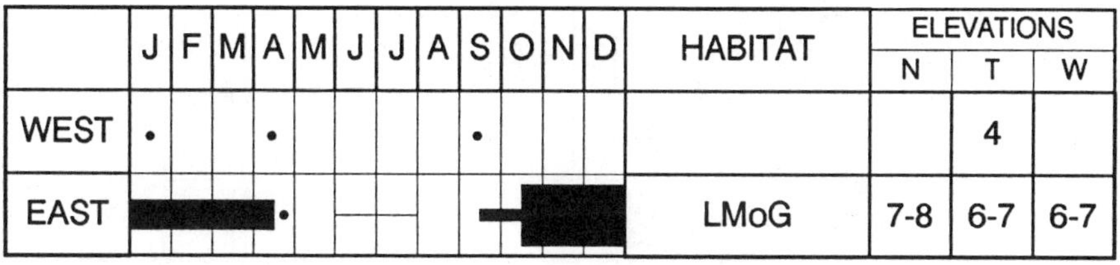

	J	F	M	A	M	J	J	A	S	O	N	D	HABITAT	ELEVATIONS		
														N	T	W
WEST	•			•					•						4	
EAST				•									LMoG	7-8	6-7	6-7

Extremely rare transient on west slope; extremely rare transient above 7500' on east slope; fairly common spring transient, uncommon summer resident, common fall transient, and fairly common winter resident below 7500' east of Sierran escarpment.

While not as numerous as other dabblers, American Wigeon gather during migrations on lakes, ponds, stream deltas and slow-moving streams east of the Sierran escarpment. They occur in largest numbers at Crowley Lake (6800') and Bridgeport Lake (6500') reservoirs, where open water is margined by extensive meadows. They sometimes feed with Green-winged Teal on mudflats, or graze with Canada Geese and cattle in nearby meadows, retreating to lakes to loaf and sleep. So long as there is open water, American Wigeon brave winter's chill. By late April, most depart for northern breeding haunts, although breeders in our area were first observed in 1989.

High counts, both Crowley Lake Reservoir: 180, 3/29/86 (DG); 330, 12/16/78 (AB 33:654; DG).

West slope records. 4000' Yosemite Valley 1/11/49 (YM) and 5, 4/12/47 (YNN 46:76); 8200' Tenaya Lake 9/14/87 (DG).

East slope and high elevation record: 9700' Tioga Lake, molting male, 10/27/77 (DeSante and Engstrom MS).

Nesting localities: 6500' Bridgeport Reservoir (AB 43:1363); 7100' Hot Creek Hatchery (AB 45:1157); 6900' Crowley Reservoir (AB 44:156).

CANVASBACK (*Athya valisineria*)

Extremely rare transient on west; rare spring and fall transient and rare sumer visitor below 7500' east of Sierran escarpment.

Of the regular diving ducks, Canvasbacks are the scarcest. They usually visit large, deep lakes and reservoirs. Most are loners, but 12 were on Bridgeport Lake Reservoir (6500') on 10/31/86 (DS, SJ), and 13 were on Crowley Lake Reservoir (6800') on 12/19/82 (AB 37:758, DG).

West slope records, both Yosemite Valley (4000'): 9/25/36 (YNN 16:23); 10/22/37 (YM).

Summer record east of crest: 6500' Bridgeport Reservoir, two females, 7/?/75 (RS).

Extreme dates excluding July record: 10/22/81 4000' Mono Lake (DW) - 12/19/82 Crowley Lake Reservoir (DG).

Extreme spring dates: 3/16/90 Bridgeport Reservoir (ESt) - 5/24/89 6400' Mono Lake (PM).

REDHEAD (*Athya americana*)

	J	F	M	A	M	J	J	A	S	O	N	D	HABITAT	ELEVATIONS		
														N	T	W
WEST																
EAST													LMo	6	6-7	

Locally common transient and uncommon summer resident below 7500' in valleys east of Sierran escarpment.

The Redhead is, after the Ruddy, the commonest diving duck east of the Sierran escarpment. I've seen several hundred, for instance, on Crowley Lake Reservoir (6800') in mid-April and mid-September. They are not as hardy as other divers, departing by and large by the end of October. A few usually linger until large lakes freeze, and possibly overwinter.

Redheads visit freshwater ponds, lakes and reservoirs, and, less often, Mono Lake as well. Small numbers probably nest, but I know of only one definite record: a hen with ducklings at Dechambeau Ponds (6500') on 7/20/85 (EB, DG). A few miles east of our area at Black Lake, Adobe Valley, there are breeding records for 1990 and 1991 (PM, DS).

Extreme dates: 2/16/82 Dechambeau Ponds (DG) - 1/1/84 Mono Lake, 3 (AB 38:793, DG).

RING-NECKED DUCK (*Athya collaris*)

	J	F	M	A	M	J	J	A	S	O	N	D	HABITAT	ELEVATIONS		
														N	T	W
WEST			•										R			4
EAST						•	•						L	7	6-8	

Formerly rare winter resident on west slope, but only one record since 1940; uncommon transient and rare summer visitor and resident below 8000' east of crest.

From 1921 through 1932 and again in 1940, four to ten Ring-necked Ducks wintered on the Merced River in Yosemite Valley (4000'—EM 2, YNN 10:23, 13:117, YM). None were seen again until 3/16/82, when a male and two females visited the river (GSt). I know of no other west slope records.

East of the crest, Ring-necked Ducks prefer lower elevation glacial lakes like Silver (7200') and Convict (7600'), where they and Common Goldeneyes are the prevalent autumn waterfowl. They also mix with other ducks on Mono Lake, Crowley, Bridgeport, and Grant reservoirs, and other lakes and ponds. They congregate in small flotillas of up to 15 individuals. Summer sightings have increased and a hen with tiny chick was seen at Crowley 7/21/91 (AB 45:1157).

Extreme dates west, all Yosemite Valley: 11/21/27 - 3/23/22.

Extreme dates east: 2/20/77 7100' Grant Lake Reservoir (T&JH) - 9/29/87 Dechambeau Ponds (PM); 12/24/76 Grant Lake Reservoir (T&JH).

GREATER SCAUP (*Athya marila*)

Status uncertain; probably a rare transient below 7500' east of Sierran escarpment.

Greater Scaup are probably more numerous than the six records suggest. Many scaup, too distant to identify to species, are plausibly this species.

Records: 6900' Crowley Lake Reservoir, 15, late March/85 (JD); 6400' Mono Lake 7/2/76 (AB 30:998), 4, 10/21/81 (DW) and 1, 11/11/90 (AB 45:146); Crowley Lake Reservoir, 6, 10/22/84 (DG) and 3, 12/19/82 (DG, AB 37:758).

LESSER SCAUP (*Athya affinis*)

	J	F	M	A	M	J	J	A	S	O	N	D	HABITAT	ELEVATIONS		
														N	T	W
WEST	•		•												4	
EAST													LMo		6-8	

Extremely rare transient on west slope; extremely rare transient above 8000' on east slope; rare spring transient and summer visitor, and uncommon fall transient below 8000' east of crest.

Small numbers of Lesser Scaup visit ponds, lakes and reservoirs east of the Sierran escarpment, including Mono Lake.

West slope records: 4000' Yosemite Valley, 3, 1/19/49 (YM), 3/5/32 (YM), 3/5/40 (YNN 19:47) and 3/?/33 (YM); 3700' Hetch Hetchy Reservoir, up to 8, 3/24-27/87 (YM).

East slope records above 8000': 8900' Lake Mary, 12, 12/7/76 (DG); 9500' Ellery Lake, 3, 10/25/59 (AFN 14:68) and 10/14/87 (DG).

Extreme dates east: 2/20/82 6400' Dechambeau Ponds (DG) - 8/13/76 Dechambeau Ponds (DG); 10/14/82 Mono Lake, 6 (DG) - 1/1/84 Mono Lake (AB 38:793).

HARLEQUIN DUCK (*Histrionicus histrionicus*)

Formerly nested from 4000' to 9000' on west slope, but current status uncertain; probably rare summer resident.

Waterfowl may be more abundant east of the Sierra, but two intriguing mountaineers have only been found to the west: Barrow's Goldeneyes and Harlequin Ducks. Both formerly bred in the mountains—goldeneyes on timber-bordered lakes and Harlequins on turbulent streams. The goldeneye has disappeared, but the harlequin may be staging a comeback.

No one can read Enid and Charles Michael's article on the nesting of Harlequin Ducks along Yosemite's Merced River (4000') without wondering why these birds vanished (Michael 1922). Until the 1920s these exquisitely patterned waterfowl bred along swift-flowing streams from 4000' nearly to treeline. While never common, they were found in virtually every major watershed. According to the Michaels, they "appeared quite at home [in Yosemite Valley], accepting crumbs from the back windows of the hotel and sunning on the float across the river."

From 1928 until 1972, however, there was but a single sighting of a Harlequin Duck, and that the only fall record. Were the birds driven from their nesting haunts by human disturbance?

On 4/9/72 a male on Tenaya Creek (4200') below Snow Creek raised hopes for the Harlequin Duck's return (YM). Another six years passed, however, before another was seen: a pair on the South Fork Merced River near Wawona (4000') on 5/6/78 (YM). Since then individuals or pairs have summered almost annually on the south fork (YM). In Yosemite Valley (4000'), a male appeared on the Merced River on 5/2/80 (AB 35:974). These birds are probably nesting; why else would they summer in the mountains?

Extreme dates: 3/30/22 - 7/28/20 Yosemite Valley (Auk 39:14-23); 10/20/40, female, Wawona (Gull 22:47).

Historical nesting localities: Tuolumne River "from about 4000' upward" (Zoe 2:97, Osprey 2:77); Yosemite Valley (C 27:10, GS 255, Michael 1922); 4000' South Fork Merced River (CFG 1:237); 7500' Cherry Creek (C 27:116); 9300' Lake Ediza (C 27:70-71).

Additional references: YNN 13:117, EM 2, AB 23:101.

OLDSQUAW (*Clangula hyemalis*)

Extremely rare vagrant east of Sierran escarpment.

Records: 6400' Mono Lake, found dead, 4/?/84 (JJ) and 12/30/90-1/8/91 (AB 45:316); 6900' Crowley Reservoir 11/29/78 (AB 33:210) and 12/15/79 (DG; AB 34:651).

BLACK SCOTER (*Melanitta nigra*)

Extremely rare vagrant at Mono Lake (6400').

Record: n. shore Mono Lake, pair, 11/16/82 (JJ).

Male Harlequin Duck on the Merced River in Yosemite Valley. The blurry image in the foreground is a hen. Photographed in 1921 or 1922 by Charles Michael, courtesy the Yosemite Museum.

SURF SCOTER (*Melanitta perspicillata*)

Irregularly rare fall vagrant (0-11/year) below 7500' and extremely rare vagrant at higher elevations east of crest.

Though remote from the splash of the surf, Surf Scoters occasionally stray to lakes, reservoirs and ponds, including Mono Lake, east of the Sierran crest. The records fall during a two and one-half week period in October, and all have been females or immatures.

Peak count: 11, 7100' Grant Lake Reservoir 10/24/87 (DG).

Record at 9500': Ellery Lake 10/25/59 (AFN 14:68).

Extreme dates, seven records since 1959 and six since 1979: 10/11/79 7100' Grant Lake Reservoir (AB 34:196) - 10/29/86 6400' Mono Lake (DS, SJ).

WHITE-WINGED SCOTER (*Melanitta fusca*)

Rare fall vagrant below 8000' east of crest.

White-winged Scoters are more frequent than Surfs on eastside lakes and reservoirs, and usually visit later in fall. No more than two have been seen at any one time, but they are found virtually every year. There have been adult males as well as females and immatures.

Extreme dates: 10/18/86 6400' w. shore Mono Lake (Gottlieb Dandliker) - 12/24/86 6900' Grant Lake Reservoir (DG).

Additional references: AB 26:96; AB 30:761.

COMMON GOLDENEYE (*Bucephala clangula*)

	J	F	M	A	M	J	J	A	S	O	N	D	HABITAT	ELEVATIONS		
														N	T	W
WEST	•	•	•								•					4
EAST											—	—	LMo		6-8	

Extremely rare winter visitor or transient on west slope; uncommon fall and extremely rare spring transient below 8000' east of crest.

Common Goldeneyes usually frequent freshwater lakes and reservoirs, but the largest group I know of—15—were on a creek delta at Mono Lake (6400') on 11/14/82 (DG). In autumn, they and Ring-neckeds are often the commonest waterfowl on glacial lakes like Convict (7600') and Silver (7200'). They linger until the lakes freeze, but may sometimes overwinter.

Unlike the northern Sierra, Common Goldeneyes are surprisingly scarce on the lower reaches of Yosemite's west-slope rivers; I'm aware of only two records.

West slope records: 4700' Lake Eleanor Reservoir, 3, 11/23/86 (YM); 4000' Mirror Lake 1/15/40 (YM); 3700' Harden Flat Jan-March/84 (TB).

Spring record east of crest: 6800' Crowley Lake Reservoir 3/25/85 (JD).

Extreme dates east of crest excluding spring record: 11/14/82 Mono Lake (DG) - 1/15/86 Crowley Lake Reservoir (DP).

BARROW'S GOLDENEYE (*Bucephala islandica*)

Formerly nested on west slope, but no records since 1934. Extremely rare vagrant on east side.

Small numbers of Barrow's Goldeneyes formerly bred on Yosemite's mountain lakes, but none have been seen for over five decades. Did human disturbance drive them away?

Historical nesting records: 7000' Table Lake, three adults with two young, 7/24/34 (C 37:85; YNN 13:85); 8300' small lake on Kibbie Ridge, "breeding female," 6/30/22 (C 27:116); 9200' Smedberg Lake, two adults with six young, 8/25/19 (CFG 6:37).

Record east side: 6400' Mono Lake, 2 males, 11/25-26/88 (JJ).

BUFFLEHEAD (*Bucephala albeola*)

	J	F	M	A	M	J	J	A	S	O	N	D	HABITAT	ELEVATIONS		
														N	T	W
WEST			•	•						•	•					
EAST													LR		6-8	6-7

Extremely rare transient on west slope; extremely rare transient above 8000' on east slope; fairly common spring transient, rare summer visitor and locally common fall transient below 8000' and uncommon winter resident below 7000' east of crest.

Though never as numerous as dabblers, Buffleheads are, after Ruddys and sometimes Redheads, the most plentiful diving duck on freshwater lakes, reservoirs, ponds and languid streams east of the Sierran escarpment. They are rare on Mono Lake (6400'), where they usually linger near the mouths of streams. These strikingly patterned waterfowl remain until large lakes freeze, and brave most winters in small numbers.

Peak counts: approx. 75, 6900' Crowley Reservoir 4/13/86 (DG); 60, 6500' Bridgeport Reservoir 6/12/90 (PM, DS); 63, 12/19/82 (AB 37:792, DG).

Record above 8000' east slope: 8900' Lake Mary 12/7/76 (DG).

West slope records: 4000' Yosemite Valley 3/3/40 (YM), 3/5/28 (YNN 13:117), 3/12/74 (YM), 4/3/21 (YNN 13:117) and 10/29/79 (YM); 4700' Lake Eleanor 3/15/87 (YM); 6400' Laurel Lake 11/10/80 (YM); 6500' Lake Vernon 11/11/80 (YM).

HOODED MERGANSER (*Lophodytes cucullatus*)

Formerly rare winter resident below 4000' on west slope, but no records since 1940; extremely rare transient east of Sierran escarpment.

Hooded Mergansers have not been seen in Yosemite Valley (4000') for almost five decades, but were recorded ten times between 1925 and 1940. Bellrose (1976) claims they "breed...in the Sierra Nevada Mountains as far south as Yosemite," but I've been unable to locate confirming evidence south of Lassen County (AFN 18:483).

Records east of crest, all females or immatures: 7100' Grant Lake Reservoir 10/27/77 (DG) and 11/19/79 (DG); 6400' Mono Lake 8/26/89 (Chris Corben) and 11/21/76 (ES:98).

Extreme dates west, all Yosemite Valley: 11/26/28 - 4/18/40 (YM).

Additional references: YNN 10:26; YNN 19:27.

COMMON MERGANSER (*Mergus merganser*)

	J	F	M	A	M	J	J	A	S	O	N	D	HABITAT	ELEVATIONS		
														N	T	W
WEST													RL	F-5		F-5
EAST													LR	7	6-8	6-7

Rare resident below 5000' and extremely rare visitor at higher elevations on west slope; rare summer resident or visitor and locally fairly common fall transient below 7500', and irregularly rare to uncommon winter resident below 7000' east of crest.

Along wooded rivers, lakes and reservoirs, especially in reaches that are seldom disturbed by hikers or fishermen, one may chance upon breeding Common Mergansers. While a nest has yet to be found, adults with flightless young have been seen in the Merced and Tuolumne River drainages on the west slope, and at Lower Twin Lake (7100') and Bridgeport Reservoir east of the crest.

East of the Sierran escarpment, Common Mergansers gather during migrations on large, freshwater lakes, reservoirs and streams, sometimes in sizable flocks. They favor stream deltas, where they roost on shoreline rocks and sand bars. They have yet to be found on Mono Lake's alkaline waters, which attract their Red-breasted relatives. They linger as long as there is open water, and often overwinter in small numbers.

Peak count: 75, 6500' Bridgeport Lake Reservoir 12/8/76 (DG).

West slope records above 5000': 8200' Tenaya Lake, 2, 10/14/87 (DG) and 6, 10/28/86 (DS, SJ); 8600' Tuolumne Meadows, pair, 6/1/77 (TB).

Representative nesting localities: 3800' Hetch Hetchy Reservoir (YNN 17:156, YM); 4000' Yosemite Valley (YNN 19:47; no records since 1939); 4200' Tuolumne River, Pate Valley (DG); 7100' Lower Twin Lake (Dan Keller).

RED-BREASTED MERGANSER (*Mergus serrator*)

Irregularly rare spring (0-2/year) and extremely rare summer visitor and fall transient east of crest.

Red-breasted Mergansers have seen on various eastside lakes, reservoirs, creeks and ponds. On Mono Lake they sometimes appear miles from shore. All have been in henny plumage. Most are loners; the one fall record is also exceptional in being the only flock.

Summer and fall records: 6500' Rush Creek 8/4/84 (DS); 7000' Alkali Ponds, 2, 9/13/87 (DG); 6900' Crowley Reservoir 2/96/87 (PM, DG, ESt); Mono Lake, 6/10-12/89 (PM) and 7, 10/21/82 (DW).

Extreme dates excluding August, September and October records, 14 records since 1976: 4/6/87 Grant Lake Reservoir (DG) - 7/21/91 Crowley Reservor (AB 45:1157).

Additional references: AB 30:998, AB 31:1184, AB 39:957, ES:98.

RUDDY DUCK (*Oxyura jamaicensis*)

	J	F	M	A	M	J	J	A	S	O	N	D	HABITAT	ELEVATIONS		
														N	T	W
WEST				•		•							LR		F-5	
EAST													LMo		6-8	6-7

Extremely rare spring and rare fall transient below 5000' and extremely rare transient at higher elevations on west slope; extremely rare transient above 8000' on east slope; common transient and uncommon summer visitor below 8000' and locally common winter resident below 7000' east of crest.

Though frequently the most numerous duck on large lakes and reservoirs east of the Sierran escarpment, Ruddy Ducks do not remain to nest within the boundaries encompassed by the endleaf map. At Black Lake, a few miles to the east of Granite Mountain, a hen Ruddy Duck was seen with a chick on June 14, 1991 (PM,DS). During migrations and winter, they amass by the hundreds on Mono Lake (6400') and on Bridgeport Lake (6500'), Crowley Lake (6900') and Grant Lake (7100') reservoirs. An estimated 1,500, for example, were on Crowley Lake on 12/31/83 (AB 38:792, DG), and over 1,000 were on Mono Lake on 9/26/90 (ESt) and 1/9/40 (J.T. Emlen, journal). At Mono, they are the only duck that frequently ventures far from freshwater streams or springs, mingling with Eared Grebes on the lake's remote shores. They also visit other lakes and ponds. Nonbreeding birds summer on Crowley Lake and Bridgeport Lake reservoirs, and occasionally visit Mono Lake as well.

Ruddy Ducks are hardy, staying in large numbers until lakes freeze, and braving the winter wherever there is open water. Usually several hundred remain on Mono Lake, outnumbering grebes from December through March. On frigid, foggy January days, when not another living thing relieves the silence, I've seen them materialize, apparition-like, among the tufa.

West slope records above 5000': 7600' Harden Lake 11/28/53 (AFN 8:38); 8200' Tenaya Lake 10/15/87 (DG).

East slope record above 8000': 8900' Lake Mary, 2, 12/7/76 (DG).

Spring records west slope: 4700' Lake Eleanor Reservoir 4/11/38 (YNN 19:43); 4000' Yosemite Valley 4/22/29 (YM); 3700' Hetch Hetchy Reservoir, several, 6/3/77 (SG).

Extreme dates west slope excluding spring records: 10/10/34, 9, Lake Eleanor Reservoir (YNN 14:26) - 12/6/28 4000' Yosemite Valley (YNN 10:126).

Order FALCONIFORMES: DIURNAL BIRDS OF PREY

Of the region's 19 raptors, nine nest on the west slope and 12 east of the crest; six occur only as winter visitors or transients. One, the Swainson's Hawk, is a long-distance migrant to the pampas of South America, where land-use changes have depleted its numbers (Stanley Temple). Other nesting species—with the possible exception of Peregrine Falcons—are short-distance migrants or, at lower elevations and east of the crest, year-round residents; none winter regularly at elevations that are prone to deep winter snows.

Like owls and mammalian predators, raptors are rarely numerous, but play critical roles in nature's economy. Except for vultures, which like their meals dead and aged, they feed on living animals. Our smallest species, the American Kestrel, dines primarily on insects, whereas our largest, the Golden Eagle, preys on mammals as large as rabbits and marmots; others, like the Sharp-shinned Hawk and Peregrine Falcon, feed mainly on other birds. For this reason, the presence of a raptor, even high overhead, sparks panicky alarm notes from squirrels and songbirds, and flushes flocks of shorebirds and waterfowl; the price of survival is constant vigilance.

In the early part of this century, rangers routinely shot Yosemite's raptors because they sometimes preyed on songbirds. Some ranchers and sheepherders still blast away at every one they see. As a result of persecution as well as pesticides and habitat destruction, most species have declined to some extent.

Family CATHARTIDAE: AMERICAN VULTURES

TURKEY VULTURE (*Cathartes aura*)

	J	F	M	A	M	J	J	A	S	O	N	D	HABITAT	ELEVATIONS		
														N	T	W
WEST											•		A	2	F-6	
EAST		•											GA		6-8	

Common summer resident in vicinity of Mariposa (2000'); rare transient and summer visitor below 6500' and extremely rare transient at higher elevations elsewhere on west slope; fairly common spring transient and uncommon summer visitor below 8000' and extremely rare transient at higher elevations east of crest.

The mountains, by and large, are too wooded for Turkey Vultures. On the west slope, they are common only in the vicinity of Mariposa (CL). Yet just a few miles west, in the oak savannahs and grasslands of the foothills, they are a ubiquitous part of the summer skyscape. When they visit higher elevations, they are usually soaring overhead en route to someplace else.

East of the crest, Turkey Vultures are partial to meadows and other open habitats, but soar over wooded slopes as well. Flocks migrate through in spring and fall, but rarely if ever stop to nest.

Records above 6500' west slope and 8000' east of crest: 9800' Dana Meadows 7/17/84 (JZ); 10,000' Mt. Dana 8/5/31 (YNN 10:82); Hall Natural Area 10,500'+, 12, 3/26/80 and 11,000'+, 2, 5/18/80 (DeSante and Engstrom MS).

Extreme dates west slope: 4/2/85 4000' Yosemite Valley (YM) - 11/10/22 Yosemite Valley (YM).

Extreme dates east of crest: 2/25/89 6800' Lee Vining (Sally Gaines)- 9/26/87 6900' Long Valley (DG).

Additional references: YNN 21:22, YNN 22:25.

Family ACCIPITRIDAE: KITES, EAGLES, HAWKS AND ALLIES

OSPREY (*Pandion haliaetus*)

Rare transient at all elevations both west and east of the crest; extremely rare summer resident on west slope; in recent years, summer resident at Mono Lake (6400') east of crest.

Ospreys, which are also called "fish-eagles," are usually seen at freshwater lakes, reservoirs and rivers, but migrate over all types of habitat. One near Mt. Lyell on 10/6/73, for example, was at 13,000' (YM), and there are numerous records for Tuolumne Meadows (8600') and the rim of Yosemite Valley (to 7500'—YM, SG, DG). East of the Sierran escarpment, I have seen them over arid, treeless sagebrush scrub.

Ospreys have nested at single localities west and east of the crest. In 1976, a pair built a nest on Yosemite's Laurel Lake (6400'—D&SJ); I don't know if they fledged young, or have bred at this remote, backcountry locality in subsequent years.

East of the Sierran escarpment, Ospreys set up housekeeping on a Mono Lake tufa tower in 1984 (6400'), and returned in 1985, 1986 and 1987, but had failed to produce young (AB 39:957, DG) until 1989 when two chicks were seen (AB 43:1363) Young were produced in 1990 and 1991 also. They fish the lakes in the June Lake loop as well as the nearby waters of lower Rush Creek, which have been thriving with trout since flood flows breached Grant Lake dam in 1982. The Los Angeles Department of Water and Power seeks to divert the water and dry up the creek, but have been temporarily thwarted by a court order. Meanwhile the tufa tower, which lies several hundred yards offshore, affords a safe as well as spectacular nesting site.

To the south of our region, Ospreys are also known to nest as close as Tinnemaha Reservoir, which lies approximately 80 miles south of Mono Lake in Inyo County. In recent years, up to four pairs have bred at this locality (CMc).

Extreme dates west slope: 2/25/76 4000' Yosemite Valley (YM) - 10/22/83 2000' near El Portal (YM).

Extreme dates east of crest: 3/26/82 Mono Lake (BE) - 9/24/89 Lundy Lake (Estel Sitze).

BLACK-SHOULDERED (WHITE-TAILED) KITE (*Elanus caeruleus*)

Rare summer visitor in Mariposa region (2000'); extremely rare spring transient and summer visitor to treeline elsewhere on west slope; extremely rare transient east of the Sierran escarpment.

West slope records excluding Mariposa region: 7000' 0.5 mile w. of Bridalveil Creek 5/2/81 (YM); 4000' Yosemite Valley 5/24/03 (Auk 21:66-78); 6600' Crane Flat Lookout 7/16/80 (YM); 4400' Big Meadow 8/29/80 (GS); 10,600' near Vogelsang Pass 8/?/40 (YM).

Record east of crest: 6900' Cain Ranch 10/5-14/84 (DG, DDeS).

MISSISSIPPI KITE (*Ictinia mississippiensis*)

Extremely rare vagrant east of crest.

Record: 6400' n. shore Mono Lake, subadult, 5/31/81 (AB 35:858; WB 16:110); (a bird thought to be this species was seen near Hetch Hetchy Reservoir on 6/27/83, but the record was rejected by the California Bird Records Committee).

BALD EAGLE (*Haliaeetus leucocephalus*)

	J	F	M	A	M	J	J	A	S	O	N	D	HABITAT	ELEVATIONS		
														N	T	W
WEST							•	•	•				LRA		F-12	F-5
EAST						•	•						LRGA		6-12	6-8

Locally uncommon winter resident below 5000', rare winter visitor to at least 8200' and extremely rare summer visitor or transient on west slope; locally fairly common transient, uncommon winter resident and extremely rare summer visitor below 8000' east of crest.

In late fall and winter, especially on large lakes and reservoirs east of the Sierran escarpment, Bald Eagles hunt for fish, waterfowl and carrion. Less frequently they patrol languid streams, ponds and moist meadows. Unlike Goldens, they prefer wetland habitats, but also search dry terrain for carrion. During migrations, they soar over all types of country.

On the west slope, Bald Eagles regularly winter at Cherry Lake Reservoir (4700'), Lake Eleanor Reservoir (4700') and probably Hetch Hetchy Reservoir (3700'), and rarely elsewhere. Four were at Cherry Lake, for example, on 1/21/80 (TB, SG). Wintering birds occasionally roam into the higher mountains; one was at Tenaya Lake (8200'), for instance, on 12/15/59 (AFN 14:338), and they have soared over Badger Pass (7200') in January, February and March (YM).

East of the crest, Bald Eagles concentrate at Crowley Lake Reservoir (6800'), where a high count of 18 were tallied on 12/16/78, many sitting on the ice (DG, AB 33:654). Large numbers also gather at Crowley Lake after the spring thaw; 17, for instance, were there in mid-March, 1987 (CMc). Lesser numbers patrol the June Lake Loop lakes (7100'-7600'), lower Rush Creek (6400'-7100'), Mono Lake (6400'), Bridgeport Lake Reservoir (6500'), Twin Lake (7100') and nearby fields and meadows. The population thins in December when the large lakes freeze, but some usually brave eastside winters.

Six decades ago, Bald Eagles were nesting on the west slope a few miles west of our region along the north fork of the Merced River near its confluence with Bull Creek (2000'—YNN 4:7), and possibly elsewhere as well.

High elevation record: 12,800'+ over Mt. Gibbs 9/2/84 (YM).

Summer records west slope: 7/3/74 7200' Glacier Point (YM) and 7/4/74 10,100' Parker Pass (YM)—possibly same bird; 8/27/78 11,000'+ over Cathedral Peak, 2 adults (YM); 9/2/84 12,800'+ over Mt. Gibbs (YM).

Summer records east of crest: 6/13/89 10,500' Long Lake, upper Rock Creek, 1 immature, (CH); 7/10/89 10,700' Hilton Lake, 2, (CH); 7/22/86 6900' Crowley Lake, adult (DP).

Mississippi Kite near the north shore of Mono Lake, May 31, 1981. Photograph by Marie Mans.

Extreme dates west slope excluding summer records: 11/10/57 4000' Wawona (YM) - 5/11/76 4000' Yosemite Valley (YM).

Additional reference: AFN 7:232.

NORTHERN HARRIER (MARSH HAWK) (*Circus cyaneus*)

	J	F	M	A	M	J	J	A	S	O	N	D	HABITAT	ELEVATIONS		
														N	T	W
WEST	•											•	GA		F-11	
EAST													GMaA	6-7	6-11	6-7

Rare spring transient below 5000', rare summer visitor and fall transient to and occasionally above treeline and extremely rare winter visitor on west slope; rare summer visitor and fall transient on east slope; fairly common transient, uncommon summer resident and irregularly rare to fairly common winter resident east of Sierran escarpment.

A slim hawk quartering over meadows or marshes is likely a Northern Harrier. They are down-to-earth raptors, gliding low over vegetation in pursuit of mice and other small mammals, and roosting and perching on the ground. During migrations, however, sometimes soar high overhead.

East of the Sierran escarpment, nesting Northern Harriers were undoubtedly more numerous before grazing, water diversions, reservoirs and recreational developments reduced or degraded their marsh and meadow nesting haunts. These raptors conceal their nests in dense, high herbaceous vegetation. In recent years, they have bred near

Mono Lake (6400'—SJ, DS, JL) and along the Owens River (6900'—CMc); they formerly nested near June Lake as well (7600'—C 36:36).

Eastside wintering populations vary depending on snowfall. When deep snow buries fields and meadows, Northern Harriers retreat to balmier climes. On the Mono Lake Christmas Bird Count, for example, tallies have ranged from 16 to 0.

High elevation record: 12,000' Mt. Conness 9/26/84 and 10/14/77 (DeSante and Engstrom MS).

Winter records west slope: 4000' Yosemite Valley 12/28/81 (YM) and 1/20/81 (YM).

Extreme dates west slope excluding winter records, both 4000' Yosemite Valley: 4/1/28 (YM) - 12/1/26 (YM).

Extreme dates above 5000' west slope or 8000' east of crest: 6/30/75 7800' White Wolf (YM); 8/2/79 - 10/14/77 12,000' Hall Natural Area (DeSante and Engstrom MS).

Additional references: AFN 8:39; YNN 13:84.

SHARP-SHINNED HAWK (*Accipiter striatus*)

	J	F	M	A	M	J	J	A	S	O	N	D	HABITAT	ELEVATIONS		
														N	T	W
WEST													POWA	4-7?	F-11	F-4
EAST													PWA	8-9?	6-11	6-8

Status uncertain; rare winter resident below 4000', rare summer and possibly winter resident from approximately 4000' to 7000' and uncommon fall transient from foothills to and rarely above treeline on west slope; rare resident below 8000' and uncommon fall transient from valleys to and rarely above treeline east of crest.

Summering Sharp-shinned Hawks are fleeting phantoms of open coniferous forests and the edges of meadows or clearings. Transient and wintering birds are more catholic in choice of habitat, hunting wherever small birds are numerous; they terrorize passerines in thickets and scrub as well as in woodlands and forests. The sharp alarm notes of birds, chipmunks and squirrels often betray their presence.

Sharp-shinned Hawks are most numerous from late August through early November, when transients soar over all types of habitat. Their numbers seem to vary from year to year; at Hall Natural Area (10,000'), for example, there are many records some years, none at all in others (DeSante MS).

This smallest accipiter probably nests in the forested parts of our region, but I'm only aware of one definite record. In 1930, a Sharp-shinned's nest was discovered in Yosemite Valley (YM). In recent years, nesting has been suspected on the west slope at Crane Flat (6200'—DG), and on the east slope near Walker Lake (7900'—CMc) and in the Glass Mountain region (8000'-9000'—CMc); to the south, these agile predators have bred at Dinkey Creek (5700') in Sequoia National Forest (SH).

High elevation record: 11,700' Koip Peak 10/10/32 (YM).

Extreme dates above 8000', both Hall Natural Area (10,200'): 8/8/80 - 10/15/78 (DeSante MS).

COOPER'S HAWK (*Accipiter cooperi*)

	J	F	M	A	M	J	J	A	S	O	N	D	HABITAT	ELEVATIONS		
														N	T	W
WEST													OWPA	F-5	F-10	F-5
EAST													WPA	8	6-10	6-8

Rare resident below 5000' and uncommon fall transient to treeline on west slope; rare resident below 8000' and uncommon fall transient to treeline east of crest.

Cooper's Hawks have become one of our scarcest birds of prey, occuring mostly during fall migration. But in 1920, Grinnell and Storer judged them "moderately common residents chiefly in upper sonoran and transition zones on both slopes" (GS 284). Contrary to Grinnell and Storer, who considered Cooper's Hawks "partial to growths of tall trees in the vicinity of streams," these woodland raptors usually nest in stands of live oak (Asay 1987), and have also bred in second-growth oak-conifer forests. Transients and wintering birds are even more catholic, hunting a wide variety of wooded habitats, and occasionally scrub as well. In late summer and early fall, they range to treeline.

On the west slope, Cooper's Hawks formerly bred in at least three localities in and around Yosemite Valley (4000'-6000'—GS 284-286, YNN 16:23, YM), but not in recent decades. I know of only three active sites, both below 5500'.

Cooper's Hawks have also declined on the east slope, where I only know of one nesting record since the 1930s. East of the Sierran escarpment, however, they still breed in several localities circum Glass Mountain (approximately 8000') (DS,CMc).

In general, Cooper's Hawks appear to be scarcer than Sharp-shinneds, especially during winter. I suspect some birds, especially on Christmas Bird Counts, are misidentified. Care should be taken in separating these two similar species.

High elevation record: 10,500' Hall Natural Area, many records in late summer (DeSante MS).

Extreme dates above 6000' west slope and 8000' east, all Hall Natural Area (10,000'): 7/1/79; 8/3/77 - 9/28/84 (DeSante MS).

Active nesting localities west slope: 2200' near Mariposa (CL); 4600' near Ackerson Meadow in second-growth coniferous forest (SG, JW); 5200' 2.8 mile NE Ackerson Meadow (JW).

Active nesting locality east slope: approx. 8000' Lee Vining Canyon (CMc).

NORTHERN GOSHAWK (*Accipiter gentilis*)

	J	F	M	A	M	J	J	A	S	O	N	D	HABITAT	ELEVATIONS		
														N	T	W
WEST													PA	5-9	5-10	3-5
EAST													PA	7-9	7-10	6-8

Rare summer resident from 5000' to 9000', rare summer visitor to treeline, rare winter resident below 5000' and extremely rare winter visitor at higher elevations on west slope; rare summer resident from 7000' to 9000', rare summer visitor to treeline and rare winter resident below 8000' east of crest.

Except near a nest, Northern Goshawks are among the most difficult birds to find. Most encounters are brief and unexpected. I usually glimpse them hurtling through the woods, hunting in meadows or soaring overhead. Alarm notes of chipmunks, squirrels and birds often betray their presence.

These fierce predators favor moderately dense forests that are broken by meadows, lakes, streams, brush or other openings. Northern Goshawks lay claim both to level terrain and steep slopes and canyons. Nests are usually concealed in dense, but sometimes small groves of large pines, firs or aspens (CMc). During winter, they sometimes hunt in treeless sagebrush scrub.

While most Northern Goshawks are probably resident in the sense they remain in the mountains throughout the year, they apparently move up and down slope seasonally, and winter below their nesting range. In summer they regularly cruise to and even above treeline. By autumn, however, most move to lower elevations. Between mid-October and mid-March, I'm aware of but a single record above 5000' on the west slope, and none at all above 8000' east of the crest. In Yosemite Valley, which at 4000' is below their known nesting range, most records fall between November and February. At this season, birds occasionally range as low as 2000' in the Merced River Canyon near El Portal (MR). The earliest record at Tuolumne Meadows (8600') is 5/3/83 (YM).

No other birds are so aggressive in defense of eggs and young. Goshawks may furiously attack bears, humans and other large animals who venture near their nests. Their sharp talons are capable of inflicting painful wounds. Recently the National Park Service, to mollify terrified hikers on Yosemite's Four-Mile Trail, chopped down a nest tree and drove a pair away. Whose park is this, anyway?

High elevation record: 10,800' Mt. Hoffmann 8/23/76 (SG).

Winter record above 5000' west slope: 1/20/84 8600' Tuolumne Meadows (YM).

Extreme dates above 5000' west slope excluding winter record: 3/19/77 Tuolumne Meadows - 10/3/15 7800' Glen Aulin (GS 287).

Representative nesting localities: 5400' Merced Grove (TB, SG); 6000' Little Yosemite Valley (EM 3); 7000' Indian Canyon (YM); 7400' Snow Creek switchbacks north of Indian Rock (YNN 38:168-169); 7600' near Ostrander Rocks (GS 287); 8600' Tuolumne Meadows (YM); 9000' and 8000' near Virginia Lakes (C 36:35-36; C 41: 247); 8500' near June Lake (C 40:3-11); 8000' Lee Vining Canyon (DG); 7900' Walker Lake (DG); 8500' Glass Mountain (CMc).

Additional references: AFN 8:327; AFN 14:475; YNN 13:85; YNN 16:93; YNN 29:45; GS 287.

RED-SHOULDERED HAWK (*Buteo lineatus*)

Rare resident in Mariposa region (2000'); extremely rare transient elsewhere on west slope; rare fall and extremely rare spring transient and summer visitor below 7000' east of Sierran escarpment.

Small numbers of Red-shouldered Hawks probably nest in the Mariposa region, where they dwell along timbered streams (CL). Of the five other west slope records, four were at high elevations.

East of the Sierran escarpment, Red-shouldered Hawks visit cottonwoods, willows and other riparian trees near streams or moist meadows. I've also seen them wheeling overhead, sometimes with Ravens or Red-taileds. Sometimes I hear their screams before I see the birds.

West slope records excluding Mariposa region: 8200' Tenaya Lake 7/19/85 (SGu); 9800' 0.5 mile west of Tioga Pass 7/31/82 (DeSante and Enstrom MS); 10,500' s. of Tioga Pass 8/24/85 (YM); 4600' Ackerson Meadow 9/1/81 (JW); 8600' Tuolumne Meadows 9/14/83 (DG); the Tenaya Lake bird was an adult, the others immatures.

High elevation record: 10,500' Hall Natural Area 8/5/89 (AB 44:156)

Additional references: AB 26:635, AB 36:213, AB 43:1363.

SWAINSON'S HAWK (*Buteo swainsoni*)

Extremely rare spring transient and irregularly rare summer visitor and fall transient mostly near or above treeline on both west and east slopes (0-2/year); rare transient and summer resident below 8000' east of Sierran escarpment.

Of all the raptors that regularly visit the high mountains, Swainson's Hawks are the scarcest. I know of nine records between mid-May and early October scattered from Glacier Point (7200'—YM) on the west slope to the Hall Natural Area (11,000'—DeSante and Engstrom MS) and Virginia Lakes (9800'—AB 27:913) on the east. They have ranged to 11,000' near Upper McCabe Lake, at Triple Divide Peak (YM) and in the Hall Natural Area (DeSante and Engstrom MS). While usually loners, a flock of six flew by Shepherd's Crest (approx. 11,000') on 8/11/77 (YM). These mountaineering hawks forage in dry meadows and fell-fields, but soar over all types of habitat.

East of the Sierran escarpment, Swainson's Hawks are a scarce transient and summer resident. In recent years two or three pairs have bred along the Owens River (7000'—CMc, T&JH) and on Parker Bench (approx. 8500'—Peter Bloom). Pairs require extensive, dry meadows in which to forage and stout trees in which to place nests. Migrating birds cruise over all types of habitat.

Swainson's Hawks have declined seriously throughout western North America, probably due to habitat changes on their wintering grounds. They journey to South American grasslands, completing annual round-trip journeys of 11,000 to 17,000 miles. Much of their grassland wintering habitat, as on the Argentine pampas, has been lost to agriculture (Stanley Temple).

Spring records west slope and above 8500' east of crest: 5/18/80 11,000' Hall Natural Area (DeSante and Engstrom MS); 6/17/40 7200' near Glacier Point (YM).

Extreme dates above 9000' excluding spring records: 7/12/73 9800' Virginia Lakes (AB 27:913) - 9/10/75 10,000' Hall Natural Area (MC); 10/17/76 9800' Tioga Pass (TB).

Extreme dates east of crest below 9000': 3/17/81 7000' Long Valley (DP) - 9/8/87, 3, 6500' Bridgeport Valley (DS).

RED-TAILED HAWK (*Buteo jamaicensis*)

	J	F	M	A	M	J	J	A	S	O	N	D	HABITAT	ELEVATIONS		
														N	T	W
WEST													GSA	F-5	F-13	F-5
EAST													GSA	6-8	6-13	6-8

Fairly common resident below 5000' and fairly common summer and uncommon fall visitor at higher elevations on west slope; fairly common resident below 8000' and fairly common summer and uncommon fall visitor at higher elevations east of crest; locally common fall transient below 7500' east of Sierran escarpment.

Overall Red-tailed Hawks are the region's most numerous and widespread raptors. They favor open terrain where they can spot small mammals and other ground-dwelling prey from the air. They forage in meadows, clearings, rock outcroppings, granite shelves, fell fields, talus and other open or openly wooded terrain, but shun dense forests. Breeding pairs build nests on stout trees and cliff ledges.

While not known to breed above 5000' on the west slope or 8000' to the east, Red-tailed Hawks range to high elevations even before the last of the snow melts from meadows and other open habitats. At Tuolumne Meadows, for example, one soared over eight feet of snow on 4/27/75, another over eight inches on 3/6/77 (TH). Until mid-summer, however, they are rare mountaineers. Between mid-July and mid-October, their numbers increase, and they cruise over the highest peaks.

East of the Sierran escarpment, an influx of northern birds swells Red-tailed Hawk populations in late fall and some winters. They may be locally common, especially in Bridgeport Valley (6500') and Long Valley (7000'). I've tallied 80 individuals between Bridgeport and Lower Twin Lake in early December. They brave most winters, but retreat to balmier climes when deep snow buries meadows and fields.

High elevation record: 13,000'+ Mt. Dana 8/19/65 (DG).

Representative nesting localities: (4400' Big Meadow —DG); 4600' Ackerson Meadow (JW); 7400' Lee Vining Canyon (DG); 6400' near Mono Lake (DG).

Additional reference: YNN 21:22.

FERRUGINOUS HAWK (*Buteo regalis*)

Irregularly rare to uncommon winter resident in Mariposa region (2000'); extremely rare transient elsewhere on west slope; irregularly rare fall transient (0-3/year) east of the Sierran escarpment.

Ferruginous Hawks are regular only in open, oak savannah habitat near Mariposa (2000'), where they winter some years and not in others (CL). They are surprisingly scarce east of the Sierran escarpment; a few miles east of the region, however, in Hammil Valley (4400'), they are uncommon winter residents (DG).

Record west slope excluding Mariposa region: 4600' Ackerson Meadow 10/5-7/87 (JW); (just west of the region, one was seen at Burch Meadow near Groveland on 11/7/81—JW, CL).

Extreme dates east of crest, six records since 1984: 9/14/85 6800' near Crowley Lake Reservoir, 3 (RS) - 6900' Dechambeau Creek 10/8/87 (JM); 6500' Bridgeport Valley 11/11/75 (T&JH).

ROUGH-LEGGED HAWK (*Buteo lagopus*)

	J	F	M	A	M	J	J	A	S	O	N	D	HABITAT	ELEVATIONS		
														N	T	W
WEST	•	•	•								•	•			8-10	9
EAST	▒	▒	▒						•	•	▒	▒	GMaSA		6-8	6-8

Rare winter resident in Mariposa region (2000'); extremely rare transient and winter visitor elsewhere on west slope; irregularly rare to fairly common winter resident below 8000' east of the Sierran escarpment.

East of the Sierran escarpment, Rough-legged Hawks often outnumber wintering Red-taileds. Some years bring dozens of these northerners, others few or none; Mono Lake Christmas Count tallies, for example, range from 20 to 0. Almost all are black-bellied immatures; an adult, however, visited Dechambeau Ponds (6500') on the exceptionally early date of 9/11/85 (DG).

Unlike Red-taileds, Rough-legged Hawks are confirmed valley dwellers. Except when migrating, they shun ridges and hillsides in favor of level or rolling meadows, fields and marshes.

West slope records excluding Mariposa region: 9900' Cloud's Rest, 2, 11/6/84 (YM); approx. 8000' Old Glacier Point Road 11/23/84 (YM); 8600' Tuolumne Meadows 12/1/74-2/2/75 (until first major snowfall—TH), 1/16/83 (YM), 3/31-4/2/83 (YM), 3/19/84, 2 (YM).

Extreme dates excluding September record: 10/22/84 7000' Long Valley (DG) - 3/23/81 6400' Mono Lake County Park (DW).

GOLDEN EAGLE (*Aquila chrysaetos*)

	J	F	M	A	M	J	J	A	S	O	N	D	HABITAT	ELEVATIONS N	T	W
WEST	━	━	━	━	━	━	━	━	━	━	━	━	GSCA	F-10	F-13	F-5
EAST	━	━	━	━	━	━	━	━	━	━	━	━	GSCA	6-10	6-13	6-8

Rare resident in Mariposa region; uncommon resident below 5000', rare summer resident to treeline and uncommon summer and extremely rare winter visitor to 12,000' elsewhere on west slope; uncommon resident below 8000', rare summer resident to treeline and uncommon summer visitor to 12,000' east of crest.

Like Red-tailed Hawks, Golden Eagles favor open terrain where they can spot small mammals and other ground-dwelling prey from the air. They hunt in meadows, clearings, rock outcroppings, granite shelves, fell fields, talus and other open or openly wooded habitats, but avoid dense forests. At Mono Lake, they regularly pluck gulls and their chicks from island rookeries (JJ, DS). While most breeding birds place their nests on precipitous, rocky ledges, a pair near Tioga Pass (9500') employed a lodgepole pine (YM).

Most Golden Eagles nest at lower elevations, moving into the higher mountains as the snow melts. Pairs have bred, however, at 10,000', and regularly cruise the highest peaks. Most winter at lower elevations, but one near Tuolumne Meadows roamed to 12,000' on 12/29/75 (TH).

Representative nesting localities: (approx. 3000' vicinity Arch Rock Entrance Station—SG); approx. 3500' below Hetch Hetchy Reservoir, three nests (TB); approx. 5000' near Royal Arches, Yosemite Valley (TB, YM); 6000' near Nevada Falls (YNN 3:2); 7000' ridge above Mono Meadow (KC); 10,000' Mt. Hoffmann (YNN 18:6); approx. 8500' Lundy Canyon (CMc).

Additional references: AFN 7:232; YNN 17:159.

Family Falconidae: FALCONS

CRESTED CARACARA (*Polyborus plancus*)

Record: 6600'-7000' Mono County dump, Cain Ranch and vicinity, adult or subadult 9/13-10/16/87 (RS, DG, PP, JD); rejected by California Bird Records Committee. It was judged a bird escaped from captivity.

AMERICAN KESTREL (*Falco sparverius*)

	J	F	M	A	M	J	J	A	S	O	N	D	HABITAT	ELEVATIONS		
														N	T	W
WEST													GCWO	F-9	F-12	F-4
EAST													GCW	6-8	6-12	6-8

Fairly common winter and uncommon summer resident in Mariposa region (2000'); uncommon resident below 4000', rare summer resident to 8500' and uncommon summer visitor from 4000' to 12,000' on west slope; fairly common summer resident below 8000', uncommon summer visitor to 12,000' and irregularly rare to uncommon winter resident below 8000' east of crest.

In open, grassy habitats ranging from valleybottom meadows to alpine fields, American Kestrels hunt for grasshoppers, ground-dwelling insects and small mammals. They perch on poles and fences as well as trees, and frequently hover like Mountain Bluebirds.

Most American Kestrels nest at lower elevations, then follow the flower bloom upslope. These beautiful little falcons raise their young in tree cavities, holes in buildings, cliffs and, east of the crest, old magpie nests; I've found them in cottonwoods, aspens and oaks. Usually they locate in the vicinity of meadows or other open terrain. A nest near Illilouette Falls (5500'), however, was ensconced on a cliff ledge in a wooded gorge (YM).

From mid-summer through early fall, post-breeding or immature American Kestrels drift into high meadows and alpine fell fields. One near Harden Lake (7600') on 10/31/53 (AFN 8:39) suggests they linger until driven down by snow.

On the east side, wintering American Kestrels are uncommon some years, absent in others, with no obvious correlation to the severity of the winter.

High elevation record: 12,500' Dana Plateau 7/14/76 (DG).

Representative nesting localities: 2000' near Mariposa (CL); 4000' McCauley Ranch (DG); 4000' Yosemite Valley (EM 4, YM); 8600' Tuolumne Meadows (PL); 8700' Mt. Clark (YM);

7400' Lee Vining Canyon (DG); 7000' Convict Creek (C 41:248); 6400' Mono Lake County Park (DG).

MERLIN (*Falco columbarius*)

Rare fall transient below treeline and rare winter resident below 4000' on west slope; rare fall transient below treeline and rare winter resident below 8000' east of crest.

Merlins are fleeting apparitions. Many times, alerted by panic among songbirds, I've glimpsed this swift falcon hurtling into the distance. Unlike Kestrels, they never hover and rarely seem to stop, capturing birds and even dragonflies on the wing. They hunt wherever small birds abound, shunning only dense forests. I've seen them in open woodlands, willow and buffalo-berry thickets, sagebrush scrub, meadows and mudflats.

Old June records near Mammoth Lakes (D 1631) and June Lake (C 40:9) suggest that Merlins used to nest in the eastern Sierra, but this remains conjectural.

High elevation record: 10,000' Hall Natural Area 10/28/77 (D&E).

Extreme dates excluding June records: 9/22/79 6400' near Crane Flat (YM) - 4/11/82 near Mono Lake (HG); (I've rejected an unsupported 8/19 record from Vogelsang Peak—YM).

Additional reference: YNN 4:15.

PEREGRINE FALCON (*Falco peregrinus*)

Rare transient and summer resident below 5000', rare summer visitor to 12,000' and irregularly rare winter resident below 5000' on west slope; rare transient and summer resident below 8000', rare summer visitor to 12,000' and irregularly rare winter resident below 8000' east of crest.

Where there are ducks, shorebirds, pigeons, woodpeckers, jays and other sizable birds, one may glimpse a Peregrine Falcon plummeting from the blue. These swiftest of raptors hunt in open woodlands, meadows, marshes and mudflats, often killing their prey in mid-air. Nesting birds seek precipitous cliff ledges with expansive, vertiginous views.

Peregrine Falcons nest below 6000' on the west slope and 8500' east of the crest, but cruise to treeline from mid-summer through early fall. Until the 1980s, there were no winter records; in recent years, however, they have lingered in Yosemite Valley (YM) and near Mono Lake (DG).

Peregrine Falcons were formerly more numerous, but suffered a precipitous decline during the 1950s. DDT and other chlorinated hydrocarbon pesticides, which Sierran birds probably contracted while migrating or wintering in the lowlands, caused eggshell thinning and widespread nesting failures. In our region every historic nesting eyrie was abandoned, including sites overlooking Yosemite Valley (YNN 18:97-98; EM 4), near the mouth of Lundy Canyon (C 40:262) and on Mono Lake's Negit Island ("possible site" GS 295). Plundering of nests by falconers may have hastened their decline.

In recent years, with the banning of DDT in the United States and Canada, Peregrine Falcons have begun to stage a comeback. Even before biologists began to meddle, pairs returned to Yosemite's El Capitan and Hetch Hetchy Valley in the late 1970s, but eggshell thinning remained a problem (Asay and Davis 1984). In response biologists removed fragile, pesticide-laden eggs to incubate in the lab, and placed newly-hatched chicks in the eyries. West of the crest they have hacked captive-reared birds in

Peregrine Falcon

Yosemite and Hetch Hetchy valleys; to the east in Lee Vining Canyon and near Grant Lake Reservoir. By 1991 a pair in Yosemite nested successfully.

High elevation record: 12,400' Mt. Conness 8/18/84 (DeSante MS).

Extreme dates above 8500', both Hall Natural Area (10,000'): 7/28/79 - 9/1/85 (DeSante MS).

Additional references: AFN 6:297; AFN 9:354; YNN 4:35; YNN 13:63; YNN 21:22; YNN 22:73.

PRAIRIE FALCON (*Falco mexicanus*)

	J	F	M	A	M	J	J	A	S	O	N	D	HABITAT	ELEVATIONS		
														N	T	W
WEST													GCA		8-12	
EAST													GCSA	7-8	6-12	6-8

Extremely rare visitor below 8000' and uncommon summer visitor and extremely rare spring transient at higher elevations on west slope; uncommon resident below 8000' and uncommon summer visitor at higher elevations east of crest.

While Prairie Falcons nest in the low foothills west of the region and in the open sagebrush country east of the crest, they avoid the Sierra's wooded midsection. At higher elevations, they arrive in July, become more numerous in August, and linger into October. They hunt for rodents and birds in meadows, fell-fields, ridges and other open habitats, often cruising high overhead.

East of the Sierran escarpment, Prairie Falcons patrol the vast expanses of meadow and sagebrush which clothe flats and gentle slopes. They also hunt the margins of Mono and other lakes and ponds (see preface, p. ix). They nest on steep, rocky cliffs, and brave all but the harshest winters.

High elevation records: 12,000' Mt. Dana 9/11/77 (SG, TB); 12,000' Mt Conness (DeSante MS).

Spring record above 8000': 8600' Tuolumne Meadows 3/3/84 (YM).

West slope records below 8000': approx. 5,500' Snow Creek switchbacks 5/2/76 (YM); 4000' Yosemite Valley 6/24/35 (YM); 4600' Ackerson Meadow 9/6/81 and 10/14/85 (JW).

Extreme dates above 8,000': 6/8/79 9700' Sawmill Campground (DDeS) - 10/14/78 11,000' Hall Natural Area (DeSante MS).

Representative nesting localities: approx. 8500' Lee Vining Canyon (DG); approx. 7500' Clark Canyon (CMc); 7800' north of Mammoth Airport (CMc); 8000' McLaughlin Cliffs (CMc).

Order GALLIFORMES: Grouse and Quail

Family PHASIANIDAE: GROUSE AND QUAIL

Of the six species of gallinaceous birds that are well-established in our region, two—Chuckars and White-tailed Ptarmigans—have been introduced to augment the ranks of huntable fowl. In addition, California Quail have been introduced in the Mono Basin. As birds go, they are a sedentary tribe; only Mountain Quail make a short migration to winter at lower elevations. Sage Grouse have been drastically reduced in numbers, and could disappear if not protected from hunting and grazing. A seventh species, Wild Turkey, has been introduced on the west slope, but its status is uncertain; I discuss it in Appendix I, p. 336.

CHUCKAR (*Alectoris chukar*)

Introduced; uncommon resident below 8500', mostly east of Sierran escarpment.

Chuckars inhabit arid, scrub-covered slopes, usually with scattered rock outcroppings. They require a spring, creek or other source of water within their daily foraging radius.

These natives of arid Eurasia and the Middle East have become established in the Bodie Hills, Cowtrack Mountain and Granite Mountain. Chuckars also range into the Sierra from Bridgeport Valley south to Reversed Peak, but have not been reported from June Lake south to lower Rock Creek. In addition to the rocky basin ranges, they also dwell on Mono Lake's two large islands (AB 38:1057). I suspect Sierran birds, like Mountain Quail, migrate eastward to avoid winter snows.

BLUE GROUSE (*Dendragapus obscurus*)

	J	F	M	A	M	J	J	A	S	O	N	D	HABITAT	ELEVATIONS		
														N	T	W
WEST													SPG	6-9	6-10	6-9
EAST													SPG	7-10	7-10	7-9

Rare resident between 4000' and 6000', uncommon resident to 9000' and rare summer visitor to treeline on west slope; uncommon resident between 7000' and 9500' and rare summer visitor to treeline east of crest.

Though fairly numerous, Blue Grouse are difficult to locate. The broader bar on the graph reflects, not an increase in absolute numbers, but the period when the cocks' deep resonant booming betrays their presence. I've spent hours searching for these chicken-sized fowl, for despite their size, their markings camouflage them in pines and firs, and their booming is ventriloqual. Of all spring's voices, theirs is the most mysterious, a sound you feel as much as hear.

The booming of cock Blue Grouse often echoes among the polished rock of glaciated canyons, for here they find ideal habitat conditions. Males boom for hour after hour from scattered pockets of conifers. Hens seek shelter and nest sites beneath dense scrub. After the snow melts, adults and chicks forage for seeds, shoots, berries and insects along the edges of meadows and clearings as well as on shrub-covered slopes. Hens raise families without assistance from their mates, who sometimes wander to treeline after courtship is consumated. Hens and young may follow later in the summer.

Little is known about Blue Grouse' winter ecology. Observations from Sequoia and Kings Canyon national parks suggest they linger in shrub and meadow habitats until the first heavy snows, gorging themselves on manzanita berries, rosehips and other fruit, green forage and even grasshoppers. With the onset of winter they sequester themselves in dense-foliaged conifers and apparently subsist primarily on conifer needles (Sumner and Dixon 1953). A male shot on the Warren Fork of Lee Vining Creek (10,500'), for instance, contained 1,520 tips of lodgepole pine needles in its crop (GS 273-274). On the other hand, droppings at Peregoy Meadow (7000') largely consisted of staghorn lichen (YM).

Despite its monotony, John Muir envied this winter diet. "Able to live on the buds of pine and fir," he wrote, Blue Grouse "are forever independent in the matter of food supply, which gives so many of us trouble, dragging us here and there away from our best work. How gladly I would live on pine buds, however pithy, for the sake of this grand independence" (Muir 1898).

High elevation record: 10,800' Sheperd Crest, female and young, 8/6/39 (YM).

Low elevation records: 4000' Yosemite Valley, many records from throughout most of year (YM).

Extreme dates for hooting males: 3/14/82 8000' Lundy Canyon (KC) - 7/14/79 8200' Olmsted Point (JL).

Representative nesting localities based on presence of booming males or females with young: 4600' near Mather (JW); 5200' San Joaquin River (SG); 7200' Glacier Point (YNN 24:104); 8200' Olmsted Point (ABR, DG); 9700' Saddlebag Lake Road (DDeS); 9000' Warren Fork of Lee Vining Creek (DG); 7800' near Lundy Lake (DG); 9300' near Sentinel Meadow, Glass Mountain (DG).

Additional references: AB 25:901; YNN 6:51; YNN 7:104; YNN 34:128.

WHITE-TAILED PTARMIGAN (*Lagopus leucurus*)

Introduced; uncommon resident between 10,000' and 12,000' both west and east slopes; irregularly rare winter resident at lower elevations on east slope.

The California Department of Fish and Game brought White-tailed Ptarmigans from the Rocky Mountains to the Sierra "to introduce another game bird in an area lacking a huntable species" (*Outdoor California* 37(6):18-19). Released near Eagle Peak in 1971 and 1972, they have spread north to at least Matterhorn Peak, west to Mt. Hoffmann and south to the Ritter Range (YM, CMc). Within this area, they are now well-established above treeline, favoring areas with sod-forming alpine vegetation and abundant water. In the fall of 1989 the first hunt was allowed in the Inyo Forest.

During harsh winters, White-tailed Ptarmigan may descend the east slope to lower elevations. In May 10, 1983, for example, 10 to 15 were munching aspen catkins at Lundy Lake (7800') while Northern Orioles chattered and sang in the branchwork overhead (DG; photograph on following page). That same year, they also appeared near Silver Lake (7200'—DB).

White-tailed Ptarmigan, which naturally range from the Rocky Mountains and Cascade Range north to Alaska, were introduced to the Sierra in blithe disregard for their impact on native plants and animals. We can only hope they don't overgraze the Sierra's unique alpine flora, or outcompete native birds and animals.

Additional reference: AB 31:1184.

SAGE GROUSE (*Centrocercus urophasianus*)

	J	F	M	A	M	J	J	A	S	O	N	D	HABITAT	ELEVATIONS		
														N	T	W
WEST								•	•						10	
EAST	—	—	—	—	—	—	—	—	—	—	—	—	SG	7-8	7-10	7-8

Extremely rare visitor near 10,000' just west of the crest; rare summer visitor to 10,000' on east slope; locally uncommon resident below 8500' east of Sierran escarpment, moving upslope to at least 9500' in summer.

On at least two occasions, small groups of Sage Grouse have wandered across the Sierran crest into Yosemite National Park. These birds were late summer wayfarers from their true home: the vast, rolling seas of sagebrush that carpet hills and valleys east of the Sierran escarpment.

Common, even abundant in the nineteenth century, Sage Grouse have been virtually extirpated from much of their former range, including most of the Mono Basin and Bridgeport Valley, by hunting and grazing (GS 117; CMc). Small breeding populations, numbering in the hundreds, persist in three principal areas, and have even increased since hunting was prohibited in 1983 (CMc): Bodie Hills (8000'-8500'), the vicinity of Sagehen Meadow (8200') and Long Valley (7000'). In these areas, one may espy these turkey-sized birds foraging in meadows at dawn, or flush them unexpectedly from the

White-tailed Ptarmigan at 7800' near Lundy Lake in May, 1983, driven downslope by heavy winter snows. When this photograph was taken, Northern Orioles were singing in the aspens overhead. Photograph by Linda LaPierre.

sagebrush. In summer, some move upslope to at least 9500' on Glass Mountain, the Bodie Hills and the eastern slope of the Sierra.

The only time Sage Grouse are easy to find is from late February to mid-April, when males gather on display grounds called *leks* to perform one of nature's most remarkable courtships. In the Bodie Hills, I've watched over 200 cocks strutting about comically with dropped wings and spread tails, emitting cackling, rumbling and popping sounds. "It is to be suspected," writes William Leon Dawson (1923), "that Dame Nature takes a special delight in making some of the most staid and prosaic of her male progeny appear in a ridiculous light when under the influence of the tender passion... Do you suppose we ever make such fools of ourselves?"

Strutting Sage Grouse return to the same leks, which are usually short-grass meadows or barren areas, year after year. To spy on them one must shiver in the frosty dawn, for the cocks fly off soon after sunrise. Under a gibbous or full moon, however, they will strut all night long (CMc). We should not disturb these revelries, but observe from a discreet distance.

Unlike most gallinaceous birds, Sage Grouse can fly for miles. In February, 1984, Clint McCarthy mistook a distant flock for blackbirds. Pursued by a Golden Eagle, 150 to 200 grouse climbed about 500 feet, then spilled down in all directions. This ability to fly long distances explains one's appearance on Mono Lake's Paoha Island (6400') in November, 1982 (Larry Ford).

With protection from hunting and the elimination of grazing, Sage Grouse could again become abundant east of the Sierra. Or they could follow Pronghorn Antelope into oblivion. As Dawson wrote many years ago, "if only our people can be brought to see that the glory of the wilderness—that little portion of it still remaining to us—lies in the presence and abundance and *happiness* of its wild things—not in their destruction—then generations to come may make unceasing pilgrimages to these desert shrines, and they will find these quaint, ungainly and most diverting fowls in the full enjoyment of their ancient tenure."

West slope records: 10,400' vicinity of Granite and Gaylor Lakes 9/?/43 (YNN 23:28); 10,000' west of Parker Pass 8/28-9/5/66 (AFN 21:73).

Additional reference: C 34:198.

CALIFORNIA QUAIL (*Callipepla californica*)

	J	F	M	A	M	J	J	A	S	O	N	D	HABITAT	ELEVATIONS		
														N	T	W
WEST	▒	▒	▒	▒	▒	▒	▒	▒	▒	▒	▒	▒	GSO	F-4		F-4
EAST					See Text								WS	6		6

Fairly common resident near Mariposa (2000'); irregularly rare to uncommon resident to 3000', rare visitor to 4000' and extremely rare visitor at higher elevations on west slope; introduced in Mono Basin east of crest, where current status uncertain

California Quail are lowland birds that appear to dispatch scouts and settlers up the west slope. Except near Mariposa, the mountains are too high, steep, wooded and brushy to suit these denizens of rolling hills, oak savannahs and open scrub. Yet I have repeatedly heard their soft "cui'dado" calls as high as 4000' at the McCauley Ranch above the Merced River Canyon. Along the Tuolumne River, they are "sparse but regular" as high as 3800' along Hetch Hetchy Reservoir (MM). The Yosemite Christmas Bird Count has tallied small numbers near El Portal (2100') for four of the past ten years. Do population pressures in the lowlands force small coveys of youthful pioneers into the mountains, where they tend to settle where humans have opened up the habitat? Do they linger until harsh winters or other disasters drive them away or kill them off?

On the east slope, the status of California Quail is unclear. A small population was introduced near the northwest shore of Mono Lake, where they dwelt in shrubby vegetation around streams and seeps, but none have been observed there since 1987. Thirteen were seen at Tom's Place (7200') 10/2/90 (CH), and four at Dexter Canyon (6700') 6/12/91 (PM,DS)

West slope records above 4000': 4400' Big Meadow 5/14/81 (SG, TB, KH); 4500' Hodgdon Meadow 6/4/82 (MM); 4600' Ackerson Meadow 6/16/82 (JW); 7200' near Smoky Jack 8/11/77 (SG); 7300' near Indian Meadow 6/25/81 (SG).

MOUNTAIN QUAIL (*Oreortyx pictus*)

	J	F	M	A	M	J	J	A	S	O	N	D	HABITAT	ELEVATIONS		
														N	T	W
WEST													SPO	2-9		F-4
EAST													SP	7-10		6-7

Fairly common resident below 4000', locally fairly common summer resident to 9000' and extremely rare visitor at higher elevations on west slope; uncommon summer resident below 9500' and extremely rare visitor at higher elevations on east slope, in Bodie Hills and on Glass Mountain; rare winter resident below 8000' east of Sierran escarpment.

Like grouse, Mountain Quail are more easily heard than seen. The broader bar on the graph reflects, not an increase in absolute numbers, but the period when courting males are most vociferous. Their loud, whistled notes, which the neophyte may mistake for those of Pygmy Owls, announce their presence a mile or more away.

Seeing these gregarious birds is another matter. Unlike their valley cousins, Mountain Quail mostly keep to brushy, steep and rugged slopes and canyons, but also haunt the wooded edges of mid-elevation meadows and clearings. They prefer mixtures of ceanothus, manzanita, huckleberry oak, chinquapin, sagebrush and other thicket-forming shrubs, often with an open canopy of pines, firs or oak. In the higher mountains, they range to the upper limit of montane chaparral.

I usually glimpse the plump forms of Mountain Quail fleeing from the edges of roads or clearings into the nearest cover. But once I saw a lone bird descend from the heavens into the large elm tree in my yard in Lee Vining (6800'), where it remained for several hours.

Before the first heavy snows, Mountain Quail retreat from the higher parts of their range. The west slope population mostly winters below 4000', a migration made entirely on foot. East side birds must undertake a similar trek, but whether they cross the range to the west or head east into the Great Basin is not definitely known. I suspect the latter, for birds have wintered at a feeder on Mono Lake's west shore, and been flushed from pinyon woodlands and sagebrush scrub in the Bodie Hills.

Records above 9500': 10,200' Summit Lake 9/22/85 (MR); 10,500' Hall Natural Area 5/25/85 (DeSante and Engstrom MS).

Representative nesting localities based on calling males or females with young: 2000' Merced River Canyon (DG); 4000' Yosemite Valley (YNN 32:80); 4600' Ackerson Meadow (JW); 4600' Hodgdon Meadow (DG); 6000' Chinquapin (DE); 7000' Gin Flat (DS); 7800' near Glen Aulin (YM); 9000' Polly Dome (DG); 9000' near Tenaya Lake (DG); 9200' Minaret Summit (DG); 9000' Warren Fork of Lee Vining Creek (DG); 8000' ridge west of Lee Vining (DG); 7800' Lundy Canyon (PM); 10,200' Hall Natural Area (DDeS).

Order GRUIFORMES: CRANES, RAILS AND ALLIES

Family RALLIDAE: RAILS, MOORHENS AND COOTS

Five species visit our region, primarily east of the Sierran escarpment. All but Common Moorhens are known to breed, but, except for coots, keep their lives well hidden.

YELLOW RAIL (*Coturnicops noveboracensis*)

Extremely rare transient on west slope; formerly summer resident below 7000' east of Sierran escarpment, but only one recent record.

Of all California's nesting birds, Yellow Rails are the most elusive. On 6/6/22, William Leon Dawson chanced on a nest in a Long Valley marsh (6900'—Dawson 1923); it was the first ever found west of the Rocky Mountains. The marsh was subsequently drowned by the Los Angeles Department of Water and Power's Crowley Lake Reservoir.

The following decades added little to our knowledge of this furtive marsh-dweller. In the 1930s, several more nests were discovered near Bridgeport Lake Reservoir (6500'—Oologist 57:39), but none thereafter. Nor have any been found elsewhere in California. In *Rare Birds of the West Coast*, Roberson concludes that Yellow Rails had "been extirpated by 1940," and that "land-clearing and cattle grazing are most responsible for their demise."

Then again, they may be overlooked. On 7/15/80, Yosemite naturalist Michael Ross flushed a Yellow Rail from a marsh in Tuolumne Meadows (8600')—the only west slope record.* Exactly five years later, on 7/15/85, I flushed another from a wet meadow below the Mono Lake County Park (6400'—accepted by California Bird Records Committee).

Do Yellow Rails still nest in eastside marshes? To the north, several colonies have recently been discovered in similar habitat to the east of Oregon's Cascade Mountains (Steve Summers). Wee *Coturnicops* has flung the gauntlet at our feet; it's up to us to answer the challenge.

*While this record has not been submitted to the California Bird Records Committee, I find the details convincing.

VIRGINIA RAIL (*Rallus limicola*)

	J	F	M	A	M	J	J	A	S	O	N	D	HABITAT	ELEVATIONS		
														N	T	W
WEST						—	—		•				G	4-7?		
EAST	•				▬	▬	▬	▬				•	Ma	6-7		6

Status uncertain, but probably rare summer resident and extremely rare fall transient between 4000' and 7000' on west slope; uncommon summer resident and probably rare winter resident below 7500' east of Sierran escarpment.

On the west slope, Virginia Rails probably nest in boggy mid-elevation meadows. In 1943, a pair bred in Yosemite Valley (4000'—YNN 22:88). In recent years, birds have been heard in Yosemite Valley (JL), Hodgdon Meadow (4600'—AB 26:804; MM, JW, DG) and McGurk Meadow (7000'—JW). At all of these localities, there are ponds of standing water margined by relatively tall growths of bulrushes, sedges or other vegetation.

East of the Sierran escarpment, Virginia Rails are undoubtedly more numerous than they seem. They are rarely glimpsed as they thread their way along the margins of bulrush- or cattail-lined ponds. But if one plays recordings of their calls—or even claps loudly—an answer can usually be coaxed from even small patches of marsh (AB 29:1026). On 6/30/90 one was heard singing (ESt) at the small restored delta of Lee Vining Creek, flowing again by court order after 50 years of diversion.

While I only know of two winter records, I suspect Virginia Rails are furtive winter residents east of the Sierran escarpment.

Fall record west slope: Yosemite Valley 9/30/34 (YNN 13:85).

Winter records east of Sierran escarpment, both Mono Lake (6400'): 12/3/81 (AB 36:746) and 1/1/84 (AB 38:793).

Extreme dates west slope: 5/27/72 Hodgdon Meadow (AB 26:804) - 8/7/83 7000' Peregoy Meadow (JL).

Extreme dates east of crest excluding winter records: 4/12/80 Mono Lake (KC) - 9/26/87 Dechambeau Ponds (DG).

Representative nesting localities: (7600' June Lake—DG); 7200' at spring NE of Grant Lake dam (DG); 6900' along McGee Creek (C 41:248); 6900' w. Crowley Lake Reservoir (DFG); 6500' near Bridgeport Reservoir (DG).

SORA (*Porzana carolina*)

Extremely rare transient on west slope; probably uncommon summer resident below 7000' east of Sierran escarpment.

While probably not as numerous as Virginia Rails, Soras also skulk in marshes east of the Sierran escarpment. These furtive birds secrete themselves in dense, marsh vegetation, especially cattails and bulrushes that margin ponds and sloughs. They linger in fall and maybe into winte. Like Virginia Rails, Soras are reinhabiting old haunts, like lower Rush Creek where Ilene Mandelbaum saw one 4/19/91.

West slope records: 4000' Yosemite Valley 4/27/23 (EM 2) and 4/9-14/83 (YM); 4500' near Mather 6/7/82 (MM).

Nesting locality: 6400' near Mono Lake (C 45:201).

Extreme dates, both Dechambeau Ponds (6400'): 4/3/82 (BE) - 9/4/83 (HG).

COMMON MOORHEN (GALLINULE)
(*Gallinula chloropus*)

Rare spring transient in Mariposa region (2000'—CL); rare spring transient and extremely rare summer visitor and fall transient below 7000' east of Sierran escarpment.

Though they resemble coots, Common Moorhens are much more furtive, hiding in the marsh vegetation that margins ponds, sloughs and languid streams. They occasionally stray to open water, where they are probably overlooked among flotillas of coots. While usually loners, three gathered on Dechambeau Ponds (6400') on 4/10/82 (HG).

Extreme dates, with no August records: 4/7/82 Mono Lake (BE) - 9/23/88 June Lake Marina (AB 43:162).

AMERICAN COOT (*Fulica americana*)

	J	F	M	A	M	J	J	A	S	O	N	D	HABITAT	ELEVATIONS		
														N	T	W
WEST						•	•						LR		F-9	F-4
EAST													LMoMu	6-8	6-8	6-7

Rare transient and winter visitor and extremely rare summer visitor below 4000' and extremely rare spring and rare fall transient to 9000' on west slope; rare fall transient below 9500' on east slope; common transient and locally common summer and winter resident below 8000' east of Sierran escarpment.

On 10/10/34, at least 1,200 American Coots were on the west slope's Lake Eleanor (4700'—YNN 15:28). Someone chancing on so many would not think them "rare," yet I only know of 17 other west slope records, mostly of lone birds. At Tuolumne Meadows (8600'), rangers found one "nestled in the snow" on 11/21/84, and "passed it several times thinking it a rock" (YM); another was "hiding in a woodpile" on the wintry date of 3/16/75 (TH). They are "regular in winter" on the South Fork Tuolumne River at Harden Flat (3500'—TB), and probably elsewhere at lower elevations as well.

East of the crest, it's a different story. Only Mono Lake's Eared Grebes are more abundant fall transients. By late August, American Coots gather by the thousands on large reservoirs and lakes. On 9/16/84, for example, approximately 25,000 were on Crowley Lake Reservoir (6900'—RS). They linger by the thousands until large lakes freeze. During the winter, they remain locally common on open water, as near the Owens River delta on Crowley Lake Reservoir and on the thermally heated waters of Dechambeau Ponds (6400'), Hot Creek (7000') and the Hot Creek Fish Hatchery (7000'). Not as many pass through in spring, but they still gather by hundreds on open water, including Mono Lake, from mid-March through April. These fall and spring influxes are not depicted on the graph, for coots are locally common throughout the summer, nesting in small numbers on ponds and lakes that are margined by cattails or bulrushes.

High elevation record: 9600' tarn near Tioga Lake 10/27/77 (DeSante and Engstrom MS).

Peak count spring: 418, Mono Lake 4/7/78 (GP, DW).

Summer record west slope: 4000' Wawona 7/1/77 (YM).

Additional west slope spring record above 5000': Tuolumne Meadows 6/4/77 (SG, TB).

Extreme dates west slope above 4000' excluding spring and summer records: 9/6/57 8200' Tenaya Lake (YM) - 4/9/24 4000' Yosemite Valley (EM 2).

Representative nesting localities: 6400' Dechambeau Ponds (DG); 6800' Crowley Lake Reservoir (DG); 7100' pond near junction of U.S. 395 and Hwy. 203 (DG); 7600' June Lake (DG); 7900' Walker Lake (DB).

Additional references: AFN 9:354; EM 2.

Family GRUIDAE: Cranes

SANDHILL CRANE (*Grus canadensis*)

Formerly a transient (fairly common?) east of Sierran escarpment, but only one recent record.

Until the 1950s, flocks of Sandhill Cranes migrated through Bridgeport Valley, Mono Basin and Long Valley east of the Sierran escarpment during spring and fall, and wintered in the Owens Valley (DB). Since that time, however, I know of only one record.

Reports of Sandhill Cranes in Yosemite National Park are probably misidentified Great Blue Herons (YM; Muir 1898).

Recent record: 6500' Bridgeport Valley, 2, 9/8/85 (JH).

Order CHARADRIIFORMES: SHOREBIRDS, GULLS, AUKS AND ALLIES

Suborder CHARADRII: SHOREBIRDS

Of the 35 species of shorebird that have reached the region, most frequent the muddy shores and deltas of lakes and ponds east of the Sierran escarpment. Only Spotted Sandpipers and Killdeer nest in the mountains proper, and, except for Common Snipe, their relatives shun the heights. East of the Sierra, however, shorebirds pass through in spring and mid- to late summer, and some, like Snowy Plovers, Black-necked Stilts, American Avocets, Willets, Common Snipe and Wilson's Phalaropes, remain to nest. Only Killdeer, Common Snipe and Least Sandpipers are regular in winter.

In general, shorebirds gather in greatest numbers near the delta of the Owens River on Crowley Lake Reservoir (6900'), on the muddy west shore of Bridgeport Lake Reservoir (6500'), and near seeps and springs along the northern, eastern and southern shores of Mono Lake (6400'). Their numbers and whereabouts, however, vary from year to year; in early August of 1985, for example, Mono Lake's east shore harbored far fewer shorebirds than it had the two previous years (DS).

While most species are scarce compared to the coast, Wilson's and Red-necked phalaropes occur in exceptional abundance on Mono Lake's salty waters, where they and other shorebirds fatten on brine shrimp and brine flies. Unless the Los Angeles Department of Water and Power curtails diversions from Mono's tributary streams, however, the lake's increasing salinity will poison its invertebrates. Phalaropes, shorebirds, grebes, gulls and other water birds will have to search elsewhere for sustenance or starve along its shores). The phalaropes, especially Wilson's, may have nowhere else to go (Gaines 1981, Patten 1987; p. 21).

Family CHARADRIIDAE: PLOVERS

BLACK-BELLIED PLOVER (*Pluvialis squatarola*)

	J	F	M	A	M	J	J	A	S	O	N	D	HABITAT	ELEVATIONS		
														N	T	W
WEST																
EAST													MuMoGL		6-7	

Uncommon spring and rare fall transient below 7000' east of Sierran escarpment.

Black-bellied Plovers, usually in small flocks of several to several dozen individuals, gather on mudflats, muddy shores, deltas and rarely short-grass meadows. Spring and early summer birds are frequently in "black-bellied" nuptial dress.

Peak count: 100, 6400' ne. shore Mono Lake, 4/4/78 (AB 32:1051).

Extreme dates: 3/25/85 6900' Crowley Lake Reservoir (JD) - 6/4/78 Mono Lake (GP, DW); 7/5/80 Mono Lake, 20 (KC) - 10/9/76 Mono Lake (BE); 10/19/87 6900' Crowley Lake Reservoir, 3 (DS); 11/10/84 Mono Lake, 3 (JJ).

Additional reference: AB 31:1184.

LESSER GOLDEN PLOVER (*Pluvialis dominica*)

Extremely rare transient east of Sierran escarpment.

Records: 6400' n. shore Mono Lake, 2, 5/16/79 (KC); Mono Lake 7/23/81 (AB 36:213); Simon's Spring 8/4/82 (JJ); Dechambeau Ponds 9/16/85 (JH, SG, TB) and 10/8/77 (AB 32:252); Crowley Lake Reservoir, *dominica* subspecies, 9/27/87 (Guy McCaskie).

SNOWY PLOVER (*Charadrius alexandrinus*)

	J	F	M	A	M	J	J	A	S	O	N	D	HABITAT	ELEVATIONS		
														N	T	W
WEST																
EAST													MoMu	6	6-7	

Common summer resident at Mono Lake (6400'); rare transient and summer resident below 7000' elsewhere east of Sierran escarpment.

Approximately 400 Snowy Plovers, ten percent of California's breeding population, nest along Mono Lake's bleak, windswept shores, primarily from Black Point on the north clockwise to Navy Beach on the south. A handful of pairs nest at Bridgeport and Crowley reservoirs, and just to the east in Adobe Valley. Transients also visit the muddy shores of other freshwater and alkaline lakes and ponds.

Snowy Plovers are almost invisible until they flit from underfoot. At Mono Lake, these diminutive, delicately plumaged shorebirds place their nests on unvegetated gravel and sand ridges from 300 feet to almost a mile from the shoreline. Within hours after hatching the chicks, mere fluffs of mottled down, are able to run about—a necessity if they are to elude gulls, ravens and other perils of ploverdom. Guided by their parents, the chicks scrounge their own meals, walking over two miles to choice feeding areas (Page and Stenzel 1981; Page, Stenzel, Winkler and Swarth 1983).

Unlike Mono Lake's gulls, phalaropes, grebes and other water birds, Snowy Plovers are not primarily dependent on the lake's brine shrimp and alkali flies, feeding on many other aquatic insects as well (Swarth 1983). If the lake is permitted to shrink, they will probably continue to nest in the vicinity of seeps and springs, as they have, for instance, at Owens Dry Lake.

Extreme dates: 3/25/85 6900' Crowley Lake Reservoir (JD) - 10/15/83 Mono Lake (DG).

Snowy Plover

SEMIPALMATED PLOVER (*Charadrius semipalmatus*)

	J	F	M	A	M	J	J	A	S	O	N	D	HABITAT	ELEVATIONS		
														N	T	W
WEST																
EAST													MoMu		6-7	

Fairly common transient at Mono Lake (6400'), and uncommon transient below 7000' elsewhere east of the Sierran escarpment.

Semipalmated Plovers visit the muddy margins of lakes, ponds and deltas.

Peak counts, both Mono Lake: 286, 4/22-23/89 (AB 43:533); 105, 8/20/76 (ES:98).
Extreme dates: 4/15/78 Mono Lake (GP) - 5/17/82 Mono Lake (GP); 6/13/78 Mono Lake (GP); 7/4/75 6500' Bridgeport Lake Reservoir (AB 29:1026) - 10/9/78, 6, Mono Lake (BE).

KILLDEER (*Charadrius vociferus*)

	J	F	M	A	M	J	J	A	S	O	N	D	HABITAT	ELEVATIONS		
														N	T	W
WEST													GRL	F-9		F-4
EAST													LMuMoGR	6-8	6-8	6-7

Fairly common resident in Mariposa region (2000'); rare resident below 4000', rare summer resident to 9000' and rare summer visitor to treeline elsewhere on west slope; rare summer resident below 8000' and rare summer visitor to treeline on east slope and in mountains east of Sierran escarpment; common summer resident and irregularly rare to fairly common winter resident below 7500' east of Sierran escarpment.

Killdeer are alert, noisy watchbirds of mudflats, muddy shores, pond margins, deltas, wet meadows and languid streams. No matter how stealthy one's approach, their shrill complaints alert the heavens to the presence of intruders.

On the west slope, Killdeer are only numerous in the vicinity of Mariposa, where they frequent golf courses, pond margins and other moist, open habitats (CL). Elsewhere, as shown on the graph, they are exceedingly scarce. Those who bird Tuolumne Meadows may garner a different impression, for one or two pairs have nested for decades near Soda Spring (8600'), and, true to their name, are vociferously conspicuous. But this is exceptional, as I know of no other montane locality where they are of regular occurence, though they have nested at Ackerson Meadow (4600'—JW) and Crane Flat (6200'—DG), and have wintered in Yosemite Valley (YNN 14:36).

East of the Sierran escarpment, Killdeer are most numerous during the mid-April to May and August to mid-October migration periods; this isn't shown on the graph, for they are common all summer as well. During mild winters, they may be fairly common; during snowy ones, most flee to balmier climes.

High elevation record: 10,500' Lake Helen, 2, 9/?/26 (YM).

Peak counts: 214, 6400' Mono Lake 5/17/78 (AB 32:1051); 314, Mono Lake 8/21/76 (ES:98); 400+ Bridgeport Lake Reservoir 9/30/87 (DG, ESt).

Earliest date Tuolumne Meadows: 4/6/77 (YM).

Additional representative nesting localities: 6500' Bridgeport Valley (DG); Mono Lake (ES:98); 6900' Crowley Lake Reservoir (DG).

MOUNTAIN PLOVER (*Charadrius montanus*)

Rare transient east of Sierran escarpment.

Records: 6400' NE shore Mono Lake 8/8/78 (KC)and 3, 8/24/91 (ESt); 6400' Warm Springs 8/31/78 (KC); 6400' Simon's Spring, 2, 9/2/78 (KC); 6900' Crowley Lake Reservoir 9/24/87 (PP, DWi); (just east of the region, on 10/10/78, I flushed a flock of six from a dirt road in Chidago Canyon—4500').

Family RECURVIROSTRIDAE: STILTS AND AVOCETS

BLACK-NECKED STILT (*Himantopus mexicanus*)

	J	F	M	A	M	J	J	A	S	O	N	D	HABITAT	ELEVATIONS		
														N	T	W
WEST							•	•							4-8	
EAST				——	——	——	——	▬	•				MuMoL	6-7	6-7	

Extremely rare transient on west slope; rare spring transient and summer visitor and uncommon fall transient below 7000' east of Sierran escarpment.

Black-necked Stilts frequent the shallow margins of saline and freshwater ponds and lakes as well as adjacent mudflats. They have nested in Long Valley (6900'—CMc) and probably along Mono Lake's southeastern shore near Simon's Spring (6400'—AB 38:1058), but do not breed in the same areas every year. We usually see from one to several individuals.

Peak count: 133, Mono Lake 8/19-21/89 (Pacific Flyway Census).

West slope records: 8200' Tenaya Lake 7/24/56 (YM) and 8/6/54 (YM); 4000' Yosemite Valley 8/14/39 (YNN 18:114-115).

Extreme dates: 4/10/86 Mono Lake (DH) - 9/23/89 6900' Crowley Lake Reservoir (HG et al.).

AMERICAN AVOCET (*Recurvirostra americana*)

	J	F	M	A	M	J	J	A	S	O	N	D	HABITAT	ELEVATIONS		
														N	T	W
WEST					•								R		4	
EAST				■	■	■	■	■	■	–			MoLMu	6-7	6-7	

Extremely rare transient on west and east slopes; common transient and locally common summer resident below 7000' east of Sierran escarpment.

American Avocets favor the shallow margins of saline and freshwater ponds, lakes and stream deltas, but also forage on adjacent mudflats. Nesting pairs are partial to low, muddy, ephemeral islets and sandbars. Numbers peak during the April to mid-May and especially the July to mid-September migration periods; this isn't shown on the graph, as they are locally common all summer long.

Peak counts, all Mono Lake (6400'): 650, 4/21-22/90 (Pacific Flyway Census); 8,467, 8/19-20/89 (Pacific Flyway Census); 200, 10/16/87—extraordinary for so late in the year (ESt).

West slope record: 4000' Wawona, 17, 5/6/50 (AFN 14:418); (Stebbins and Stebbins [1963] mention "a single record for Yosemite Valley" and "several for Tenaya Lake and Tuolumne Meadows," but I have not found substantiating details).

East slope and high elevation record: 9600' tarn below Tioga Lake 7/14/79 (DeSante and Engstrom MS).

Extreme dates: 2/18/89,5, south shore Mono Lake (Ilene Mandelbaum) - 10/19/87, 5, Crowley Reservoir (DS).

Representative nesting localities: 6400' Paoha Island (DG); 6400' Mono Lake (DG); 6900' Long Valley (DG); 6500' Adobe Valley, east of Granite Mountain (DS).

Family SCOLOPACIDAE: Sandpipers, Phalaropes and Allies

GREATER YELLOWLEGS (*Tringa melanoleuca*)

	J	F	M	A	M	J	J	A	S	O	N	D	HABITAT	ELEVATIONS		
														N	T	W
WEST								•					LR		8-9	
EAST													MuMoL		6-7	

Extremely rare transient on west slope; uncommon transient, rare summer and winter visitor below 7000' east of Sierran escarpment.

Greater Yellowlegs visit the margins and muddy shores of alkaline and freshwater lakes, ponds, vernal pools, deltas and, rarely, languid streams.

Peak counts: 23, 6400' Mono Lake 4/15/78 (AB 32:1051); 60, 6900' Crowley Lake Reservoir 10/6/86 (DG).

West slope records: 8000' Huckleberry Lake 8/1/37 (YM); 8600' Tuolumne Meadows 8/13/76 (SG) and 8/16/86 (DG).

LESSER YELLOWLEGS (*Tringa flavipes*)

	J	F	M	A	M	J	J	A	S	O	N	D	HABITAT	ELEVATIONS		
														N	T	W
WEST																
EAST													MuMoL		6-7	

Rare spring and uncommon fall transient below 7000' east of Sierran escarpment.

Lesser Yellowlegs visit the margins and muddy shores of alkaline and freshwater lakes, ponds and deltas. From mid-August through early September, they may outnumber their Greater cousins; later in the year, the situation reverses.

Peak count: 55, 6900' Crowley Lake Reservoir 8/31/87 (DG).

Extreme dates, all but one Mono Lake (6400'): 4/15/78 - 5/9/78 (AB 32:1051); 7/6/91 Bridgeport Reservoir (AB 45:1157) - 9/30/85, 2 (DG).

SOLITARY SANDPIPER (*Tringa solitaria*)

Extremely rare transient in high mountains both west and east of crest; extremely rare spring and rare fall transient below 8000' east of crest.

Unlike most shorebirds, Solitary Sandpipers covet cover. They are usually found among the sedge- or bulrush-lined margins of ponds or languid streams, though I have also seen them on open mudflats. These reclusive pipers may visit the subalpine Sierra more often then we know; in addition to our three mountaineers, one was recorded in King's Canyon National Park at 10,600' (C 45:208).

Peak count: 6, 6500' Bridgeport Reservoir 8/27/90 (AB 45:147).

West slope records: 9000' Slide Canyon 7/30/34 (YM); 8600' Tuolumne Meadows 10/1/76 (AB 31:218).

East slope record above 8000': 10,200' Lundy Pass 8/26/84 (AB 39:97).

Spring records: 6400' Dechambeau Ponds 4/21-28/90 (AB 44:492); 6900' Crowley Reservoir 5/31/68 (DE).

Extreme dates east of crest excluding spring records, both Dechambeau Ponds: 7/28/87 (PM) - 9/16/85, 4 (JH, TB, SG).

WILLET (*Catoptrophorus semipalmatus*)

	J	F	M	A	M	J	J	A	S	O	N	D	HABITAT	ELEVATIONS		
														N	T	W
WEST				•	•										4	
EAST				—	■	■	■	—		•			MaGLMuMo	7	6-7	

Extremely rare transient on west slope; locally fairly common summer resident at 6900' to 7100' in Long Valley; uncommon transient and rare summer visitor below 7000' elsewhere east of Sierran escarpment.

Willets frequent wet meadows and the muddy margins of saline and freshwater lakes, ponds and deltas. These vociferous pipers breed in Long Valley, where they usually place their nests in dry, upland sagebrush scrub (CMc). A few miles east of the region, a few pairs also nest in Adobe Valley (6500'—ESt).

Peak count: 31, Mono Lake 8/19-20/89 (Pacific Flyway Census).

West slope records, both Yosemite Valley (4000'): 4/12/74 (YM); 5/24/71 (YM).

Extreme dates: 4/13/86 Long Valley (DG): - 10/1/89 Mono Lake (ESt).

WANDERING TATTLER (*Heteroscelus incanus*)

Extremely rare spring and irregularly rare fall vagrant (0-2/year) at Mono Lake (6400').

While most Wandering Tattlers travel along the coast, a few have wandered to Mono Lake's tufa towers as well as its shores. All have been loners.

Spring record: 5/11/80 (AB 34:812).
Extreme dates, nine records since 1976: 8/20/86 (ESt) - 9/14/76 (ES:99, AB 31:218).
Additional references: AB 33:210, AB 36:213.

SPOTTED SANDPIPER (*Actitis macularia*)

	J	F	M	A	M	J	J	A	S	O	N	D	HABITAT	ELEVATIONS		
														N	T	W
WEST		•		—	▬	▬	▬	▬	—	•		•	RL	F-10		4
EAST				—	▬	▬	▬	▬	—			•	RL	6-10		6-7

Locally uncommon summer resident below 9000', rare summer resident to treeline and extremely rare winter visitor on west slope; uncommon summer resident below 9000' and rare summer resident to treeline on east slope; locally fairly common summer resident and extremely rare winter visitor below 7000' east of Sierran escarpment.

Spotted Sandpipers are the most far-ranging of our shorebirds, nesting from the foothills across the Sierran crest to the floors of Great Basin valleys. In a few places, like Yosemite Valley (4000'), Tuolumne Meadows (8600') and stream deltas around Mono Lake (6400'), their whistled cries are a significant element in the avian chorus. Yet overall these diminutive pipers are not numerous, and are entirely absent from many areas of seemingly suitable habitat.

Nesting Spotted Sandpipers favor sand or gravel bars along languid streams and deltas, but also haunt small rills in subalpine meadows. Transients visit the margins of ponds, tarns and lakes, including fish hatcheries and sewage ponds.

Peak Count: 53, Mono Lake 8/25-26/90 (Pacific Flyway Census).

Winter records: Yosemite Valley 12/28/57 (YNN 37:4); Mono Lake, 4, 12/31/77 (DW) and 12/82 (LF); 7000' Hot Creek, 3, 12/19/82 (AB 37:758, LW).

High elevation record: 10,200' Hall Natural Area, regular summer resident (DeSante MS).

Extreme dates west slope excluding winter record: 2/24/86 1300' Merced River (MR); 4/24/28 Yosemite Valley (YM) - 9/17/28 Yosemite Valley (YM); 10/25/72 Yosemite Valley (YM).

Extreme dates east of crest excluding winter records: 4/17/82 6800' Lee Vining (BE) - 10/2/86 Mono Lake, 2 (DG).

Earliest date above 8000': 5/23/83 Tuolumne Meadows (YM).

Representative nesting localities: (1300' Merced River—DG); (2000' Mariposa—DG); 4000' Yosemite Valley (GS 265); 8600' Tuolumne Meadows (GS 265); 10,200' Hall Natural Area (DeSante MS); 6400' Mono Lake (ES:99).

Additional references: YNN 31:5-6; AFN 9:52.

WHIMBREL (*Numenius phaeopus*)

Rare transient below 7000' east of Sierran escarpment.

Whimbrels visit meadows as well as the margins of freshwater and alkaline lakes, ponds and deltas. While most are loners, a flock of at least 200 descended on Mono

Lake's northwestern shore (6400') on 5/9/82, perhaps forced down by inclement weather the previous night (BE, VN, DW).

Extreme dates, all Mono Lake: 4/18/78 (GP, DW) - 5/23/89 (PM); 7/24/89 (PM) - 10/8/81 (JJ).

LONG-BILLED CURLEW (*Numenius americanus*)

Rare transient and summer visitor below 7000' east of Sierran escarpment.

Though both are rare "rare," Long-billed Curlews are more numerous than Whimbrels. Both visit meadows as well as the margins of freshwater and alkaline lakes, ponds and deltas. We usually see lone birds or small groups of less than five individuals. While they have yet to stray to Yosemite's higher mountains, one in Sequoia National Park was at 11,200' on 5/28/87 (Sally Miller).

Peak count: 33, 6400' Mono Lake 8/4/76 (ES:99).
Extreme dates, both Mono Lake: 4/4/82 (PJ, BE) - 10/16/88, 3, (PM); 11/19/83 (MK).

MARBLED GODWIT (*Limosa fedoa*)

Rare transient below 7000' east of Sierran escarpment.

Marbled Godwits visit the muddy margins of freshwater and alkaline lakes, ponds and deltas, often in small flocks. August seems to be their big month.

Peak count: 124,(54 in one group) 6400' Mono Lake 8/25-26/90 (Pacific Flyway Census).
Spring records: Alkali Lakes 4/25/90 (ESt); Mono Lake 5/2/78 (AB 32:1051); 6400' Negit Islets 5/27/85 (DS).
Extreme dates excluding spring records, both Mono Lake: 7/1/76 (ES:98) - 10/8/78 (BE).

RUDDY TURNSTONE (*Arenaria interpres*)

Extremely rare spring and rare fall transient (1-4/year) at Mono Lake (6400').

While they have only been found at Mono Lake, Ruddy Turnstones must also visit the muddy margins of other lakes and ponds east of the Sierran escarpment. The only spring record is also the only flock.

Spring records, both e. shore Mono Lake, 12, 5/12/78 (AB 32:1051); 5/21/81 (CS).
Extreme dates excluding spring record: 7/22/84 (DS, SJ) - 9/6/83 (DS) and 9/6/87 (DS).
Additional references: AB 30:998, AB 31:219, AB 32:252, ES:98.

RED KNOT (*Calidris canutus*)

Rare transient at Mono Lake (6400').

Though they have only been found at Mono Lake, Red Knots undoubtedly visit the muddy margins of other lakes, ponds and deltas east of the Sierran escarpment as well. They are usually alone or in small flocks.

Peak count: 15, 4/21/78 (AB 32:1051).

Extreme dates: 4/19/78 (AB 32:252) - 5/16/79 (KC); 7/21/76 (ES:99; AB 31:2318) - 9/4/83, 3 juveniles (RW).

Additional references: AB 32l1051, AB 35:221.

SANDERLING (*Calidris alba*)

Rare transient below 7000' east of Sierran escarpment.

Sanderlings stray to the muddy margins of saline and freshwater lakes, ponds and deltas east of the Sierran escarpment as well. They are usually in small flocks.

Peak counts, both Mono Lake (6400'): 21, 5/17/78 (AB 32:1061); 14, 9/27/84 (JJ).

Extreme dates: 4/21/78 Mono Lake (AB 32:1051) - 6/11/79 Mono Lake (KC); 7/7/80 Mono Lake, 12 (AB 34:926) - 9/27/84 Mono Lake, 14 (JJ); 10/19/87 6900' Crowley Lake Reservoir (DS); 11/10/84 Mono Lake, 5 (JJ).

Additional references: AB 31:218, AB 34:196, AB 35:974, AB 38:242, AB 38:1058.

SEMIPALMATED SANDPIPER (*Calidris pusilla*)

Extremely rare spring and rare fall vagrant (1-5/year) below 7000' east of Sierran escarpment.

Semipalmated Sandpipers visit the muddy margins of lakes, ponds and deltas east of the Sierran escarpment (photograph on following page).

Peak counts: 3 juveniles, Mono Lake 8/6/86 (JD); 3 juveniles, Mono Lake 8/6/87 (JD); 2-3 juveniles, 6900' Crowley Lake Reservoir, 8/19/87 (JD).

Spring records: 5/24/79 (KC); 5/21/81, 4 (AB 35:829, CS--AB incorrectly reported only one individual).

Extreme dates excluding spring records: 7/18/80 (AB 34:926) - 9/4/83 (RW).

Additional references: AB 31:218, AB 35:221.

WESTERN SANDPIPER (*Calidris mauri*)

	J	F	M	A	M	J	J	A	S	O	N	D	HABITAT	ELEVATIONS		
														N	T	W
WEST																
EAST				■	■	—	■	■	■	•	•		MuMoL		6-7	

Common transient below 7000' east of Sierran escarpment.

Of the sandpipers that pause to rest and fatten on the muddy shores of alkaline and freshwater lakes, ponds and deltas east of the Sierran escarpment, Westerns and Leasts are the most numerous. During the spring and fall migration periods, Westerns may

Juvenile Semipalmated Sandpiper at Mono Lake, August 18, 1987. Photograph by Jon L. Dunn.

congregate in large, close-knit flocks. A few trickle through in June; are they heading north or south?

Peak counts, both Pacific Flyway Census at Mono Lake (6400'): 18,412 4/21-22/90; 3,371 8/25-26/90.

Extreme dates: 4/15/78 Mono Lake (AB 32:1051) - 9/30/83 Mono Lake (DG); 10/19/87 6900' Crowley Lake Reservoir, approx. 15 (DS); 11/23/76 Mono Lake (DW).

LEAST SANDPIPER (*Calidris minutilla*)

	J	F	M	A	M	J	J	A	S	O	N	D	HABITAT	ELEVATIONS		
														N	T	W
WEST							•								7	
EAST													MuMoL		6-7	6-7

Extremely rare transient on west slope; common transient and irregularly rare to uncommon winter resident below 7000' east of Sierran escarpment.

The least of our sandpipers is also the hardiest. In contrast to Westerns, with which they often consort, Least Sandpipers arrive earlier in spring, linger later in autumn, and brave mild winters in small numbers. They congregate on the muddy shores of alkaline and freshwater lakes, ponds and deltas, sometimes in large flocks.

Record west slope: 8600' Tuolumne Meadows 7/16/87 (MR).

Peak counts, all Mono Lake (6400'): 4,666, 4/21-22/90 (Pacific Flyway Census); 1,151, 8/15-16/90 (Pacific Flyway Census); 200, 10/8/78 (BE); 44, 12/29/79 (AB 34:652).

Extreme dates: 7/6/91 Bridgeport Reservoir (RT) - 5/12/78 Mono Lake (AB 32:1051).

WHITE-RUMPED SANDPIPER (*Calidris fuscicollis*)

Extremely rare vagrant at Mono Lake (6400').

Record: near Warm Springs 6/6/81 (AB 35:974); accepted by California Bird Records Committee.

BAIRD'S SANDPIPER (*Calidris bairdii*)

	J	F	M	A	M	J	J	A	S	O	N	D	HABITAT	ELEVATIONS		
														N	T	W
WEST																
EAST				•			▬	▬	—				MuMoL		6-7	

Extremely rare spring and uncommon fall transient below 7000' east of Sierran escarpment.

In comparison to other small sandpipers, Baird's prefer drier, upland shores and beaches, sometimes thinly vegetated with salt or alkali grass, as on the eastern and southern shores of Mono Lake. They also visit the shores of other lakes, ponds and deltas, alone or in small flocks.

Peak counts: 31, 6400' Mono Lake, 8/25-26/90 (Pacific Flyway Census); 100, 6900' Crowley Reservoir 9/6/87 (AB 42:129).

Spring records, all Mono Lake: 4/17/78, 5 (AB 32:1051); 4/21/78 (AB 32:1051); 4/23/80 (KC).

Extreme dates excluding spring records, all Mono Lake: 6/30/81, 2 (CS); 7/8/80 (AB 34:926) - 10/8/78 (BE).

Additional references: AB 26:121, AB 38:1058.

PECTORAL SANDPIPER (*Calidris melanotos*)

Rare fall transient below 7000' east of Sierran escarpment.

Unlike most sandpipers, Pectorals prefer marshy ponds to mudflats, but also visit the muddy margins of lakes and deltas.

Extreme dates and peak count: 8/23/88 Crowley Reservoir (PM) - 10/20/79 Mono Lake, 10 (DG).

STILT SANDPIPER (*Calidris himantopus*)

Extremely rare vagrant east of Sierran escarpment.

Two records: 6900' Crowley Reservoir 9/23/89, 3, (AB 44:157); 6400' Mono Lake 9/1/90 (AB 45:147).

DUNLIN (*Calidris alpina*)

	J	F	M	A	M	J	J	A	S	O	N	D	HABITAT	ELEVATIONS		
														N	T	W
WEST																
EAST	•			—■	■			•		—	—	•	MuMoL		6-7	

Locally fairly common spring transient, extremely rare summer visitor and rare fall transient below 7000' east of Sierran escarpment.

Dunlin congregate on the muddy margins of lakes, ponds and deltas, often in sizable flocks. Spring birds are usually garbed in elegant nuptial plumage. They are surprisingly scarce during the fall migration.

Peak count, Mono Lake (6400'): 802, 5/2/78 (AB 32:1051).
Summer records: Crowley Reservoir 7/25/90 (AB 44:1182); Mono Lake 8/19/85 (DS).
Extreme dates excluding summer records: 3/25/85, 3, 6900' Crowley Lake Reservoir (JD) - 5/18/79, 6, Mono Lake as all the rest (KC); 10/1/89 (ESt); 12/9/90, 75 (AB 45:147); 1/1-2/91 (AB 45:316).

RUFF (*Philomachus pugnax*)

Extremely rare vagrant east of Sierran escarpment.

Record: 6900' Crowley Lake Reservoir 10/12/86 (DG).

SHORT-BILLED DOWITCHER (*Limnodromus griseus*)

	J	F	M	A	M	J	J	A	S	O	N	D	HABITAT	ELEVATIONS		
														N	T	W
WEST																
EAST				■			•	—■	■—				MuMoL		6-7	

Fairly common transient below 7000' east of the Sierran escarpment.

Short-billed Dowitchers visit the margins of lakes, ponds and deltas.

Peak counts, all Mono Lake (6400'): 135, 4/25/78 (AB 32:1051); 30, 8/29/86 (DS).

Extreme dates, all Mono Lake: 4/5/78, 38 (AB 32:1051) - 5/2/78, 26 (AB 32:1051); 7/21/76, 2 (DW, BE) - 9/30/85, 10 (DG).

Additional reference: AB 38:242.

LONG-BILLED DOWITCHER (*Limnodromus scolopaceus*)

	J	F	M	A	M	J	J	A	S	O	N	D	HABITAT	ELEVATIONS		
														N	T	W
WEST																
EAST			•										MuMoL		6-7	

Fairly common spring and common fall transient and extremely rare winter visitor below 7000' east of Sierran escarpment.

Like their Short-billed cousins, Long-billed Dowitchers visit the margins of lakes, ponds and deltas, but are more partial to muddy substrates.

Peak counts: 44, 6400' Mono Lake 5/12/78 (AB 32:1051); 200+, 6900' Crowley Lake Reservoir 10/12/86 (DG).

Winter record: 7000' Hot Creek 12/22/85 (AB 40:994; LW).

Extreme dates excluding winter record: 3/23/86 6400' Dechambeau Ponds (DG) - 5/12/78 Mono Lake (AB 32:1051); 7/6/91 Bridgeport Reservoir, 4 (BS) - 10/19/87 Crowley Reservoir, 20 (DG).

COMMON SNIPE (*Gallinago gallinago*)

	J	F	M	A	M	J	J	A	S	O	N	D	HABITAT	ELEVATIONS		
														N	T	W
WEST		•			•						•	•	GMaR		F-9	4-5
EAST													GMaR	6-8	6-8	6-8

Rare spring transient below 5000', rare fall transient below 9000' and extremely rare winter visitor on west slope; fairly common summer resident and irregularly rare to fairly common winter resident below 8000' east of crest.

From late winter through early summer, especially at dusk and on moon-lit nights, the ventriloqual winnowing of Common Snipe seems to wander through the sky above large, wet meadows east of the Sierran escarpment. These long-billed shorebirds probe for invertebrates in the soft mud or sod of boggy meadows and marshes as well as along the grassy margins of languid streams. Except during the nesting season, they keep well concealed among sedges and bulrushes. If one slogs through their haunts, however, they flee in wild, zigzag flight.

While nesting Common Snipe favor large meadows, transients and winter residents are often satisfied with small, boggy places along streams or below springs and seeps. After rains or snowmelt have moistened the soil, I have even flushed them from sagebrush scrub. They frequently winter, for example, in a boggy aspen grove near the west shore of Mono Lake (6600'), on Mill Creek below Lundy Lake Dam (7800') and in the vicinity of thermal springs at Hot Creek (7000'). During harsh years, most seek balmier climes; numbers on the Mono Lake Christmas Bird Count, for instance, have varied from 35 to 2.

While most Common Snipe nest in the valleys east of the Sierran escarpment, I've also found them breeding on the moist floors of east-slope Sierran canyons. During the nesting season, they perch on fence posts and, at the north end of Mono Lake, the summits of tufa towers.

Common Snipe may occasionally nest on the west slope as well. Two males at Ackerson Meadow (4600') winnowed continuously from 3/31 to 5/5/87, but subsequently disappeared (JW).

On the west slope, Common Snipe are usually loners; to the east, transient and wintering birds gather in flocks of up to 15 individuals.

High elevation record: 9000' Lyell Canyon 10/24/43 (YNN 13:12).

Winter records west slope: 4000' Yosemite Valley 12/23/48 (YM);

4400' Big Meadow 12/18/79 (GS); 4600' Ackerson Meadow 2/21/87 (JW); 7600' near Red's Meadow 12/30/77 (Bill LeDain).

Extreme dates of winnowing: 2/22/86 Mono Lake (LF) - 7/16/85 7400' Lee Vining Canyon (DG).

Extreme dates west slope excluding winter records: 3/13/85 Yosemite Valley (YM) - 5/5/87 2, Ackerson Meadow (JW); 8/6/84 8600' Tuolumne Meadow (YM) - 11/9/86 Ackerson Meadow (JW).

Representative nesting localities: (7400' Horse Meadow—DG); (7400' Lee Vining Canyon—DG); 6900' near McGee Creek (C 41:248); 6900' w. Crowley Lake Reservoir (DFG); 6400' Mono Lake (ES:98).

Additional reference: AFN 12:55.

WILSON'S PHALAROPE (*Phalaropus tricolor*)

	J	F	M	A	M	J	J	A	S	O	N	D	HABITAT	ELEVATIONS		
														N	T	W
WEST					•	•	•						LR		4-9	
EAST										•			MoLMu	6-7	6-7	

Extremely rare transient on west slope; fairly common summer resident and common fall transient at Mono Lake (6400'); fairly common summer resident and transient elsewhere below 7000' east of Sierran escarpment.

Wilson's Phalaropes breed in Bridgeport Valley, the Mono Basin and Long Valley, where they seek out open, shallow water margined by low marsh or meadow vegetation. Small flocks appear on freshwater ponds, lakes, reservoirs and deltas during migrations.

Wilson's Phalaropes at Mono Lake, from Checklist of North American Birds.

But these flocks are dwarfed by the tens of thousands that descend on Mono Lake in summer.

Of all Mono Lake's shorebirds, Wilson's Phalaropes are the most numerous, graceful and trusting. Sit quietly, and they will feed at your feet. Float in the lake, and these curious birds will paddle within arm's reach. Their euphonious name is Greek for "coot-foot," for, like coots and unlike other shorebirds, phalaropes have evolved lobed toes. These propel them about on the water, where they daintily pick brine flies off the surface film and dab brine shrimp from the lake's upper inch. Sometimes they seem to unwind, swimming in tight little circles to stir up food. Hunched along the shore they seize passing flies with lightning thrusts of their bills. Females feed mainly on brine shrimp, the smaller males to a large extent on brine flies (JJ).

Phalaropes reverse the usual avian sex roles. Breeding plumage females wear vivid shades of orange, maroon and silver, the males dull grays. The females are also larger and more aggressive, and actively court the males. After courtship is consummated, the females depart, leaving their mates behind to incubate the eggs and raise the chicks. As a consequence, female phalaropes reach Mono's shores weeks ahead of males. Last of all come the young, on their own on their first migration.

And an impressive migration it is! In mid-June, long before the plovers, gulls and other nesting birds have fledged the last of their young, the first female Wilson's

Phalaropes descend on Mono Lake, probably from breeding haunts in southern Canada and the intermountain west. By the end of the month, they arrive in large flocks. Joined later by smaller numbers of males and a small fraction of juveniles, an estimated 80,000 to 125,000 pause at the lake during their southward migration (JJ). Tens of thousands crowd together along seep-lined portions of the lake shore. At a distance I've mistaken them for mud flats. Airborne, they look like clouds of gnats wheeling and diving among the tufa spires. At night they roost near the middle of the lake (JJ).

Wilson's Phalaropes not only rest and feed during their four to six week sojourn on Mono Lake, they change their clothes as well. The lake's bountiful food provides the energy they need to molt nearly all their feathers and grow new ones; in fact, theirs may be the quickest molt of any bird (JJ).

Once clothed in winter plumage, Wilson's Phalaropes lay on stores of fat that almost double their weight, becoming so heavy that some can barely fly (JJ). Then they embark on nonstop journeys of over 3,000 miles to saline lakes high in the Andes of Bolivia, Peru and northern Argentina. As blizzards blast the tufa towers, they cavort with flamingos at places like Bolivia's Laguna Laromay, which lies at 15,100 feet, has a salinity similar to Mono's, and supports large numbers of brine shrimp (Hurlbert, Lopes and Keith 1984). For these two ounce puffs of feathers, Mono Lake is a crucial stop on journeys of thousands of miles.

In the years ahead, however, Wilson's and Red-necked phalaropes as well as other shorebirds and waterfowl may find little to eat at Mono Lake. Unless the Los Angeles Department of Water and Power curtails diversions from Mono Lake's tributary streams, increasing salinity will poison the brine shrimp and flies on which these birds depend for sustenance (p. 21).

Peak counts, all Mono Lake: 240, 4/30/78 (GP, DW); 15,000-20,000 in one flock, 6/27/85 (CS); approx. 93,000, 7/26/76 (AB 30:999).

West slope records: 4000' Yosemite Valley 7/21/38 (YNN 17:156); 8600' Tuolumne Meadows 6/22/77 (TB) and 7/12-31/81 (MR, MM); 9100' Dog Lake 5/21/76 (YM).

Extreme dates, both Mono Lake: 4/17/82 (GP, DW) - 10/8/78 (BE).

Representative nesting localities: 6400' Mono Lake (DG); (6500' Bridgeport Lake Reservoir—DG); 6900' McGee Creek (C 41:248); 6900' w. Crowley Lake Reservoir (DFG).

RED-NECKED (NORTHERN) PHALAROPE (*Phalaropus lobatus*)

	J	F	M	A	M	J	J	A	S	O	N	D	HABITAT	ELEVATIONS		
														N	T	W
WEST								•	•	•			LR		4-10	
EAST													MoL		6-7	

Extremely rare transient on west slope; fairly common spring transient, rare summer visitor and common fall transient on Mono Lake (6400'); fairly common transient below 7000' elsewhere east of Sierran escarpment.

While Red-necked Phalaropes visit freshwater lakes and ponds, they concentrate by the thousands only on Mono Lake's briny water. They are most numerous in the

Red Phalarope in Yosemite Valley, October, 1928—the only record on the west slope. Photograph by Charles Michael, courtesy the Yosemite Museum.

vicinity of submerged tufa formations and rocky shoals, where they feast on pupating alkali flies. Often they climb onto tufa or tufa-encrusted boulders to rest and preen.

Unlike Wilson's, Red-necked Phalaropes linger at Mono Lake for only a short period (5-14 days), and do not undergo a complete molt. But they do lay on fat to fuel the next leg of their migratory journeys. The early arrivals are mostly adult females, followed by males and juveniles; by late September, only youngsters remain (Jehl 1986). They winter far from land on the southern oceans, feeding on tiny crustaceans and sea snails, and occasionally picking parasites from the backs of resting whales.

From 1980 to 1984, with one exception, an estimated 52,000 to 65,000 Red-necked Phalaropes passed through Mono Lake. In 1983, that total declined to 36,000, a drop that might be attributable to high mortality on the wintering grounds in the southern oceans. The previous winter, changes in ocean temperature and pelagic food supplies ("El Nino") adversely affected other water birds in the phalaropes' wintering range (Jehl 1986).

Peak counts: 1,200, 5/17/78 (AB 32:1251); 800-1,000, 5/13/84 (Jehl 1986); 40,000, 8/22/58 (Jehl 1986); 21,600, 8/30/76 (AB 31:218; ES:99); 14,000, 9/2-3/82 (Jehl 1986).

West slope records: 4000' Yosemite Valley 9/4/38 (YNN 18:126) and 10/12-22/25 (EM 2); 9800' near Tioga Pass 8/8/77 (YM).

Extreme dates east side, all Mono Lake: 4/17/78, 4 (GP, DW) - 10/21/82 (Jehl 1986).

Additional reference: AB 34:926.

RED PHALAROPE (*Phalaropus fulicaria*)

Extremely rare vagrant on west slope; irregularly rare fall vagrant (0-2/year) on Mono Lake (6400').

Though most Red Phalaropes are pelagic migrants, a few have strayed to Mono Lake, often feeding far offshore. Just east of the region, one was reported on Black Lake (7300') on the unusual date of 7/4/77 (AB 31:1185).

West slope record: 4000' Yosemite Valley 10/?/28.
Extreme dates, both Mono Lake: 9/1/80 (AB 35:221)- 11/16/82 (JJ).
Additional reference: AB 37:220.

Family LARIDAE: Jaegers, Gulls and Terns

Of 18 species, only California Gulls nest in significant numbers and frequently range onto the west slope. Except for Caspian and possibly Forster's terns, the rest occur primarily as transients, several extremely rare.

POMARINE JAEGER (*Stercorarius pomarinus*)

Extremely rare fall vagrant east of Sierran escarpment.

Records: 6400' Mono Lake 9/5/91 (TB) and 9/13/64 (AFN 19:64); 7100' Grant Lake Reservoir 9/11/85 (DG).

PARASITIC JAEGER (*Stercorarius parasiticus*)

Extremely rare spring and rare fall vagrant (1-4/year) below 7000' and extremely rare transient at higher elevations east of Sierran escarpment.

Though most Parasitic Jaegers migrate off the coast, a few stray to Mono Lake (6400') and other freshwater and saline lakes and ponds, where they are often seen chasing gulls. With two exceptions, all have been juveniles or subadults. The June bird at Dechambeau Ponds was a trusting youngster that could be approached within several feet; it seemed to be healthy, however, and was dining on teal chicks (DG, ESt, DS).

Record at 9600': over meadow north of Glass Mountain 9/23/63 (AFN 18:20).

Spring records: Mono Lake 6/13/80 (AB 34:926); Dechambeau Ponds 6/21-29/86 (DG, ES, DS).

Records of adults: Mono Lake 6/13/80; Glass Mountain 9/23/63 (AFN 18:20).

Extreme dates excluding spring records: Mono Lake 7/26/86 (DG) -Glass Mountain 9/23/63 (AFN 18:20).

Additional references: AB 32:253; AB 35:221; AB 38:242.

LONG-TAILED JAEGER (*Stercorarius longicaudus*)

Extremely rare fall vagrant east of Sierran escarpment.

Records: 6400' Mono Lake 8/10/80 (adult—AB 35:221), 8/24/83 (adult—MJ) and 8/28/80 (immature—AB 35:221); 6900' Crowley Reservoir 9/16/89, immature, (AB 44:157), 9/2/79 (AB 34:196) and 8/28/87 (adult—JD, see photograph on next page).

Adult Long-tailed Jaeger, Crowley Lake Reservoir, August 28, 1987. Photograph by Jon L. Dunn.

(JAEGER species.?)

An unidentified jaeger thought to be an immature Long-tailed flew over Tuolumne Meadows on 9/4/85 (Doug Greenberg). This is the only record for a jaeger on the west slope.

LITTLE GULL (*Larus minutus*)

Extremely rare vagrant east of Sierran escarpment.

Record: 6900' Crowley Lake Reservoir 8/6-9/28/87 (AB 42:130 -photograph on following page).

FRANKLIN'S GULL (*Larus pixixcan*)

Extremely rare spring and rare fall transient east of Sierran escarpment.

There are two spring and six fall sightings since 1988, at Mono Lake, Bridgeport and Crowley reservoirs.

First spring, last fall dates: 4/21/90 e.shore Mono Lake (AB 44:492) - 9/16/88 Mono Lake County Park (AB 43:163).

BONAPARTE'S GULL (*Larus philadelphia*)

	J	F	M	A	M	J	J	A	S	O	N	D	HABITAT	ELEVATIONS		
														N	T	W
WEST																
EAST	•		•	—	▒	—	—	▒	▒	▒	•	•	LMo		6-7	

Irregularly uncommon to common transient and rare summer visitor below 7000' east of Sierran escarpment.

In some years, Bonaparte's Gulls flock to alkaline and freshwater lakes, ponds and deltas in considerable numbers. In other years, these tern-like gulls are scarce. Unlike their relatives, they are not found at dumps, but snatch their meals on open water.

Stebbins and Stebbins (1963) allude to records in Yosemite, but I have been unable to locate details.

Peak counts: 100, 5/13/77 (DT) and 50, 9/1/77 (DDeS) 6400' Mono Lake; 120, 7/21-22/91 (AB 45:1157) and 130, 10/5/86 (DG) 6900' Crowley Reservoir.

Extreme dates: 3/21/91 mouth Lee Vining Creek (Ilene Mandelbaum), 4/15/78 Mono Lake, 2 (GP) - 12/3/83 Mono Lake (MK); 1/12/91 S. Tufa, Mono Lake (Allen Brown).

First summer Little Gull in molt to adult winter plumage, Crowley Lake Reservoir, August 6, 1987. Photograph by Jon L. Dunn.

HEERMAN'S GULL (*Larus heermanni*)

Extremely rare vagrant east of Sierran escarpment.

Record: 6400' Mono Lake 5/24-25/89, adult, (AB 43:533); 6900' Crowley Reservoir, 7/27/91, juvenal, (AB 45:1157).

RING-BILLED GULL (*Larus delawarensis*)

	J	F	M	A	M	J	J	A	S	O	N	D	HABITAT	ELEVATIONS		
														N	T	W
WEST				•	•						•		R		4	
EAST													LMoDMuG		6-8	6-7

Extremely rare transient on west slope; rare summer visitor, uncommon spring and fairly common fall transient and rare winter visitor below 8000' and extremely rare transient at higher elevations east of Sierran escarpment.

Like other large gulls, Ring-billeds loiter at saline and freshwater lakes, ponds, deltas, meadows and dumps. Usually small groups mingle with hordes of California Gulls. Occasionally, however, they occur in much larger numbers. During November, 1982, for example, up to 500 congregated along the south shore of Mono Lake (DG). During winter, Ring-billed and California gulls occur with approximately equal frequency.

Record above 8000' east of crest: 10,100' Saddlebag Lake 10/15/78 (3 adults and one second-year) and 10/23/78 (1 adult—DeSante and Engstrom MS, AB 33:210).

West slope records, all Yosemite Valley (4000'): 4/8/48 (YM); 5/?/32 (YNN 47:82); 5/13/41 (YNN 47:82); summer/46 (YNN 47:82); 11/11/78 (YM).

CALIFORNIA GULL (*Larus californicus*)

	J	F	M	A	M	J	J	A	S	O	N	D	HABITAT	ELEVATIONS		
														N	T	W
WEST													LDGA		4-10	
EAST													MoLDMUGA	6	6-10	6-7

Uncommon summer visitor in Yosemite Valley (4000'); rare summer visitor below 8000', locally fairly common summer visitor from 8000' to 10,000' and rare summer visitor at higher elevations elsewhere on west slope; common summer resident and rare winter resident at Mono Lake (6400'); common summer visitor below 8000', locally fairly common summer visitor to 10,000', rare summer visitor at higher elevations and rare winter resident below 7000' elsewhere east of crest.

Few people associate gulls with mountains and desert lakes. Yet for centuries California Gulls have been crossing the Sierra each spring to raise their young on Mono Lake's islands. From this center of abundance they range to lakes, meadows, rivers, picnic areas, campgrounds, parking areas and dumps on both slopes of the Sierra, and even to outposts like Bodie (8400').

On the west slope, California Gulls are most numerous at places like Tenaya Lake (8200'), Olmsted Point (8400') and Tuolumne Meadows (8600'), where they importune picnicking tourists for morsels. Yet they also scavenge virtually every backcountry lake, consuming, among other things, the garbage left by hikers and fishermen. They seen to enjoy the alpine scenery; certainly those which soar over glaciers find little to eat above 10,000'.

East of the crest, California Gulls also range from high country lakes to garbage dumps, but their natal home is Mono Lake. The colonies were first described, somewhat hyperbolically, by J. Ross Browne in an 1865 issue of *Harper's New Monthly Magazine* (31:411-419): "Immense swarms of gulls visit these islands during the spring of the year and deposit their eggs on every available spot. Myriads upon myriads of them hover over the rocks from morning till night, deafening the ear with their wild screams, and the water is literally covered with them for a distance of many miles... The open spaces between the rocks are so thickly covered with eggs that the pedestrian is at a loss to find a vacant spot for his foot."

Most of Mono Lake's California Gulls arrive in March and April, soaring across the Sierra Nevada when the passes are buried in snow. Eggs are laid in May, chicks hatch in June, and by August the young and their parents are winging to coastal wintering areas from British Columbia to San Diego (C 53:57-77). Many of the gulls seen about bays, schoolyards and fields were raised at Mono.

By the 1880s, however, commercial harvesting of gull eggs for sale in nearby mining towns had depleted the colonies. "It is a common practice," wrote Browne, "for the settlers to go over in their boats and in the course of a few hours gather as many eggs as they can carry home." In later years, the commercial eggers would remain on the gulls' principal nesting island, Negit, during the entire season (Denton 1949). In 1882, a local newspaper, the *Homer Mining Index*, noted a paucity of eggs, and concluded that "depradations on the birds' nests have probably caused them to seek some safer spot to rear their young" (6/3/1882). The following year the same newspaper reported that "gulls are becoming very scarce on Mono Lake" (6/23/1883).

Between 1916 and the 1970s, Mono Lake's nesting California Gull population increased from a few thousand to approximately 50,000. Jehl, Babb and Power (1985) attribute this increase "largely...to the formation of new nesting islands, exposed by the decline of the lake since 1941, and to immigration from other colonies." Others interpret the increase as a gradual recovery from commercial egg harvesting augmented by declines in winter mortality (Winkler and Shuford, in press). In fact, since most of the increase took place on the elevated portions of Negit Island, it could have had little if anything to do with the shrinkage of the lake or the emergence of new islands.

Nesting gulls did not colonize the islets west of Paoha Island until 1979, when mainland predators forced them from Negit. By that year, Mono Lake's receding waters—a result of stream diversions by the Los Angeles Department of Water and Power—had exposed a landbridge between Negit Island and the mainland. Coyotes invaded the island and routed its estimated 33,000 breeding birds.

Since 1979, most of Mono's nesting California Gulls have moved onto small islets northeast of Negit and west of Paoha islands. Their nesting success fluctuates greatly from year to year. The Mono Lake Committee's quarterly newsletters contain current updates. Leading biologists hotly debate the long term sustainability of the population.

Of equal concern is the threat to the food supply. California Gulls are lured to Mono Lake, not only by safe island nesting sanctuaries, but by plentiful food. With hungry mouths to feed, abundant food is a necessity, and Mono's bounty of brine shrimp and brine flies keeps the gull chicks fat and satisfied. Garbage, fish and other invertebrates round out the menu (Shuford 1985).

Both food supply and nesting sanctuaries are in jeopardy. Unless the Los Angeles Department of Water and Power curtails water diversions from Mono Lake's tributary streams, virtually all of Mono Lake's islands will become connected to the mainland. Moreover the increasing salinity of Mono's waters will poison the shrimp and flies on which the gulls depend to feed their chicks (p. 21). Unless the lake is stabilized, the mountains will lose a raucous but elegant avian inhabitant. At press time (1992), the court has ordered a temporary halt to diversions until the lake rises three feet, restoring a moat around Negit Island. If we have average precipitation this will take at least two more years.

High elevation record: 13,000' Mt. Dana 8/5/43 (YM).

Peak winter count: 100, Mono Lake 12/31/80 (AB 35:716, DG).

Extreme dates west slope or east slope over 8000': 3/28/81 4600' Ackerson Meadow, 50 (JW) - 10/19/85 8200' Tenaya Lake (MCh); 11/3/87 9700' Tioga Lake (DG).

Additional references: ES:88-113, Johnston 1956, Mahoney and Jehl 1985, Schwan and Winkler 1984, Shuford, Strauss and Hogan 1984, Shuford, Super and Johnston 1985, Shuford 1986, Winkler 1985, YNN 18:126.

HERRING GULL (*Larus argentatus*)

Rare winter and extremely rare summer visitor below 7000' east of Sierran escarpment.

Our scarcest regular gull, Herrings visit freshwater and alkaline lakes and ponds as well as dumps.

On the west slope, Stebbins and Stebbins (1963) consider them "infrequent," but I have found no substantiated records. Summer records: 6400' Mono Lake 7/10/80 (JJ); 6900' Crowley Reservoir 6/11-7/21/91 (AB 45:1157) and 8/31/87 (AB 42:130).

Peak count: 4, 6900' Crowley Lake Reservoir 3/25/85 (JD).

Extreme dates excluding summer records: 9/26/89 Mono Lake (ESt) - 3/28/76 Long Valley Dump (T&JH).

Additional reference: AB 31:1043.

YELLOW-FOOTED GULL (*Larus livens*)

Extremely rare vagrant east of Sierran escarpment.

Record: 6900' Crowley Reservoir, 7/21-29/91, juvenal, (AB 45:1157). First northern California record.

Sabine's Gull at Mono lake, September 24, 1985. Photograph by Joseph R. Jehl Jr.

GLAUCOUS-WINGED GULL (*Larus glaucescens*)

Extremely rare vagrant east of Sierran escarpment.

Record: 6500' Bridgeport 6/20/88 (AB 42:1337)

SABINE'S GULL (*Xema sabini*)

Irregularly rare fall vagrant below 7000' east of Sierran escarpment (0-5/year—6400').

While primarily pelagic migrants, Sabine's Gulls stray to alkaline and freshwater lakes east of the Sierran escarpment. Of all our gulls, they are the most dramatically garbed.

Peak count: 5, 6900' Crowley Lake Reservoir 9/26/87 (DG, ESt, PM).
Extreme dates: 8/6/88 Crowley Reservoir (AB 43:163) - 10/19/88 Mono Lake (ESt).
Additional references: AB 37:220, C 4:10; C 54:115.

CASPIAN TERN (*Sterna caspia*)

	J	F	M	A	M	J	J	A	S	O	N	D	HABITAT	ELEVATIONS		
														N	T	W
WEST						•							RL		5-9	
EAST				—	—	—	—	—					MoLMuR	6	6-10	

Extremely rare transient on west and east slopes; uncommon summer resident below 7500' east of Sierran escarpment.

Among the flocks of gulls that gather on the muddy margins of Crowley Lake and Bridgeport Lake reservoirs, blood red bills sometimes betray small groups of Caspian Terns. At Mono Lake, these large, raucous fisherbirds nest among the gulls on the Negit and Paoha Islets (6400'—ES:100, JJ, ESt); they have bred at Bridgeport Lake Reservoir as well (6500'—RS). They also range to, ponds, languid streams and high elevation lakes such as George (9000') and Saddlebag (10,100').

At Mono Lake, the number of nesting Caspian Terns has declined from a high of approximately 14 pairs in 1982-83 to approximately six pairs in 1991, probably due to predation by California Gulls (JJ, ESt). Since gulls were driven from Negit Island in 1979, their densities have increased on the islets where the terns nest.

Records west slope: 3700' Hetch Hetchy Reservoir 6/3/77 (MM); 8600' Tuolumne Meadows, 2, 6/21/78 (AB 32:1205).

Records above 7500' east slope: 7800' Lundy Canyon 6/11/82 (MM); 10,100' Saddlebag Lake, 2, 7/26/77 (AB 38:1185) and adult and begging juvenile 9/20/79 (DeSante and Engstrom MS).

Extreme dates: 3/29/86, 10, 6900' Crowley Lake Reservoir (DG) - 9/24/90 Mono Lake (ESt).

COMMON TERN (*Sterna hirundo*)

Extremely rare spring transient and irregularly rare fall transient (0-5/year) below 7000' and extremely rare transient at higher elevations east of crest.

Though primarily coastal migrants, Common Terns occasionally stray to lakes, ponds and stream deltas east of the Sierran escarpment. Unlike Forster's, they have even mountaineered to treeline.

Spring records: 6400' Mono Lake 5/27/84 (AB 38:1058) and 6/15/83 (DS); 6900' Alkali Ponds 6/30/87 (DG).

Record above 7000': 10,100' Saddlebag Lake 9/9/72 (AB 27:115).

Extreme dates east of crest excluding spring records: 8/16/91 6900' Crowley Reservoir (DS) - 10/8/86 6400' Rush Creek delta, Mono Lake, 6 immatures (DG).

Peak counts: 6, one adult, Crowley Lake Reservoir 9/18/87 (JD); 6 immatures, Mono Lake 10/6/86 (DG).

ARCTIC TERN (*Sterna pardisaea*)

Extremely rare vagrant east of Sierran escarpment.

Records: 6500' Bridgeport, found dead, 5/22/73 (AB 27:815); 6900' Crowley Reservoir 7/6/91 (AB 45:1157), 9/24/87 (PP, KH), and 9/15/91, 1 adult, (JD).

FORSTER'S TERN (*Sterna forsteri*)

	J	F	M	A	M	J	J	A	S	O	N	D	HABITAT	ELEVATIONS		
														N	T	W
WEST																
EAST					▬	▬	▬	▬	▬				LRMuMo	6?	6-8	

Uncommon transient and locally uncommon summer visitor below 7500' east of the Sierran escarpment.

Forster's are the most numerous small tern east of the Sierran escarpment, but have yet to stray into the higher mountains or onto the west slope. These graceful birds dive for fish on lakes, ponds, deltas and languid streams. Small numbers may breed at Bridgeport Lake Reservoir (6500'), where juveniles have been seen begging for food (RS).

Peak counts: 30-40, Bridgeport Lake Reservoir 6/21/87 (DS); 24, 6400' Mono Lake 5/9/78 (GP); 27, Mono Lake 8/17/77 (DG); 20, 6900' Crowley Lake Reservoir 9/20/86 (DG).
Extreme dates, both Crowley Reservoir: 4/20/91, 2, (JHu) - 9/30/85 (DG).

(FORSTER'S OR COMMON TERN)

Four terns which were either Forster's or Commons were at Lake Eleanor Reservoir (4700') on 4/27/86. Though they were reported as "Commons," the observer did not distinguish them from Forster's (YM, Charles Fullam). This is the only record for this "species pair" in Yosemite National Park.

LEAST TERN (*Sterna antillarum*)

Extremely rare vagrant east of Sierra escarpment.

Record: 6500' Bridgeport Reservoir 7/4/91, 2 adults, (AB 45:1157).

BLACK TERN (*Chlidonias niger*)

Rare transient and summer visitor below 7000' east of Sierran escarpment.

Black Terns visit freshwater and alkaline ponds and lake margins.

Peak counts: 5, 5/11/79 6400' Mono Lake (KC); 40, 8/19/91 Crowley Reservoir (DS).
Extreme dates: 4/30/77 Mono Lake (DW) - 9/6/87 6900' Crowley Lake Reservoir (HG).

Family ALCIDAE: Auks, Murres and Puffins

MARBLED MURRELET (*Brachyramphus marmoratus*)

Extremely rare vagrant on Mono Lake (6400').

No one has seen a live Marbled Murrelet on Mono Lake. On four occasions, however, their carcasses have been found along its shores.

One would suppose these Marbled Murrelets blundered to Mono Lake from nesting areas along the Pacific Coast of North America, perhaps even Northern California, but such is not the case. The Mono Lake birds all belong, not to the North American subspecies *B. m. marmoratus*, but to the Asiatic race *B. m. perdix*, whose breeding range seems to be concentrated along the east coast of the Kamchatka Peninsula and on the mainland coast of the Sea of Okhotsk at least 2,500 miles away (Jehl 1981; S. G. Sealy).

Records: 8/3/83 (ES, MK); 8/6/86 (DS); 8/9/81 (Jehl 1981); 9/29/83 (ES, DS).

ANCIENT MURRELET (*Synthliboramphus antiquus*)

Extremely rare vagrant at Mono Lake (6400').

Record: found freshly dead 12/9/85 (JJ).

Order COLUMBIFORMES: Pigeons and Doves

Family COLUMBIDAE: Pigeons and Doves

Of five species, only two—Band-tailed Pigeons and Mourning Doves—are widespread natives.

ROCK DOVE (*Columba livia*)

Introduced; rare visitor below 7000' and extremely rare visitor to treeline throughout the region.

Rock Doves occasionally wander to meadows, pastures and towns. It is impossible to know how many are truly feral. The small flocks which forage in meadows near Mono Lake, for example, are from local cotes, and most of the other birds are probably strays or errant "homing pigeons."

High elevation record: 10,000' Tioga Pass 9/15/81 (DeSante and Engstrom MS).

BAND-TAILED PIGEON (*Columba fasciata*)

	J	F	M	A	M	J	J	A	S	O	N	D	HABITAT	ELEVATIONS		
														N	T	W
WEST													OPDA	F-6	F-10	F-5
EAST													PWA	8	6-10	

Uncommon summer resident below 5000', uncommon summer visitor to 8000', rare summer visitor to treeline and irregularly rare to common winter resident below 5000' on west slope; irregularly rare summer visitor below treeline east of crest.

Oaks, be they blacks, canyons or interior lives, are the Band-tailed Pigeons' home and dining commons. They may be mixed with Douglas fir, white fir, ponderosa pine, Sequoias or other conifers, but it's acorns that lure Columba's favor. They swallow acorns whole, using their muscular gizzards to crack the hard shells. They also feast on the fleshy fruits of elderberry, dogwood, chokecherry and other shrubs, and visit stables to scrounge for grain.

Because of their predilection for berries and mast, Band-tailed Pigeons nest later in the year than other birds. Near Nevada Fall (6000'), for example, a pair was still feeding young on 9/29/27 (C 30:126-27). Even when nesting, they are gregarious, and several pairs may place bulky nests in the same tree. In autumn, when black oaks are laden with acorns, I've seen flocks of hundreds explode from the trees, their powerful wings beating the air with the sound of rushing wind.

Oaks are fickle, however, and do not produce bountiful crops of acorns every year. In lean years, empty bellies force Band-taileds to forsake the oaks and wander the foothills in search of madrone, toyon, manzanita and other fruits. If all else fails, they resort to the grain fields and orchards of the Central Valley. Some winters they leave the mountains entirely. Numbers on the Yosemite Christmas Bird Count, for example, have varied from 1,150 to 0.

This does not explain the irregular presence of Band-tailed Pigeons in coniferous forests above the oak belt and east of the crest. In fact, they sometimes follow the pines to treeline, and have been seen at 10,300' just east of the crest in the Hall Natural Area at least 10 times since 1979 (AB 33:894; AB 34:197; DeSante MS). Elsewhere on the east slope and in the valleys and ranges beyond, flocks or individuals appear unpredictably in canyonbottom woodlands, jeffrey pine forests, riparian habitats and meadows. In 1972, a widespread flight throughout the West brought them in numbers; at least one pair nested near Mammoth Lakes (8000'—AB 26:789; AB 26:884). I suspect these peregrinating pigeons are youthful pioneers driven from the oaks by population pressures.

Extreme dates east of crest: 4/18/82 6400' near Mono Lake (DG, BE) - 9/28/83 7800' Lee Vining Canyon (HG).

Extreme dates above 8000', both Hall Natural Area (10,000'): 6/24/81 - 9/8/84 (B&E).

Representative nesting localities: (2200' near Mariposa—CL); 4000' Yosemite Valley (YNN 6:54); 6000' Mariposa Grove (YNN 29:45).

Additional reference: YNN 31:132.

WHITE-WINGED DOVE (*Zenaida asiatica*)

Extremely rare vagrant east of crest.

Record: 7200' Lee Vining Canyon 8/5-10/76 (MC).

MOURNING DOVE (*Zenaida macroura*)

	J	F	M	A	M	J	J	A	S	O	N	D	HABITAT	ELEVATIONS		
														N	T	W
WEST													GWSO	F-5	F-10	F-4
EAST											•	•	GWS	6-7	6-10	

Uncommon summer resident below 5000', rare transient and summer visitor to treeline and rare winter resident below 4000' on west slope; fairly common summer resident below 7500' and rare transient and summer visitor to treeline east of crest.

Though primarily lowlanders, Mourning Doves follow meadows, grassy openings and roadsides into the mountains. They favor open, grassy areas that are margined by woodland or scrub. Like other seedeaters, they require a stream, spring or other source of fresh water within their daily cruising radius. Hence they often frequent riparian habitats.

Mourning Doves forage on the ground, but resort to thickets and woods for shelter and nesting sites. Though they usually nest in trees, I have also discovered nests beneath sagebrush scrub. During the breeding season, mated birds travel in pairs; after the young have fledged they gather in small flocks.

High elevation record: 10,300' near Vogelsang Lake 9/14/15 (GS 278).

Extreme dates east of crest: 4/6/86 Lee Vining (DG) - 12/18/88 n. shore Mono Lake (AB:43:363)

Extreme dates above 4000' west slope or 7500' east of crest: 4/25/80 8500' Tioga Road (DG) - 10,000'+ Hall Natural Area 10/20/85 (DeSante MS).

Representative nesting localities: (2000' near Mariposa—CL); (4400' Big Meadow—DG); 4600' Ackerson Meadow (JW); 5200' Miguel Meadow (YM); 7000' Dechambeau Creek (EB); 6500' near Mono Lake (DB); 7000' near Owens River (DG).

Additional reference: AB 29:115.

COMMON GROUND-DOVE (*Columbina passerina*)

Extremely rare vagrant east of Sierran escarpment.

Record: 8100' Sagehen Summit 8/19/87 (Joel Hornstein).

Order CUCULIFORMES: Cuckoos and Allies

Family CUCULIDAE: Cuckoos, Roadrunners and Anis

BLACK-BILLED CUCKOO (*Coccyzus erythopthalmus*)

Extremely rare vagrant east of Sierran escarpment.

Record: 6400' Mono Lake County Park 8/29/86 (41:139); accepted by the California Bird Records Committee.

YELLOW-BILLED CUCKOO (*Coccyzus americanus*)

Extremely rare transient east of Sierran escarpment.

Records, both Mono Lake County Park (6400'): 6/14/75 (DG); 6/20/86 (AB 40:1251).

GREATER ROADRUNNER (*Geococcyx californianus*)

Status uncertain—probably rare resident below approximately 3000' on west slope; extremely rare visitor east of Sierran escarpment.

Greater Roadrunners are rare near Mariposa (2000'—CL), and have strayed as high as Yosemite Valley (4000') on one occasion. While I know of no records elsewhere on the west slope, I suspect these elusive ground-dwelling cuckoos dwell in parts of the Merced and Tuolumne River canyons as well as other localities. They favor chaparral interspersed with sparsely vegetated grassland.

Record in Yosemite Valley: 11/13/24 (EM 4).

Records east of crest: 8000' Mammoth Lakes 8/29/90 (lisa Horn); 6400' near Mono Lake 8/15/84 (Sally Gaines); 7000' s. of Conway Summit, fall, early '50s (DB).

Order STRIGIFORMES: Owls

A haunting call, a form flying silent in the moonlight, a pair of solemn eyes glowering in a flashlight beam—such is our acquaintance with these gnomes of night. Consequently much remains to be learned about the habits, haunts and distribution of the 11 owls which occur in our area. All but Great Grays, Spotteds and Flammulateds regularly range both west and east of the crest, and all but the Burrowing nest or used to nest in our area.

Of our breeding species, only the insectivorous Flammulated Owl departs entirely in winter. As the others prey predominantly on mammals or birds, they can find sustenance throughout the year. Nonetheless, some are at least partially migratory or prone to winter wanderings.

Two species—Great Gray and Spotted owls—persist in only small numbers, and are vulnerable to logging of old-growth forests. East of the crest, breeding Short-eared Owls have been nearly or entirely extirpated by habitat destruction.

Family TYTONIDAE: Barn-Owls

BARN OWL (*Tyto alba*)

Fairly common resident in Mariposa region (2000'—CL); extremely rare transient elsewhere on west slope; rare transient below 7000' east of Sierran escarpment.

Barn Owls are decidedly uncommon in the mountains. They dwell in the rolling, oak savannah country near Mariposa, and occasionally visit valleys east of the Sierran escarpment. They hunt for mice and other furry edibles in meadows, grasslands and on openly wooded hillsides, roosting in buildings, cliffs, thick-foliaged trees and, at Mono Lake (6400'), tufa towers. On 8/28/84, 25 were discovered in a buffalo-berry grove near Simons Spring (6400'—LF).

West slope records excluding Mariposa region: 4000' Yosemite Valley 11/27/31 (YNN ll:4) and 8/28/63 (YM); 4400' Big Meadow 6/3/86 (JW); 4600' Ackerson Meadow 4/2-8/22/81 (AB 35:975) and 4/15/84 (JW); 6200' Crane Flat 6/21/80 (AB 35:975); (I have rejected reports of birds heard at Glacier Point [AB 38:1058] and Tuolumne Meadows (RG) because Long-eared Owls have similar calls—JW).

Extreme dates east of crest: 4/7/79 6400' near Mono Lake (DG) - 6/13/84 6500' Dechambeau Ranch (DS); 7/25/80 near Mono Lake (DC) - 10/14/89, it spooked everyone on the South Tufa Halloween walk; (I have rejected the 11/21/76 report of a bird heard near Mono Lake—Gaines [1977]).

Family STRIGIDAE: Typical Owls

FLAMMULATED OWL (*Otus flammeolus*)

	J	F	M	A	M	J	J	A	S	O	N	D	HABITAT	ELEVATIONS		
														N	T	W
WEST													OP	3-6		
EAST					•	•		•							6-8	

Uncommon summer resident from 3000' to 6000' and extremely rare summer visitor or transient at higher elevations on west slope; extremely rare transient east of crest.

"If a martian in black livery were to sidle up on the dark side of our planet to spy upon us, he could scarcely keep his business so well concealed as this ghoulish avian mystery." Since William Leon Dawson (1923) penned these words over six decades ago, we've become slightly better acquainted with Flammulated Owls. Late at night, in favored localities, it is not difficult to hear their low-pitched hoots; the broader bar on the graph reflects, not an increase in numbers, but the period when birds are calling.

Glimpsing these gnomes, however, is one of the Sierra's greatest avian challenges. The ventriloqual calls of Flammulated Owls are difficult to trace, and even in places where they are relatively numerous, one is lucky to descry a fleeting shadow fleeing into the foliage.

Flammulated Owls favor open forests of black oak, pondersosa pine, white fir and other trees interspersed with small, shrubby openings. But I have sought them in vain in seemingly perfect habitat.

While Flammulated Owls cease hooting during midsummer, they resume again on warm nights after completing their molts. Like other insectivorous birds, but unlike most owls, they are migratory, wintering from central Mexico to Central America.

While I know of only three records east of the crest, I would not be surprised if Flammulated Owls are secretly nesting among conifers at lower elevations. They are probably regular, but unseen, transients.

High elevation record west slope: 7000' Peregoy Meadow 5/10/61 (AFN 15:491).

East side records: 6400' near Mono Lake, found dead 5/24/77 (AB 38:1044); 7100' near Twin Lakes sw. of Bridgeport, early June/26 (GM 189); 8200' near Parker Lake, 8/?/58 (Winter 1974).

Extreme dates: 4/15/81 4600' Ackerson Meadow (JW) - 10/30/66 6000' Henness Ridge (AFN 15:491).

Nesting localities: 5400' Merced Grove (Winter 1974); 6000' Henness Ridge (AB 28:945).

Additional references: AFN 17:431, AB 24:640.

WESTERN SCREECH-OWL (*Otus kennicottii*)

	J	F	M	A	M	J	J	A	S	O	N	D	HABITAT	ELEVATIONS		
														N	T	W
WEST													O	F-4	F-7	F-4
EAST								•				•			7-10	

Fairly common resident below 3000', uncommon resident to at least 3700' (Hetch Hetchy), extremely rare spring and rare fall transient or visitor to 5000' and extremely rare transient at higher elevations on west slope; extremely rare transient east of crest.

Among the live and blue oaks of the western foothills, the voices of Western Screech-Owls haunt warm, spring nights. To be sure, they seem "fairly common" only when vocalizing, and this, not a change in abundance, is reflected by the graph.

Above 3000' on the west slope, the status of Western Screech-Owls is more problematical. Stebbins and Stebbins (1963) say they are resident as high as Yosemite Valley (4000'), "especially among canyon live oaks," but I suspect they occur at 3000' to 5000' primarily as post-breeding or juvenile wanderers.

Records above 5000' west slope: approx. 7000' Tioga Road e. of Crane Flat 8/25/87 (DDeS); approx. 7500' Badger Pass 8/15/86 (JW); 8600' Tuolumne Meadows, flushed from culvert in road during snowstorm, 12/18/86 (Marilyn Muse).

Records east of crest: 7200' Silver Lake, 1 immature found freshly drowned, 8/3/89 (DDeS); 10,000' Hall Natural Area 8/6-7/87 (DeSante and Engstrom MS) and 8/29/77 (AB 32:253, DeSante and Engstrom MS); 10,000' Tioga Pass, late Aug. or early Sept./75 (DeSante and Enstrom MS); 7000' found dead near junction of U.S. 395 and Hwy. 203 (T&JH).@SUBTEXT = Extreme dates above 4000' west slope: 4/29/85 4400' Big Meadow, hooting (JW); 7/21/77 4600' Hodgdon Meadow (SG) - 12/?/73 4000' Yosemite Valley (CM).

Representative nesting localities: (1300' Merced River—MR); (2000' Mariposa CL); (2100' El Portal—DG).

GREAT HORNED OWL (*Bubo virginianus*)

	J	F	M	A	M	J	J	A	S	O	N	D	HABITAT	ELEVATIONS		
														N	T	W
WEST													OPWSGC	F-9	F-10	F-9
EAST													PWSGC	6-9	6-10	6-9

Fairly common resident below 7000' and uncommon resident or visitor to treeline both west and east of crest.

Great Horneds are the most catholic of owls. They nest from the foothills nearly to treeline, and are equally at home in woodlands and deserts. Even mountaineers are probably resident year-round, for their sonorous hoots have echoed across the frozen expanse of Tuolumne Meadows (8600') and the snowbound Hall Natural Area (10,000') as early as February (YM, TH, AB 33:310, DeSante MS). Like most owls, they are easier to hear than see; this, not a change in absolute numbers, is reflected by the graph.

Great Horned Owls inhabit so wide a variety of habitats that it is simpler to describe what they shun. On the west slope they leave dense, old-growth mid-elevation forests to Spotted Owls, and thickly vegetated, mid-elevation meadows to Great Grays. But everywhere else—woodlands, meadows, chaparral, scrub, burns, cliffs—Great -Horneds reign supreme. Like their diurnal ecological cousins, Red-tailed Hawks, they hunt primarily in open or openly-wooded habitats for rabbits, wood rats, mice and other small mammals. On Mono Lake's islands, they dine seasonally on gulls and their chicks (JJ).

For roosting and nesting, Great Horned Owls require trees, cliffs or rocks. In desert areas east of the Sierran escarpment, the lack of timber restricts nesting pairs to cliffs, rock outcroppings, lava flows and riparian groves. At Mono Lake, they utilize tufa towers (DG). In 1990 a pair successfully nested on an historic building in Bodie (Peggy Nicholson).

High elevation record: 10,500' Lyell Canyon 10/?/32 (YM).

Representative nesting localities: (2000' near El Portal—DG); 4000' Yosemite Valley (GS:309, YM); 4600' Ackerson Meadow (JW); 7400' Lee Vining Canyon (DG); 7000' Hot Creek (DG); 6400' Negit and Paoha Islands (DG, JJ); (Great Horned Owls probably nest at higher elevations, but there are no positive records).

NORTHERN PYGMY-OWL (*Glaucidium gnoma*)

	J	F	M	A	M	J	J	A	S	O	N	D	HABITAT	ELEVATIONS		
														N	T	W
WEST													OPWG	3-7		F-7
EAST													PWG	7-8		7-8

Irregularly rare to fairly common winter visitor below 3000', uncommon resident from 3000' to 6000', rare resident to approximately 7000' and extremely rare visitor at higher elevations on west slope; rare resident below 8000' east of crest.

Like other owls, Pygmys are more easily heard than seen; the period when they actively vocalize, not a change in numbers, is reflected by the graph.

Unlike most of their night-loving confreres, however, Northern Pygmy-Owls frequently call and hunt during the day. Yet, being scarcely larger than sparrows, they are challenging to see in their forest homes. They favor open stand of black oaks, ponderosa pines, incense cedars and white firs, but also dwell among sugar pines, sequoias, riparian hardwoods and even abandoned orchards. They often hunt along the edges of meadows and clearings where the songbirds on which the prey are plentiful. Though they seldom range above the oak belt, they have bred among firs and lodgepole pines; at Peregoy Meadows (7000'), a pair appropriated an abandoned sapsucker hole in a lodgepole (JW). They shun dense old-growth forests, however, such as climax stands of red fir.

During the winter, Northern Pygmy-Owls wander irregularly below and outside their nesting range. In the Mariposa region (2000'), for example, they were fairly common during the winters of 1978-79 and 1979-80, but have not been seen since (CL). East of the Sierran escarpment, they have materialized in residential Lee Vining (6800'—DG, DB).

As Northern Pygmy-Owls dine on songbirds, one would think their calls would drive them away. Not so! By mimicking their repetitious whistles, one can attract, not only owls, but nuthatches, chickadees, warblers, juncos and other forest birds. These passerines want to ascertain their enemy's whereabouts, for Pygmys, like most predators, can capture them only by stealth and surprise. In fact, they may "mob" an owl, hawk or weasel, and noisily drive it away. And with good reason, for Pygmys prey on birds, such as robins, which are larger than they are.

Representative nesting localities: (2000' Merced River Canyon—MR); 4000' Yosemite Valley (YNN 4:47, YNN 6:58); 4600' Hodgdon Meadow (MM); 6200' near Crane Flat (AFN 7:35); 7000' Peregoy Meadow (JW); 7200' near Merced Lake (YM); (8000' Lee Vining Canyon—DG); (7800' O'Harrell Canyon—DG).

Record at 8600': Tuolumne Meadows 7/?/83 (MR).

Additional references: AFN 7:35, AFN 9:355, GS:311, C 27:110, C 28:92, C 29:161, YNN 19:86, YNN 29:45.

BURROWING OWL (*Athene cunicularia*)

Extremely rare transient on west slope; extremely rare spring and rare fall transient below 8000' and extremely rare transient at higher elevations east of crest.

Not only is the Burrowing our rarest owl, but it also holds high altitude laurels. On 9/25/74, one on the Dana Plateau was far above treeline at 12,000' (YM, MO). Yet an alpine fell-field is not that far removed from this ground-dwellers' usual haunts: arid meadows and grasslands. In sagebrush scrub, they materialize along the margins of dirt roads and in dry washes. They have even strayed to Mono Lake's Paoha Island (JP).

West slope record: 7600' top of El Capitan 10/22/80 (YM).

Spring record east of crest: 7000' Long Valley 4/11/86 (CMc).

Extreme dates east of crest excluding spring record: 9/16/82 6500' near Mono Lake (DG) - 10/25/89 dirt road e. of LV airport (Sally Gaines); 10/28/81 7000' junction U.S. 395 and Hwy. 120E, three found dead (THa, MRD).

SPOTTED OWL (*Strix occidentalis*)

	J	F	M	A	M	J	J	A	S	O	N	D	HABITAT	ELEVATIONS N	ELEVATIONS T	ELEVATIONS W
WEST	—	━	━	━	━	—	—	—	—	—	—	—	PO	3-5		3-5
EAST							•							8?		

Uncommon resident from 3000' to 5500' and extremely rare visitor at higher elevations on west slope; extremely rare visitor east of crest.

More than any other bird, Spotted Owls are wedded to dense, old-growth forests, where they usually betray their presence with wild-sounding hoots, barks, screeches and

Spotted, Flammulated and Northern Pygmy owls

whistles; the graph reflects the period when they actively vocalize, not a change in absolute numbers.

Spotted Owls inhabit the deep, multilayered old-growth forests that clothe shady slopes and canyonbottoms below the level of heavy snow, often near rivers or streams. These strigian dryads shun the red fir forests of the snow belt, but dwell below them among douglas firs, incense cedars, sugar pines, ponderosa pine, white firs, sequoias, big-leaf maples and black oaks (Gould 1974).

Spotted Owls are challenging to see, though they will respond to imitated calls, sometimes in the middle of the day. The excited voices of songbirds may betray their presence.

East slope record: approximately 8000' Deadman Creek, calling male, 6/28/80 (TH); (there is also an unconfirmed report from Mammoth Lakes—CMc; despite the paucity of records, these reclusive owls may nest in the old-growth forests of the Deadman Creek and Mammoth Creek watersheds).

West slope records above 5500': 6300' near Wawona 5/19/74 (Gould 1974); 7000' Peregoy Meadow (AFN 14:69).

Representative nesting localities: 4000' Yosemite Valley (YNN 6:60, YNN 10:77); 4600' Ackerson Meadow (JW).

Additional references: AFN 9:400, C 35:202, GS 304, YNN 15:67.

GREAT GRAY OWL (*Strix nebulosa*)

	J	F	M	A	M	J	J	A	S	O	N	D	HABITAT	ELEVATIONS		
														N	T	W
WEST													GP	4-7		3-5
EAST									•						10	

Rare summer resident from 4000' to 7000', extremely rare summer visitor to treeline and rare winter resident from 3000' to 5000' west slope; extremely rare visitor east of crest.

Of Yosemite's resident birds, Great Gray Owls are the rarest. Until 1915, their presence was not even suspected (GS:305). These boreal, circumpolar owls breed sparingly in the Cascades and northern Rockies as well as the central Sierra. Yosemite's small population is the southernmost contingent.

And a small population it is! Jon Winter estimates that approximately 50 Great Gray Owls summer and nest in the vicinity of verdant meadows from the mixed conifer forests through the red firs to the lower edge of the lodgepole pine belt. They usually choose extensive, well-watered meadows margined by old-growth coniferous forest. Their acute sense of hearing, facilitated by huge, hemispherical facial disks, allows them to prey by ear on gophers and meadow mice concealed beneath dense meadow vegetation. For nest sites they utilize the broken-off tops of large dead trees; all but one have been in red firs (JW).

During the summer, Great Gray Owls sometimes wander upslope as far as treeline. Conversely, with heavy winter snows, but not before, they forsake the higher mountains for the balmier forests and meadows of lower elevations. They usually winter near moist meadows just below the heavy snow level, such as Big Meadow (4400'), Ackerson Meadow (4600') and Wawona Meadow (4000'), but may occupy small forest openings (JW). Though the habitat is suitable, I know of only three records in Yosemite Valley (4000'), perhaps because the crowds keep them away. During some winters, they descend as low as 3000', as near Midpines and Jerseydale (CL), and there is even a nesting record at 2800' (Greeley Hill—JW).

No other birds lure so many birdwatchers to Yosemite, yet few are more elusive. At dawn and dusk, one may glimpse Great Gray Owls gliding over meadows or perched, sometimes conspicuously, on snags or trees along the forest margin. Sometimes the excited calls of robins and other birds betray their presence. Yet these largest of owls are easily missed, and deserve William Leon Dawson's epithet of great gray ghosts.

With so few individuals, Great Gray Owls are de facto endangered. In the Sierran national forests, livestock grazing has thinned meadow vegetation, favoring Great Horeds. In Yosemite National Park, the greatest threat is probably us. Let's leave these great owls in peace, shun their nest sites and roosts, and observe, if at all, from discreet distances. Let us treat them with the respect and reverence they deserve.

Records at or above 9000': 10,000' Agnew Pass 9/5/50 (JW); 9500' near May Lake 9/?/34 (YM); 9000' Ireland Creek 7/27/69 (YM); (in the eastern Sierra south of our region, one n. of Mt. Alice was at 11,000' on 10/12/74—JW).

Additional nesting localities: 4600' Ackerson Meadow (JW); 6200' Crane Flat (AB 26:902); 7000' Peregoy Meadow (AB 25:102, AB 26:902); 7000' McGurk Meadow (AB 40:1252).

High elevation records and record east of crest: 10,000' Agnew Pass 9/5/50; (just north of region, one was at Sardine Meadow [8800'] 8/13-28/60—C 64:164-65).

Additional references: AB 27:116, AB 27:815, EM 4, GM 206, YNN 10:65, YNN 21:23, YNN 37:40-42.

LONG-EARED OWL (*Asio otus*)

	J	F	M	A	M	J	J	A	S	O	N	D	HABITAT	ELEVATIONS		
														N	T	W
WEST													WPO	F-6?	F-10	F-?
EAST													WP	6-8	6-10	6-7

Status uncertain; probably rare resident below 6000' and rare fall transient to treeline on west slope; locally uncommon summer resident below 8000', rare fall transient to and probably above treeline and rare winter resident below 7000' east of crest.

Long-eared Owls may be more numerous than we think; their status and even habitat requirements are baffling.

On the west slope, Long-eared Owls are known to nest in riparian forests and oak-conifer woodlands. Pairs have been found during the nesting season as high as Swamp Lake (5200'—YM) and Henness Ridge (6000'—RS). While they may be irregular, they are more likely overlooked. Most birdwatchers are unfamiliar with their varied calls, which are mostly heard early in the year when few nocturnal birders are afield.

East of the crest, Long-eared Owls usually nest along the wooded margins of streams, springs and seeps. In arid Great Basin country like Cowtrack Mountain, the Bodie Hills and Mono Lake's margins, they are often content with a few willows, cottonwoods or buffalo-berrys clustered around a remote seep or spring. I have also encountered them in open Jeffrey pine forests east of the Mono Craters, where they may nest as well. They do not always breed in the same places every year.

In the past, Long-eared Owls may have been more numerous. In 1916, for example, seven pairs bred in old magpie nests along Walker Creek between Walker Lake and Rush Creek (GS 300-303); water diversions and grazing have devastated the habitat, and the nesting owls have disappeared.

Above 6000', I know of 15 mid-summer to early autumn records ranging from Crane Flat (6200'—YM, WC) east across the crest to the Hall Natural Area (10,200'—DeSante MS). Either Long-eared Owls disperse up-slope, or northern transients migrate south through the Sierra. In either case, they must occur in significant numbers; for every one reported, many more must pass unseen.

High elevation record: 10,200' Hall Natural Area, many records (DeSante MS); an owl identified as a Short-eared at 11,000' on Mt. Clark (8/1/41—YNN 21:22) was more likely this species.

High elevation spring record, west slope: 6200' Crane Flat 6/6/86 (JW).

Extreme dates above 7000, both Hall Natural Area: 8/7/84 - 10/7/79 (D&E).

Nesting localities west slope: 4000' Yosemite Valley (GS 300); 4600' Ackerson Meadow (AB 34:927).

Additional nesting localities east of crest: 8000' Lee Vining Canyon (CMc); 7000' Convict Creek (C 41:248); 6500' Warford Spring (DG); 6500' Simons Spring (DG); (7800' Indian Spring—DG).

Additional references: AFN 18:70; EM 4; AB 35:975; AB 36:214; AB 37:1024.

SHORT-EARED OWL (*Asio flammeus*)

Formerly nested in valleys east of Sierran escarpment, but now apparently an extremely rare summer visitor and rare fall transient below 7000'.

Short-eared Owls formerly bred near June Lake (7600'—C 36:36), Crowley Lake Reservoir (6900'—C 41:248) and undoubtedly other marshes and boggy meadows east of the Sierran escarpment, but have been nearly or entirely extirpated. Two courting birds in Bridgeport Valley (6500') on 5/31/84 are the only recent evidence of breeding (DS, SJ, PSu). Water diversions, grazing and recreational development have degraded or destroyed most of the habitat.

Short-eared Owls have been reported four times on the west slope, but without sufficient documentation to eliminate the possibility they may have been Long-eareds (YNN 21:22, YM—these reports, including an owl I identified as a Short-eared before I realized how closely they resemble Long-eareds on the wing, were published in the 1977 edition of this book).

Additional recent spring and summer records east of crest: 6500' s. Mono Lake 4/27/91 (HG); 6500' Hwy 395, old Mono Lake Marina, 1 freshy killed (AB 45:493); 6400' Simons Spring 6/15/86 (MP); 6500' near Mono Lake 8/4/76 (DW).

Extreme dates east of crest excluding spring records: 8/27/84 e. Mono Lake, 2 (DS, SJ) - 1/1/82 6500' Dechambeau Ponds (CS).

NORTHERN SAW-WHET OWL (*Aegolius acadicus*)

Status uncertain; probably rare resident below approximately 6000' and extremely rare visitor at higher elevations on west slope; probably rare summer resident below approximately 8500', extremely rare transient or visitor at higher elevations, and extremely rare winter visitor below 8000' east of crest.

The comings and goings of Saw-whet Owls, and even their habitat requirements, are cloaked in mystery. On the west slope, at least a small population dwells in the oak-conifer forests. Jon Winter, who has heard them frequently near Ackerson Meadow (4600') during the winter and early spring, believes they are more numerous than supposed, but are usually silent in summer when most people bird the mountains. The only nest was discovered in a flicker hole in a Yosemite Valley cottonwood in 1926 (4000'—EM 4), but juveniles have been seen or heard at Ackerson Meadow (JW) and Crane Flat (JW—6200').

East of the crest and in the Glass Mountain region, the story may be similar, though Saw-whets have apparently nested as high as 8000', and possibly higher. A family group was seen at 9500' on Glass Mountain in 1963 (RS), but it may have drifted upslope after nesting at a lower elevation. In June of 1991 a juvenile was seen at Mono Lake county Park by Dan Keller. I suspect these high altitude nesters are migratory, but have not searched for them extensively in winter. Transients appear outside their nesting haunts in fall and early winter; five, for example, were banded in willow thickets at the Mono Lake County Park in September, 1970 (BS), and they have materialized several times in pinyon woodlands. Their winter status is conjectural; I know of only two records, but they could easily be overlooked.

I hesitate to generalize about the Sierran haunts of Saw-whet Owls, though they seem to favor drier, more open forests than their coast range kin. A nocturnal naturalist should befriend these strigian mysteries, and share their secrets with us ordinary mortals.

West slope record above 6200': 7700' Yosemite Creek, found dead 9/9/87 (DG).

Winter records east of crest: 7900' near Lee Vining 12/16/85 (DG) and 2/2/86 (JP); 7800' Lundy Canyon Jan-Feb/84 (Linda LaPierre).

Known nesting localities east of crest: 8000' near June Lake (C 36:36); 8000' near Mammoth Lakes (AFN 4:291; AB 26:884).

Additional reference: AB 34:927.

Order CAPRIMULGIFORMES: GOATSUCKERS AND ALLIES

Family CAPRIMULGIDAE: GOATSUCKERS

COMMON NIGHTHAWK (*Chordeiles minor*)

	J	F	M	A	M	J	J	A	S	O	N	D	HABITAT	ELEVATIONS		
														N	T	W
WEST													A	?	F-12	
EAST					•				•				ALMSP	6-8?	6-10	

Rare transient and summer visitor from foothills to above treeline on west and east slopes; locally common summer resident below 8000' in valleys east of Sierran escarpment and below 9500' in the Bodie Hills.

At dusk, on summer evenings east of the Sierran escarpment, Common Nighthawks swoop like winged scimitars over ponds, lakes, meadow, sagebrush scrub and open coniferous forests. Late at night I've watched them hawk insects about the street lights of Lee Vining (6800'). Despite their names, they are often abroad by day as well. Of all the summer birds, they are the last to arrive and one of the first to depart; perhaps coincidentally, they undertake one of the longest migrations, wintering in South America.

East of the Sierran escarpment, Common Nighthawks nest in sagebrush scrub. A few probably breed on the west slope as well, but I know of no positive records. Jon Winter has heard their courtship booming near Mather (4500'—JW). In Sequoia National Park, they have bred on alpine fell fields at 10,750' (SD 79-80).

Common Nighthawks are gregarious, especially in mid-summer and during migrations. At least 250, for instance, were hawking insects over Crowley Reservoir (6900') on 8/13/88 (AB 43:63) and 200 were tilting over Bridgeport Reservoir (6500') on 8/27/90 (PM).

High elevation record: 12,000' Koip Peak, 12, 8/?/38 (YM).

Extreme dates: 5/21/86 6400' Mono Lake (DS); 5/30/87 6900' Mono City (JP) - 9/22/90 Crowley Lake Reservoir (AB 45:147)

Representative nesting locality: 7000' Black Point (JZ).

COMMON POORWILL (*Phalaenoptilus nuttallii*)

	J	F	M	A	M	J	J	A	S	O	N	D	HABITAT	ELEVATIONS		
														N	T	W
WEST				?						•			S	F-6	F-10	
EAST				•						•			S	6-8	6-10	

Fairly common summer resident below 4000', uncommon summer resident to 6000' and rare fall transient to treeline on west slope; fairly common summer resident below 8000' and rare fall transient to treeline east of crest.

At dusk, on warm spring and early summer evenings, Common Poorwills serenade the chaparral and sagebrush scrub. They fall silent in midsummer, but resume in September prior to migrating.

On the west slope, Common Poorwills dwell among chamise, manzanita, ceanothus and other chaparral shrubs as well as open stands of oaks and pines. To the east, they consort with sagebrush, bitterbrush, pinyons and other shrubs and small trees. They favor gentle to steep slopes with a diversity of moderate to large shrubs, and with scattered open spaces, clearings or roads. They shun flat sagebrush-covered flats as well as dense woodlands. Often they huddle on dirt or gravel roads, their eyes flashing orange in the beam of flash- or headlights.

While Common Poorwills are one of the few birds known to hibernate, Sierran populations are probably migratory; I know of no winter records.

High elevation and extreme dates above 8000', both Hall Natural Area: 10,500' 7/22/82 - 9900' 10/1/77 (DeSante and Engstrom MS).

Extreme dates: 4/19/91 Cemetery Rd. Mono Lake (JHu) - 10/6/33 4000' Yosemite Valley (YNN 13:12); 10/7/89 6600' Mono City (ESt). (Common Poorwills probably arrive considerably earlier at low elevations on the west slope, but I know of no records; one found dead on U.S. 395 near Lee Vining on 10/29/86 had probably been killed during the previous week—DS, SJ).

Representative nesting localities: (2000' near Mariposa—CL); 3500' near McCauley Ranch (DG); 6000' Henness Ridge (DDeS, DG); 8000' Lee Vining Canyon (DG); 7600' near June Lake (C 36:36); 7500' slope w. Mono Lake (DS).

Additional references: AFN 12:56, AB 28:102, AB 33:895, EM 5, YNN 13:12, YNN 21:23, YNN 29:76.

Order APODIFORMES: SWIFTS AND HUMMINGBIRDS

Family APODIDAE: SWIFTS

Three species nest in the region, of which, to paraphrase William Leon Dawson (1923), Vaux's are swift, Blacks are swifter and White-throateds are the swiftest of all. Compared to swallows, they are faster fliers and range farther from nest and roost sites, sometimes dining on dispersing insects a thousand feet heavenwards.

Unlike swallows, swifts' diminutive feet prevent them from perching on limbs, power lines and other horizontal resting places. Blacks and White-throateds roost and nest in crevices or ledges on vertical cliffs, while Vaux's use the interiors of hollow, vertical snags.

Swifts spend many daylight hours hawking insects on the wing. Blacks and Vaux's winter in the balmy, insect-rich climes of Mexico and Middle America. Some White-throateds, however, brave Sierran winters on the lower west slope, probably going torpid during prolonged periods of inclement weather.

BLACK SWIFT (*Cypseloides niger*)

	J	F	M	A	M	J	J	A	S	O	N	D	HABITAT	ELEVATIONS		
														N	T	W
WEST													AC	4-7	4-13	
EAST					•								A		10-13	

Locally fairly common summer resident from 4000' to 7500' and rare transient at higher elevations on west slope; rare fall transient above 10,000' on east slope and extremely rare transient at lower elevations east of crest.

Ledges on sheer, well-shaded cliffs, often behind waterfalls, cradle Yosemite's Black Swifts. From their misty nesting haunts, these shadowy scimitars range far and wide, materializing over meadows, forests, lakes and even mountain peaks. In late July and August, when parental cares are probably past, flocks of over 30 have buzzed the summits of Mt. Conness (12,600'—MC), Mt. Dana (13,100'—JH) and the Dana Plateau (11,700'—DG).

The ruggedness and inaccessibility of the Black Swifts' breeding haunts have defeated nearly everyone who has sought their nests. Not so Yosemite postmaster Charles Michael, who not only located seven nests in Tenaya Canyon (approx. 6000') in the 1920s, but also secured excellent photographs of nestlings. "It was the wild, erratic winging of a lone Black Swift," he wrote, "that first attracted my attention. Such be-

Charles Michael pointing to the nest of a Black Swift in Tenaya Canyon, July, 1926. Photograph courtesy of the Yosemite Museum.

Five-weeks-old Black Swift on nest in Tenaya Canyon, August 22, 1926. Photograph by Charles Michael, courtesy of the Yosemite Museum

wildering speed, such coordination of mind and muscle... Somehow the thought came to me of a great winged spider gone mad... While I watched, the bird suddenly swooped and fairly seemed to plaster himself to the wall not fifty feet from where I stood... The nest site was in one of the most inaccessible sections of a gorge as grand as any in all the Sierra".

"The nest was composed of the delicate pinnae of the five-fingered fern. Great banks of these ferns hung from neighboring walls, and it would be quite possible for the swifts to procure material while on the wing. Perhaps, though, the swifts may gather nesting material while clinging to a wall, as I have often seen swifts alight on a ferny ledge above Vernal Fall... The nest was placed on a bit of projecting rock...located within the shelter of an overhung wall, thirty feet directly above a deep pool in the creek. The inner chasm is here very narrow; the vertical walls stand not fifty feet apart. The channel is dark and cool; in the long summer days the sun lights its depth for but a brief hour. And at no time or season does the sun ever play on the nest of the swift—cramped quarters, I should say, for birds of the wide skies" (Michael 1927).

Records below 10,000' east of crest: 8800' Lee Vining Canyon 7/19/85 (DDeS); 6800' Lee Vining, 2, 5/28/80 (DG) and 8/14/79 (DG); 6400' Mono Lake County Park 8/29/86 (DG).

Extreme dates: 3/14/40 4000' Yosemite Valley (YM); 5/5/43 Yosemite Valley (YM) - 9/16/83 7200' Glacier Point (JZ); 10/7/81 Yosemite Valley (YM).

Additional nesting localities: 6000' Nevada Fall (YM); 7400' Rainbow Fall, Devil's Postpile National Monument (GF).

Additional references: AFN 9:355, AFN 9:400, AFN 10:407, AB 26:902, C 27:111, C 28:109, C 29:89, C 35:30, EM 6, GS 349, YNN 14:69.

CHIMNEY SWIFT (*Chaetura pelagica*)

Extremely rare vagrant east of Sierran escarpment.

Records: both 6400' Mono Lake County Park: 6/10/89 (AB 43:1364); 6/11/76, 5, one found dead (specimen at California Academy of Sciences; the July date in AB 31:221 is in error—RS).

VAUX'S SWIFT (*Chaetura vauxi*)

Rare transient below 4000, rare summer resident from 4000' to 7000' and extremely rare transient at higher elevations on west slope; rare transient and possibly summer resident below 8000' and extremely rare transient at higher elevations east of crest.

Nesting Vaux's Swifts were not discovered on the west slope until 1968, when a pair were observed entering a dead red fir at Crane Flat (6200'—AFN 22:573). Since that time, small numbers have summered and undoubtedly bred at Hodgdon Meadow (4600'), Wawona Meadow (4000'), Peregoy Meadow (7000') and other localities, and have also bred in Sequoia National Park (AB 28:945). I suspect these "cigars with wings" are thinly but widely distributed in old-growth forests where standing, hollow snags afford suitable nesting sites. The many records near meadows may reflect birder rather than chaetura preferences. Usually only a few are seen at a time.

East of the crest, Vaux's Swifts are transients, though seven at the Paha Campground near Upper Twin Lakes (7000') on 7/20-21/85 were "possibly nesting in the jeffrey pines" (AB 39:959). I know of no other June, July or August records.

Peak counts: 20-30, Crane Flat 7/15-21/85 (SGu); 60+, 6600' over w. shore Mono Lake 9/26/86 (DG).

Records above 8000': 9800' Tioga Pass, flock, 9/14/85 (SG); 12,000' Hall Natural Area, 6, 8/4/84 (DeSante and Engstrom MS).

Extreme dates west slope: 5/19/68 Crane Flat (AFN 22:573) - 10/15/81 2000' El Portal (JD).

Extreme dates east of crest excluding July record: 4/22/78 Mono Lake County Park (KC) - 5/28/71 8000' Mammoth Lakes (AB 25:778); 9/18/82 6800' Lee Vining (DG) - 10/15/85 Mono Lake County Park, 2 (DG).

Additional references: AB 23:692, AB 25:903, AB 26:902, AB 27:816.

WHITE-THROATED SWIFT (*Aeronautes saxatalis*)

	J	F	M	A	M	J	J	A	S	O	N	D	HABITAT	ELEVATIONS		
														N	T	W
WEST													AC	F-8	F-13	
EAST													AC	7-9	6-13	

Uncommon resident below 3000', common summer resident to 8000' and rare summer visitor at higher elevations on west slope; locally uncommon summer resident below 9000' and rare summer visitor at higher elevations on east slope; rare summer visitor east of Sierran escarpment.

Crevices in vertiginous walls cradle Yosemite's White-throated Swifts. From their natal cliffs, they range the airways far and wide, cruising over all types of habitat. Grinnell and Miller (1944) suggest they travel more miles each day than any other species, even California Condors. Birds have buzzed the summits of Mt. Conness (12,600'—DeSante MS), Mt. Gibbs (12,800'—MR) and Mt. Dana (13,100'—DG).

Nesting White-throated Swifts favor granite cliffs, perhaps because these afford the firmest claw-holds and attachments for nests (GM 216). But they also breed in volcanic rock east of the Sierran escarpment, as near Crowley Lake Reservoir (6900'). They roost and nest in deep crevices, and are unable to take off from the ground; a chick's first flight is successful or fatal. In fact, young have marooned on the floor of Yosemite Valley uninjured but unable to take flight; tossed skywards, they vanish into the blue (C 28:109-114; YM).

White-throated Swifts winter in the Merced River and probably the Tuolumne River canyons, but are only seen on warm days (MR). Probably they become torpid during inclement weather.

White-throateds are the swiftest of the swifts, and perhaps of any bird. Their skill and speed on the wing, as William Leon Dawson (1923) remarked, is best appreciated from the rims of Yosemite Valley and other precipices: "If one does happen to be squeamish about gazing into a 3000-foot abyss, it doesn't help matters any to have a saucy bird demonstrate the strength of his nerves by dashing within a foot of one's ears at a rate of five miles per minute."

Extreme dates west slope above 3000': 4000' Yosemite Valley 2/20/28 (YM) - 10/11/53 7600' Harden Lake (AFN 8:39).

Extreme dates east of crest: 4/16/82 approx. 8500' Lee Vining Canyon (BE) - 9/21/81 approx. 10,000' e. of Tioga Pass (HG).

Representative nesting localities: (1000'-7500'+ Merced River Canyon from foothills to Yosemite Valley—YM, MR, DG); (approx. 8000'-9000' Lee Vining Canyon—DG); (6900' near Crowley Lake dam—JH).

Additional references: AFN 7:35, AFN 7:233, C 28:111, GS 251, YNN 7:80, YNN 21:42, YNN 29:46.

Family TROCHILIDAE: Hummingbirds

Of seven species, only Calliopes are a widespread nesting species. The most numerous, Rufous Hummingbirds, use the Sierra as a flowery southward migration route to Mexico. They and their confreres dine on the nectar from paintbrush, columbines, penstemons and other red, tubular flowers as well as on insects, spiders and the sap at sapsucker drillings. Except for Anna's, which brave Sierran winters in the western foothills, all migrate to flowery, insect-rich climes in Mexico.

During the nesting season, male hummingbirds defend flowery breeding territories, engaging in spectacular pendulum-like aerial displays for hour after hour. Females usually nest in more wooded habitats, raising broods without help from their mates. In the migratory species, males depart while females are still feeding nestlings; late in the season, most hummingbirds are females and immatures.

We still have much to learn about the status and distribution of these iridescent avian meteors, especially the confusingly similar females and juveniles.

BLACK-CHINNED HUMMINGBIRD (*Archilochus alexandri*)

Rare summer resident below 4000' on west slope and below 7000' east of crest—nesting probable but unconfirmed; extremely rare fall transient in higher mountains.

In the vicinity of cottonwoods, willows, oaks, aspens and other broad-leaved, riparian trees, one sometimes espies Black-chinned Hummingbirds. They also join other hummers at flowers and feeders in meadows and gardens, but have kept their home life well-hidden. They probably breed in the region, but a nest has yet to be found.

After mid-July, virtually all Black-chinned Hummingbirds are females or juveniles, and closely resemble Costa's. While all but one have been identified as *alexandri*, some may have been the other species.

Records above 4000' west slope or 7000' east of crest: 4600' Ackerson Meadow 8/30-9/2/86 (JW); 6200' Crane Flat 7/15/73 (AB 27:911); 8200' Tenaya Lake 7/1/74 (AB 28:946); 8000' Lundy Canyon 6/6/87 (DG, HG); (the published record from the Hall Natural Area [10,000'—AB 29:115] was apparently in error).

Extreme dates west slope, both Yosemite Valley (4000'): 4/12/85 (YM) - 9/22/24 (YM).

Extreme dates east of crest: 4/23/81 7000' town of Crowley Lake (DP) - 9/30/85 6800' Lee Vining (DG).

Latest date for male: 8/6/87 6400' Mono Lake (JD).

Additional references: AFN 7:289, AB 26:899, GS 352.

ANNA'S HUMMINGBIRD (*Calypte anna*)

	J	F	M	A	M	J	J	A	S	O	N	D	HABITAT	ELEVATIONS		
														N	T	W
WEST	■	■	■	■	■	■	■	■	■	■	■	■	SOP	F-4	F-10	F-2
EAST				•	•	•	—	—	—				SWP		6-10	

Fairly common resident below 2500', fairly common summer resident to 4000', uncommon summer visitor and fall transient to 7000' and rare fall transient to treeline on west slope; rare summer visitor and fall transient below treeline east of crest.

Of all the hummingbirds, Anna's are the hardiest. West of the crest, they are the only one to brave winters, albeit mostly at feeders. To the east they linger longest into autumn, and often suffer the season's first snow.

In their native haunts, Anna's Hummingbirds favor dry slopes grown to broken chaparral, scattered trees or open woodlands. Early in the year, the flowers of manzanita and current lure them onto steep canyon slopes, where males defend flowery display and foraging areas. Once courtship is consummated, females sequester themselves in denser oak, oak-conifer and riparian woodlands.

With the advent of civilization, Anna's Hummingbirds made themselves at home in Mariposa (2000'), El Portal (2100') and other residential communities, dining at feeders and cultivated flowers, and nesting in yards and gardens.

After the breeding season, small numbers of Anna's Hummingbirds drift upslope. In contrast to the meadow-loving Rufous, Anna's prefer, or are driven into, drier, scrubbier slopes and ridges. Because they nest in late winter or early spring, they reach the higher mountains as early as June. These midget mountaineers are frequently vocal and aggressive in defense of flower fields, and have been heard singing vociferously at 10,200' (Saddlebag Lake 7/18/81—MM). High elevation record: 10,600' Upper McCabe Lake 8/5/39 (YM).

Extreme dates above 3000' west slope, both Yosemite Valley (4000'): 2/23/78 (YM) - 10/13/85 (DG).

Extreme dates above 7000', both Hall Natural Area (10,300'): 7/9/81 - 9/11/79 (DeSante MS).

Extreme dates east of crest, both 6900'Tom's Place (feeder): 4/12/90 (AB 44:493) - 10/24/91 (CH).

Additional references: AFN 18:484, AB 25:900, AB 26:899; AB 34:197.

COSTA'S HUMMINGBIRD (*Calypte costae*)

Status uncertain; one positive record on west slope.

While there is but a single record, I suspect Costa's Hummingbirds are rare but regular visitors both west and east of the crest.

Record: 7100' Glacier Point Road between Summit and Peregoy meadows, hatching year male 6/16/83 (AB 37:1024).

CALLIOPE HUMMINGBIRD (*Stellula calliope*)

	J	F	M	A	M	J	J	A	S	O	N	D	HABITAT	ELEVATIONS		
														N	T	W
WEST													SWGP	4-10	F-10	
EAST				•					•				WGSP	6-10	6-10	

Rare spring transient below 4000', locally fairly common summer resident from 4000' to 8000' and rare summer resident and irregularly rare to fairly common summer visitor and fall transient to treeline on west slope; locally fairly common summer resident below 8500' and rare summer resident and irregularly rare to fairly common summer visitor and fall transient to treeline east of crest.

Calliopes are the only hummingbird to raise young in the higher mountains. Their nesting haunts defy facile description, for they dwell in moist thickets as well as dry, montane chaparral.

At Hodgdon Meadow (4600'), for example, male Calliope Hummingbirds defend streamside willow thickets near the meadow's margin, employing the shrubbery for lookout posts and display areas. Both sexes feed at sap holes drilled in the willows by Red-breasted Sapsuckers as well as on nectar-bearing meadow flowers and small insects. Males remain in the open, but females also forage in adjacent coniferous forests, where they probably sequester their nests.

In contrast, on the Alder Creek trail near Wawona (4500'), male Calliope Hummingbirds display on arid slopes with montane chaparral and scattered conifers. They favor blooming manzanita and ceanothus, arriving about the time the shrubs begin to blossom (YNN 10:78).

East of the crest, nesting Calliope Hummingbirds are partial to moist habitats. In Lundy Canyon (7000'-8500'), for instance, males defend riparian willow thickets on steep hillsides as well on the level canyon floor. Females forage in aspen groves as well, hiding nests in dense greenery. Early in the season, both sexes range onto dry moraines and slopes in search of paintbrush and other fresh blooms.

Common to all their haunts are columbines, scarlet gilias, currents, manzanitas and other "hummingbird flowers." Since the bloom time is later east of the crest, Calliopes arrive later as well.

In some places that would seem to offer ideal habitat conditions, however, Calliope Hummingbirds are surprisingly scarce. They are uncommon, for example, in Yosemite Valley on the west slope and the floor of Lee Vining Canyon to the east. In general they prefer the smaller streams and ancillary canyons, but why I don't know. Overall their numbers and whereabouts fluctuate from year to year (AB 29:1027).

Male Calliope Hummingbirds mostly depart by early July, leaving females and juveniles to challenge our identification skills. In some years they are numerous almost to treeline; in others scarce or absent. These summer mountaineers may be wandering upslope from lower elevations, or migrating south from northern nesting haunts.

Latest date for male: 7600' Lee Vining Canyon 7/16/86 (DG).

Extreme dates west slope: 3/2/24 4000' Yosemite Valley (YM) - 8/28/83 7000' Peregoy Meadow (JL); (the 3/2 record ties the earliest I know of in California, but I see no reason to doubt the identification by an experienced observer, and there are other records during March [YNN

10:78; YM]; I have rejected, however, six September and October records in Yosemite Valley, the latest falling on 10/24/26 [YM], as I know of few September and no October records elsewhere in the state).

Extreme dates east of crest: 4/10/88 7200' Tom's Place (feeder) - 9/12/89 6500' Mono Lake County Park (AB 44:158).

Additional representative nesting localities: 7200' and 7400', Yosemite Creek Trail (TB, SG); 9900' Hall Natural Area (AB 33:895; DeSante MS); 9000' near Mammoth Lakes (GM 224).

Additional reference: GS 356, C 23:136, C 27:111, C 40:93, C 41:248, D 917-921, YNN 29:46.

BROAD-TAILED HUMMINGBIRD (*Selasphorus platycercus*)

Extremely rare transient on west slope; locally rare summer resident below 8500' and rare summer visitor to treeline east of crest.

Though common to the east in the Great Basin ranges, Broad-tailed Hummingbirds are marginal pioneers in the eastern Sierra. Only in Lundy Canyon (8000'-9000') have they been found dependably, and at a feeder established in 1988 at Tom's Place (7200').

Like Calliopes, Broad-tailed Hummingbirds favor moist thickets near streams, springs, seeps and meadows, but also range onto dry, shrubby and openly wooded slopes in search of nectar-bearing flowers. In midsummer they drift to treeline; in the Hall Natural Area, for instance, they have been identified at least seven times at over 10,000' (DeSante and Engstrom MS). Undoubtedly they are also a regular but undocumented member of Yosemite National Park's subalpine avifauna.

West slope record: 8400' Olmsted Point 7/11/87 (Guy McCaskie).

High elevation record: 11,800' Hall Natural Area, male 7/4/81 (DeSante and Engstrom MS).

Extreme dates: 4/9/89 Tom's Place (CH); 5/19/85 Lundy Canyon (RH) - 8/25/91 Mono Lake County Park (John Sterling).

Known nesting localities: 8000' Lundy Canyon (AB 40:1252) and 7600' near Wildrose Canyon, Glass Mountain (AB 44:1182).

Additional references: AB 26:805, AB 29:1027, AB 30:1000, AB 31:1186, AB 35:975, AB 43:2364.

RUFOUS HUMMINGBIRD (*Selasphorus rufus*)

	J	F	M	A	M	J	J	A	S	O	N	D	HABITAT	ELEVATIONS		
														N	T	W
WEST													GSC		F-12	
EAST				•									GSC		6-12	

Fairly common spring transient in Mariposa region (2000'—CL); locally common fall (summer) transient from 4000' below treeline and uncommon fall transient above treeline on west slope; locally common fall (summer) transient below treeline and uncommon fall transient above treeline east of crest.

Our most numerous hummingbird, the Rufous, does not even nest in the Sierra Nevada. Rather they utilize the Sierra and other western mountain ranges as flowery migration routes.

Wherever paintbrush, penstemon, scarlet gilia and other "hummingbird flowers" color meadows and slopes, they gather in large, feisty aggregations. At Crane Flat (6200'), for example, I have seen at least 100 Rufous Hummingbirds disputing possession of the nectar gardens in July and August; similar concentrations have also been encountered in Yosemite Valley (4000'—YNN 10:70). These pugnacious midgets visit shrubby slopes, rock outcroppings and even fell fields far above treeline.

Because they nest so early in spring, transient Rufous Hummingbirds arrive in the region before many of our breeding birds have fledged their young. Each year, from 1988 to 1992, an early bird male visited a feeder in late April at Tom's Place and left the next day (AB 43:533). The average adult male appears by the end of June, followed several weeks later by females and juveniles. They vanish from lower elevations and well-drained slopes as conditions dry out and flowers wither.

In late August, I have watched Rufous Hummingbirds drone through a gap in the ridge above the Conness glacier (12,300'). Grinnell describes a similar migration on Mt. Parsons in early September (GS 355).

Northward-bound Rufous Hummingbirds seem to avoid all but the low, western foothills, as they have only been found in the Mariposa region (CL).

High elevation record: 12.600' Mt. Dana 8/2/78 (DG).

Extreme dates excluding Mariposa region: 6/20/86 Crane Flat (DSu) - 9/29/76 6700' Lake Vernon (DG).

Extreme spring arrivals: 4/22/90 w. shore Mono Lake (AB 44:493).

ALLEN'S HUMMINGBIRD (*Selasphorus sasin*)

Status uncertain; probably rare fall (summer) transient on west slope.

Allen's Hummingbirds—at least the males—are the scarcest of our hummingbirds. The status of females and juveniles are anybody's guess. They are so similar to Rufous that they can only be distinguished by measuring outer tail feathers. Rufous are certainly many times more numerous, but Allen's may pass unnoticed.

I know of no evidence, however, to substantiate the notion that large numbers of Allen's precede Rufous Hummingbirds over the same Sierran migration routes (C 77:196-205). Particularly inexplicable is Dixon's observation that "most of the adult males found early in the season, from June 20 to July 20, at high altitudes in the Sierra Nevada are Allen's" (C 40:264, C 45:210). In this region no one has suspected an Allen's Hummingbird for over 50 years.

Record based on collected specimen: 4000' Yosemite Valley 8/16/34—I have not been able to locate or examine this specimen; (just west of the region, *Sasin* was collected near Dudley [3000'] on 8/5/20 and 8/10/20—these specimens are in the Museum of Vertebrate Zoology, Berkeley, and appear to have been correctly identified [GS 355]; I only know of one other sighting by an experienced observer, and I consider it questionable—5000' base of Upper Yosemite Fall, six males, 8/18/30—YM).

Order CORACIIFORMES: KINGFISHERS AND ALLIES

Family ALCEDINIDAE : KINGFISHERS

BELTED KINGFISHER (*Ceryle alcyon*)

	J	F	M	A	M	J	J	A	S	O	N	D	HABITAT	ELEVATIONS N	ELEVATIONS T	ELEVATIONS W
WEST													RL	F-5	F-10	F-5
EAST													RL	6-8	6-10	6-8

Uncommon resident below 5000' and rare summer visitor and fall transient to treeline on west slope; rare resident below 8000' and rare summer visitor and fall transient to treeline east of crest.

Along freshwater lakes and languid streams, loud, tropical-sounding rattles betray the presence of Belted Kingfishers. They are partial to clear, tree-margined waters, plunging on fish from the air or riparian perches. They sometimes stray to Mono Lake (6400'), but sour on the fishing. Young are cradled in burrows excavated in friable earthen or sandy banks. If suitable sites were not so scarce, halcyons would grace more Sierran waters.

High elevation: 10,200' Hall Natural Area, many records (DeSante MS).

Extreme dates above 5000' west slope and 8000' east: 7/15/79 Hall Natural Area (DeSante MS) - 10/28/86 8600' Tuolumne Meadows (DS, SJ); 12/25/76 9600' Tioga Lake (YM); 12/31/76 8600' Tuolumne Meadows (YM).

Representative nesting localities: 4000' Yosemite Valley (GS 315, YNN 4:64); 7000' Convict Creek (GD).

Additional reference: C 27:111.

Order PICIFORMES: WOODPECKERS AND ALLIES

Family PICIDAE: WOODPECKERS AND ALLIES

Twelve woodpeckers nest in our region, Pileated and Black-backeds only on the west slope, and Lewis' Woodpeckers only to the east. Most winter in their breeding haunts, even at high elevations, subsisting on bark beetles and other wood-boring insects. Sapsuckers, flickers and Lewis' woodpeckers, which feed on sap, fruit and aerial insects, migrate to lower elevations or balmier climes.

Except for Black-backeds, all our woodpeckers require dead, decayed trees or snags in which to gouge out commodious nesting cavities. Last years' domiciles are appropriated by birds and animals such as small owls, swallows, nuthatches, chickadees, bluebirds, chipmunks and flying squirrels. Hence the survival of woodpeckers and the health and diversity of forest ecosystems depends, not just on living trees, but on dead ones as well.

I have treated "Red-shafted" and "Yellow-shafted" Northern Flickers separately, as they are readily recognized subpecies.

LEWIS' WOODPECKER (*Melanerpes lewis*)

	J	F	M	A	M	J	J	A	S	O	N	D	HABITAT	ELEVATIONS		
														N	T	W
WEST	•					•	•						OPW		F-10	2
EAST											•		PW	7-8	6-10	

Irregularly rare to fairly common winter resident in Mariposa region (2000'—CL); irregularly rare spring transient below 5000', irregularly rare fall transient below and occasionally above treeline and extremely rare winter visitor elsewhere on west slope; locally fairly common summer resident below 8000' and irregularly rare fall transient to and occasionally above treeline east of crest.

Lewis' favor more open habitats than most woodpeckers, for they nab their meals, not by drilling into bark, but mostly by flycatching. East of the crest, they invariably nest among the open stands of jeffrey pine that extend from the glacial moraines of Sierran canyon mouths east beyond the Mono Craters and Glass Mountain. Except during migration, they shun steep slopes as well as narrow canyons.

On the west slope and in the higher mountains, Lewis' Woodpeckers are decidedly irregular. Some years many are seen, in most few or none at all.

During winter and migrations, Lewis' Woodpeckers visit hardwoods as well as conifers, especially oaks, but still prefer open woodlands or the edges of meadows, lakes

Lewis' Woodpecker, courtesy Discovering Sierra Birds

and openings. In late summer, they often feast in apple orchards. A small grove will attract wanderers to isolated ranches and springs.

Over sixty years ago, on 9/11/25, Enid Michael witnessed an incredible migration of Lewis' Woodpeckers at 11,000': "through the narrow pass east of Foerster Peak, where the birds could be easily counted, 195 birds crossed the pass in 15 minutes, and for hours the birds continued to stream through the pass at about the same rate" (EM 5). Thousands must have crossed the flank of Foerster Peak that day. Where could they all have come from? Where were they bound?

Winter record excluding Mariposa region west slope: approximately 6000' Turner Ridge 1/11/76 (YM).

Extreme dates below 5000' west slope excluding Mariposa region and winter record: 5/2/26 4000' Yosemite Valley (YM) - 6/5/39 (YNN 18:101); 7/5/39 Yosemite Valley (YM); 7/22/41 Yosemite Valley (YM) - 4600' Ackerson Meadow, 6, 9/23/80 (JW).

Extreme dates above 5000' west slope or above 8500' east of crest: 7/22/41 7000' Horse Ridge (YNN 21:22) - 9/25/85 8600' Tuolumne Meadows (MR).

Extreme dates east of crest, all Mono Lake County Park (6400'): 4/3/86 (DG) - 10/13/79 (DG); 11/5/87 (Sally Gaines).

Representative nesting localities: approx. 7000' Long Valley (Jour. Mus. Comp. Oology 2:52); 7000' ne. of Mono Craters (DG); 7800' Oh! Ridge (DG); 8000' Walker Lake (GS 341).

Additional references: AFN 15:491, YNN 18:101, YNN 30:94.

ACORN WOODPECKER (*Melanerpes formicivorus*)

	J	F	M	A	M	J	J	A	S	O	N	D	HABITAT	ELEVATIONS		
														N	T	W
WEST	█	█	█	█	█	█	█	█	█	█	█	█	OP	F-5		F-5
EAST						•		•	•				P		7-10	

Common resident below 4500', uncommon resident to 5500' and extremely rare transient at higher elevations on west slope; extremely rare transient east of crest.

As their name implies, Acorn Woodpeckers are intimately dependent on oaks. They favor open woodlands and savannahs with mature live, black or blue oaks, often mixed with ponderosa pines, white firs, incense cedars and other conifers. On the other hand, they shun dense forests, including the shady groves of canyon oaks that clothe steep slopes.

Unlike others of their clan, Acorn Woodpeckers do not drill into bark after insects, but gather acorns, sally for aerial insects and even sapsuck. They dwell in small, clamorous groups of four to eight individuals, cooperatively harvesting acorns, defending acorn stores, excavating roosting and nesting cavities and raising young. During autumn, they whack tens of thousands of acorns into storage holes in ponderosa pines, incense cedars and, rarely, telephone poles or buildings. They favor dead trees and snags for storage bins, as decaying bark is easier to quarry.

If the acorn crop fails, Acorn Woodpeckers temporarily desert parts of their range. In 1943, for instance, they vacated Yosemite Valley (4000') after a two-year acorn famine (YNN 22:25).

In Yosemite Valley, Acorn Woodpeckers winter in the black oak groves on the sunnier, north side of the Merced River; in spring, some take up quarters on the south side as well (YNN 18:105-107).

Records above 5500' and east of crest: 8400' Olmsted Point 9/7/87 (DWi); 8600' Tuolumne Meadows 8/22/78 (HF); 7200' Tom's Place 6/5-6/89 (AB: 1364); 9900' Hall Natural Area 8/3/77 (DeSante and Engstrom MS); 6800' Lee Vining 8/23/85 (DG); 7300' Mono Mills 9/23/88 (HG).

Representative nesting localities: 2000' Mariposa (CL); 2100' El Portal (DG); 4000' Yosemite Valley (GS 337, YNN 15:44); 4700' near Eleanor Lake Reservoir (DG).

Additional references: C 28:68, C 38:125, YNN 18:105, YNN 19:35, YNN 20:15.

RED-NAPED SAPSUCKER (*Sphyrapicus nuchalis*)

Rare winter resident below 4000' and extremely rare summer visitor at higher elevations on west slope; extremely rare spring transient, summer resident, winter visitor and rare fall transient east of crest.

Like closely related Red-breasteds, with which they occasionally hybridize, Red-naped Sapsuckers favor deciduous woodlands, especially aspens, willows and cottonwoods. They also visit apple orchards and residential neighborhoods.

On the east slope reported sightings throughout the calendar year have increased since 1988; February, May and November being the only bare months. Nesting has been verified at Emma Lake (8800'), upper Rock Creek (AB 43:1364).

Summer record west slope: 7000' Bridalveil Creek 6/27/26 (YNN 7:56).

Extreme dates west excluding summer record, both Yosemite Valley (4000'): 11/19/15 (GS 330) - 4/?/24 (YM).

RED-BREASTED SAPSUCKER (*Sphyrapicus ruber*)

	J	F	M	A	M	J	J	A	S	O	N	D	HABITAT	ELEVATIONS		
														N	T	W
WEST													WOP	4-8	F-10	F-4
EAST													WP	6-10	6-10	6

Locally fairly common summer resident from 4000' to 8000', irregularly rare to uncommon summer visitor and fall transient to treeline, uncommon winter resident below 3000' and rare winter resident from 3000' to 4500' on west slope; common summer resident below 8000', irregularly rare to uncommon summer visitor and fall transient to treeline, and extremely rare winter visitor below 8000' east of crest.

During the warmer months, wherever there are aspens, willows, cottonwoods, alders and other hardwoods, one finds Red-breasted Sapsuckers drilling for sap or sallying for insects like overgrown flycatchers. Unlike Williamson's Sapsuckers, they rarely drill into conifers.

While hardwoods are de rigueur, Red-breasted Sapsuckers are at home in mixed forests dominated by sugar pines, ponderosa pines, white firs, red firs, lodgepole pines and other conifers. They favor the wooded margins of meadows, lakes, streams and other openings, where there are usually hardwoods as well as plentiful aerial insects. Thickets of willow lure them into meadows. East of the crest, "strawberry-heads" are conspicuous denizens of aspen groves and willow thickets, often far from the nearest conifer.

Though transient and wintering Red-breasted Sapsuckers range outside their breeding haunts, they remain loyal to hardwoods. They drill rows of characteristic sap holes into oaks as well as orchard trees, bay trees and many ornamentals. When the weather turns cold, they trade the higher mountains for lower elevations and balmier climes with flowing sap and bountiful insects.

From summer into early autumn, Red-breasted Sapsuckers disperse irregularly both up and down slope. At 10,000' in the Hall Natural Area, for example, they are frequent during some years, absent during most (DeSante MS). Conversely, at 4000' in Yosemite Valley, where they rarely if ever nest, there is usually an influx in midsummer (YM; YNN 18:102).

High elevation record: 10,000' Hall Natural Area, many records (DeSante MS).

Winter records east of crest, all w. shore of Mono Lake: 12/31/77 (DW), 12/29/79, 2 (AB 34:652) and 12/28/82 (DG, AB 37:760).

Extreme dates above 8000', all Hall Natural Area (10,000'): 5/29/81; 6/30/75 - 10/14/78 (DeSante MS).

Extreme dates east of crest excluding winter records: 3/27/82 7400' Lee Vining Canyon (BE) - 10/14/84 6800' Lee Vining (DG).

Representative nesting localities: 4400' Big Meadow (SG), 4600' Ackerson Meadow (JW), 5200' Miguel Meadow (YM), approx. 8000' near Sentinel Dome (YM), 8100' Glacier Point Road (AFN 10:407), approx. 7500' Mammoth Creek (C 41:248), 7400' Lee Vining Canyon (DG), 6400' Mono Lake County Park (DG), 10,600' Hall Natural Area (AB 45:1158, DDeS brags this is a world record for nesting elevation!).

Summer record west slope: 7000' Bridalveil Creek 6/27/26 (YNN 7:56).

Extreme dates west excluding summer record, both Yosemite Valley (4000'): 11/19/15 (GS 330) - 4/?/24 (YM).

Additional references: AB 38:354, GS 327, C 27:111.

(RED-BREASTED X RED-NAPED SAPSUCKER)

Hybrids of these two closely related sapsuckers were observed on the west slope at Ackerson Meadow (4600') on 7/25/78 (JW), and east of the crest near Mono Lake (6400') on 6/6/83 (AB 37:1024) and in Lee Vining (6800') on 8/29/85 (JD). In 1974, a male Red-breasted mated with a female Red-naped in Lee Vining Canyon (7400'—WB 4:107-108).

WILLIAMSON'S SAPSUCKER (*Sphyrapicus thyroideus*)

	J	F	M	A	M	J	J	A	S	O	N	D	HABITAT	ELEVATIONS		
														N	T	W
WEST	—	—	—	—	—	—	—	—	—	—	—	—	P	7-9	6-10	4-6
EAST				—	—	—	—	—	—	—		·	P	7-9	6-10	7-8

Extremely rare summer visitor below 7000', uncommon summer resident from 7000' to 9000', rare summer visitor to treeline, extremely rare summer visitor above treeline, uncommon winter resident from 4000' to 6000' and extremely rare winter visitor at lower and higher elevations on west slope; uncommon summer resident from 7000' to 9000', rare summer visitor to treeline and apparently extremely rare winter resident east of crest.

Compared to Red-breasteds, Williamson's Sapsuckers dwell at higher elevations, and tap conifers rather than hardwoods. Within their altitudinally circumscribed breeding range, they dwell on dry, rocky, openly-wooded ridges as well as in moist densely-forested valley bottoms. They favor lodgepole pines, mountain white pines, mountain hemlocks and jeffrey pines, but have also bred among red firs.

For some reason, Williamson's Sapsuckers do not nest in subalpine forests. I know of no nesting records above 9200', though a mountaineering male reached 12,000' on Stanton Peak on 8/19/81 (MR), and they visit the Hall Natural Area (10,000') every summer (DeSante MS).

Though the scientific literature classifies Williamson's Sapsuckers as year-round residents in their breeding range (e.g. GM 237), I believe they are primarily short-distance migrants, at least in this region. If they didn't migrate, they could not suck sap during sub-freezing weather. On the west slope, I know of only two winter records above 6000'; east of the crest, but two anywhere. Below 5000', in contrast, they have been found numerous times between November and March in mixed oak and conifer forests, including high counts of five in Yosemite Valley (4000') on 11/5/23 (YM) and eight near Big Meadow (4600') on 12/23/73 (DG). At Tuolumne Meadows, the winter ranger—an experienced birder—first saw this sapsucker in early May of 1975 and 1976 (TH).

The winter whereabouts of Williamson's Sapsuckers east of the crest is a much greater mystery. Perhaps they vanish into pinyon pine woodlands at lower elevations to the south and east. During the latter half of September, they have appeared outside their breeding haunts in residential Lee Vining (6800'—RS, LH) and along the west shore of Mono Lake (6500'—PM).

Record below 4000': 3200' Chowchilla Mountain, female, 11/21/81 (MR).

Winter records above 6000' on west slope: 6500' Deer Camp, 2, 12/16/35; 7000' near Badger Pass 12/30/66 (YM).

Winter records east of crest: approx. 8000' Gibbs Canyon 12/31/82 (AB 37:760); 7400' Lee Vining Canyon 12/31/86 (TH).

Summer records below 7000': 4000' Yosemite Valley 6/7/43 (YM); 6200' Crane Flat 6/20/86 (DSu).

Extreme dates above 6000' excluding winter records: 3/9/76 8600' Tuolumne Meadows (YM); 3/20/27 9400' Lembert Dome, eating juniper berries and sapsucking (YNN 6:21) - approx. 10,000' Hall Natural Area 10/17/78 (DeSante MS); 8000' Deadman Creek, two males 10/25/87 (DG).

Extreme dates below 6000': 9/23/80 4600' Ackerson Meadow (JW) - 3/20/27 Yosemite Valley (YM).

Representative nesting localities: 7000' Bridalveil Creek (DG); 7400' Harden Lake (YNN 32:40); 7800' White Wolf (DG); 8600' Tuolumne Meadows (GS 331); 9200' Minaret Summit (DG); 9000' Virginia Lakes (C 41:248); 8500' Mammoth Lakes (T&JH); 8500' n. of Glass Mountain (DG).

Additional references: EM 5, YNN 29:46, YNN 40:148.

NUTTALL'S WOODPECKER (*Picoides nuttallii*)

	J	F	M	A	M	J	J	A	S	O	N	D	HABITAT	ELEVATIONS		
														N	T	W
WEST													OWP	F-3		F-4
EAST													W		6-7	

Fairly common resident below 3000', rare resident or visitor to 5000' and extremely rare visitor at higher elevations on west slope; irregularly rare fall visitor (0-2/year) below 7000' east of Sierran escarpment.

Among the blue and live oaks of the western foothills, Nuttall's Woodpeckers are noisy nesting birds. They dwell as well among large cottonwoods that line languid streams, and in orchards. East of the crest, they stray to cottonwoods and willows as well as apple trees.

After the nesting season, some Nuttall's Woodpeckers, perhaps juveniles, wander upslope into the relatively dense mixed oak and conifer forests. In Yosemite Valley (4000'), for example, they occur from mid-summer until the end of winter, but then disappear. Here is a bird that winters, in small numbers at least, above its nesting range.

Records above 5000' on west slope: 7000' Peregoy Meadow 6/18/73 (AB 27:905); 8400' Devil's Postpile National Monument 9/18/80 (AB 35:222); (in the southern Sierra, Nuttall's Woodpecker has wandered to 11,500'—AB 35:975).

Extreme dates in Yosemite Valley: 8/13/76 (YM) - 3/5/51 (YM).

Extreme dates east of crest, five records since 1982: 9/10/84 6800' Lee Vining (DG) - 12/22/84 6800' Mono Lake County Park, 2 (AB 39:789).

Representative nesting localities: 2000' Mariposa (CL); 2100' El Portal (DG); (3800' Hetch Hetchy—DG); 4500' near Mather (MM).

Additional references: EM 5, GS 319, YNN 10:23.

DOWNY WOODPECKER (*Picoides pubescens*)

	J	F	M	A	M	J	J	A	S	O	N	D	HABITAT	ELEVATIONS		
														N	T	W
WEST													W	F-4	F-7	F-4
EAST													W	6-7		6-7

Uncommon resident below 4000', rare summer and visitor or fall transient to 7500' and extremely rare transient at higher elevations on west slope; uncommon resident near west shore of Mono Lake (6400') and rare resident below 7500' elsewhere east of crest.

More than any of their relatives, Downy Woodpeckers are wedded to deciduous groves and thickets, dwelling among willows, cottonwoods, alders and dogwoods. While they usually reside along languid streams or about seeps and springs, they also forage in orchards and even in stout herbaceous vegetation, such as mullein. Less frequently, they range into oaks or conifers; a pair at Foresta (4400') nested in a black oak within 20 feet of a small stream (SG). In order to excavate nesting and roosting cavities, these diminutive peckers must find dead trees or snags well advanced in decay.

Being small does have its drawbacks. On 7/8/41, Charles Michael encountered a Downy Woodpecker in the throes of being swallowed by a Yosemite Valley rattlesnake (YM).

Records above 7500': 7800' near Smoky Jack 10/18/76 (SG); 8000' Siesta Lake 9/14/80 (HF); 8600' Tuolumne Meadows 6/29/79 (MR).

Extreme dates above 5000' west slope: 6/29/79 Tuolumne Meadow (MR) - 10/18/76 7800' near Smoky Jack (SG).

Additional representative nesting localities: (2000' El Portal—DG); 4000' Yosemite Valley (GS 318); 4600' Ackerson Meadow (JW); 7400' Lee Vining Canyon (Robert Calhoun); 6400' Mono Lake County Park (DG).

HAIRY WOODPECKER (*Picoides villosus*)

	J	F	M	A	M	J	J	A	S	O	N	D	HABITAT	ELEVATIONS		
														N	T	W
WEST	■	■	■	■	■	■	■	■	■	■	■	■	POW	3-10		3-10
EAST	■	■	■	■	■	■	■	■	■	■	■	■	POW	6-10		6-10

Fairly common resident from 3000' to treeline on west slope, but irregular at high elevations in winter; fairly common resident to treeline east of crest.

Mature timber and dead snags or trees of moderate to large size are more important to Hairy Woodpeckers then forest type or elevation. No other forest-dwelling woodpeckers are so catholic in choice of habitat. They nest in dense forests as well as open groves, foraging in living and dead conifers as well as oaks, cottonwoods, willows and orchard trees.

Hairy Woodpeckers are hardy, and winter regularly at high elevations (e.g. 10,000' Hall Natural Area—AB 33:310, DeSante MS). During times of scant food supply, however, they retreat downslope. During the winter of 1974-75, for example, they were numerous at Tuolumne Meadows (8600'), but during the milder winter the following year, only one was seen (TH).

High elevation record: 10,200' Hall Natural Area, many records (DeSante MS).

Representative nesting localities: 4000' Yosemite Valley (GS 317); 6200' Crane Flat (DG); 9000' Dog Lake (YM); 10,200' Hall Natural Area (DeSante MS); 7400' Lee Vining Canyon (DG); 6400' Mono Lake County Park (DG).

WHITE-HEADED WOOPECKER (*Picoides albolarvatus*)

	J	F	M	A	M	J	J	A	S	O	N	D	HABITAT	ELEVATIONS		
														N	T	W
WEST	━	━	━	━	━	━	━	━	━	━	━	━	P	4-8		4-8
EAST													P	7-9		7-9

Fairly common resident from 3000' to 8000' on west slope; rare resident from 7000' to 8500' and extremely rare resident or visitor at higher elevations east of crest.

Among sugar and ponderosa pines, white and red firs, sequoias, incense cedars and black oaks, White-headed Woodpeckers are sometimes so trusting that every park visitor asks their name. Even their nests, which are excavated in the soft, decayed wood of dead trees or snags, are often low and conspicuous. In the Hodgdon Meadow Campground (4600'), for instance, I once found a pair feeding young in a sawed-off round of pine about three feet in diameter and two feet high; I could have lifted up the nesting "tree" and carted it away.

White-headed Woodpeckers dwell in mature, mixed coniferous forests with trees of moderate to large girth. They do not range below the oak-conifer belt, and are extremely rare above the red firs on the west slope and the jeffrey and western white pines east of the crest; they have yet to be recorded, for example, at Tuolumne Meadows (8600'). Though they depend on dead trees or snags for nesting sites, they prefer dining on the bark of living trees. While wedded to conifers, I have also found them in large cottonwoods in Yosemite Valley (4000') and in aspen groves east of the Sierran escarpment (e.g., 7100' McGee Creek).

Records above 8100', all east of crest: 10,500' Hall Natural Area 8/3/87 (DeSante and Engstrom MS); 10,300' Hall Natural Area 10/9/77 (DeSante and Engstrom MS); approx. 10,000' Hall Natural Area 7/18/76 (DSt, DeSante and Engstrom MS); 9000' Virginia Lakes, "several nests," 1939 (C 41:249).

Additional representative nesting localities: 4000' Yosemite Valley (GS 320-236); 6000' Little Yosemite Valley (YM); 6200' Crane Flat (DG); 7100' near Gin Flat (TB); 8100' near Siesta Lake (SH); 8000' Mammoth Lakes (DG, JD).

Additional reference: YNN 19:54.

BLACK-BACKED WOODPECKER (*Picoides arcticus*)

	J	F	M	A	M	J	J	A	S	O	N	D	HABITAT	ELEVATIONS		
														N	T	W
WEST													P	7-9		7-9
EAST			•		•	•	•		•			•			8-10	

Rare resident from 6500' to 9000' and extremely rare visitor at lower and higher elevations on west slope; extremely rare visitor east of crest.

Black-backed Woodpeckers belong, with Great Gray Owls and Pine Grosbeaks, to a select company of boreal birds that range south into the mountains of central California. Our scarcest nesting woodpeckers, they dwell in lodgepole pines and, less frequently, mountain white pines, mountain hemlocks or red firs.

Over the years, I have found Black-backed Woodpeckers nesting in habitats ranging from openly wooded granite ridges to dense, shady forests. But nowhere have I found these reclusive birds dependably. I suspect they wander from year to year, settling down to nest in areas infested with the larval bark insects that are their primary fare. In 1977 and 1978, for example, they nested below their usual haunts in a partially burned fir forest near Crane Flat (6400'—SG).

Except for the importunities of hungry nestlings, Black-backed Woodpeckers are quiet birds. Often only the sound of methodical drilling betrays their presence to attentive ears. Yet, once found, they are trusting, approachable fowl. Nor do they shun the company of humans, sometimes raising young in the midst of bustling campgrounds.

Unlike other woodpeckers, Black-backeds usually excavate nesting cavities in the trunks of living conifers, stripping the bark from around the hole. These distinctive domiciles are another clue to their often invisible presence.

High elevation record west slope: approx. 9000' trail to Young Lakes 6/9/85 (RH).

Records below 6400': 6200' Little Yosemite Valley 8/8/55 (YM); 6200' Crane Flat 2/23/78 (YM) and 10/1/82 (YM); 4600' near Hodgdon Meadow, 3, 1/16/77 (TB); 4600' Ackerson Meadow 7/26/80 (JW); 4000' Yosemite Valley 8/3/68 (YM).

Records east of crest: 9900' Hall Natural Area, mid-July/74 (MC, DeSante and Engstrom MS); 8600' Mammoth Lakes 5/15/82 (DG) and 12/?/84 (Larry Abbott); 8000' Obsidian Dome 3/10/87 (DG); 7800' Lundy Lake 6/30/81 (MM); 7600' Crestview, 2, 9/15,27/90 (ESt).

Additional representative nesting localities: 7000' Bridalveil Creek (GS 326-327); 7600' Mt. Watkins, in burned area where most trees were dead (SG); 7600' Devil's Postpile National Monument (GF); 8000' Siesta Lake (RS, DG); 8200' Lukens Lake (SH); 8500' Ostrander Lake (YM).

Additional references: AFN 13:452, AFN 17:482, AB 26:652, AB 27:660, YNN 15:20.

"RED-SHAFTED" NORTHERN FLICKER
(*Colaptes auratus cafer*)

	J	F	M	A	M	J	J	A	S	O	N	D	HABITAT	ELEVATIONS		
														N	T	W
WEST													WOPG	F-10	F-13	F-5
EAST													WPG	6-10	6-13	6-8

Fairly common summer resident to treeline, rare summer visitor above treeline and irregularly uncommon to fairly common winter resident below 5000' on west slope; fairly common summer resident to treeline, rare summer visitor above treeline and irregularly rare to fairly common winter resident below 8000' east of crest.

Of all our woodpeckers, Northern Flickers are the least specialized and most widespread, dwelling in a wide range of habitats from the foothills to, and occasionally above, treeline. No other member of their family cavorts with Rosy Finches near the summits of lofty peaks. But their favored haunts are not alpine fell-fields, but meadows, grasslands and openly wooded terrain. For unlike other woodpeckers, they forage not only in trees, but beneath them and in the open as well.

During the nesting season, Northern Flickers are partial to cottonwoods, aspens and orchards, but dwell among oaks and conifers as well. Later in the summer and into autumn, they join other birds in feasting on the fleshy fruits of elderberries, dogwoods and other trees and shrubs. In migration and winter, they may forsake trees entirely, ranging into meadows, marshes, hills and scrub far from the nearest timber. At Mono Lake, for example, they frequently perch on tufa towers.

In autumn and winter, numbers of Northern Flickers vary dramatically from year to year, probably in response to weather and food conditions. In some years an influx of northern birds swells the population to the point they are locally "common." In others they vanish almost entirely. Numbers on the Mono Lake Christmas Bird Count, for example, have varied from 48 to 4. In general, eastside and high mountain populations thin as wintry weather intensifies; most return to valleys in April and to higher elevations in May.

High elevation record: 13,000' Mt. Dana 7/20/57 (YM).

Extreme dates above 5000' west slope and 8000' east of crest: 3/17/77 9100' Dog Lake (YM); 3/26/80 10,300' Hall Natural Area (DeSante MS); 4/30/76 8600' Tuolumne Meadows (YM) - 10/24/77 10,300' Hall Natural Area (DeSante MS); 12/6/55 11,000' Parker Pass (YM).

Representative nesting localities: 4000' Yosemite Valley (GS 343); 4600' Ackerson Meadow (JW); 6400' Mariposa Grove (YM); 8600' Tuolumne Meadows (DG); 10,000'+ Hall Natural Area (DeSante MS); 7400' Lee Vining Canyon (DG); 7200' Convict Creek (C 41:248); 6400' Mono Lake County Park (DG).

"YELLOW-SHAFTED" NORTHERN FLICKER
(*Colaptes auratus auratus*)

Extremely rare vagrant both west and east of crest.

Records: 2100' El Portal 12/28/57 (YNN 37:4); 4600' Ackerson Meadow 4/7/87 (JW); 11,200' Hall Natural Area 9/26/81 (DeSante and Engstrom MS); 10,200' Hall Natural Area 10/13/78 (AB 33:211, DeSante and Engstrom MS); (an intergrade was observed in Yosemite Valley [4000'] on 2/10/69—YM).

PILEATED WOODPECKER (*Dryocopus pileatus*)

	J	F	M	A	M	J	J	A	S	O	N	D	HABITAT	ELEVATIONS		
														N	T	W
WEST	—	—	—	—	—	—	—	—	—	—	—	—	POW	3-7		3-7
EAST								•								

Uncommon resident from 3000' to 7000', rare visitor to 8000' and extremely rare visitor at higher elevations on west slope. Extremely rare vagrant to the east side.

Of all our woodpeckers, Pileateds are the most woodsy. These retiring dryads dwell in old-growth forests with an abundance of large, decayed standing and fallen timber. They favor sugar pines, red and white firs, douglas firs and sequoias, but also dwell among black oaks and cottonwoods; the size and state of the trees, rather than the species, are the deciding factors.

Pileated Woodpeckers are homebodies, rarely straying outside their nesting range in the oak-conifer and red fir belts. Along the Tioga Road, they follow red firs as high as 7900' (SH), but have been seen but once among the lodgepole pines of loftier climes.

From mid-summer into autumn, Pileated Woodpeckers spice their invertebrate diets with the fruits of elderberry, dogwood and other lithe trees. I watched these heavy, crow-sized birds try to balance chickadee-like on the tips of swaying, berry-laden limbs (YNN 33:50, C 30:157).

Though our largest woodpeckers, Pileateds are furtive and elusive. The forests abound with evidence of their presence—large, rectangular tree excavations, stripped bark and piles of chips and flakes. But to know, intimately, these cocks-of-the-woods, requires patience and grace.

Record above 8000': 8600' Tuolumne Meadows 8/7/87 (MR).

Representative nesting localities: 4000' Yosemite Valley and 4200' Mirror Lake (GS 334, YM); 4600' Ackerson Meadow (JW); 6200' Crane Flat (DDeS, DG); 6900' near Yosemite Point (GS 334); 7200' Glacier Point (YM).

Records for east side: 7100' Mono Mills 8/26/90 (Arlene Reveal); 8200" Green Creek Campground 8/6/90 (Pat Dickinson, fide PM).

Additional references: AFN 13:452; AB 23:622; YNN 29:46.

Order PASSERIFORMES: PASSERINE BIRDS

Family TYRANNIDAE: TYRANT FLYCATCHERS

While many kinds of birds sally from perches in pursuit of airborne prey, our 15 species of tyrant flycatchers are full-time professionals. Eleven nest in our area, and their unique habitat preferences are often a help in identifying similar species. When the days are warm and the air alive with humming and buzzing insects, they chase down meals from conspicuous perches. Because they depend on a seasonal food supply, most winter in subtropical Mexico and Middle America, leaving the mountains in August and returning the following May.

OLIVE-SIDED FLYCATCHER (*Contopus borealis*)

	J	F	M	A	M	J	J	A	S	O	N	D	HABITAT	ELEVATIONS		
														N	T	W
WEST									•				PO	3-9	F-10	
EAST													P	7-9	6-10	

Uncommon transient below 3000', fairly common summer resident from 3000' to 7000', uncommon summer resident to 9000' and rare summer visitor and fall transient to treeline on west slope; uncommon summer resident below 9000' and rare summer visitor and fall transient to treeline east of crest.

Of all our forest flycatchers, Olive-sideds dwell closest to heaven, perching habitually in the dead tips or uppermost branches of lofty trees. From their towering look-outs, they venture on long sallies after flying insects, often returning to the same perch time after time. Compared to other flycatchers, they sally less frequently but chase down larger prey.

The physiognomy of a forest is less important to Olive-sided Flycatchers than the amount of space that can be scanned from its highest perches. They dwell, not only in dense, old-growth forests, but also where scattered tall timber overlooks saplings, chaparral or even bare rock. All kinds of trees serve as perch and nest sites, but ponderosa pines, sugar pines, douglas firs and white and red firs are especially favored. They nest in most forested habitats except subalpine forests and, east of the crest, jeffrey pine forests and pinyon woodlands. Transients appear wherever there are trees, including towns and isolated groves.

The clear, loud calls of Olive-sided Flycatchers, ringing from the woods on a morning in May, announce the return of a distant traveler. Among Sierran flycatchers, only Olive-sideds and Western Wood-Pewees winter south of Central America.

Extreme dates: 4/29/85 4600' Ackerson Meadow (JW) - 9/12/77 8000' Mammoth Lakes (DG).

Representative nesting localities: 4000' Yosemite Valley (YM); 4500' Hodgdon Meadow (MM); 6200' Crane Flat (DG); 7400' Dewey Point Ski Trail (SH); (8200' below Olmsted Point—DG); (9500' Lee Vining Creek—DDeS); (8000' Lundy Canyon—DG).

Additional references: AFN 11:56, C 38:86, GS 364, YNN 3:3.

WESTERN WOOD-PEWEE (*Contopus sordidulus*)

	J	F	M	A	M	J	J	A	S	O	N	D	HABITAT	ELEVATIONS		
														N	T	W
WEST													POW	3-9	F-9	
EAST													PW	6-9		

Uncommon transient below 3000', common summer resident from 3000' to 9000' and rare summer visitor to treeline on west slope; common summer resident below 9000' and rare summer visitor to treeline east of crest.

Of all our flycatchers, Western Wood-Pewees are the most numerous, ubiquitous and conspicuous. They nest in nearly every timbered habitat within their elevational range, shunning only the deeply-shaded interiors of dense forests on one extreme, and arid pinyon woodlands on the other. Where the woods are dense, they dwell along the edges of meadows, streams, lakes and other openings. They live among hardwoods as well as conifers, nesting, for example, in ponderosa pine-black oak woodlands, mixed conifer forests, lodgepole pine forests, riparian cottonwood-willow forests and aspen groves. Transients are even more widespread, appearing wherever there are trees or large shrubs, including woodlands and towns.

Western Wood-Pewees choose conspicuous lookout posts at middle heights beneath the crowns of trees. They also perch on the tops of small to medium-sized trees as well as on fallen logs and stout herbaceous plants. Their sallies take them farther from foliage than their *Empidonax* relatives, but not so far as the larger Olive-sideds'.

From May into August, our forests have no more constant voice than that of Western Wood-Pewees. From dawn until dusk their lugubrious calls toll the passing hours. Yet, to mated pairs, these nasal drawls bespeak comradeship and courage, for few small birds defend their nests and young so vigorously against jays, hawks, chipmunks and other predators. And well they might, for pewees take scant pains to conceal their nests, saddling them on horizontal limbs with little or no leafy cover. No skulking in the shadows for these birds! They advertise their presence by voice and behavior, and challenge the world to welcome their fellowship.

Extreme dates: 4/26/80 Big Meadow (GSt) - 10/3/83 6500' w. shore Mono Lake (DS).

Representative nesting localities: 3000' Chowchilla Mountain (MR); 4000' Yosemite Valley (GS 365); 4600' Ackerson Meadow (JW); 6200' Crane Flat (TB); 6400' Mariposa Grove (YM); 8600' Tuolumne Meadow (DG); 10,000' Virginia Lake (C 41:249); 8000' Mammoth Lakes (DG); 7400' Lee Vining Canyon (DG).

Additional references: AB 34:812, EM 6, GS 365.

EMPIDONAX FLYCATCHERS

Some of the small Sierran flycatchers, especially the five species of the genus *Empidonax*, the "gnat kings," are so similar that most birdwatchers despair of telling them apart. When Theodore Roosevelt met John Muir, he reputedly asked, "How does one distinguish the Hammond from the Dusky Flycatcher?" Muir, who knew more about rocks than birds, probably had no idea. Yet these gnat kings and their relatives differ enough in voice, behavior, habitat and plumage to be recognizable to cognoscenti, especially in their breeding haunts.

Until the 1983 publication of the National Geographic Society's *Field Guide to the Birds of North America*, however, the guides were more confusing that helpful. In the National Geographic, the excellent text concisely covers the basics, and the illustrations, if not outstanding, are at least serviceable. Without repeating what is there, I will proffer some additional advice on learning to recognize songs and calls.

Singing, territorial *Empidonax* are best recognized by voice and habitat. The high pitched, whistled "su-wheet" of the Western, the sneezy "fitz-bew" of the Willow and vigorous "chi-bit" of the Gray, though difficult to verbalize, are easily distinguished. Even the songs of Hammond's and Duskys are discernably different to the experienced ear, even though many a birdwatcher, after reading in Peterson's *Field Guide to Western Birds* that "the author can hear no great difference," despairs of succeeding where the master has failed. In fact their voices are easier to identify than some of the warblers.

Describing bird sounds in words, however, is almost impossible. One can "tsui-i-i-p," "tseep," and "prrddrt" for page after page, and still not convey a difference in tone that is obvious to the trained ear. One's best strategy, then is to identify singing, territorial birds in late spring and early summer based on their choice of habitat, and listen persistently to their voices.

If your perception is similar to mine, the songs of Hammond's will sound, overall, "burred" or "sneezy" in comparison to the cleaner Dusky. With Hammond's, the sneezy notes predominate; with Duskys, you wait for those notes. Other parts of their repertoires are also distinctive. Hammond's, for example, have sharp "peek" calls that are reminiscent of Pygmy Nuthatches. Duskys sometimes utter plaintive whistled and short emphatic notes that have been transcribed as "tee, tee, tee-hick"(H208). If you get confused, don't despair, keep listening, and the "gnat kings" will gradually turn from tiresome little flycatchers into unique avian personalities.

WILLOW FLYCATCHER (*Empidonax traillii*)

Formerly fairly common; now locally rare summer resident from 4000' to 5000' and extremely rare at higher elevations on west slope; locally rare summer resident below 8000' and extremely rare at higher elevations on east slope.

Once considered "common" in our region, Willow Flycatchers have become our scarcest nesting tyrannid. I doubt that more than 30 pairs still nest in scattered, mid-elevation meadows and canyonbottoms both west and east of the crest.

Willow Flycatchers were not always sparse. Until at least the 1930s, in suitable habitat, they were vocal, conspicuous birds below 5000' west of the crest and below 8000' to the east. Enid Michael, for example, called them "common" nesters in Yosemite Valley (4000'—YNN 3(6):3), and Ralph Hoffmann said "their song mingles with that of the Lincoln's Sparrow in open mountain meadows, as in Yosemite" (H 206). But that is rarely the case today.

While the Sierra's Willow Flycatchers have dwindled to the brink of extinction, their confreres in the rest of California have fared even worse. Once among the commonest birds along the willow-choked waterways of the lowlands and foothills, they have disappeared almost entirely. The marginal mountain populations, of which the largest are to our south on the south fork Kern River and to our north on the Truckee River, are their last stand; probably less than 150 pairs remain in the entire Sierra Nevada, and very few more in the rest of California (Serena 1982, JH).

While Willow Flycatchers have not been found nesting in Yosemite Valley since 1966 (DDeS), they continue to return to Wawona (4000'), Hodgdon Meadow (4600') and especially Ackerson Meadow (4600') each year; the latter site has harbored up to eight pairs, but only four remained in 1986 (JW). East of the crest one to two pairs still nest in Lundy Canyon (MM, DG), but they have not been seen in Lee Vining Canyon or along Rush Creek since 1982 (DG). Surveys in 1982 and 1986 failed to discover them elsewhere in our region, but I suspect a few were overlooked (Serena 1982, JH). In 1974, a pair bred near Mammoth Creek (7100'—DG), and others were seen in Bridgeport Valley (6500') during the 1973 nesting season (AB 27:915).

Two possible new nesting locales have been reported since 1988: a pair nest building 6/16/91 at headwaters of Green Creek (PM) and suspected nesting at nearby Barney Lake, Hoover Wilderness (8400') (AB 43:1364).

Willow Flycatchers may occasionally breed at higher elevations as well. Singing birds were found on the west slope at Peregoy Meadow (7000') in June 1974 (DDeS), Westfall Meadow (7000') on 6/7/86 (JW) and just east of the crest near Ellery Lake (9500') on 6/18-20/73 (AB 27:915).

True to their name, Willow Flycatchers are wedded to willows, especially the large, shrubby ones that line languid streams or gather around seeps in moist meadows. They prefer clumps to dense, continuous thickets, and shrubby to arborescent willows. Often they perch on the uppermost dead tips, calling persistently for hour after hour. From their willowy homes, they embark on foraging expeditions into adjacent meadows and openings, deigning to perch on stout herbaceous vegetation, fences or handy trees of every description. Transients share a predilection for shrubby haunts in the vicinity of water.

But why have Willow Flycatchers become so scarce? In lowland California, they have probably fallen victim to habitat destruction in concert with high levels of Brown-headed Cowbird parasitism (see p 318). In the Sierra, however, grazing may be the major factor. Cowbird parasitism may not have played a major role, since most cowbirds lay their eggs before the flycatchers arrive (Stafford and Valentine 1985). Only Common Nighthawks are equally tardy migrants.

Outside Yosemite National Park, most lower elevation Sierran meadows are still heavily grazed. Recent studies indicate that Willow Flycatchers shun willows if the lowermost foliage has been denuded by livestock (Serena 1982, JH). While most of Yosemite National Park has not been grazed in this century, there is probably not enough habitat within the park itself to sustain a viable population without immigration from neighboring Sierran and lowland areas.

Extreme dates, both Yosemite Valley (4000'): 5/15/26 (YM) - 10/1/26 (YM).

Additional references: AB 27:915, AB 29:905, AB 29:1028, C 18:27, C 36:24, D 885, EM 7, GS 371, YNN 3:3.

LEAST FLYCATCHER (*Empidonax minimus*)

Extremely rare transient east of Sierran escarpment.

Record: 6400' n. shore Mono Lake 9/22/84—carefully identified by experienced observer (DDeS).

HAMMOND'S FLYCATCHER (*Empidonax hammondii*)

	J	F	M	A	M	J	J	A	S	O	N	D	HABITAT	ELEVATIONS		
														N	T	W
WEST				•									PO	5-7	F-10	
EAST			•										PW		6-10	

Uncommon transient below 4500', rare summer visitor (resident?) from 3000' to 4500', common summer resident from 4500' to 7000', rare summer resident to 8000' and rare fall transient to treeline on west slope; extremely rare spring and rare fall transient below treeline east of crest.

Of all our common birds, Hammond's Flycatchers and Golden-crowned Kinglets are the most difficult to see. Though both are easily heard, they defy intimacy as they flit through firs and pines high overhead. Spotting them can strain the staunchest of necks.

During the nesting season, Hammond's Flycatchers sequester themselves in the deeply shaded foliage underneath the crowns of conifers. They dwell among sugar pines, white firs, red firs, Douglas firs and sequoias. Where there is little understory, as in old-growth red fir forests, they live high in the crowns. But where young conifers, dogwoods, alders and other saplings grow beneath a canopy of larger trees, they sing and forage almost to the forest floor. They are not restricted to old-growth, but inhabit moderately dense second-growth forests as well.

Shade is the common factor. Except during migrations, Hammond's Flycatchers rarely forage in the open. Dusky Flycatchers, in contrast, prefer open forests, forest edges and shrub-covered slopes where there is plenty of sun (Johnson 1963).

Contrary to most field guides, Hammond's Flycatchers generally nest at lower elevations than Duskys, at least on the west slope of the Sierra Nevada. Marie Mans has heard territorial birds during May and June at 3000' (AB 37:909; AB 34:812), and nests have been found as low as 4600'. They follow red firs to 8000', but shun the lodgepole pine forests of higher altitudes. While I have not found them nesting east of the crest, a few may breed in pockets of dense forest, particularly in the Deadman Creek drainage.

Transient Hammond's Flycatchers are more catholic in choice of habitat. They visit deciduous as well as coniferous trees, and appear in isolated groves and thickets. They and other *Empidonax* cannot be identified by habitat or elevation during migrations.

Hammond's is the last of our *Empidonax* to abandon the mountains. Any small flycatcher seen in September or early October is likely, but not positively, this species. Most Dusky and Gray flycatchers depart in August and molt on their wintering grounds. Hammond's, like most Sierran passerines, molt before they migrate. Hence they embark several weeks after their relatives (Johnson 1970).

High elevation records: 10,500' Mt. Clark 8/22/15 (GS 370); 10,200' Hall Natural Area, many records (DeSante MS).

Extreme dates west slope: 4/24/87 4600' Ackerson Meadow (JW) - 10/15/85 2100' El Portal (AB 36:214).

Extreme dates east of crest: 5/23/89 Mono Lake County Park, 9 (PM); 8/9/86 10,000'+ Hall Natural Area (D&E) - 10/15/85 6400' Mono Lake County Park (DG).

Representative nesting localities: 4600' Ackerson Meadow (AB 35:976); 5000' along Tuolumne Grove Road (MM, DG); 6200' Crane Flat (DG).

DUSKY FLYCATCHER (*Empidonax oberholseri*)

	J	F	M	A	M	J	J	A	S	O	N	D	HABITAT	ELEVATIONS		
														N	T	W
WEST													PS	4-10	F-10	
EAST													PS	7-10	6-10	

Uncommon transient below 4000', uncommon summer resident from 4000' to 6000', fairly common summer resident to 8000' and common summer resident to treeline on west slope; fairly common summer resident from 7000' to 8500' and common summer resident to treeline east of crest.

Duskys are the hardiest of flycatchers, braving frost and snow to raise broods in storm-battered pines at treeline. In contrast to Hammond's and Westerns, they like the sun, sallying over clearings, meadows and brush-covered slopes.

At lower elevations, Dusky Flycatchers prefer montane chaparral with scattered trees, consorting with manzanita, ceanothus, chinquapin, huckleberry oak and other shrubs on the west slope, desert mahogany, bitterbrush and sagebrush to the east. Usually, but not invariably, pines, firs or black oaks overlook the shrubbery. At higher elevations, they inhabit open stands of lodgepoles and other pines, especially near meadows, lakes, streams and clearings. Less frequently, they dwell in willow thickets and aspen groves. Among the shady, forested haunts of Hammond's Flycatchers, they sometimes

Hammond's and Dusky "gnat-kings", courtesy Discovering Sierra Birds.

nest near meadows and openings. Transients visit a wide variety of woodland and scrub habitats.

Extreme dates, both 6400' Mono Lake County Park: 4/20/91 (JHu) - 9/27/70 (BS).

Representative nesting localities: 4600' Ackerson Meadow (JW); 6000' Henness Ridge (DG); 6400' Crane Flat Fire Lookout (DG); 7800' White Wolf (DG, TB); 8600' Tuolumne Meadow (DG); to 10,600' Hall Natural Area (DeSante MS); 7800' Lee Vining Canyon (DG).

GRAY FLYCATCHER (*Empidonax wrightii*)

	J	F	M	A	M	J	J	A	S	O	N	D	HABITAT	ELEVATIONS		
														N	T	W
WEST					•	•		•	•				SG		5-7	
EAST				—	■	■	■	■	—				S	6-8		

Extremely rare transient on west slope; extremely rare on east slope; locally fairly common summer resident below 8000' east of Sierran escarpment.

Of all our small flycatchers, Grays are the most desert-loving. Some forsake timber altogether, dwelling among the scented sagebrush east of the Sierran escarpment. They nest in open woodlands as well as sagebrush scrub, but require large, dense-foliaged shrubs or Utah junipers.

On well-drained, gentle slopes, Gray Flycatchers nest among large, mature sagebrush and bitterbrush. The shrubs, usually four to six feet in height, may be mixed with rabbitbrush, desert peach and scattered pinyon or jeffrey pines.

On rocky hillsides and in other areas where the sagebrush scrub is not so large, nesting Gray Flycatchers associate with shrubby Utah junipers. The junipers may be the only tree present, as northeast of Mono Lake (6600'), or may be mixed with pinyon pines, as on Cedar Hill (7200').

On the other hand, nesting Gray Flycatchers shun pinyon pine woodlands, jeffrey pine woodlands and other xeric habitats where large shrubs or Utah junipers are lacking. They also avoid montane chaparral and saline or alkaline soils where sagebrush scrub is relatively dwarfed.

This said, I must add that I sometimes fail to find Gray Flycatchers in patches of seemingly perfect habitat. Transients are more widespread, and visit riparian thickets and open woodlands as well as scrub.

West slope records: 4600' Ackerson Meadow 6/23/87 (JW) and 8/23/87 (JW); 7000' Peregoy Meadows 5/16/70 (AFN 24:641) and 5/8/87 (Gary Lester); 4600' Hodgdon Meadow 9/27/82 (AB 37:221).

East slope record above 8000': 11,000' near Gardisky Lake 7/14/77 (DeSante and Engstrom MS); (the published record from Sawmill Campground [9700'—AB 33:895] is probably erroneous—DDeS).

Extreme dates east of crest: 4/19/80 6400' near Mono Lake (DG) - 9/19/81 7000' near Mono Mills (HG).

Additional representative nesting locality: 7000' w. of Mono Craters (D 897).

Additional reference: GS 373.

WESTERN FLYCATCHER COMPLEX includes PACIFIC-SLOPE FLYCATCHER (*Empidonax difficilis*) and CORDILLERAN FLYCATCHER (*Empidonax occidentalis*)

	J	F	M	A	M	J	J	A	S	O	N	D	HABITAT	ELEVATIONS		
														N	T	W
WEST													PW	F-5	F-10	
EAST													PW	8-9?	6-10	

In 1989 the American Ornithologists Union split the Western Flycatcher into two species. Because they are indistinquishable in the field except by call, the status of the two forms is not well understood. It is certain that all individuals breeding on the west slope are Cordilleran Flycatchers, but positive evidence is lacking to specific identification. Most migrating through on the west side are probably Pacific-slope Flycatchers, but the possibility of other species should not be ruled out. It is likely that both species migrate through on the east side. Pacific-slope Flycatchers breeding west of the Cascade Range bound for Mexican wintering grounds would pass well to the east of Mono Lake if migrating in a straight line. Because details of range, breeding areas and migrating routes are lacking, the following information applies to the complex as a whole.

Locally uncommon summer resident below 5000', rare summer resident to 6500' and rare fall transient to treeline on west slope; rare summer resident below 9000' and rare fall transient to treeline east of crest.

Western Flycatchers share with Hammond's a love for shady nesting haunts. But they are not so common and widespread, being restricted, on the west slope at least, to the vicinity of running water below the level of deep winter snows. They typically dwell in moist, shady forests of douglas fir, big-leaf maple, alder, cottonwood and other trees in forested canyonbottoms at lower elevations. In the Mariposa Grove, however, they have nested "between the bark plates of a large sugar pine" at the exceptional elevation of 6400' (YNN 29:46, YM).

East of the crest, Western flycatchers summer and probably nest in streamside groves of mixed aspens and conifers. They are scarce and local, however, and cannot be found dependably in any given place. In recent years, birds have been singing on territories near Mammoth Lakes (8000'—AB 33:895), in Lee Vining Canyon (8000'—DG, AB 34:927), Lundy Canyon (7800'—MM) and near Green Lake (9000'—DG). Based on their songs, I suspect they are Cordilleran flycatchers.

High elevation records: 10,000' May Lake 7/22/66 (AFN 20:597); to 10,100' Hall Natural Area, 7 records (DeSante and Engstrom MS).

Extreme dates: 4/8/40 4000' Yosemite Valley (YM); 4/20/80 6400' Mono Lake (DW, KC) - 10/3/83 6500' w. shore Mono Lake (DS).

Extreme dates above 6500' west slope and 8000' east of crest, both Hall Natural Area (10,000'+): 6/20/87 - 9/13/79 (AB 34.197, DeSante and Engstrom MS).

Additional representative nesting localities: (1300' Merced River—MR); 4000' Mirror Lake (YM, YNN 3:3); (4500' Tuolumne Grove Road—MM, DG); 4600' Ackerson Meadow (JW).

Additional references: AB 33:894, GS 372.

BLACK PHOEBE (*Sayornis nigricans*)

	J	F	M	A	M	J	J	A	S	O	N	D	HABITAT	ELEVATIONS		
														N	T	W
WEST													RGW	F-5		F-4
EAST	•												RGW		6-7	

Locally fairly common resident below 3000', uncommon summer and irregularly rare to uncommon winter resident to 5000', and extremely rare transient at higher elevations on west slope; rare transient below 7000' and extremely rare transient at higher elevations east of crest.

Along the margins of languid streams, ponds and meadows, Black Phoebes perch on trees, shrubs, herbaceous vegetation, fences and buildings in watch for passing insects. In our region they nest exclusively on houses, barns and under bridges. Like Barn and Cliff swallows, they invaded as people provided, albeit unintentionally, suitable breeding sites. In Yosemite Valley, the first nest was found in 1932 (YM). In addition to sites, they also need supplies of mud for plastering nests. Of all the flycatchers, they are the only one to regularly brave Sierran winters.

Records above 5000' west slope and above 7000' east of crest: 6200' Crane Flat 7/12/85 (AB 39:959); 7100' Merced Lake 8/4/28 (YNN 7:90); 7700' Crescent Lake 7/27/76 (YM); 8600' Tuolumne Meadows 7/12/81 and 8/5/87 (MR); 10,100' Hall Natural Area 7/9/81 and 8/3/87 (DeSante and Engstrom MS); 7800' Lundy Lake 3/7/82 (LW); 7400' Lee Vining Canyon 9/5/87 (DG, DS).

Extreme dates east of crest: 1/27/89 6400' w. shore Mono Lake (AB 43:363); 3/2/86 6400' n. shore Mono Lake (LF) - 5/15/84 Dechambeau Ponds (DS); 7/4/85 Dechambeau Ponds (AB 39:959) - 9/20/85 Dondero Ranch (DG).

Representative nesting localities: 1300' Merced River (MR); 2100' El Portal (DG); 4000' Yosemite Valley (YM); 4000' Wawona (RG); 4400' Big Meadow (DG); 4600' Ackerson Meadow (JW); 4600' Hodgdon Meadow (SM).

Additional references: EM 6, GS 362.

EASTERN PHOEBE (*Sayornis phoebe*)

Extremely rare vagrant east of Sierran escarpment.

Record: 6500' Mono Lake County Park 5/31/90 (AB 44:493).

SAY'S PHOEBE (*Sayornis saya*)

	J	F	M	A	M	J	J	A	S	O	N	D	HABITAT	ELEVATIONS		
														N	T	W
WEST			—	—			• —	—	—			•	G		F-5	2
EAST	•		▬	▬	▬	▬	▬	▬	—			•	GS	6-8		6

Rare transient below 5000', extremely rare transient to treeline and extremely rare winter visitor on west slope; extremely rare transient above 7000' on east slope; fairly common transient, uncommon summer resident and extremely rare winter visitor below 7000' and rare summer resident to 8500' east of Sierran escarpment.

Unlike most birds, Say's Phoebes like desolation. A drab flycatcher sallying over sparse and overgrazed meadows, meagerly vegetated alkali flats, exposed lakebottoms, gullies, eroded stream channels and lava flows is apt to be this species. These xerophilous anchorites tolerate scattered shrubs, but shun dense stands of sagebrush as well as timber. Shrubs, weed tips, rocks, fence posts, buildings and even clods of earth suffice for look-out posts from which to sally after aerial insects. If these are lacking, as in meadows, they will hover in the manner of Mountain Bluebirds. On the west slope, for lack of anything bleaker, they visit the drier parts of meadows.

While transients are widespread, nesting Say's Phoebes are restricted to rocks, cliffs, undercut banks or buildings with ledges suitable for anchoring nests. I've discovered nests, for example, in lava flows, abandoned miner's cabins, a motel in Lee Vining (6900') and in Mono Lake's tufa towers (6400').

East of the Sierran escarpment, Say's Phoebes are harbingers of spring. They arrive in the sagebrush at the end of February—in time to brave the last fierce snowstorms.

West slope records during March and early April, including a mountaineering Say's Phoebe at 10,000' near Tioga Pass on 3/19/85 (MR), suggests a west-to-east migration from Central Valley wintering areas to Great Basin breeding haunts. In the southern Sierra, one on Mt. Williamson on 9/29/80 was at 12,000' (DG).

Records above 5000' west slope and above 7000' on east slope: 6200' Crane Flat 9/15/72 (MM); 7000' Peregoy Meadow 9/15/57 (AFN 12:56); 8600' Tuolumne Meadows 9/2/85 (MR); 10,000' Tioga Pass 3/19/85 (MR).

Winter records west slope: 2000' El Portal 12/19/77 (LMcK; AB 32:892); another was reported on the Yosemite Christmas Bird Count on 12/18/76, but I've been unable to ascertain the locality (AB 31:895).

Winter records east of crest: 6400' Mono Lake 12/29/81 (DG); 6500' Dechambeau Ponds 1/1/82 (CS, HG).

Extreme dates west slope excluding winter record: 2000' El Portal 3/4/79 (MR) - 4/18/27 4000' Yosemite Valley (YM); 4600' Ackerson Meadow 7/24/81 (JW) - 6200' Crane Flat 9/27/90 (ESt).

Extreme dates east of crest excluding winter records: 2/12/91 Mono City (AB 45:317) - 10/15/85 Dechambeau Ponds (DG).

Additional representative nesting localities: 6500' Negit Island, Paoha Island and Negit Islets (C 40:262, DW, ESt, DS); 7000' Black Point (Tom Curdts); 8400' Bodie (DG).

VERMILION FLYCATCHER (*Pyrocephalus rubinus*)

Extremely rare vagrant east of Sierran escarpment.

Record: 6500' Dechambeau Ponds, male and female, 10/4/81 (EB).

ASH-THROATED FLYCATCHER (*Myiarchus cinerascens*)

	J	F	M	A	M	J	J	A	S	O	N	D	HABITAT	ELEVATIONS		
														N	T	W
WEST				?					•				SWO	F-4		
EAST													SP		6-8	

Fairly common summer resident below 3000', locally uncommon summer resident to 4500' and extremely rare transient in higher mountains on west slope; rare transient below 8000' and extremely rare transient at higher elevations east of crest.

Ash-throated Flycatchers are, by and large, foothill rather than mountain dwellers. On the west slope, their haunts range from chaparral-covered slopes with dense shrubbery and a few scattered oaks and digger pines to open pine-oak forests with discontinuous understories of ceanothus, manzanita and other shrubs. They also inhabit moist, riparian thickets.

Wherever Ash-throated Flycatchers nest, there must be nearby trees with natural or woodpecker-excavated holes or hollows. While they usually avail themselves of live or black oaks, I've also found nests in an abandoned apple orchard at 4000' and in a large ponderosa pine at 4500'.

East of the Sierran escarpment, Ash-throated Flycatchers may nest in areas, such as Cedar Hill, which are clothed with Utah junipers. They breed in similar habitat throughout the Great Basin.

Records above 5000' west slope and 8000' east of crest: 6200' Crane Flat 6/11/85 (YM); 7000' McGurk Meadow 8/27/86 (JW); 8100' near Glen Aulin 8/7/31 (YNN 10:83); 8600' Tuolumne Meadow 8/8/87 (JW); 9700' Clouds Rest 7/19/31 (YNN 10:83); 8200' Bald Mountain 8/17/77 (DG).

Extreme dates west slope: 5/4/31 4400' Big Meadow (YM) - 8/27/86 McGurk Meadow (JW); 9/27/82 4600' Hodgdon Meadow (YM); (they probably arrive about three weeks earlier in the western foothills, but I have no records).

Extreme dates east slope: 5/22/84 6400' Negit Island (DS) - 6/28/78 7000' Hot Creek (Gary Fugle); 8/1/78 6400' w. Mono Lake (DG) - 8/27/78 n. Mono Lake (KC).

Representative nesting localities: 2000' near Mariposa (CL); 2100' El Portal (DG); 3700' Hetch Hetchy (MM); 4000' McCauley Ranch (DG, YM); 4500' near Wawona (DG).

Additional references: AB 38:1058, YNN 3:2, YNN 18:126.

TROPICAL KINGBIRD (*Tyrannus melancholicus*)

Extremely rare vagrant east of Sierran escarpment.

Record: 7000' near Tom's Place 9/20/86 (DG); as this bird was silent, I cannot dismiss entirely the very similar Couch's Kingbird, which has yet to be recorded in California or the Great Basin; as I was able to study this beautiful bird under excellent conditions, however, I believe it was indeed a young Tropical.

WESTERN KINGBIRD (*Tyrannus verticalis*)

	J	F	M	A	M	J	J	A	S	O	N	D	HABITAT	ELEVATIONS		
														N	T	W
WEST													GO	F-2	F-5	
EAST													GS	6-7	6-7	

Fairly common summer resident in Mariposa region (2000'); locally uncommon summer resident below 2500', rare transient and summer visitor to 5000' and extremely rare transient at higher elevations on west slope; uncommon transient and rare summer resident below 7500' east of Sierran escarpment.

Except in the western foothills, Western Kingbirds visit the region primarily as transients. These elegant flycatchers favor open, level or gently sloping terrain with scattered trees, living or dead, for look-out posts and nesting sites. In the absence of trees, they are satisfied with telephone or power poles, windmills, fence-posts, stout herbaceous vegetation and, at Mono Lake, tufa towers. From these look-outs, they sally for insects over grasslands, meadows, pastures and other open, grassy habitats. They inhabit savannahs with scattered trees, but avoid dense woodlands and forests except at the edge of large meadows and clearings.

Western Kingbirds may occasionally nest at mid-elevations, as at McCauley Ranch (4000'—DG) and Big Meadow (4600'—MM), but this has yet to be confirmed. Nesting has also been suspected at Dechambeau Ranch east of the Sierran escarpment (6500'—DS), and verified near Bridgeport Reservoir (6500') (AB 45:1158).

Records above 5000' west slope: 7000' McGurk Meadows 7/28/89 (AB 43:1364); 8400' Olmstead Point 7/26/80 (AB 34:927); 8600' Tuolumne Meadows 7/18/72 (AB 26:899), 2, 8/14/77 (YM) and 8/2/43 (YM).

Extreme dates west slope: 4/4/79 2100' El Portal (DG) - 9/27/73 4000' Yosemite Valley (EM 6).

Extreme dates east of crest: 4/7/72 "Mono County" (AB 26:789) - 9/17/85 7000' n. Mono Lake (JH).

Additional references: GS 359, YNN 3:2.

EASTERN KINGBIRD (*Tyrannus tyrannus*)

Extremely rare vagrant east of Sierran escarpment.

Records: 6500' Dechambeau Ponds 6/24-25/82 (Debby Parker, DG); 6400' near Mono Lake 7/19/21 (C 23:195); 6400' n. Mono Lake 7/24/78 (DG, DW) and 8/30-9/1/86 (AB 41:140).

SCISSOR-TAILED FLYCATCHER (*Tyrannus forficatus*)

Extremely rare vagrant east of Sierran escarpment.

Record: 6400' S. Tufa, Mono Lake 6/28/89 (AB 43:1365); accepted by California Bird Record Committee.

Family ALAUDIDAE: LARKS

HORNED LARK (*Eremophila alpestris*)

	J	F	M	A	M	J	J	A	S	O	N	D	HABITAT	ELEVATIONS		
														N	T	W
WEST													G	11	F-12	4-5
EAST													G	6-12		6-7

Locally fairly common summer resident above treeline, rare fall transient below treeline and extremely rare winter visitor on west slope; locally common summer resident and irregularly rare to uncommon winter resident below 7000' and locally fairly common summer resident to 12,000' east of crest.

Elevation makes no difference to Horned Larks, so long as the habitat is suitably bleak. They nest both above treeline in the Sierra Nevada, the Bodie Hills and on Glass Mountain, and below treeline in the arid, often alkaline valleys and playas of the Great Basin.

The Horned Lark's latin name, *Eremophila* or desert-loving, befits birds wedded by plumage and habits to the bleakest parts of the wilderness. They thrive on windswept, treeless plains, plateaus, slopes and ridges that often shelter no other birds. Alkali flats, pumice flats, the muddy shores of ponds, lakes and deltas, sparsely vegetated and over-grazed meadows, dry alpine meadows and fell fields as well as small, well-spaced sagebrush are all to their liking. On the lower west slope, transients seek out meadows, dirt roads or muddy shores.

Except when nesting, Horned Larks are gregarious. East of the Sierran escarpment, especially in late summer and autumn, one may espy half a dozen only to flush a wheeling cloud of over a hundred. Though I've seen large flocks in winter, most retreat to warmer climes that remain free of snow.

But they don't stay away for long. As early as late February, the Horned Larks' sweet, skylarking songs are mocking winter's grip and welcoming the returning sun.

Peak count below 9000' west slope: 20, 4600' Ackerson Meadow 10/13/85 (JW).

Winter and spring records below 9000' west slope: 1/27/84, 5 and 2/20/86, 3, Ackerson Meadow (JW); 3/1/22 4000' Yosemite Valley (EM 7); 4/?/25 Yosemite Valley (YM); 4/29/82, 4, 7000' Peregoy Meadow (YM).

Extreme dates above 9000': 4/15/79 9600' ridge nw. of Lee Vining (DG) - 11/23/75 9200' near Dog Lake (YM).

Representative nesting localities: 10,000' Parker Pass (DG); 12,000' Mt. Dana and Dana Plateau (DG); 11,000' e. of Mt. Warren (DG); 9000' summit of ridge w. of Lee Vining (DG); 7000' Long Valley (DG); 6400' Mono Lake (DG).

Family HIRUNDININAE: Swallows

The return of swallows from wintering areas as far away as South America is a harbinger of spring, not only in the Sierra, but throughout North America. Of our seven nesting species, five are widespread both west and east of the crest. Purple Martins and Bank Swallows, however, are known to breed only at single localities.

Swallows differ more in nest sites than in foraging habitats. During migration, I've seen all but martins sharing the airways above ponds east of the Sierran escarpment. Like swifts, with which they sometimes mingle, they are usually seen aloft gracefully hawking aerial insects.

Nesting Bank Swallows may be threatened by the proposed enlargement of Crowley Lake Reservoir.

PURPLE MARTIN (*Progne subis*)

Uncommon summer resident in Mariposa region (2000'); extremely rare transient elsewhere on west slope and east of Sierran escarpment.

Purple Martins are inexplicably scarce in the region, and have never been positively recorded in Yosemite National Park. A small colony summers and nests near Mariposa, arriving at the end of May and remaining through July (CL). I know of only two other records, one east of the Sierran escarpment. I have discarded an old Yosemite record (6/20 25/1893) that was based on hearing "notes...from some old oaks" (GS 497). Just west of our region, these large swallows have been seen "occasionally in spring" near Coulterville (GS 497).

West slope record excluding Mariposa region: 4700' Cherry Lake Dam, female, 6/28/84 (JW).
Record east of Sierran escarpment: 7000' Hot Creek 9/15/73 (AB 28:103).

TREE SWALLOW (*Tachycineta bicolor*)

	J	F	M	A	M	J	J	A	S	O	N	D	HABITAT	ELEVATIONS N	T	W
WEST		•											WGRL	F-9		
EAST													WGRL	6-8		

Uncommon summer resident below 4000' and rare summer resident to 8500' on west slope; uncommon summer resident below 8000' and extremely rare transient at higher elevations east of crest; fairly common transient in valleys east of Sierran escarpment.

Though much less numerous than Violet-greens, Tree Swallows are almost as widespread. They are closely wedded to watery haunts, nesting almost invariably in the vicinity of languid streams, ponds, lakes and meadows, and foraging over quiet water or damp ground. Even transients favor ponds and meadows, though they travel over all types of habitat.

Tree Swallows usually nest in trees or snags with woodpecker-excavated or natural cavities, though they also avail themselves of nesting boxes and holes in buildings. East of the crest, they nest in aspen groves; on the west slope, they have also used cottonwoods and even lodgepole pines. As they never nest in rocks or cliffs, they are generally restricted to timbered habitats. Mono Lake's treeless tufa groves, for example, though otherwise perfect, have been claimed by tufa-nesting Violet-greens.

Record above 9000': 10,000' Hall Natural Area 6/26/79 and 7/3/87 (DeSante and Engstrom MS).

Extreme dates, both Dechambeau Ponds (6500'): 2/20/82, 3 (DG) - 9/28/83 (HG).

Representative nesting localities: 4000' Yosemite Valley (EM 11, YM); 4600' Ackerson Meadow (JW); 8000' Siesta Lake (DG); 8600' Tuolumne Meadows (DDeS, DG); 8000' Lundy Canyon (DG); 7400' Lee Vining Canyon (DG); 6800' Lee Vining (DG).

Additional reference: GS 500.

VIOLET-GREEN SWALLOW (*Tachycineta thalassina*)

	J	F	M	A	M	J	J	A	S	O	N	D	HABITAT	ELEVATIONS N	T	W
WEST													WGCPOA	F-9	F-10	
EAST													WGCPA	6-10		

Common transient and uncommon summer resident below 3000', common summer resident to 5000', uncommon summer resident to 9000' and rare summer resident or visitor to treeline on west slope; common summer resident below 8500' and rare summer resident or visitor to treeline east of crest.

Of all our swallows, Violet-greens are the most numerous and ubiquitous. They pursue their aerial prey over all types of habitat. Their haunts range from precipitous cliffs to open forests. They shun dense woods, however, keeping to the margins of meadows, lakes and other openings.

Violet-green Swallows concentrate where there are suitable crevices or cavities in which to nest. These range from cliff-faces and precipitous canyon walls, where they consort with White-throated Swifts, to trees and snags with woodpecker-excavated or natural cavities. They also utilize bird boxes, crannies in buildings and, at Mono Lake, tufa towers. While they nest in virtually every kind of tree, they favor oaks, cottonwoods and aspens, often congregating in loose colonies. Unlike Trees, they often nest far from water; east of the Sierran escarpment, for example, they breed on the parched rock walls of desert mountains.

Violet-greens, like other swallows, are among the earliest spring arrivals. I have seen them cavorting with snowflakes during a February storm. Most appear with warm weather in late March and early April. Migrating flocks mill overhead, feeding as they journey. In spring of 1975, for instance, Tina Hargis saw them passing east to west over Tuolumne Meadows (8600') at a rate of over 100 per hour; where were they coming from, and where were they going?

Violet-green Swallows are also one of the last migrants to depart. From the end of August through much of September, the skies fill with hundreds of migrating birds. They gather in especially large flocks in the valleys east of the Sierran escarpment, perching and roosting on power wires or in pond and streamside willows. They mass on the west slope as well; 300 were still at El Portal (2100'), for example, on the late date of 10/15/81 (JD).

From late spring into mid-summer, Violet-green Swallows sun-bathe, sometimes by the hundreds, on the shingled roofs of barns and buildings. I've seen them soaking up the rays, for example, at Big Meadow (4400') and Ackerson Meadow (4600'), presumably to rid themselves of parasites.

No birds anywhere are lovelier, but their beauty is fleeting and elusive. William Leon Dawson captured the Violet-green Swallow's numinous qualities: "The livid green of back and crown reflect the ardent glances of the sun with a delicate golden sheen...the violet of upper tail-coverts and rump comes to view only in changing flashes...but one catches such visions as a beggar flung coins... At such a time, if one is clambering about the skirting of some rugged precipice in Yosemite, he feels as if the dwellers of Olympus had come down in appropriate guise to inquire his earth-born business" (Dawson 1923).

High elevation records: 10,200' Hall Natural Area, many records (DeSante MS).

Peak numbers: 800-1000, Ackerson Meadow 7/16/80 (JW); 300, 2100' El Portal 10/15/81 (JD); 300, 6800' Lee Vining 9/17/83 (DS).

Extreme dates west slope: 2/24/78 4900' east of Foresta (YM) - 10/15/81 6000' near Chinquapin and 2100' El Portal (JD).

Extreme dates east of crest: 2/17/83 Lee Vining (DG) - 10/15/85, 2, 6500' Mono Lake County Park (DG).

Extreme dates above 8000': 4/13/82 9000' Lee Vining Canyon (BE) - 8/15/79 10,200' Hall Natural Area (DeSante MS).

Representative nesting localities: 1300' Merced River (MR); 2100' El Portal (DG); 4000' Yosemite Valley (GS 501); 4400' Big Meadow (DG); 7000' Upper Yosemite Falls (DG); 8600' Tuolumne Meadows (DG); 9700' Virginia Lakes (C 41:249); 9500' Ellery Lake (DSu); 7400' Lee Vining Canyon; 6500' Negit and Paoha Islands (DW).

Additional references: AFN 7:35; C 38:86; JMCO 2:53.

Tree Swallows, courtesy Checklist of North American Birds

NORTHERN ROUGH-WINGED SWALLOW
(*Stelgidopteryx serripennis*)

	J	F	M	A	M	J	J	A	S	O	N	D	HABITAT	ELEVATIONS		
														N	T	W
WEST			•										RLG	F-5		
EAST			•										RLG	7	6-7	

Locally uncommon summer resident below 4500' and extremely rare transient at higher elevations on west slope; uncommon transient and rare summer resident below 7500' and extremely rare transient at higher elevations east of crest.

Rough-winged Swallows are scarce in the region, probably due to a paucity of suitable nest sites. They raise their young in natural or rodent-excavated holes in the earthen banks of gullies, washes and streams. Unlike other swallows, they rarely flock, even during migrations. Transients travel over most habitats, but favor ponds and languid streams.

Records above 5000' west slope or 7000' east of crest: 8600' Tuolumne Meadows 6/4/77 (TB); 10,100' Hall Natural Area 9/2/85 (DeSante and Engstrom MS).

Early date west slope: 3/27/57 4000' Yosemite Valley (AFN 9:398).

Extreme dates east of crest: 3/23/81 6500' Bridgeport (DW) and 3/23/82 6500' Mono Lake County Park (DW) - 6400' Mono Lake 9/11/76 (DW).

Representative nesting localities: (2000' Mariposa—DG); 4000' Yosemite Valley (YNN 3:12; YNN 4:64; YM); 4400' Big Meadow (SG); 4600' Ackerson Meadow (JW); 6800' Virginia Creek (RS).

Additional references: AFN 11:374, C 27:113, C 38:86, GS 503, YNN 21:23.

BANK SWALLOW (*Riparia riparia*)

	J	F	M	A	M	J	J	A	S	O	N	D	HABITAT	ELEVATIONS		
														N	T	W
WEST						•									4	
EAST													see text	7	6-7	

Extremely rare transient on west slope; locally common summer resident at nesting sites and rare transient elsewhere below 7000' east of Sierran escarpment.

Bank Swallows are abundant at several locations, and rare everywhere else. Approximately 2,000 pairs nest at Crowley Lake Reservoir, where they share vertical bluffs with Cliff Swallows (DG, JHu). Numbers there were down to 500 plus in 1988 (AB 42:479, 43:164).

California Department Fish and Game recently listed the Bank Swallow as a state threatened species, so it is heartening to report two new nesting bluffs. In 1989 a new colony of approximately 30 pairs was found at a quarry outside Bridgeport (AB 43:1365) and by 1990 it had swelled to about 100 pairs (AB 44:1182-1183). In 1991 the quarry colony was still active and 450 birds were seen swarming near 50 active nestholes in the eroded cliffs on the w. shore of Bridgeport Reservoir (PM).

At Crowley Lake, Bank Swallows forage over the reservoir and adjacent meadows and sagebrush scrub. Transients favor ponds, marshes and meadows, but materialize almost anywhere.

West slope record: 4000' Yosemite Valley 6/4/76 (AB 30:1000).

Extreme dates: 6500' Mono Lake County Park 4/10/82 (DG) - 6500' Simons Spring 9/7/84 (SJ, DS); 9/29/87 Dechambeau Ponds (PM).

CLIFF SWALLOW (*Hirundo pyrrhonota*)

	J	F	M	A	M	J	J	A	S	O	N	D	HABITAT	ELEVATIONS		
														N	T	W
WEST													BCRGA	F-5		
EAST													BCRGA	6-7		

Locally common summer resident below 2500', irregularly rare to uncommon summer resident or visitor to 4500' and extremely rare at higher elevations on west slope; extremely rare transient on east slope; locally common summer resident below 8500' east of Sierran escarpment.

Except during migrations, Cliff Swallows are plentiful only in the vicinity of their nesting colonies. These sociable birds plaster nests on the rough vertical faces of cliffs, banks and rock outcroppings as well as on buildings, bridges and culverts. Since the nests are constructed of mud, they are situated near streams, ponds, lakes or other sources of mud and fresh water. Breeding pairs do not stray far, racing to and fro over nearby waters and meadows in tireless pursuit of flying insects. Transients range over many habitats, but favor moist meadows and open water.

Like Black Phoebes and Barn Swallows, Cliff Swallows have followed white settlement into many parts of the region. While they nest on cliffs in the Bodie Hills and Hot Creek Gorge, other sites have all been on human-made structures. Now that water is back in Rush Creek, there is a new colony beneath that Highway 395 bridge. Cliff Swallows may colonize higher elevations during mild years, only to be repulsed by cold springs. For many years, for example, a small colony plastered nests to the side of O'Shaughnessy (Hetch Hetchy) Dam (3700'—YNN 17:126; YM). On 5/17/74, however, an unusual spring snowstorm left the swallows squatting under shrubs unable to fly (MM); they have not bred there since.

East of the Sierran escarpment, at least in Mono Basin, nesting Cliff Swallows exploded between 1982 and 1987. Their numbers increased from zero to several hundred in Lee Vining, for instance, and they colonized Bodie (8400') as well. The latter may be the highest breeding locality.

Records above 5000' west slope or on east slope: 6200' Crane Flat 9/21/79 (JW); 8600' Tuolumne Meadows 7/24/81 (MR); 12,000' Hall Natural Area 5/7/81 (DeSante and Engstrom MS); (there is a record at 12,300' in the southern Sierra—AB 30:122).

Extreme dates, both Mono Lake (6400'): 3/5/81, 2 (JJ) - 9/29/83 (HG).

Additional representative nesting localities: 1000'-2000' Merced River Canyon (MR); 4600' Ackerson Meadow (JW); 8100' Conway Summit (C 42:249).

Additional reference: GS 497.

BARN SWALLOW (*Hirundo rustica*)

	J	F	M	A	M	J	J	A	S	O	N	D	HABITAT	ELEVATIONS		
														N	T	W
WEST													GRL	F-5		
EAST													GRLA	6-7		

Locally common summer resident below 4500' and extremely rare transient at higher elevations on west slope; uncommon summer resident and fairly common fall transient below 7500' east of Sierran escarpment.

Above meadows, ponds, languid streams and other moist habitats, Barn Swallows gracefully hawk flying insects. Yet, except in the western foothills and Great Basin valleys, they were probably not part of the pristine avifauna. Anglo settlement, with its houses, barns and bridges, has enabled them to colonize mid-elevations.

Until 1949, Barn Swallows were not reported in Yosemite National Park (YM). Yet now they are plentiful in mid-elevation meadows, plastering mud nests onto ledges in houses and barns. The only natural site I know of was discovered east of the Sierran escarpment in Long Valley (7000'); the nest was ensconced "on the face of a sandstone bank four feet above the rushing water...and just beneath the pendant rootlets of the sod above" (Grinnell, MVZ journal, 7/11/22).

Barns are not the first swallows to arrive, but they are the last to depart. Until mid-October, especially east of the Sierran escarpment, they straggle southward over sagebrush, woodlands and other uncharacteristic habitats. They have a long way to go, for they winter from Panama south to the tip of South America, the farthest south of any Sierran passerine.

Peak concentration: approx. 2,000, 6900' Crowley Lake Reservoir 9/7/87 (DS).

Record above 5000' west slope: 8600' Tuolumne Meadows 9/11/77 (SG).

Extreme dates west slope, both El Portal (2100'): 3/24/78 (Don Roberson) - 10/15/81 (JD).

Extreme dates east of crest: 3/5/81 6400' Mono Lake (JJ); 3/22/86, 4, 7100' Hot Creek Fish Hatchery (DG) - 10/20/85 Mono Lake (DG).

Additional representative nesting localities: 2100' El Portal (Don Roberson); 4000' Yosemite Valley (YM); 4400' Big Meadow (DG, SM); 4600' Ackerson Meadow (JW); 7900' near Mammoth Lakes (GM 278); 6500' w. Mono Lake (DS).

Additional references: YNN 21:23.

Family CORVIDAE: Jays, Magpies and Crows

Of eight corvids, six nest in our area. These inquisitive, intelligent and garrulous birds have the most varied diets of any passerines, feeding on nuts and berries as well as insects, carrion and the eggs and young of other birds. Most can scrounge enough to winter in or near their nesting haunts.

STELLER'S JAY (*Cyanocitta stelleri*)

	J	F	M	A	M	J	J	A	S	O	N	D	HABITAT	ELEVATIONS N	ELEVATIONS T	ELEVATIONS W
WEST													POW	2-10		F-9
EAST													POW	6-10		6-8

Locally uncommon summer resident and irregularly uncommon to common winter resident below 3000', common summer and irregularly uncommon to common winter resident to 5000', common summer resident and locally uncommon winter resident to 7000', locally common summer resident and locally uncommon winter resident to 8500' and locally uncommon summer resident to treeline on west slope; common summer resident to 9000', locally uncommon summer resident to treeline and irregularly rare to common winter resident below 8000' east of crest.

Steller's Jays, while one of our most conspicuous birds, are not nearly so numerous overall as they seem around places of human habitation. These rowdy opportunists have been quick to take advantage of the crumbs and handouts available at campgrounds, picnic areas and about human habitations. Ever alert to new sources of food, they have even learned to scavenge road-killed carrion.

Because they will eat almost anything, Steller's Jays inhabit a wide variety of wooded habitats. While they favor pines and firs, they also dwell among oaks, maples, alders, aspens, cottonwoods and other hardwoods. They forage from the tops of lofty trees to the forest floor.

As one travels east of the crest, Steller's Jays grow more tolerant of arid conditions. On the east slope, they nest sparingly in mountain mahogany woodlands. In the Bodie Hills and other basin ranges, they breed in pinyon woodlands, though usually in the vicinity of streams or springs.

At higher elevations, most Steller's Jays keep to the vicinity of campgrounds, picnic areas, roads and other places of human habitation, following people, for instance, all the way to Tioga Pass (10,000'). They invaded the heights during this century; in 1924, for instance, Joseph Grinnell observed that their range "ends abruptly at the Canadian-Hudsonian boundary [i.e., below the lodgepole pines], above which is found the Clark's Nutcracker" (GS 379-380). While no longer the case overall, this still holds true in the remoter backcountry, where jays are rare summer visitors above 8000'.

While incubating eggs and feeding nestlings, Steller's Jays grow uncharacteristically quiet and shy. Their nests are usually sequestered in dense, well-shaded forest and woodland habitats.

Wintering Steller's Jays are more widespread, invading, depending on food conditions, all types of wooded habitats, including pinyon woodlands, oak woodlands, riparian hardwoods, willow thickets and residential areas. Rarely they range in chaparral and sagebrush scrub as well. They linger in the high country as long as they can scrounge or beg hand-outs, harassing nordic skiers, for instance, at Tuolumne Meadows (8600') and Tenaya Lake (8200'—TH). In towns like Mammoth Lakes (8000') and Lee Vining (6800'), flocks hang out near feeders. But most winter in oak-conifer forests west of the crest and pinyon woodlands to the east.

Acorns and pine nuts are important winter staples; in lean years, Steller's Jays may desert the mountains in large numbers. In the winter of 1943, for instance, a two-year dearth of acorns drove all the jays from Yosemite Valley (4000'—YNN 22:25). In such years, large numbers invade the foothills. Tallies on the Yosemite Christmas Bird Count have varied from 261 to 25.

In the early days of Yosemite National Park, rangers routinely shot Steller's Jays because they preyed on the eggs and nestlings of other birds (GS 383). We now better understand the role jays, chipmunks and other "nest-robbers" play in the balance of nature. Far from threatening the survival of other birds, they are penalizing the inexperienced and less fit. As William Leon Dawson remarked, "It takes the touch of adversity, well met, to bring out the admirable traits in bird character, as well as human" (Dawson 1923).

High elevation record: 10,000' Tioga Pass, summer resident.

Representative nesting localities: (2100' El Portal—DG); 4000' Yosemite Valley (GS 379); (6200' Crane Flat—DG); 7800' White Wolf (DG); (8600' Tuolumne Meadows—DG); 7400' Lee Vining Canyon (DG); 6800' Lee Vining (DG).

Additional references: C 17:58; YNN 13:67; YNN 18:93.

SCRUB JAY (*Aphelocoma coerulescens*)

	J	F	M	A	M	J	J	A	S	O	N	D	HABITAT	ELEVATIONS		
														N	T	W
WEST													SO	F-4		F-4
EAST													SP	6-8	6-10	6-8

Common resident below 3500', rare visitor to 5000' and irregularly rare summer visitor from 8500' to treeline on west slope; irregularly rare fall visitor to treeline and rare winter resident below 8000' on east slope; uncommon resident below 8000' in mountains east of Sierran escarpment; rare summer visitor and locally uncommon winter resident below 7000' in valleys east of Sierran escarpment.

There are really two Scrub Jays in the region: *A. c. superciliosa*, which reside in the western foothills, and *A. c. woodhouseii*, which dwell east of the Sierran escarpment. These races, which once were considered distinct species, differ in plumage, voice, habits and habitat (see National Geographic Society *Field Guide*, p. 300).

On the west slope, "California" Scrub Jays favor dry, open woodlands mixed with chaparral, but also inhabit riparian thickets, orchards and residential gardens. They are partial to oaks, for acorns are a staple part of their diets. But they also consort with digger pines, manzanitas, ceanothus and other xerophilous shrubs.

East of the Sierran escarpment, "Woodhouse's" Scrub Jays nest in pinyon and juniper woodlands in the Bodie Hills, on Granite Mountain and in other basin ranges. In contrast to their west slope cousins, they are shy, reclusive and relatively quiet, and rarely visit human habitations; even their squawks are not as grating. In fall and winter they are more widespread, wandering into sagebrush scrub, willow thickets and cottonwoods.

At high elevations, Scrub Jays stray into open woodlands, meadows and montane chaparral, though one in Tuolumne Grove (5800') on 8/5/77 was in dense forest (TB). Those which mountaineer to high elevations usually, perhaps invariably, belong to the Great Basin subspecies (AB 36:214, DeSante MS, DG); those which drift into oak-conifer forests presumably belong to the west slope race. Both seem to shun mid-elevations, for they have yet to be reported between 5800' (Tuolumne Grove—TB) and 8600' (Tuolumne Meadows—YM).

High elevation record: 11,000' Young Lake (EM 7).

Extreme dates above 8500': 6/26/81 10,000' Hall Natural Area (DeSante MS); 8/24/78 Hall Natural Area (DeSante MS) - 10/8/77 8600' Tuolumne Meadows (YM).

Representative nesting localities. 1300' Merced River (MR); 2000' Mariposa (CL); 2100' El Portal (DG); (3700' below McCauley Ranch—DG); (7200' Cedar Hill—DG).

Additional reference: GS 392.

PINYON JAY (*Gymnorhinus cyanocephalus*)

	J	F	M	A	M	J	J	A	S	O	N	D	HABITAT	ELEVATIONS		
														N	T	W
WEST				•			•	—	—	—	—		P		4-13	
EAST	▒	▒	▒	▒	▒	▒	▒	▒	▒	▒	▒	▒	PS	6-8	6-13	6-8

Extremely rare spring and irregularly rare fall transient from 4000' to 12,000' on west slope; extremely rare spring transient and irregularly rare fall transient below 12,000' on east slope; locally common summer resident and irregularly rare to common winter resident below 8000' east of Sierran escarpment.

True to their names, Pinyon Jays dwell in woodlands of pinyon pine, but range into sagebrush scrub as well. They also inhabit open, park-like jeffrey pine forests east of the Mono Craters. As these gregarious corvids do not nest in the same places every year, they are sometimes difficult to locate.

Pinyon Jays favor gentle slopes and flats, shunning—for no obvious reason—the pinyons that clothe the eastern slopes of the Sierra. They forage in trees and shrubs as well as on the ground.

In late summer and early autumn, Pinyon Jays wander widely. Noisy, peregrinating flocks fly over all types of habitat. In some years, they gypsy westwards across the Sierran crest, reaching, exceptionally, the oak-conifer forests and places like Yosemite Valley (4000'). These flights occur only in certain years, such as 1955, 1960, 1972, 1979, 1982 and 1987, which correlate with pinyon and Jeffrey pine nut failures.

A lone Pinyon Jay is exceptional. Usually they group in flocks of several dozen to several hundred individuals. North of Mono Lake, in mid-October, I once watched several thousand stream overhead for hour after hour.

High elevation record: 12,600' Mt. Conness 9/9/78 (DeSante MS).

Peak count west slope: 55 Yosemite Valley 9/19/35 (YM).

Spring records west slope and above 8000' east of crest: Yosemite Valley, "flock," 4/27/23 (YNN 15:44); 10,000' Hall Natural Area 5/5/82 (DeSante MS).

Extreme dates west slope and above 8000' east of crest excluding spring records: 7/6/60 10,000'+ Mt. Dana (AFN 14:475); 8/15/81 10,400' Hall Natural Area (DeSante MS) - 11/16/60 Yosemite Valley (YM).

Representative nesting locality: 7000' near Mono Mills (DG).

Additional references: AB 27:112, AB 30:122, AFN 10:53.

CLARK'S NUTCRACKER (*Nucifraga columbiana)*

	J	F	M	A	M	J	J	A	S	O	N	D	HABITAT	ELEVATIONS		
														N	T	W
WEST													P	8-10?	4-10	8-10
EAST													P	7-10		7-10

Common summer and irregularly rare to fairly common winter resident from 8000' to and occasionally above treeline and irregularly rare fall and winter visitor from 4000' to 8000' on west slope; common summer and irregularly rare to common winter resident to and occasionally above treeline east of crest.

Clark's Nutcrackers are the high country's noisiest, most conspicuous avian inhabitants. These obstreperous fowl are sworn to greet all intruders. Wander where you will among the storm-bent whitebarks and glacier-carved cirques, they will bid you grating but exuberant welcome.

The domain of Clark's Nutcrackers begins on the sparsely wooded granite shingles of the west slope, and extends across the crest and down into open forests east of the Sierran escarpment. In the higher mountains, they dwell among lodgepole and especially whitebark pines, following the latter to treeline. On the dry, steep slopes of the eastern escarpment, they consort with pinyon pines, Jeffrey pines, Sierran junipers and mountain mahogany. East of the escarpment, they favor tall but open groves of Jeffrey pines.

From these wooded headquarters, Clark's Nutcrackers cruise far and wide, buzzing the summits of the highest peaks. Like their Steller's Jay cousins, they scout roads for carrion, rob birds' nests of eggs and chicks, and stoop to beg for hand-outs at feeders, campgrounds and viewpoints. They forage on the ground as well as in trees and shrubs.

Though Clark's Nutcrackers venture into cottonwoods, aspens and other deciduous trees, pines are their staff of life. A single bird may harvest and store more than 30,000 pine nuts, caching them, a few at time, in small holes. Diana Tomback has found that many birds harvest large numbers of whitebark pine seeds at subalpine elevations in late summer, then migrate to lower elevations to harvest and store jeffrey pine and pinyon pine seeds. These not only fodder the adults throughout the winter, but nourish nestlings, which hatch as early as March (Tomback 1978, 1982).

Although some Clark's Nutcrackers probably nest on the west slope, most probably raise young east of the crest. Among Sierran birds, only Red Crossbills are earlier nesters. In the pinyon pines west of Lee Vining (7500'), for instance, Brett Engstrom found nests nearing completion in the first week of March. In large junipers near June Lake (8000'), Dixon found eggs and young in early April (C 36:229-234). After fledging, families troop en masse to higher elevations, arriving before the summer tourists and feeding on whitebark seed stores from the previous fall (Tomback 1982).

This is not to say Clark's Nutcracker do not nest at high elevations. At 10,500' in the Hall Natural Area, they are building nests in late April, and have nearly grown nestlings in mid-June (DeSante MS). Some undoubtedly nest at high elevations west of the crest as well, but I know of only one sixty-year old record, and that at an exceptionally low elevation (8100' Sentinel Dome—YNN 6:56).

The relationship between Clark's Nutcrackers and whitebark pines is mutually beneficial. The birds depend on whitebarks for sustenance, the pines on birds for seed dispersal. Nutcrackers, in fact, have planted most of the whitebarks growing at high elevations (Tomback 1982). When the pines fail to produce, the birds may desert the mountains to scrounge food in lowland valleys and deserts (AFN 10:361; C 59:297-307).

Peak count below 8000' west slope: 119, 4400' Big Meadows 12/27/60 (YNN 40:14).

Summer records below 8000': 6200' Crane Flat 7/26/77 (SG); 6400' Mariposa Grove 8/12/50 (YNN 30:94).

Extreme dates below 8000' excluding summer records, both Yosemite Valley (4000'): 9/11/40 (YNN 13:7) - 5/24/78 (YM).

Additional references: AFN 10:361; AFN 16:71, C 58:3-23, C 58:386, GS 393, YNN 13:7, YNN 30:94, YNN 35:165.

BLACK-BILLED MAGPIE (*Pica pica)*

	J	F	M	A	M	J	J	A	S	O	N	D	HABITAT	ELEVATIONS		
														N	T	W
WEST		•					•		•	•					4-10	
EAST	■	■	■	■	■	■	■	■	■	■	■	■	WGSD	6-7		6-9

Extremely rare vagrant on west slope; locally common resident below 7500' east of crest.

East of the Sierran escarpment, Black-billed Magpies are conspicuous denizens of well-watered valleys. They occasionally wander into the Bodie Hills, the mouths of Sierran canyons or onto the flanks of glacial moraines.

Black-billed Magpies usually dwell near streams, springs, seeps and other sources of water, not only to slack their thirst, but for the mud they use in nest construction. They roost and nest in dense thickets and groves of low, deciduous shrubs and trees, such as willows, buffalo-berries and cottonwoods. From these shelters they range into sagebrush, meadows, pastures and dumps, and infrequently, towns and residential areas.

Like other corvids, Black-billed Magpies feed on anything edible, including the carcasses that disgrace our highways. Toward sunset, they gather to spend the night in communal roosts.

Records on west slope: 4000' Yosemite Valley 10/19/53 (AFN 8:40) and 7/1-28/73 (YM); 8200' Tenaya Lake, 2, 2/1/57 (YM); 9500' Lyell Canyon 9/26/37 (YNN 16:87).

Additional reference: GS 376.

YELLOW-BILLED MAGPIE (*Pica nuttallii)*

Extremely rare visitor on west slope.

Record: 4000' Yosemite Valley 9/5/31 (YNN 10:85).

AMERICAN CROW (*Corvus brachyhynchos)*

Rare transient and extremely rare summer visitor below 5000' and rare transient at higher elevations on west slope; rare transient below 7500' east of crest.

American Crows, usually alone, occasionally stray to meadows, fields and pastures. One was reported on the Yosemite Christmas Bird Count on 12/28/80, but I've been unable to track down details (AB 35:737).

Peak count: 6, 6800' Cain Ranch 10/28/79 (DG).

Records above 5000' west slope: 6200' Crane Flat 10/14/75 (AB 30:122); 8200' Tenaya Lake 10/19/78 (AB 33:211).

Summer and winter records: 7/23/81, 2, 4600' Ackerson Meadow (JW); 8/5/79 8600' Tuolumne Meadow (YM); 6/3/19 (D 16) and 7/22-25/76 6400' Mono Lake (DSt, DG).

Extreme dates excluding summer and winter records west slope: 3/13/56 Yosemite Valley (AFN 10:279) - 5/1/23 Yosemite Valley (YM); 10/4/26 Yosemite Valley (YM) - 12/8/74 4000' Wawona (YM).

Extreme dates east slope excluding summer record: 3/9/82 Mono Lake (BE) - 4/19/78 Mono Lake (KC); 9/17/81 8000' Conway Summit (JZ) - 11/19/79, 2, 6900' Grant Lake Reservoir (DG).

Additional references: AB 30:122, EM 8.

COMMON RAVEN (*Corvus corax*)

	J	F	M	A	M	J	J	A	S	O	N	D	HABITAT	ELEVATIONS		
														N	T	W
WEST													DGSCA	F-9	F-12	F-9
EAST													DGSCA	7-9	6-12	6-9

Fairly common resident below 3000', fairly common summer and rare winter resident to 9000' and rare summer and early fall visitor to 12,000' on west slope; locally common resident below 7500', uncommon resident to 9000' and rare summer visitor and fall transient to 12,000' east of crest.

Common Ravens, like other corvids, have seized the foraging opportunities afforded by burgeoning resorts and hordes of motorized tourists. They cruise highways in search of road-killed squirrels, chipmunks, marmots and other animals. They scrounge campgrounds, picnic areas and vista points. They gather at garbage dumps. While they also scavenge meadows, lake and stream shores, sagebrush scrub and other open habitats, their fortunes are tied to the traffic on our highways and the garbage in our dumps. In fact, until 1950, they were unreported in Yosemite National Park (YNN 29:117).

While Ravens prefer to forage in open or openly wooded terrain, they follow roads and campgrounds into the forested heart of the mountains. They have even nested in the dense red fir forest at Crane Flat (6200'), where busy highways and a bustling campground assure plenty of food (SG). Most nesting pairs, however, eschew trees in favor of ledges on cliffs and rock walls.

Like eagles, vultures and Red-tailed Hawks, Common Ravens spend much of their time soaring overhead. Though presumably searching for meals, they often seem to be sporting, turning cartwheels and engaging in aerial acrobatics.

Even in mid-winter, Common Ravens occasionally cruise the higher elevations. During the exceptionally snowy 1983 winter, for example, they were seen over Tuolumne Meadows (8600') during periods of clear weather (YM).

High elevation record: 12,600' Mt. Dana 6/11/86 (DG).

Peak count: approximately 150, 6500' Mono Lake dump, 9/12/87 (DG).

Additional representative nesting localities: (approx. 2000' Merced River Canyon—MR); approx. 8500' Mono Dome (KC); approx. 8000' near Grant Lake (CMc); 7000' near Crowley Lake dam (CMc); (approx. 9000' Glass Mountain—CMc).

Family PARIDAE: TITMICE

Of four species, only Mountain Chickadees are widespread mountaineers. All flit through trees and shrubbery, gleaning insects and other invertebrates from foliage and bark. They brave Sierran winters in their breeding haunts, sustaining themselves on insect eggs and overwintering larvae and pupae.

MOUNTAIN CHICKADEE (*Parus gambeli*)

	J	F	M	A	M	J	J	A	S	O	N	D	HABITAT	ELEVATIONS		
														N	T	W
WEST													POW	3-10		F-10
EAST													PW	6-10		6-10

Fairly common resident from 3000' to 4000', common resident from 4000' to treeline and irregularly rare to uncommon winter resident below 3000' on west slope; common resident below treeline east of crest.

Mountain Chickadees are the conifers' most constant companions. Even in winter, when less hardy fowl flee to balmier climes, these midget mountaineers glean meals from pines and firs all the way to treeline. At Tuolumne Meadows (8600'), for example, they are "by far the most common winter resident" (TH).

Mountain Chickadees are at home among most coniferous trees, shunning only the digger pines of the western foothills. While they nest among pinyon pines east of the crest, they are more numerous in the lusher evergreens of higher elevations. They also breed in oaks, old apple orchards and, east of the crest, aspen groves, cottonwoods and large mountain mahoganies. At Mono Lake County Park (6500'), for example, they nest in cottonwoods and willows far from the nearest evergreen (DG). They dwell in open woodlands as well as dense forests, even breeding in burns or montane chaparral with scattered trees or snags. For nesting sites they usually avail themselves of woodpecker-excavated or natural tree cavities, but also use holes or crannies in buildings as well as drain pipes and nest boxes.

While many Mountain Chickadees reside year-round in their nesting haunts, others wander during fall and winter. In some years, they invade the western foothills and spread east into pinyons, junipers and deciduous trees and thickets. They appear, for example, in the willow and buffalo-berry thickets that margin Mono Lake (6400'), and stray occasionally into treeless sagebrush scrub.

High elevation record: 12,400' Kuna Crest 10/6/55 (AFN 10:53).

Representative nesting localities: 4000' Yosemite Valley (GS 574); 4400' Foresta (DG); 4600' Ackerson Meadow (JW); 6200' Crane Flat (DG); 8600' Tuolumne Meadow (DG); 10,200' Hall Natural Area (DeSante MS); 7400' Lee Vining Canyon (DG); 9000' Glass Mountain (DG).

Additional reference: C 41:250.

CHESTNUT-BACKED CHICKADEE (*Parus rufescens*)

	J	F	M	A	M	J	J	A	S	O	N	D	HABITAT	ELEVATIONS		
														N	T	W
WEST													OWP	3-5		3-5
EAST																

Locally uncommon resident from 3500' to 5000' on west slope.

Chestnut-backed Chickadees were not discovered in the Sierra Nevada until 1951 (C 54:115, AFN 5:307), nor in the Yosemite region until 1958 (AFN 13:60). They are probably recent immigrants, as Yosemite's skilled early birdwatchers would not have overlooked them. They belong to the northern rather than the coastal California race (*P. r. rufescens*—AB 30:673).

The moist, densely forested homes of Sierran Chestnut-backed Chickadees are reminiscent of their haunts in the north coast ranges. They are partial to Douglas firs, big-leaf maples, alders and madrones, but also consort with ponderosa pines, sugar pines, incense cedars, sequoias, black oaks and other trees.

High elevation record: 5400' w. Fireplace Creek 3/1/86 (GSt).

Representative nesting localities: 4000' Yosemite Valley (AB 36:891, DG); 4100' Mirror Lake (DG); 4600' Hodgdon Meadow (DG); 4600' Ackerson Meadow (AB 37:910).

Additional references: AB 26:652, AB 27:116, Western Tanager 32:82.

PLAIN TITMOUSE (*Parus inornatus*)

	J	F	M	A	M	J	J	A	S	O	N	D	HABITAT	ELEVATIONS		
														N	T	W
WEST													OP	F-3		F-4
EAST													PS	6-8		6-8

Fairly common resident below 3000', rare visitor to 4000' and extremely rare visitor at higher elevations on west slope; rare winter resident below 8000' on east slope; rare summer and uncommon winter resident below 8000' east of Sierran escarpment.

Like Scrub Jays and Bushtits, Plain Titmice on the west slope belong to a different subspecies than their east side cousins. These races differ subtly in voice and plumage, and more dramatically in habitat (see National Geographic Society *Field Guide*, p. 308).

On the west slope, *P. i. inornatus* nests among oaks and digger pines in the sun-drenched foothills. To the east, *P. i. zaleptus* dwells among pinyon pines and Utah junipers on hills and flats.

Both races of Plain Titmice favor open woodlands with tree cavities in which to rear young. In the absence of woodpecker excavations, rotted-out knot holes or other suitable natural sites, they avail themselves of bird boxes and even drain pipes. They forage on the ground as well as in trees.

In fall and winter, Plain Titmice wander outside their nesting haunts into atypical habitats. On the west slope they wander upslope, where they forage in ponderosa pines, black oaks and other forest trees; most Yosemite Valley records (4000'), for instance, fall between November and February (EM 13, YNN 10:31, YM). East of the crest they stray into cottonwood groves, willow and buffalo-berry thickets and even treeless sagebrush scrub.

Records above 5000' west slope: 7000' near Jackass Meadow 7/7/81 (SG); 7800' White Wolf 7/22/76 (SG) and 9/16/80 (HF).

Representative nesting localities: 2000' Mariposa (CL); 2100' El Portal (DG); 6800' near Goat Ranch (DG); 7500' Rancheria Gulch, Mono Basin (HG); 6900' North Canyon, Glass Mountain (DS).

Additional reference: GS 572.

BUSHTIT (*Psaltriparus minimus*)

	J	F	M	A	M	J	J	A	S	O	N	D	HABITAT	ELEVATIONS		
														N	T	W
WEST													SOWP	F-4	F-10	F-4
EAST													SWP	6-8	6-10	6-8

Common resident below 3000', uncommon resident to 4000', uncommon summer visitor to 7000' and rare summer and early fall visitor to treeline on west slope; uncommon winter resident and rare summer resident below 8000' and rare summer and early fall visitor to treeline east of crest.

Bushtits which nest on the west slope belong to a different subspecies than their east slope relatives, and differ recognizably in plumage and haunts (see National Geographic Society *Field Guide*, p. 312). In fall and winter, however, both Pacific and interior races flock together east of the Sierran escarpment (*P. m. californicus, P. m. providentialis* and possibly others—BE, DG, GS 579).

Bushtits are marginal mountaineers, preferring the foothills and valleys both west and east of the crest. They dwell in dry as well as moist situations provided there are large shrubs or small trees in which to forage and nest. Their haunts range from dry slopes and canyons to moist streams and meadows. On the west slope, they nest on chaparral-covered slopes with scattered oaks or pines, in oak savannah and open oak woodlands and in riparian thickets of cottonwood, willow and other hardwoods. East of the crest they usually consort with pinyons and junipers, but also range into mountain mahoganies, sagebrush scrub and, especially in fall and winter, riparian willow and buffalo-berry thickets. They forage almost entirely in trees and shrubs, flitting through the foliage in loose, cheerful flocks.

During summer, Bushtits drift upslope into montane chaparral, willow thickets and open woodlands. They often flock along the margins of meadows. While most of these mountaineers were born at lower elevations, a few may nest as high as 8000'. On the west slope, they breed irregularly in Yosemite Valley (4000'—EM 14; DG), and I have seen wobbly fledglings between Vernal and Nevada Falls (5500'). East of the crest there is a nesting record at the extraordinary elevation of 9600' (Glass Mountain—AFN 18:70); no other records top 7800'.

Bushtits, like Plain Titmice, Scrub Jays and Bewick's Wrens, are not considered migratory. Yet in valleys east of the Sierran escarpment, they are all more numerous in fall and winter than during the nesting season. Where do these wintering birds come from?

Because of their gregarious habits, Bushtits may seem locally abundant, even at higher elevations. A flock of 46, for instance, was at Crane Flat (6200') on 9/7-9/74 (AB 29:116).

High elevation record: 10,300' Hall Natural Area, 3, 6/30/81 and 7, 7/10/81 (DeSante and Engstrom MS).

Extreme dates above 5000' west slope: 6/6/64 8600' Tuolumne Meadows (AFN 19:575) - 10/20/87 9000' McGee Canyon, 15 (DS, JM).

Additional representative nesting localities: 1300' Merced River (MR); 2000' Mariposa (CL); (7800' moraine s. of Lee Vining Canyon—DG); 6500' w. Mono Lake (AB 38:1059).

Additional references: AB 26:899, AB 27:912, C 23:35, C 27:113, D 637, YNN 29:47.

Family SITTIDAE: NUTHATCHES

Unlike woodpeckers and creepers, which use their tails to brace themselves on vertical trunks, nuthatches rely entirely on strong, elongate toes and claws to climb about, sometimes upside down, on the bark of trees. The name "nuthatch," a corruption of "nut-axe," derives from their habit of wedging plant seeds in bark and pounding them open with their bills. The bulk of their diets, however, consists of insects and spiders gleaned from the bark of trees. Even during winter, nuthatches can usually find sufficient insect eggs and other foods to subsist at high elevations. Our three resident species differ in habitat as well as plumage and voice.

RED-BREASTED NUTHATCH (*Sitta canadensis)*

	J	F	M	A	M	J	J	A	S	O	N	D	HABITAT	ELEVATIONS		
														N	T	W
WEST													PO	3-8	F-10	F-10
EAST													P	7-8	6-10	6-10

Irregularly rare to common winter resident below 3000', uncommon summer resident and irregularly rare to common winter resident from 3000' to 4000', common summer resident and irregularly rare to common winter resident from 4000' to 8000', and rare summer resident and irregularly rare to fairly common summer visitor and winter resident to treeline on west slope; fairly common summer resident and irregularly rare to common winter resident below 9000' and rare summer resident and irregularly rare to fairly common summer visitor and winter resident to treeline east of crest.

Shady, mid-elevation coniferous forests have no more distinctive voice than the nasal "yanks" of Red-breasted Nuthatches. Bold, inquisitive and cheerfully loquacious, they are the forest's most forward avian inhabitants. Their excited, nasal calls, which make me think of troops of children blasting away on toy horns, announce and welcome every intruder. And should a Pygmy Owl, Pine Marten or other guest harbor hostile intentions, these fearless fellows lead their feathered brethren in driving it away.

During the nesting season, Red-breasted Nuthatches are partial to dense, shady forests of mature red firs, sugar pines, ponderosa pines, sequoias, incense cedars, white firs, douglas firs, black oaks and other trees. They shun the sun-baked digger pines of the western foothills, the open lodgepole pine forests of high elevations and the pinyon woodlands east of the Sierran escarpment. At lower elevations, they reside in the cooling shadows of densely wooded canyons and north-facing slopes.

Like woodpeckers, they excavate their own nesting cavities, but require dead trees and snags in advanced states of decay. They forage from the tops of lofty trees to the forest floor, and sometimes sally for insects in the manner of flycatchers (YNN 19:20).

Red-breasted Nuthatches wander both above, below and outside their nesting haunts, but their numbers and whereabouts vary from year to year. Some years they winter from the foothills to treeline; in others, they desert large portions of the region entirely, invading lowland California in large numbers. Tallies on Christmas Bird Counts, for instance, have varied from 80 to 0 in Yosemite, 47 to 0 in Mammoth and 58 to 0 at Mono Lake; in 1983 they were abundant on the east side, absent to the west. In Yosemite Valley (4000'), hundreds may arrive as early as mid-August and linger until the following April (YM). Are they Sierran-born, or do they hail from further north?

Non-nesting Red-breasted Nuthatches are much more catholic in choice of habitat. They still favor dense, mature conifers, but also wander into lodgepole and whitebark pines, pinyon pines, oak woodlands, aspen groves, cottonwoods, desert mahogany and residential neighborhoods. They mingle with White-breasted Nuthatches in open woodlands, and with Pygmy Nuthatches in long-needled jeffrey and ponderosa pines; particularly in late summer and fall, one may encounter all three "nuts" in the same tree (YNN 19:4, DG, HG).

In sum, non-breeding Red-breasted Nuthatches can appear in any terrestrial habitat. In the southern Sierra I have found them foraging among rocks at Kearsarge Pass (11,800'); in this region, they have reached 11,000' above Convict Lake (DG) and 10,500' in Glacier Canyon (DG). Jon Miller, while climbing on Yosemite Valley's Washington Column (approximately 5000'), observed nuthatch mountaineers stuffing nuts into cracks and behind flakes on the granite wall hundreds of vertical feet above the valley floor. Undoubtedly they have planted most of the pines that cling tenaciously to Yosemite's walls.

Representative nesting localities: 4000' Yosemite Valley (EM 13); 4600' Ackerson Meadow (JW); 6000' Chinquapin (GS 570); 6200' Crane Flat (DG); 7000' Peregoy Meadow (DG); 8000' Siesta Lake (DG); 10,100' Hall Natural Area—only in 1987 (DeSante and Engstrom MS); 8000' Mammoth Lakes (DG).

Additional references: C 36:113, YNN 9:60.

WHITE-BREASTED NUTHATCH (*Sitta carolinensis*)

	J	F	M	A	M	J	J	A	S	O	N	D	HABITAT	ELEVATIONS		
														N	T	W
WEST	■	■	■	■	■	■	■	■	■	■	■	■	OP	F-10		F-10
EAST	■	■	■	■	■	■	■	■	■	■	■	■	P	6-10		6-10

Fairly common resident below 3000', rare resident or visitor between 3000' and 8000' and uncommon resident from 8000' to treeline on west slope; uncommon resident below treeline east of crest.

White-breasted Nuthatches have a disjunct distribution. Numerous in the western foothills, they are scarce at mid-elevations, but increase in numbers above 8000'. The birds of the western foothills belong to the subspecies *S. c. aculeata*, which differs most obviously from *S. c. tenuissima* of the high mountains and east side in its call notes (*aculeata* give one or two nasal "keers," *tenuissima* a longer series of high-pitched notes—JD). It remains for some keen-eared sittaphile to trace their ranges; *Tenuissima* occurs west to at least Siesta Lake (8000'), and *aculeata* has been suspected at Glacier Point (7200'—JD).

Both races of White-breasted Nuthatch prefer open forests and woodlands with large-trunked trees. In contrast to Red-breasteds, they shun shady, deep woods. In the western foothills, they nest among oaks and digger pines; at higher elevations, jeffrey, western white, lodgepole and other pines. East of the crest, they also dwell among large pinyon pines and, less frequently, aspens and cottonwoods. Unlike Red-breasteds, they rarely excavate their own nesting holes, but appropriate woodpecker-excavated or natural cavities.

In fall and winter, White-breasted Nuthatches may wander outside their nesting haunts, but not to the extent of their Red-breasted cousins. They appear, for example, in isolated groves of trees and in the wooded parts of towns. At high elevations, they winter most but not every year; they abandoned Tuolumne Meadows (8600'), for example, during the exceptionally snowy 1983 winter, reappearing on 5/9/83 (YM).

Representative nesting localities: 2100' El Portal (DG); 6000' Henness Ridge (DG); 6800' Tamarack Flat (GS 567); 7800' White Wolf (ABR); 8600' Tuolumne Meadow (DG); 10,200' Hall Natural Area (AB 31:1186, DeSante MS); 9200' Minaret Summit (DG); 8000' Lee Vining Canyon (DG); 7000' Mono Mills (DG).

Additional references: C 27:113, C 38:86, GS 564.

PYGMY NUTHATCH (*Sitta pygmaea*)

	J	F	M	A	M	J	J	A	S	O	N	D	HABITAT	ELEVATIONS		
														N	T	W
WEST	▬	▬	▬	▬	▬	▬	▬	▬	▬	▬	▬	▬	P	3-7	3-10	3-7
EAST	█	█	█	█	█	█	█	█	█	█	█	█	PW	6-8	6-10	6-8

Locally uncommon resident from 3000' to 7000' and rare summer visitor to treeline on west slope; fairly common resident below 8000' and rare summer visitor to treeline east of crest.

Pygmys are the most gregarious nuthatch, trooping in small, chattering bands from pine to pine. Because of their small size, "p-nuts" are difficult to see among thick clusters of needles. Sharp, staccato cries, which suggest the notes of crossbills, betray their presence.

No other birds are so partial to particular kinds of trees. On the west slope, Pygmy Nuthatches rarely forage in anything but ponderosa pines; to the east, jeffrey pines. They will nest, however, in aspens and cottonwoods, chiseling nesting cavities in the soft, decaying wood.

Pygmy Nuthatches favor open, park-like forests, shunning dense woods. On the west slope, they generally keep to the ponderosa pines that grow on dry slopes and benches. East of the crest they follow jeffrey pines from Sierran canyonbottoms eastward into the Mono Craters and Glass Mountain regions. Unlike their bark-gleaning cousins, they spend most of their time foraging among the thick clusters of pine needles, small branchwork and cones.

High elevation record: 10,300' Hall Natural Area, many records (DeSante MS).

Extreme dates above 8000', both Hall Natural Area (to 10,300'): 7/27/81 - 9/9/80 (DeSante MS).

Representative nesting localities: 4600' Ackerson Meadow (JW); 4900' north of Arch Rock in Yosemite Valley (YNN 23:41); 6900' Yosemite Point (EM 13); 7400' Lee Vining Canyon (DG); 7000' Mono Mills (DG).

Additional references: C 27:113, GS 571.

Family CERTHIIDAE: CREEPERS

BROWN CREEPER (*Certhia americana)*

	J	F	M	A	M	J	J	A	S	O	N	D	HABITAT	ELEVATIONS		
														N	T	W
WEST													POW	3-10		F-8
EAST													PW	6-10		6-8

Irregularly rare to fairly common winter resident below 3000', fairly common summer resident and irregularly rare to fairly common winter resident from 3000' to 8000' and irregularly rare to uncommon summer resident or visitor to treeline on west slope; fairly common summer resident and irregularly rare to uncommon winter resident below 8000' and irregularly rare to uncommon summer resident or visitor to treeline east of crest.

Brown Creepers are much more numerous than they seem to birdwatchers unattuned to their high-pitched calls and plaintive whistled songs. While not particularly shy, their woodsy brown plumage conceals them as they hitch up the boles of tree after tree. Yet the Sierra's shady forests have no more constant avian companion.

Brown Creepers favor dense groves of conifers, but also dwell among oaks, aspens, cottonwoods and other deciduous trees, particularly in fall and winter. Though they sometimes nest near treeline, they are most numerous among the red and white firs, incense cedars, sugar and ponderosa pines, sequoias and douglas firs of lower elevations. They cradle their young in hammock-like nests slung between the boles of large or dead trees and pieces of loosened bark. I have found such nests in incense cedars, red firs, ponderosa pines, sugar pines, sequoias, lodgepole pines, jeffrey pines and even black oaks.

Above 8000', in the lodgepole pine forests of higher elevations, Brown Creepers are markedly irregular. In some years, they nest to treeline; in others, non-breeding birds visit in mid- to late summer, or do not appear at all.

During most winters, Brown Creepers brave storms and blizzards in their breeding haunts, even at high elevations. They glean pupae, grubs and other fare from the snow-free vertical trunks of trees. In some years, however, they desert the mountains, invading the foothills and materializing in towns and isolated groves; numbers on Christmas Bird Counts, for example, have varied from 36 to 1 in Yosemite and from 22 to 1 at Mono Lake. At such times, they may materialize in any type of wooded habitat.

Representative nesting localities: 3200' Olive Creek (MR); 4000' Yosemite Valley (YM); 4000' Wawona (YM); 4600' Ackerson Meadow (JW); 7000' Peregoy Meadow (DG); 7800' White

Wolf (DG); 8600' Tuolumne Meadow (DG); 10,000' Hall Natural Area (DeSante MS); 8000' Mammoth Lakes (DG).

Additional references: GS 561, YNN 11:2, YNN 17:123.

Family TROGLODYTIDAE: WRENS

Our six nesting species differ more dramatically in habitat and voice than they do in coloration. All are energetic bughunters who forage close to the earth or in low vegetation. Bewick's, Canyon and Winter wrens remain in or near their nesting haunts all year; the others migrate, at least from the higher parts of their ranges, to balmier winter quarters.

ROCK WREN (*Salpinctes obsoletus*)

	J	F	M	A	M	J	J	A	S	O	N	D	HABITAT	ELEVATIONS		
														N	T	W
WEST	━	━	━	━	━	━	━	━	━	━	━	━	C	F-12		F-3
EAST			─	━	━	━	━	━	━	─			C	6-12		

Locally uncommon resident below 3000', rare summer resident to 9000' and uncommon summer resident to 12,000' on west slope; uncommon summer resident below 12,000' east of crest.

Of all our breeding birds, Rock Wrens have the greatest altitudinal range, nesting from foothill canyons to alpine fell fields. Yet they are inexplicably scarce at mid-elevations on the west slope, shunning, for example, the talus below Yosemite's vertical walls.

True to their names, Rock Wrens dwell among rock outcroppings, rock slides, talus slopes, fractured cliff faces, lava flows and, at Mono Lake, tufa towers. They care nought about elevation or climate so long as there be crevices, fissures and other small openings in which to forage, shelter and nest. The rocks themselves need not be large, and may be interspersed with shrubs or grasses. Lacking large rocks, shrubs suffice for song and look-out posts. Yet only during migrations do these tiny bughunters occasionally stray from their rocky haunts onto dry, earthen banks, dilapidated buildings, fallen logs and wood piles.

Rock Wrens vie with White-tailed Ptarmigans, Horned Larks, Mountain Bluebirds, American Pipits and Rosy Finches for the honor of nesting highest in the Sierra. In the vastness of the alpine landscape, their bright songs and jaunty bearing cheer the mountaineer on his or her lonely rambles.

Extreme dates above 4000', both Mono Lake (6400'): 3/22/86 (LF) - 10/13/79 (DG).

Representative nesting localities: 2000' Mariposa (CL); 3800' Hetch Hetchy (MM, SG); 6000' Little Yosemite Valley (YM); 9200' near Tuolumne Meadow (MR); 11,000' Hall Natural Area

(DeSante MS); 12,000' Dana Plateau (DG); 8000' Mono Craters (DG); 6400' Negit and Paoha Islands (C 40:262; DS).

Additional references: GS 550; YNN 21:79, YNN 23:41, YNN 29:47.

CANYON WREN (*Catherpes mexicanus*)

	J	F	M	A	M	J	J	A	S	O	N	D	HABITAT	ELEVATIONS		
														N	T	W
WEST													C	F-6		F-6
EAST													C	6-8		6-8

Locally fairly common resident below 4500', uncommon resident to 6000' and extremely rare summer visitor at higher elevations on west slope; uncommon resident below 8000' and extremely rare summer visitor at higher elevations east of crest.

Canyon Wrens are not easily seen as they pick their way through boulder fields and steep canyon walls. But, in spring and early summer, their loud, joyous songs are readily heard. Ralph Hoffmann (1927) has likened their rich, descending whistles to "the spray of a waterfall in sunshine." Be that as it may, theirs is a song that can never be forgotten.

Canyon Wrens favor steep, rocky stream canyons, but also dwell on rock outcroppings, slides and boulder-strewn hillsides. They shelter and nest in crevices and fissures. Compared to Rock Wrens, they are more shade-tolerant and water-loving. Around Yosemite Valley, for example, they inhabit narrow, water-scoured canyons as well as the large boulders that slough off vertical walls. Though their haunts are usually treeless, they follow boulders into shaded woodlands, as beneath canyon oaks west of the crest and pinyon pines to the east.

Unlike Rock Wrens, which desert the higher elevations during the colder months, Canyon Wrens are year-round residents. During winter, however, they sometimes stray outside their breeding haunts. They have appeared, for example, on tufa-covered boulders along Mono Lake's west shore (DG).

Records above 6000' west slope and 8000' east of crest: 7200' Merced Lake 8/23-9/1/15 (GS 552); 7600' one mile n. of Smoky Jack 7/12/78 (SG); 10,000' Lower Young Lake 7/29/79 (MR); 10,500' Hall Natural Area 9/29/81 (AB 36:215, DeSante and Engstrom MS); 9000' Fern Lake 8/3/79 (DG); (there is also a record at 12,200' in the southern Sierra—AB 38:243).

Representative nesting localities: 1300' Merced River Canyon (MR); 4000' Yosemite Valley (GS 554, YNN 21:77); 4700' above Lake Eleanor Reservoir (TB); 5500' in Illilouette Gorge (YM); (7500' Lee Vining Canyon—DG); (7300' Cottonwood Canyon—DG).

BEWICK'S WREN (*Thryomanes bewickii*)

	J	F	M	A	M	J	J	A	S	O	N	D	HABITAT	ELEVATIONS		
														N	T	W
WEST	■	■	■	■	■	■	■	■	■	■	■	■	SOW	F-3	F-5	F-3
EAST	—	—	—	—					—	—	—	—	SW	6-7		6-7

Fairly common resident below 2000', locally uncommon resident to 3500', rare summer and fall visitor to 5000', extremely rare summer visitor above 5000' and extremely rare winter visitor above 3500' on west slope; rare summer and uncommon winter resident below 7500' east of crest except on Cedar Hill, where fairly common summer resident.

Bewick's Wrens are vociferous denizens of the foothills, especially on the lower west slope. They favor shrubby vegetation with scattered trees or open, woody overstories. In the western foothills, they dwell on chaparral-covered hillsides, in live oak-digger pine woodlands and along thicket-lined watercourses. East of the Sierran escarpment, they nest in sagebrush scrub, riparian thickets and pinyon woodlands, but are most numerous among Utah junipers.

In fall and winter, in the lower portions of the Mono Basin, Bewick's Wrens—like Scrub Jays, Plain Titmice, Bushtits, Mountain Chickadees and other small birds—move into dense riparian thickets of willow, buffalo-berry and adjacent sagebrush scrub. They appear in September about the time House Wrens depart, and leave in April about the time House Wrens return.

Records above 5000' west slope: 6400' Deer Camp Road 9/9/81 (JL); 6300', 2, Snow Creek Trail 6/?/42 (YNN 21:78); 7600' near Smoky Jack 8/16/76 (SG).

Extreme dates and winter record above 3500' west slope: 5/?/28 approx. 6000' Snow Creek Trail (YNN 21:78) - 11/16/53 4000' Yosemite Valley (AFN 8:40); 1/30/84 4600' Ackerson Meadow (JW).

Representative nesting localities: 1300' Merced River Canyon (MR); 2000' Mariposa (CL); approx. 4500' Indian Canyon (YNN 21:78); (6800' s. Lee Vining—DG); (7200' Cedar Hill—DG); 6500' Negit Island (DS, SJ, PS).

Additional references: AFN 8:40, GS 555.

HOUSE WREN (*Troglodytes aedon*)

	J	F	M	A	M	J	J	A	S	O	N	D	HABITAT	ELEVATIONS		
														N	T	W
WEST													WOS	F-5	F-10	
EAST													WS	6-8	6-10	

Locally common summer resident below 3000', uncommon summer resident to 5000' and fairly common summer visitor or fall transient from 4000' to treeline on west slope; common summer resident below 8500' and fairly common summer visitor and fall transient to treeline east of crest.

About the time aspens and cottonwoods unfurl their leaves, House Wrens return to Sierran nesting haunts. From spring through early summer, their bubbling songs are a constant, pleasing voice of deciduous groves and woodlands, especially east of the Sierran escarpment.

Though partial to the aspens, cottonwoods, willows and other deciduous trees that grow about streams and springs, House Wrens also nest in live oak woodlands and, true to their name, in buildings and sheds. From their nesting haunts, they embark on foraging expeditions into nearby scrub, such as chaparral west of the crest and sagebrush to the east. In the higher mountains, they are partial to moist willow thickets, but materialize in drier habitats as well. Few birds can equal the energy of these bug-hunters as they busily search for insects among shrubbery, fallen logs and root tangles.

The numbers of nesting House Wrens are probably limited by the availability of suitable nesting cavities. Nowhere are they more numerous than in eastside aspen groves, where there is a surfeit of woodpecker-excavated and natural holes. They also nest in oaks, cottonwoods, willows and apple trees as well as buildings and bird boxes.

High elevation record: 10,300' Hall Natural Area, many records (DeSante MS).

Extreme dates: 4/10/86 6500' w. of Mono Lake (DG) - 9/27/87 6600' Dechambeau Creek (ESt).

Representative nesting localities: 2100' El Portal (MR); 4000' Yosemite Valley (YNN 21:79); 4600' Ackerson Meadow (JW); 7200' Harden Lake—exceptional elevation for west slope (SG); 8500' Lundy Canyon (DG); 8500' Virginia Creek (C 43:250); 7400' Lee Vining Canyon (DG); 6500' Mono Lake County Park (DG).

Additional references: AB 27:912, C 27:113, EM 13, GS 556, YNN 23:41.

WINTER WREN (*Troglodytes troglodytes*)

	J	F	M	A	M	J	J	A	S	O	N	D	HABITAT	ELEVATIONS		
														N	T	W
WEST	—	—	—	—	—	—	—	—	—	—	—	—	RPOW	F-5	F-8	F-5
EAST	—	—	—		•				•	—	—	—	RPW		7	6-8

Locally uncommon resident below 5000', rare summer resident and extremely rare winter visitor to 6000', rare summer visitor to 8000' and extremely rare fall transient to treeline on west slope—may nest as high as 8000'; extremely rare fall transient to treeline and rare winter resident below 8000' east of crest.

In the moist, shady depths of old-growth forests, Winter Wrens skulk among logs, root tangles, undercut banks and log jams. These mousy birds are more easily heard than seen. During spring and early summer, their long, joyous songs ring through the woods, but are not always easy to trace.

Winter Wrens only nest on the west slope, where they are most numerous along languid streams below the level of heavy snow. These smallest and darkest of forest-dwelling birds live beneath douglas firs, sugar pines, sequoias, alders, maples and other trees. At higher elevations, they summer and probably nest in old-growth red fir forests; singing, territorial birds, for example, have been heard at Crane Flat (6200'—DG, JW), near the Glacier Point Road (6900' and 7300'—SH) and near White Wolf (7900'—SH).

East of the crest, Winter Wrens winter in groves with deep shade, moist soil and a plenitude of fallen logs. They have been found in aspens as well as lodgepole pines. I know of no evidence to support the contention that they reside year-round on the "east slope...south to Mammoth" (SU 294).

Winter record above 5000' west slope: 6200' Crane Flat 1/15/77 (TB, DG).

Records above 8000': 8600' Tuolumne Meadows 10/17/86 (TB) and 9/16/82 (MR); 8800' near Tuolumne Meadows 9/13/79 (MR); 9800'-10,200' Hall Natural Area late 8/9/86, 8/17/84, Aug./74 and 10/28/77 (DeSante and Engstrom MS).

Extreme dates below 8000' east of crest: 9/29/87 6500' w. Mono Lake (PM); 10/13/77 8000' Mammoth (John Derby); 3/28/87 7400' Lee Vining Canyon (DG); 5/26/91 w. shore Mono Lake (AB 45:493).

Representative nesting localities: 4000' Yosemite Valley (GS 560); 4800' Crane Creek (RS); 4600' Ackerson Meadow (JW); 4800' near Henness Ridge (JS); (5800' Tuolumne Grove—DG; a report of nesting at 11,000' in the southern Sierra is probably specious—Bent 1964).

Additional references: AFN 17:431, AB 28:849, EM 13, YNN 21:78

MARSH WREN (*Cistothorus palustris*)

	J	F	M	A	M	J	J	A	S	O	N	D	HABITAT	ELEVATIONS		
														N	T	W
WEST		•		•				•				•	MaGW		F-5	4
EAST													MaGW	6		6-7

Rare fall transient and extremely rare winter visitor and spring transient below 5000' and extremely rare transient at higher elevations on west slope; extremely rare transient on east slope; rare summer resident, fairly common fall transient and rare winter resident below 7000' east of Sierran escarpment except at Simons Spring on se. shore of Mono Lake, where fairly common summer resident.

True to their name, Marsh Wrens dwell in marshes, boggy meadows and adjacent shrubbery. While they nest in beds of tall cattails, they tarry and winter in all types of dense, low herbaceous and woody vegetation, provided it is in or near water or damp ground. East of the Sierran escarpment, wintering birds huddle near hot springs, as along Hot Creek (7000') and at Dechambeau Ponds (6500').

Records above 5000': 8600' Tuolumne Meadows 8/24/54 (AFN 9:53); 10,500' Gardisky Lake 8/10/79 (AB 36:328, DeSante and Engstrom MS).

Winter and spring records west slope, both Yosemite Valley (4000'): 2/13/72 (JZ); 4/25/43 (YNN 22:73); (there is also a 12/22/74 Yosemite Christmas Bird Count record , but I have been unable to determine where the bird was observed).

Extreme dates west excluding above records: Yosemite Valley 8/24/34 (YNN 13:77) and 8600' Tuolumne Meadows 8/24/54 (AFN 9:53) - Yosemite Valley 11/1/15 (GS 561).

Representative nesting localities: 6400' Simons Spring (DG); (6400' w. shore Mono Lake—SJ).

Additional references: YNN 18:127, YNN 21:78, YNN 22:73.

Family CINCLIDAE: DIPPERS

AMERICAN DIPPER (*Cinclus mexicanus*)

	J	F	M	A	M	J	J	A	S	O	N	D	HABITAT	ELEVATIONS		
														N	T	W
WEST													RL	F-10		F-8
EAST													RL	6-10		6-8

Fairly common resident below 8000', uncommon summer resident and rare winter visitor to treeline and rare summer visitor above treeline on west slope; fairly common summer resident and uncommon winter resident below 8000', uncommon summer resident and rare winter visitor to treeline and rare summer visitor above treeline on east slope.

No Sierran river or stream is too cold or swift for American Dippers. John Muir called them "the mountain streams' own darling, the hummingbird of blooming waters, loving rocky ripple-slopes and sheets of foam as a bee loves flowers", adding "among all the mountain birds, none has cheered me so much in my lonely wanderings" (Muir 1878). They rarely forsake the company of flowing water, following every sinuous curve of even the smallest creeks.

While they often sport in the rapids, American Dippers dwell along quiet waters as well, including the margins of glacial lakes. If there are suitable nest sites, they will breed along small streams as well as large rivers. They usually place their large, globular nests on ledges in steep rock walls that rise above flowing water or sit behind waterfalls. I've also found nests, however, ensconced on log jams, beneath dense bank vegetation and under bridges.

Above 9000', most American Dippers are juvenile or post-breeding birds that wander up from lower elevations from mid-summer through early fall. A few are "continuously resident, even under the rigors of the Sierran winter, up as high as any water remains open" (GS 544), but most retreat to winter downstream.

It does not take American Dippers long to colonize new habitat. Three years after wet winters and court orders forced the Los Angeles Department of Water and Power to rewater Rush Creek, at least three pairs were nesting along the ten miles of resurrected stream (DG).

When rivers begin to swell and roar with snowmelt, the strong warbles and trills of singing American Dippers rise in sweet melody above the boisterous water. "While water sings, so must he; in heat or cold, calm or storm, ever attuning his voice in sure accord" (Muir 1878).

American Dipperlets at nest, courtesy Discovering Sierra Birds

High elevation record: 11,600' McClure Lake 9/29/55 (YM).

High elevation winter record: 9800' Lee Vining Creek 1/1/79 (AB 33:311, DeSante MS).

Representative nesting localities: 1500' Merced River (AFN 7:289); 2000' Merced River near El Portal (MR); 4000' Yosemite Valley (GS 543-546); 7800' Glen Aulin (YM); 10,200' Hall Natural Area (DeSante MS); 9000' Warren Fork Lee Vining Creek (DG); 7500' Lee Vining Creek (DG); 6600' Rush Creek (DG).

Additional references: AFN 16:71, YNN 10:70, YNN 17:134.

Family MUSCICAPIDAE: MUSCICAPIDS

Taxonomists have recently lumped the kinglets and gnatcatchers, thrushes and wrentits, formerly of separate families, into this new, large and variable group.

Subfamily SYLVIINAE: : Kinglets and Gnatcatchers

GOLDEN-CROWNED KINGLET (*Regulus satrapa)*

	J	F	M	A	M	J	J	A	S	O	N	D	HABITAT	ELEVATIONS		
														N	T	W
WEST													PWO	4-10		F-8
EAST													PW	7-10		6-8

Common summer and irregularly rare to common winter resident from 4000' to 8000', rare summer resident to treeline and irregularly rare to common winter resident below 4000' on west slope; locally uncommon summer resident below 9000', rare summer resident to treeline and irregularly rare to fairly common winter resident below 8000' east of crest.

To one unattuned to their high-pitched, creeper-like notes, Golden-crowned Kinglets would hardly seem the most numerous avian inhabitants of mid-elevation coniferous forests. Yet wherever one wanders in the west slopes' old-growth fir and mixed conifer forests, one will hear—and occasionally glimpse—these tiny birds.

During the nesting season, Golden-crowned Kinglets favor mature, well-shaded forests, especially stands of old-growth red firs. Below the fir belt, as in Yosemite Valley (4000'), they sequester themselves in shady groves of douglas firs, sugar pines, ponderosa pines and other conifers in deep canyons and on north-facing slopes. East of the crest, they dwell in scattered pockets of dense firs and pines. They glean insects high in the canopy, forsaking lofty trees only to drink and bathe at seeps, springs and streams.

During winter, Golden-crowned Kinglets are more widespread but less predictable. In contrast to the nesting season, they are not tied to conifers, but range into oaks, cottonwoods, willows and other hardwoods. Moreover their numbers and whereabouts fluctuate. In most years, they brave winter's fury in the forests where they nest. In others, they descend en masse to lower elevations, occasionally wintering in open, sunny habitats such as live oak woodlands on the west slope and pinyon woodlands to the east. Or they desert the mountains entirely. On the Yosemite Christmas Bird Count, for example, tallies have varied from 483 to 0.

High elevation record: 10,100' Hall Natural Area, many records (DeSante MS).

Representative nesting localities: 4000' Yosemite Valley (GS 588-89, EM 14); (4600' Hodgdon Meadow—DG); 4600' Ackerson Meadow (JW); (6200' Crane Flat—DG); 7800' Porcupine Creek (TB, SH); (8000' Siesta Lake—DG); 9000' Mammoth Pass (GM 371); 10,100' Hall Natural Area (DeSante MS); (8000' Lee Vining Canyon—DG).

RUBY-CROWNED KINGLET (*Regulus calendula*)

	J	F	M	A	M	J	J	A	S	O	N	D	HABITAT	ELEVATIONS		
														N	T	W
WEST													POWS	8-10	F-10	F-4
EAST													PWS	8-10	6-10	6-7

Uncommon summer resident between 7000' and 9000', rare summer resident or visitor to treeline, uncommon fall transient throughout, irregularly rare to common winter resident below 3000' and rare winter resident to 4000' on west slope; rare summer resident from 8000' to treeline, common spring transient below 7500', fairly common fall transient below treeline and rare winter resident below 7000' east of crest.

Of our summer resident songbirds, Ruby-crowned Kinglets are among the scarcest. Like Golden-crowneds, they nest in coniferous forests, but usually at higher elevations. They consort with lodgepole pines or mountain hemlocks, favoring open woodlands and the edges of meadows where they can sally for flying insects.

Transient and wintering Ruby-crowned Kinglets are more numerous and much more catholic in choice of habitat. They glean insects and other invertebrates from shrubs and trees as well as dense herbaceous vegetation. Nor are they restricted to conifers, ranging into oaks, willows, cottonwoods, aspens, chaparral, sagebrush scrub, meadows and even marshes and lakeshores. On the west slope, the wintering population varies from year to year; tallies on the Yosemite Christmas Bird Count, for example, have varied from 111 to 0.

In mid-April, waves of Ruby-crowned Kinglets pass through valleys east of the Sierran escarpment. At times, every tree and shrub seems to flit with small flocks. Among passerine migrants, only Wilson's Warblers materialize in comparable numbers.

One would suppose that the Ruby-crowned Kinglets nesting in Yosemite's mountains move downslope to winter in the foothills, but this is probably not the case. Our breeding kinglets, like Hermit Thrushes, White-crowned Sparrows and Fox Sparrows, may winter in Mexico, while our wintering birds may come from far to the north (see p. 16).

Extreme dates above 6000' west slope and above 8000' east of crest: 4/27/77 6200' Crane Flat (SG) and 6800', 3, Snow Creek Trail (YM) - 10/23/77 10,000' Hall Natural Area (DeSante MS).

Representative nesting localities: (7800' White Wolf—DG); 10,000' Hall Natural Area (DeSante MS); 9400' near Virginia Lakes, parasitized by Brown-headed Cowbird (AFN 16:505).

BLUE-GRAY GNATCATCHER (*Polioptila caerulea)*

	J	F	M	A	M	J	J	A	S	O	N	D	HABITAT	ELEVATIONS		
														N	T	W
WEST										•			SOP	F-5	F-8	
EAST											•	•	SP	6-8		6

Uncommon summer resident below 4500', rare summer visitor to 8000' and extremely rare transient at higher elevations on west slope; uncommon summer resident and extremely rare winter visitor below 8000' east of crest.

While nowhere numerous, Blue-gray Gnatcatchers are jaunty denizens of arid scrub and woodland habitats west and east of the crest. They dwell primarily in the sun-baked foothills, rarely straying into the higher mountains.

Though they sometimes nest in treeless stands of chaparral and sagebrush scrub, Blue-gray Gnatcatchers favor an admixture of small or large trees. On the west slope, they are most numerous in woodlands or open forests of live oaks, knobcone pines, digger pines, ponderosa pines or black oaks with understories of manzanita, ceanothus or other chaparral shrubs. East of the crest, they dwell among desert mahoganies, pinyon pines, jeffrey pines and Utah junipers with understories of bitterbrush, sagebrush and desert peach. When they do nest in treeless scrub, the shrubbery is diverse and relatively large.

Though not a montane species, Blue-gray Gnatcatchers bred near Glacier Point at the extraordinary elevation of 8000' in 1926 (YNN 7:62). This is 3500' above the next highest west slope record.

During migrations, Blue-gray Gnatcatchers are more widespread, appearing in willow and buffalo-berry thickets, the wooded margins of meadows and open forests. At higher elevations, they usually keep to dry slopes and montane chaparral. One singing at McGurk Meadow (7000') on 6/16/86, however, was in moist coniferous forest.

In the western foothills, as in many parts of lowland California, Blue-gray Gnatcatchers may have declined in numbers. In the 1920s they were considered "common" near El Portal (2100'--YNN 9:40), but are now scarce throughout the lower Merced River canyon.

Winter record: 6500' w. Mono Lake 12/31/86 (DG).

Records above 8000': 8400' Olmsted Point 8/5/87 (JD); 8600' Tuolumne Meadows 7/31/81 (MR); 10,300' Tuolumne Pass 10/14/15 (GS 598).

Extreme dates west slope: 3/14/27 4000' Yosemite Valley (YM) - 9/22/75 7200' Glacier Point (DG).

Extreme dates east of crest excluding winter record: 4/13/86 7000' Long Valley (DG) - 11/5/83 6800' Lee Vining (DG).

Additional representative nesting localities: 2000' Merced River Canyon (MR); 4000' Yosemite Valley (EM 14); (4500' Alder Creek Trail near Wawona—DG); 7500' Lee Vining Canyon (DG); (7400' Williams Butte—DG); (6900' near Lee Vining—DG); (7000' Mono Mills—DG).

Townsend's Solitaire, courtesy Discovering Sierra Birds.

Subfamily TURDINAE: SOLITAIRES AND THRUSHES

Seven species nest in the region. All except bluebirds are celebrated songsters, and they more than compensate with brilliance in dress. This diverse group varies in plumage, behavior, habitat and migratory proclivities. Their kinship is betrayed by the speckled breasts of juvenile-plumaged young, and perhaps by a common appetite for fruit.

WESTERN BLUEBIRD (*Sialia mexicana*)

	J	F	M	A	M	J	J	A	S	O	N	D	HABITAT	ELEVATIONS		
														N	T	W
WEST													GOP	F-5		F-3
EAST													BS	7	7	

Fairly common resident below 2500', locally fairly common summer and irregularly rare to uncommon winter resident to 5000', rare summer resident to 8000' and extremely rare visitor to treeline on west slope; locally uncommon summer resident and rare transient east of crest.

In the foothills on the west slope, Western bluebirds dwell among open stands of blue and live oaks on dry, grassy hillsides. At mid-elevations, they choose large, forest-margined meadows and, less frequently, dry, rocky ridges with scattered conifers and a grassy understory. From look-out posts on trees, fences or stout herbaceous plants they sally after aerial and ground-dwelling insects in meadows or grassy openings. They are partial to dead trees and snags, for these afford look-out posts as well as woodpecker-excavated or natural nesting cavities.

In light of the above, I'm surprised by a report that Western Bluebirds are "common breeders" in "closed crown conifer forests" in Sequoia and Kings Canyon National Parks (AB 28:946); they shun such habitat in the Yosemite Sierra.

In late summer and autumn, many Western Bluebirds forsake their nesting haunts to search for berries in both more forested and shrubbier habitats. Flocks visit chaparral-covered slopes, for example, to feast on toyon berries and other fruits, and invade oak-conifer forests in quest of mistletoe berries. They will linger in dense canyon oak woodlands until they have devoured the mistletoe crop (EM 15). In years when mast is abundant, large numbers winter at mid-elevations, such as Yosemite Valley (4000'); when the crop fails, they don't appear at all. Numbers on the Yosemite Christmas Bird Count, for example, have varied from 189 to 0.

On the east side, Western Bluebirds were first seen in Lee Vining in 1987 and were breeding there in 1988 and 1989, both in boxes and natural tree cavities.

Records above 8000': 8600' Tuolumne Meadows, flock, 7/27/39 (YM) and 2, 9/20/81 (DG); 9400' Ten Lakes 10/8-9/16 (GS 616); 10,500' near top of Mt. Hoffmann 8/20/83 (SG).

Extreme dates above 6000': 4/28/77 7800' near Smoky Jack (SG) - 10/27/85 7400' Dewey Point Ski Trail (SH).

Representative nesting localities: 1300' Merced River Canyon (MR); 2100' El Portal (MR); 4000' Yosemite Valley (YNN 15:77); 4400' Big Meadow (TB, DG); 4600' Ackerson Meadow (JW); 7000' near top of Yosemite Falls (DG); 7800' near Smoky Jack (SG); 8000' Moraine Dome (YM).

MOUNTAIN BLUEBIRD (*Sialia currucoides)*

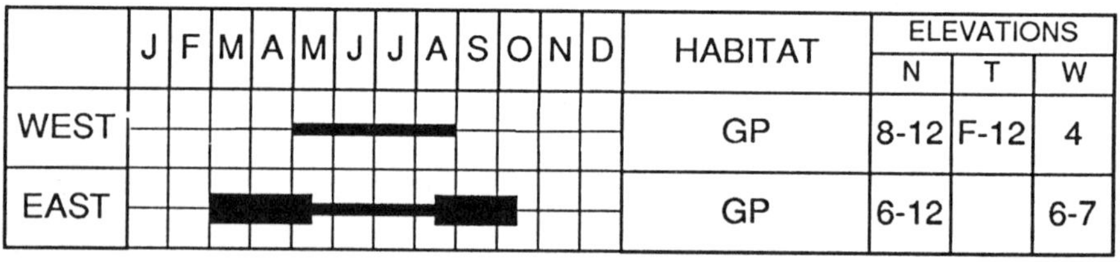

	J	F	M	A	M	J	J	A	S	O	N	D	HABITAT	ELEVATIONS		
														N	T	W
WEST													GP	8-12	F-12	4
EAST													GP	6-12		6-7

Uncommon summer resident from 8000' to 12,000', rare transient below 8000' and rare winter visitor below 4000' on west slope—one nesting record at 4000'; uncommon summer resident below treeline, rare summer visitor to 12,000' and fairly common transient and rare winter resident below 7500' east of crest.

Though they lack the dulcet songs of other thrushes, I fancy Mountain Bluebirds the loveliest of all Sierran birds. As they hover over flowery meadows or glide to perches atop rocks or trees, their delicate grace lifts the heart. The sun catches their plumage, turning it bluer than the mountain sky above. They are not merely birds; they are feathered epiphanies.

During the nesting season, the distribution of Mountain Bluebirds reflects a preference for open, relatively dry short-grass foraging areas rather than high elevations per se. They range from the west slope's glaciated granite shingles and large subalpine and alpine meadows across the crest to the floors of Great Basin valleys. Whether at 12,000' on the Dana Plateau or at 6400' at Mono Lake, they sally after aerial and ground-dwelling insects in treeless openings, meadows and fell-fields. While they perch on trees and shrubs, they shun dense forests and unbroken scrub. They also avoid meadows with thick, high herbaceous vegetation. During migrations, however, they forage in open sagebrush scrub east of the Sierran escarpment.

Most Mountain Bluebirds nest in woodpecker-excavated or natural tree cavities. East of the crest, they are attracted to aspen groves by their surfeit of suitable holes and proximity to meadows. Above treeline, they resort to rock crevices. At Mono Lake, they utilize crannies in tufa towers. A pair has even bred on a ledge in a wood shed (GS 623).

In 1934, Mountain Bluebirds in Yosemite Valley nested at the extraordinarily low elevation of 4000' (YNN 15:77). This is the only west slope breeding record below 7800'.

In the sagebrush country east of the Sierran escarpment, Mountain Bluebirds are one of spring's earliest arrivals. While a few may brave the winter, many more appear in mid- to late February. At this time of year, and again from mid-summer through mid-autumn, they congregate in flocks that number 10 to 30 individuals, and sometimes more. On 1/3/84, approximately 100 were in the sagebrush near Simons Spring (6500')—the largest flock I know of, and one of few winter records (MLTSR).

At the same time Mountain Bluebirds are flocking through Great Basin valleys, small numbers appear on the west slope in meadows below their breeding range. These are probably birds in transit from San Joaquin Valley wintering to Sierran breeding areas, or vice versa. Virtually all materialize between mid-February and mid-May, and mid-October to mid-November, often in small flocks of up to 15 individuals. These seasonal movements are not depicted on the graph, since there are seven December or January records from Yosemite Valley (GSt), El Portal (2100'--YM) or somewhere in the Yosemite Christmas Bird Count circle. Thirteen remained in Yosemite Valley until the surprisingly late date of 6/30/21 (EM 15).

After heavy winters, Mountain Bluebirds linger in eastside valleys and canyonbottoms late into spring, apparently awaiting the thaw at higher elevations. Yet long before the snow melts, some inspect their high mountain breeding haunts. At Tuolumne Meadows (8600'), for example, small flocks have appeared as early as 2/4/56 (YM) and 3/20/27 (YNN 6:22). One on Kavanaugh Ridge on 3/29/78 was at 11,000' (LW); another on Buena Vista Crest (approx. 9400') had to contend with eight feet of snow on 4/10/79 (YM). Do flocks dispatch scouts to assess conditions in the high country?

Extreme dates below 7000' west slope excluding June and nesting record: 10/2/30 4000' Yosemite Valley (YM) - 5/31/53 El Portal (AFN 7:289).

Extreme dates above 8000', both Tuolumne Meadows (8600'): 2/4/56 (YM); 3/20/27 (YM) - 11/16/76 (YM); 12/6/75 (YM).

Additional representative nesting localities: 7800' near Smoky Jack (SG); 8600' Tuolumne Meadows (GS 623); 9800' Tioga Pass (DG); 11,200' Helen Lake (YM); 12,000' above Virginia Lakes (C 41:250); 7400' Lee Vining Canyon (DG); 6400' Mono Lake (DG).

Additional references: C 38:85, EM 15, YNN 4:68, YNN 6:22.

TOWNSEND'S SOLITAIRE (*Myadestes townsendi*)

	J	F	M	A	M	J	J	A	S	O	N	D	HABITAT	ELEVATIONS		
														N	T	W
WEST													PO	5-10		F-9
EAST													P	7-10		6-9

Uncommon summer and locally uncommon winter resident between 4500' and 9000', irregularly rare to uncommon summer resident to treeline, extremely rare transient above treeline and rare winter resident below 4500' on west slope—one nesting record at 2200'; uncommon summer and fairly common winter resident below 9000' and irregularly rare to uncommon summer resident to treeline east of crest.

In coniferous forests, Townsend's Solitaires materialize unexpectedly, like slim gray ghosts. In contrast, among the polished granite of glacier-scoured canyons, they perch like statuesque sentinels on gnarled junipers. Suddenly they arc into graceful flight, snatch an insect from the ground, air or the trunk of a tree, and vanish silently into the shadows.

During the nesting season, Townsend's Solitaires favor forests and woodlands with shrubby understories, especially on ridges or well-drained slopes. Trees may be scattered or dense, provided they possess shrubby understories, an abundance of downed wood or margin montane chaparral. At one extreme, they nest on rockbound, shrubby slopes with scattered Sierra junipers, mountain white pines and jeffrey pines. At the other, they dwell in shady forests of ponderosa pines, sugar pines, lodgepole pines, firs, mountain hemlocks or other conifers. The understory usually consists of chinquapin, huckleberry oak, ceanothus or manzanita. Of all our thrushes, they are the most earthly nester, concealing nests under rocks, logs or shrubbery.

In late summer, Townsend's Solitaires forsake their breeding haunts in search of ripening berries. In the higher mountains and east of the crest, they are especially fond of junipers. On the west slope, they descend into the oaks, especially groves of canyon live oaks, to gorge on mistletoe berries, and, less often, into the foothills to feast on toyon, elderberry and other fleshy fruits.

While some Townsend's Solitaires winter in juniper groves at elevations as high as 9000', as near Tuolumne Meadows (YM), most retreat to lower elevations. Their numbers vary from year to year depending on the abundance of juniper berries and other mast.

Of all Sierran birds, Townsend's Solitaires are one of the few to sing persistently in autumn. When the aspens turn gold, their rich, melodic voices ring through the frosty air of eastern Sierran canyons. They are not just enjoying themselves, but earnestly defending winter larders. True to their names—and unlike most other thrushes—they are truly solitary at this time of year, driving others of their kind as well as robins and waxwings away from fruitful junipers. I wonder if females are as songful and contentious as males.

High elevation record: 13,000' Mt. Dana 6/11/86 (DG).

Representative nesting localities: 2200' El Portal—begging juvenile at this extraordinarily low elevation on 7/1/81 (MR); 4600' Ackerson Meadow (JW); (5000' Fireplace Creek—DG); 5500' below Nevada Fall (YM); 6000' Henness Ridge (DG); 7000' above Chinquapin (GS 598); 7600' below Glen Aulin (DG); 10,300' Hall Natural Area (DeSante MS); (9000' Warren Fork Lee Vining Creek—DG); (7600' Lee Vining Canyon—DG).

Additional references: AFN 7:289, YNN 6:22.

SWAINSON'S THRUSH (*Catharus ustulatus*)

Formerly fairly common on west slope; now rare summer resident below 8000' and extremely rare transient at higher elevations on both west and east slopes.

Earlier in this century, Swainson's Thrushes were considered fairly common summer residents in Yosemite Valley (4000') and elsewhere on the west slope. In the 1920s, for example, Charles and Enid Michael recorded them almost daily in June and July (EM 14; C 34:221). Yet none have been seen in Yosemite Valley for decades.

Swainson's Thrushes have declined, but why? There are no obvious answers. In Yosemite Valley, some of the dense, moist understory thickets they favor has been destroyed, but much remains. Brown-headed Cowbirds have parasitized their nests, but as far as we know, only a small proportion.

Whatever the reasons, one seldom hears the vibrant ascending songs of Swainson's Thrushes rising from Yosemite's woods. When one does encounter these moisture-loving birds, it is usually in dense, shrubby understory vegetation on moist, forested slopes near streams and meadows. While the overstory trees may be douglas firs, red or white firs, sugar pines and other conifers, the understory consists predominantly of hardwoods. On the west slope, dogwoods, hazelnut, blackberry and even bracken ferns provide cover; to the east, willow thickets, aspens and labrador tea. In general east-side birds, which presumably belong to the Rocky Mountain subspecies *C. u. almae*, are tolerant of sunnier, drier conditions than their west slope relatives, *C. u. ustulata*.

Transient Swainson's Thrushes, while extremely scarce, are not as wedded to mesic settings, appearing in woodlands and residential gardens as well.

Record above 8000': 9500' Lyell Canyon 9/?/25 (YM).

Extreme dates, both Yosemite Valley: 5/9/23 (YM) - 10/3/22 (YM).

Possible current west slope nesting localities based on presence of singing birds: 4700' North Crane Creek (MM, DG); 6200' Crane Flat (SG); 7800' White Wolf (DG, RS).

Representative east side nesting localities: (8000' Lundy Canyon—KC, DG); (8000' Mammoth Lakes—D 757; C 27:37); (7800' Lee Vining Canyon—DG).

Additional reference: GS 600.

HERMIT THRUSH (*Catharus guttatus*)

	J	F	M	A	M	J	J	A	S	O	N	D	HABITAT	ELEVATIONS		
														N	T	W
WEST													PS	5-10	F-10	F-3
EAST													P	7-10	6-10	6-7

Fairly common summer resident from 5000' to treeline, uncommon transient below 5000', uncommon winter resident below 3000' and rare winter resident to 5000' on west slope; fairly common summer resident from 8000' to treeline, uncommon transient below 8000' and rare winter resident below 7000' east of crest.

Were it not for their song, heard from May through early summer, nesting Hermit Thrushes would often pass unnoticed. Their woodsy brown plumage, while attractive, blends with their haunts on the forest floor, where they spend much of their time searching for insects. Moreover they are shyer than most woodland birds, slipping unseen into the shadows. Even their songs—most ethereal of avian music—seem to flee before a hurried or noisy approach.

During the nesting season, Hermit Thrushes favor coniferous forests, though they also dwell in aspen groves and, locally east of the crest, dense groves of mature mountain mahogany. At mid-elevations on the west slope, they are reclusive inhabitants of deep, shady forests of red and white firs, sugar pines, sequoias and other conifers. At higher elevations they live in more open, drier forests of lodgepole and whitebark pines. In fact, as one travels east, they tolerate increasingly arid conditions, especially at high elevations. They shun, however, pinyon pine and jeffrey pine woodlands.

East of the crest, David Shuford has discovered Hermit Thrushes apparently nesting in arid mountain mahogany woodlands on glacial moraines above Rock Creek (approx. 8500'). While such dry, insolated conditions are out of character for the Sierran subspecies, *C. g. sequoiensis*, they match the habitat Grinnell and Miller describe for the Great Basin race *C. g. polionota*, which nests in the White Mountains to the east (C 20:89; GM 361).

Transient and wintering Hermit Thrushes desert conifers in favor of thickets, chaparral and forest edge situations. As they are gluttonous frugivores, they are partial to toyons, manzanitas, elderberry, madrone and other berry-producing shrubs.

The Hermit Thrushes that nest in the Sierra are not the ones that winter here. Our nesting birds, *C. g. sequoiensis*, depart for northern Mexican wintering haunts by the end of August (GS 603). Our fall and winter thrushes belong to darker-hued northern subspecies (*D. g. guttata* and *C. g. nanus*), which breed in Alaska and Canada (GS 603). They occur mostly below 6000', but are rare in fall to treeline. Like robins they descend to the foothills during autumn as the weather turns cold and the mountain berry crops dwindle.

You don't befriend the Hermit Thrush by storm, but with quietude and reverance. For, as William Leon Dawson wrote, this thrush—and especially its song—is "a thing apart...it is sacred music, not secular... Mounted on the chancel of some low-crowned fir tree, the bird looks calmly at the setting sun, and slowly phrases his worship in such dulcet tones, exalted, pure, serene, as must haunt the corridors of memory forever after" (Dawson 1923).

As Elna Bakker adds, it "makes little difference to the listener that the singer may be merely reestablishing his territorial boundaries or communicating with his mate. His song is of firs and pines darkening against the sundown sky."

High elevation record: 10,100' Hall Natural Area, summer resident (DeSante MS).

Extreme dates above 8000', both Hall Natural Area (10,000'): 5/1/81 - 10/27/77 (DeSante MS).

Representative nesting localities: 4000' Yosemite Valley (YM—only one record at this low elevation); (5800' Tuolumne Grove—DG); (6200' Crane Flat—DG); (6400' Mariposa Grove—YM); 8600' Tuolumne Meadows (GS 602); 10,100' Hall Natural Area (DeSante MS); 9700' near Virginia Lake (C 41:250); 9000' near Mammoth Lakes (MVZ); 8500' near June Lake (C 36:35).

Additional references: EM 14; YNN 5:26; YNN 12:98.

AMERICAN ROBIN (*Turdus migratorius*)

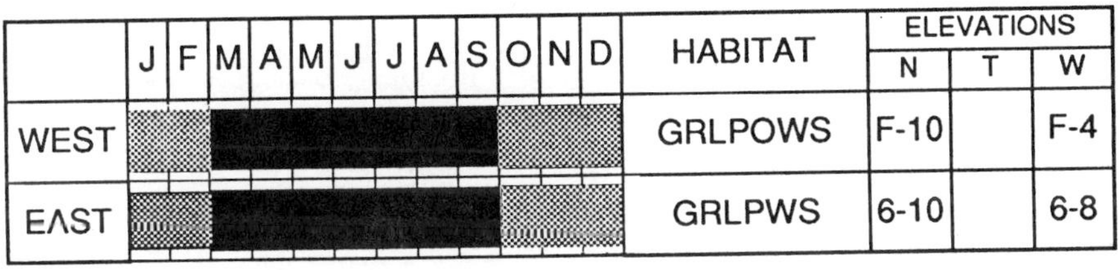

	J	F	M	A	M	J	J	A	S	O	N	D	HABITAT	ELEVATIONS		
														N	T	W
WEST													GRLPOWS	F-10		F-4
EAST													GRLPWS	6-10		6-8

Locally common summer resident below 3000', common summer resident from 3000' to treeline, irregularly rare to common winter resident below 4000' and rare winter resident or visitor to at least 6000' on west slope; common summer resident below treeline and irregularly rare to common winter resident below 8500' east of crest.

From the foothills to treeline, nesting American Robins are conspicuous denizens of moist, tree-margined meadows, streambanks, lake shores, parks, lawns and yards. Their requirements are earthy: the ground must be rich in invertebrates, soft enough for probing bills and well-supplied with mud for plastering nests. Beyond this, any sort of timber serves for roosting, nesting and singing. Every kind of Sierran tree—from oaks, maples and aspens to pines, firs and junipers—hosts their nests and young.

Even during the nesting season, some American Robins stray from their nesting haunts into arid habitats such as chaparral, sagebrush scrub, montane chaparral and pinyon pine woodlands. From late summer through winter, this peregrinating tendency intensifies. They gather in flocks, sometimes by the hundreds or rarely thousands, to scour the hills for ripening fruits. On the west slope, they feast on toyon, chokecherry, bittercherry, dogwood, elderberry, mistletoe and manzanita; to the east, they also relish juniper, whose bitter fruits sustain them through the bitterly cold winters. When the ground has been softened by rain or melting snow, they also forage on grassy hillsides and even in openings in sagebrush scrub.

The numbers of wintering American Robins varies with the mast crop. When fruit is plentiful, they roam the lower elevations in flocks of hundreds or rarely thousands (AFN 7:233); in other years, they are rare or absent. Tallies on the Yosemite Christmas Bird Count, for example, have varied from 423 to 0; on the Mono Lake Christmas Bird Count from 511 to 0.

Of all our migrants, American Robins are among the first to arrive and the last to depart. Their vigorous, pleasing songs are an early sign that spring is spreading north.

In places like Yosemite Valley (4000') on the west slope and Mono Lake (6400') to the east, they return in numbers by mid- to late February. Flocks linger at lower elevations, especially meadows, through early May, presumably waiting for the snow to melt in the higher mountains. They have been heard singing at 10,000', however, as early as late March (DeSante MS). Of all Sierran migrants, they are the first to nest and fledge young, frequently rearing second broods.

If fruit is abundant or the weather is mild, American Robins linger in the higher mountains late into autumn. At 6000', Enid Michael found a "small flock...wintering on North Dome...where steep slopes and a warm exposure kept the ground free of snow and manzanita berries were plentiful" (EM 14). During dry winters, if patches of ground are free of snow, small bands stray at least as high as Tuolumne Meadows (8600'—Marilyn Muse).

The American Robins that winter in our region are probably not the ones that nest here. One banded in Yosemite Valley on 2/21/31, for example, was recaptured at Sandpoint, Idaho on 5/24/34 (YM). I suspect the wintering flocks are composed mostly if not entirely of northerners.

Representative nesting localities: 2000' Mariposa (CL); 4000' Yosemite Valley (GS 605); 6200' Crane Flat (DG); 7000' Peregoy Meadow (DG); 7800' White Wolf (DG); 8600' Tuolumne Meadows (DG); 10,300' Hall Natural Area (DeSante MS); 7400' Lee Vining Canyon (DG); 6800' Lee Vining (DG); 6500' Mono Lake County Park (DG).

Additional references: AB 25:624, YNN 12:26, YNN 13:72, YNN 16:73, YNN 21:42.

VARIED THRUSH (*Ixoreus naevius)*

	J	F	M	A	M	J	J	A	S	O	N	D	HABITAT	ELEVATIONS		
														N	T	W
WEST	▓	▓	▓	▓		•		•		▓	▓	▓	OPSW			F-5
EAST	•						•			—	—	—	PSW		6-10	

Irregularly rare to fairly common winter visitor below 5000' and extremely rare summer visitor and irregularly rare fall visitor to treeline on west slope; extremely rare summer visitor and irregularly rare fall visitor below treeline and extremely rare winter visitor east of crest.

During most winters, Varied Thrushes are scarce or absent. But every few years, they descend in numbers on dense forests and thickets west of the crest. Tallies on the Yosemite Christmas Bird Count, for example, range from 86 to 0.

Varied Thrushes favor shady woodlands, dense thickets and tall chaparral, especially on hillsides and in ravines. These reclusive birds venture only rarely into the open habitats preferred by American Robins. As they dine largely on acorns and berries, they are partial to live and canyon oaks as well as madrones, dogwoods, mistletoes, toyons and manzanitas. In the higher mountains and east of the crest, they favor dense, shady woods and thickets, but can appear in any wooded habitat, including isolated groves and residential areas.

High elevation record: 10,000' Hall Natural Area, up to 3, 10/8-27/77; on the latter date, two greeted a snowstorm by singing an ethereal duet (DeSante and Engstrom MS).

Summer records: 6/23/77 9900' Hall Natural Area (AB 31:1186, DeSante and Engstrom MS); 7/?/78 8600' Tuolumne Meadows (MR); 8/10/79 9500' Warren Fork canyon, Lee Vining Creek (BE).

Winter records east of crest: 4, 12/31/77 7500' Lee Vining Canyon (DW); 1/1/84 7400' Lee Vining Canyon (AB 38:793).

Extreme dates west slope excluding summer record: 10/4/52 6300' near Chinquapin (AFN 7:35) - 4/24/25 4000' Yosemite Valley (YM).

Extreme dates east slope excluding summer and winter records: 10/8/77 Hall Natural Area (DeSante and Engstrom MS) - 11/26/81 6800' Lee Vining (DG).

Subfamily TIMALIINAE: BABBLERS

WRENTIT (*Chaemaea fasciata*)

	J	F	M	A	M	J	J	A	S	O	N	D	HABITAT	ELEVATIONS N	ELEVATIONS T	ELEVATIONS W
WEST	■	■	■	■	■	■	■	■	■	■	■	■	S	F-5	F-7	F-5
EAST																

Common resident below 3000', locally fairly common resident to 4500', and rare summer resident and fall visitor to 7000' on west slope—possibly resident to 6000'.

Like California Thrashers, Wrentits are wedded to thickets and chaparral. On the lower west slope they consort with chamise, ceanothus, manzanita, scrub oak and other shrubs. In the higher mountains, they inhabit montane chaparral, especially large manzanitas and ceanothus, and, less frequently, the shrubby understories of open forests. The shrubbery need not be extensive; an acre of brush surrounded by pines and oaks will lure a nesting pair.

Wrentits may be "resident...at 6,000'" (YNN 10:21), but I'm only aware of records between June and December, suggesting up-mountain drift. Nor do I know how often they breed in the higher mountains; in 1978 I discovered a pair feeding young at 6000' near Union Point, but know of no other nestings above 4000'. Along the Snow Creek trail, they have been found as high as 7000' on several occasions (YNN 7:90; YNN 18:127).

Additional representative nesting localities: 1300' Merced River Canyon (MR); 3000' above El Portal (DG); 3700' near Hetch Hetchy Reservoir (MM, DG); 4500' Alder Creek Trail near Wawona (DG).

Extreme dates above 4000': 6000' Union Point 6/22/78 (DG) - 5200' between Vernal and Nevada Falls 12/30/30 (YNN 10:21).

Additional references: GS 582; C 42:127; EM 14.

Family MIMIDAE: MOCKINGBIRDS AND THRASHERS

Thrashers are reluctant mountaineers, visiting higher elevations only as occasional strays. California Thrashers reside year-round in the western foothills, whereas Sage Thrashers spend summers in the eastern sagebrush scrub. The remaining threesome are errant easterners or rare visitors.

GRAY CATBIRD (*Dumetella carolinensis*)

Extremely rare vagrant on east slope.

Record: 8000' Mammoth Lakes 9/19-23/74 (AB 29:116); record accepted by California Bird Records Committee.

NORTHERN MOCKINGBIRD (*Mimus polyglottos*)

Rare summer visitor and extremely rare winter visitor below 4000' and extremely rare visitor at higher elevations on west slope; rare summer visitor and extremely rare winter visitor below 7500' east of crest.

Northern Mockingbirds occasionally stray to wooded habitats with scattered large shrubs or small trees, including residential areas. They are partial to ripe berries; east of the crest, I've found them feasting on buffalo-berries with Sage Thrashers and American Robins.

Record above 4000' west slope: 8600' Tuolumne Meadows 5/12/87 (MR).

Winter records west slope: 2000' El Portal 12/18/76, 12/18/77 and 12/22/79 (AB 31:895, AB 32:892, AB 34:670, LMcK); 4000' Yosemite Valley 3/21/29 (YNN 18:102-103) and 3/1-31/31 (YNN 10:63).

Winter record east of crest: 12/13/79-1/8/80 6800' Lee Vining (DG; AB 34:652).

Extreme dates east of crest excluding winter record: 5/3/78 Lee Vining; 5/11/79 6400' n. shore Mono Lake (KC); 5/20/84 6400' Mono Lake (DS); 6/13/89 6400' Dechambeau Ponds (PM) - 9/28/83 w. Mono Lake (HG).

SAGE THRASHER (*Oreoscoptes montanus*)

	J	F	M	A	M	J	J	A	S	O	N	D	HABITAT	ELEVATIONS		
														N	T	W
WEST				•		•		•	•	•					4-9	
EAST			—■	■	■	■	■	■	■—		•	•	S	6-8	6-9	6-7

Extremely rare transient on west slope; common summer resident below 8500', uncommon summer visitor to 10,000' (Bodie Hills) and extremely rare winter visitor east of Sierran escarpment.

Of the sagebrush birds, Sage Thrashers are the sweetest singers, and one of the first to return from desert wintering haunts. By the end of March, they are ecstatically welcoming spring's return.

Sage Thrashers are confirmed valley dwellers, rarely straying onto steep slopes. I have never seen one, for example, on the Sierra's eastern escarpment. Yet just to the east, they are plentiful among the sagebrush and greasewood scrub which carpet flats and rolling hills.

During the breeding season, Sage Thrashers appropriate large shrubs for nesting sites. They frequently utilize big sagebrush (*Artemisia tridentata*), which grows to several feet or more in height, but shun its smaller cousins, such as *Artemisia nana*. In alkaline soils, as around Mono Lake (6400'), they nest in large greasewoods.

While paired during the breeding season, Sage Thrashers gather in flocks in mid- to late summer to strip buffalo-berries, currants and other shrubs of ripening fruits. I've seen over 60 swarming in a single thicket.

High elevation record: 10,100' Bodie Mountain 8/19/87 (DG).

West slope records: 4000' Yosemite Valley 4/29/33 (YNN 12:66); 10/16/81 4400' Big Meadow (AB 36:215); 4600' Ackerson Meadow 6/16/85, 8/23/87 and 9/6/82 (JW); 8600' Tuolumne Meadows 8/5/87 (MR).

Late fall and winter records, east slope: 6400' South Tufa 11/10/79 (DG); 7000' Hot Creek 12/15/79 (DG, AB 34:651); 6900' Conway Ranch 12/31/80 (DG, AB 35:716).

Extreme dates excluding above records: 3/5/81 6400' Mono Lake (JJ) - 10/14/79 South Tufa (DG).

Additional representative nesting localities: 7000' Long Valley (DG); 6500' Bridgeport (DG).

BROWN THRASHER (*Toxostoma rufum*)

Extremely rare vagrant east of Sierran escarpment.

Records: Parker Creek early June/91 (TB); Mono Lake County Park 6/10/91 (AB 45:1159); 7000' Benton's Crossing on Owens River 6/19/82 (Jean Brandt); Lee Vining Creek mouth 8/10/88 (AB 43:164).

CALIFORNIA THRASHER (*Toxostoma redivivum*)

	J	F	M	A	M	J	J	A	S	O	N	D	HABITAT	ELEVATIONS		
														N	T	W
WEST	■	■	■	■	■	■	■	■	■	■	■	■	S	F-3		F-3
EAST																

Fairly common resident below 3500' and extremely rare visitor at higher elevations on west slope.

California Thrashers seldom venture far from the impenetrable chaparral that carpets canyon slopes. From mid-winter through spring, their rich, varied songs cascade from thickets of chamise, manzanita, buckbrush, scrub oak and toyon.

While I know of only two records within Yosemite National Park, I suspect they nest in the park's seldom-birded lower elevations.

Records in Yosemite National Park: 4000' McCauley Ranch 5/10/87 (Rob Hayden); 4000' Yosemite Valley 1/15/84 (AB 38:355); approx. 4500' Alder Creek Trail near Wawona, date unknown (Beedy and Granholm 1985).

Family MOTACILLIDAE: PIPITS

AMERICAN PIPIT (*Anthus rubescens*) (Water Pipit)

	J	F	M	A	M	J	J	A	S	O	N	D	HABITAT	ELEVATIONS		
														N	T	W
WEST	•											•	GL	10+	F-12	5
EAST													GL	10+	6-12	6-7

Locally uncommon summer resident from 10,000' to 12,000', rare transient below 10,000' and extremely rare winter visitor on west slope; locally uncommon summer resident from 10,000' to 12,000' on east slope; uncommon spring and common fall transient and irregularly rare to uncommon winter resident below 7500' east of Sierran escarpment

Like Chestnut-backed Chickadees, nesting American Pipits are Johnny-come-latelys. On 8/1/75, California's first known nest was discovered near an alpine lake at 10,500' in the Hall Natural Area (AB 29:1028), not far from where a pair had been seen four years earlier (AB 25:904). That same year nests were also found in Sequoia and Kings Canyon National Parks (WB 13:39-40). Since that time, many nests or nesting pairs have been encountered from Yosemite's Tower Peak south to Sequoia's Franklin Lakes; a disjunct population is also nesting on the arid summit of Mt. San Gorgonio in Southern California (Miller and Green 1987).

This is not to say that American Pipits were unknown in the High Sierra prior to the 1970s. Between 1933 and 1943, for example, C. A. Harwell observed "pipits on the moraines and on the ice well above timberline" on "almost all glacier trips" (YM). But these, like all other pre-1970 alpine records, fall in September and October when transients would be expected. No one found or suspected nesting birds, probably because none were there.

Jon Miller and Michael Green, who have studied the Sierra's nesting American Pipits, believe the Rocky Mountain race, *A. s. alticola*, has invaded during the past several decades. They speculate that dry "temperature maxima," such as the hypsithermal of approximately 2,900 to 5,000 years ago, eliminated both pipits and their moist tundra habitat from the Sierra. In recent centuries, the climate has become cooler and wetter again, and "chance dispersal, or the attainment of some threshold population density," has permitted pipits to spread and thrive (Miller and Green 1987).

American Pipits nest in moist, alpine meadows, often in the vicinity of tarns and lakes. The presence of water and water-dependent vegetation distinguishes their haunts from those of alpine-nesting Horned Larks. They dwell on gentle slopes as well as level terrain, and often perch on rocks and boulders.

Transient and wintering American Pipits, primarily of the western subspecies *A. s. pacificus*, inhabit moist, bare ground such as mudflats, muddy shores and the edges of streams as well as open, level terrain covered with sparse grass or stubble. In spring and especially fall, they are characteristic denizens of Mono, Crowley and Bridgeport lakes' muddy shores and stream deltas, where they often consort with shorebirds, starlings, Savannah Sparrows and blackbirds. At Mono Lake, they often perch on tufa towers. In winter, they linger in moist, sparsely vegetated meadows, or near hot springs, as along Hot Creek (7000').

Transient and wintering American Pipits are gregarious, gathering in flocks of up to 100 individuals east of the Sierran escarpment. Even on the lower west slope, where they are scarce, they may appear in small flocks; 12, for example, were at Crane Flat (6400') on 4/23/85 (MR).

Being ground foragers, American Pipits are intolerant of snow, but do not begrudge cold weather. East of the Sierran escarpment, they linger in valleys until heavy snow drives them to balmier climes, often overwintering.

Winter records west slope: 12/26/62 4400' Big Meadow (YM); 12/29/48 4000' Yosemite Valley (YM); 1/19/85 4600' Ackerson Meadow (JW).

Extreme dates above 10,000': 4/25/82 11,800' Hall Natural Area (D&E) - 10/25/77, 2, 10,400' Hall Natural Area (DeSante and Engstrom MS).

Extreme dates below 10,000' west slope, excluding winter record: 4/4/81 Ackerson Meadow (JW) - 5/18/77 6200' Crane Flat (YM); 9/13/39 - 12/8/23 Yosemite Valley (YM).

Extreme dates below 7500' east of crest: 9/4/87 6900' Crowley Lake Reservoir (DS) - 5/10/82 6400' Mono Lake (BE).

Family BOMBYCILLIDAE: WAXWINGS

BOHEMIAN WAXWING (*Bombycilla garrulus*)

Extremely (irregularly?) rare transient and winter visitor both west and east of the crest.

Though one of our scarcest birds, large flocks of Bohemian Waxwings have strayed to Tuolumne Meadows (8600'), where there is still no record for Cedars.

Records west slope: 8600' Tuolumne Meadows 40-50, 1/13/87 (Marilyn Muse) and 75-100, 3/1/84 (YM); 7000' near Glacier Point 5/3/76, an "invasion" year elsewhere in California (YM); 4000' Yosemite Valley 9/28/20 (EM 11), 12/23/38 (YNN 18:83) and 4, 12/18/27 (EM 11).

Records east of crest: 6500' Mono Lake County Park, 2, 1/22/88 (AB 42:318); 8000'-9000', approx. 15 in several small flocks, Lee Vining Canyon, 11/29/81 (AB 36:215); 7000' Dechambeau Creek 12/19/85 (Jon Miller).

CEDAR WAXWING (*Bombycilla cedrorum*)

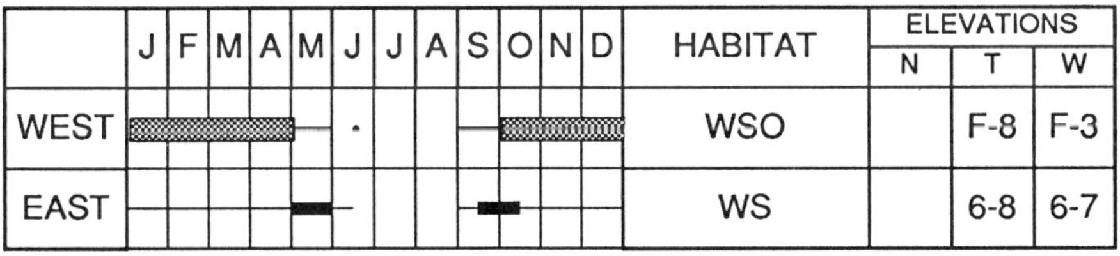

	J	F	M	A	M	J	J	A	S	O	N	D	HABITAT	ELEVATIONS		
														N	T	W
WEST													WSO		F-8	F-3
EAST													WS		6-8	6-7

Irregularly rare to fairly common winter resident below 2500', rare transient and extremely rare summer visitor to 8000' and extremely rare transient at higher elevations on west slope; uncommon transient and rare winter visitor below 8000' and extremely rare transient at higher elevations east of crest.

The whereabouts of Cedar Waxwings are governed by berries, fruits and buds. They nab insects now and then, but are by and large frugivorous. On the west slope, they favor toyon, mistletoe and madrone berries; to the east, elderberry and juniper berries as well as cottonwood buds. They also raid orchards and gardens for cherries, pyracantha berries and other exotic delicacies.

Flocks of Cedar Waxwings, often in company with American Robins, gypsy about the countryside, stripping fruits from trees and shrubs, then moving on. The search lures them into many habitats, including foothill and montane chaparral, riparian woodlands, oak-conifer woodlands, residential areas and occasionally coniferous forests.

In the higher mountains and east of the crest, most Cedar Waxwings occur in two periods: late May through early June, and early September through October. They are among the last migrants to pass northwards in spring. As late as mid-June, when most eastside birds are sitting on eggs or raising young, garrulous flocks are oblivious to familial cares. "What's the hurry?," they seem to say. "Up north the berries have yet to ripen, and there's plenty of time for children later in the summer."

In the western foothills, numbers of wintering Cedar Waxwings vary from year to year depending on the availability of fruits and berries. In some years, they descend in flocks numbering hundreds; in others, they are scarce or absent.

Summer record west slope: 7/7/66 4000' Yosemite Valley (AFN 20:598).

Records above 8000': 9000' Lee Vining Creek 9/17/15 (GS 504); 9100' Virginia Lakes, 2, 5/30/81 (MM); Hall Natural Area 9900'—9/1/79, 10,300'—8, 9/29/78 and 10.100'—9, 10/6/79 (AB 33:21, AB 34:198, DeSante and Engstrom MS).

Extreme dates west slope excluding summer record, both Yosemite Valley: 8/19/38, 3 (YNN 18:126) - 6/12/27 (C 30:250).

Extreme dates east of escarpment: 8/22/88 6500' Mono Lake County Park (PM) - 6/18/84 west of Mono Lake (SJ, DS).

Additional references: EM 11; AB 35:860.

Family PTILOGONATIDAE: SILKY FLYCATCHERS

PHAINOPEPLA (*Phainopepla nitens*)

Uncommon resident in Mariposa region (2000'—CL); extremely rare visitor elsewhere on west slope and east of Sierran escarpment.

Phainopeplas dwell in open woodlands and scattered groves of small trees, especially those with berries or mistletoe.

Records west slope: 4000' Yosemite Valley 10/5/29 (YM) and 5/30/82 (AB 36:891); 4600' Ackerson Meadow 5/24/86 (JW); *in the southern Sierra, one at Mineral King on 10/14/85 was at 7900' (AB 40:332).*

Records east of crest: 6400' Mono Lake 9/8/76 (DG), 9/11/83 (AB 38:244) and 10/15/82 (AB 37:221); 7500' Lee Vining Canyon 11/7/82 (AB 37:221).

Family LANIIDAE: SHRIKES

NORTHERN SHRIKE (*Lanius excubitor*)

	J	F	M	A	M	J	J	A	S	O	N	D	HABITAT	ELEVATIONS		
														N	T	W
WEST	•	•										•				5-10
EAST	—	—									—	—	WSP			6-7

Extremely rare winter visitor on west slope and above 7500' on east slope; rare winter resident below 7500' east of crest.

During the coldest months of the year, in deciduous thickets east of the Sierran escarpment, Northern Shrikes terrorize flocks of wintering songbirds. These rapacious passerines favor open country with willows and cottonwoods, as along the west shore of Mono Lake (6400'). But they also hunt wherever there are flocks of birds, including sagebrush scrub, pinyon woodlands, riparian woodlands and occasionally coniferous forests. Along Lee Vining Creek (7200'), for example, I saw one swoop into a dense grove and kill a Hairy Woodpecker—a bird almost as heavy as the shrike itself. Most of these northerners are immatures.

During late autumn, before snow mantles montane meadows, Northern Shrikes may hunt as high as treeline. There are only two records, but birders seldom visit the higher moutains at this time of year.

Records west slope and above 7500' east of crest: 4600' Ackerson Meadow, sub-adult 1/19-2/26/85 (JW); 9800' Tioga Pass 12/6/76—immature—the only record within Yosemite National Park (DG); 9300' Virginia Lakes 11/30/75 (AB 30:122).

Extreme dates: 11/1/81 6900' east of Conway Ranch (DG) - 3/31/79 6600' Bridgeport Valley (DG).

LOGGERHEAD SHRIKE (*Lanius ludovicianus*)

	J	F	M	A	M	J	J	A	S	O	N	D	HABITAT	ELEVATIONS		
														N	T	W
WEST													GS		F-9	F-2
EAST													GS	6-7		6-7

Rare winter resident in Mariposa region (2000'—CL); irregularly rare spring transient (0-2/year) below 5000', irregularly rare fall transient (0-2/year) below 9000' and extremely rare transient at higher elevations elsewhere on west slope; uncommon summer resident and rare winter resident below 7500' and extremely rare transient at higher elevations east of crest.

In open country east of the Sierran escarpment, a shrike between November and March is usually a Northern, between April and October, always a Loggerhead. These passerine predators dwell in arid habitats with scattered shrubs or small trees, fence posts or other well-spaced lookout posts. At the south end of Mono Lake, they perch on tufa towers. The surrounding terrain is usually bare or sparsely vegetated, leaving insects, reptiles and other potential meals little place to hide. They shun timber, dense sagebrush scrub, chaparral and lush meadows in favor of pinyon pine woodlands, open scrub and the margins of dry, stubbly grasslands.

Records above 9000': 11,500' Red Slate Mountain 9/10/77 (AB 32:254); 10,000' Hall Natural Area 5/21/80 and 7/31/84 (D&E).

Extreme dates west slope excluding Mariposa region, 13 records: 4/3/20 - 5/10/27 4000' Yosemite Valley (YM); 8/9/81 4600' Ackerson Meadow (JW) - 9/20/52 7000' Peregoy Meadow (AFN 7:32).

Representative nesting locality: *6900' Panum Crater (DG).*

Additional references: YNN 15:3; AB 30:122; AB 38:244; AB 38:793.

Family STURNIDAE: STARLINGS

EUROPEAN STARLING (*Sturnus vulgaris*)

	J	F	M	A	M	J	J	A	S	O	N	D	HABITAT	ELEVATIONS		
														N	T	W
WEST													GWOBD	F-5		F-4
EAST													GWBD	6-7		6-7

Common resident in Mariposa region (2000'—CL); locally common resident below 3000' and locally common summer and rare winter resident below 4500' elsewhere on west slope; common summer resident below 7500' and locally common winter resident below 7000' east of crest.

Since their introduction in New York in 1890, European Starlings have spread throughout North America. One near Mono Lake (6400') on 12/8/47 was among the first to reach California (C 49:89). Almost two decades later, on 4/27/66, they appeared in Yosemite Valley (4000'—YM).

Like the argonauts, these starling-pioneers were harbingers of hordes to come. By the 1970s, flocks of hundreds were disputing eastside garbage dumps with gulls, ravens and blackbirds, and wresting nesting cavities from bluebirds, swallows and other native birds. By the 1980s, small numbers were nesting in Yosemite Valley (4000'), Wawona (4000'), Big Meadow (4400'), Hodgdon Meadow (4600') and other mid-elevation localities within Yosemite National Park, and were numerous in foothill towns, oak woodlands and riparian areas as well.

Moreover the European Starling population may still be on the rise. On the west slope at Ackerson Meadow (4600'), Jon Winter has noted "increasing numbers every year" since 1981. To the east, in a Lee Vining Canyon aspen grove (7500'), they have been appropriating more and more of the cavities and nest boxes formerly used by Violet-green Swallows, Mountain Bluebirds and House Wrens (JZ, DG).

European Starlings have heretofore shunned the backcountry and higher elevations, following closely the white man's footsteps. Garbage dumps, stables, campgrounds, towns, ranches, pastures, grazed meadows, stubble fields and orchards are favored haunts. They often mingle with livestock, sometimes perching on the backs of cattle, sheep or horses. On mudflats and muddy shores, they mingle with shorebirds, Horned Larks, pipits and blackbirds. They range into remote areas, as east of Mono Lake, but only in places that are heavily grazed.

In spring and summer, however, some breeding Starlings invade more virginal habitats to nest in woodpecker-excavated or natural tree cavities. This brings pairs into oak and riparian woodlands and mid-elevation meadows on the west slope, and canyon bottoms—especially aspen and cottonwood groves—to the east. They usually choose timber that margins large, open meadows or fields; they avoid deep woods. In addition to tree cavities, they avail themselves of almost any kind of hole, including nest boxes, openings in buildings and barns, and, at Mono Lake (6400'), crevices in tufa towers.

It is all too easy to vilify European Starlings for tipping nature's balance against native species. Because their behavior, at times, mirrors our own greed and aggression, we greet them with opprobrium. But let us not forget that we, through our use and abuse of the land, have allowed them to thrive and multiply. Moreover they are handsome fowl, devoted parents and among the first to sing of spring's return. They are travellers like ourselves on life's uncertain evolutionary journey.

Family VIREONIDAE: Vireos

The vireos' latin name, which means "I am green," befits their habitat better than their dress. Like warblers, they glean invertebrates from the greenery, but are not as hyperactive as their colorful cousins. Of our three nesting species, Hutton's reside year-round while Warblings and Solitaries winter mostly in Mexico.

I have treated "Plumbeous" Solitary Vireos separately, as they belong to a recognizable race which may eventually be granted "species" status.

WHITE-EYED VIREO (*Vireo griseus*)

Extremely rare vagrant east of Sierran escarpment.

Record: 8000' Glass Creek 9/2/88 (DS); under review by California Bird Records Committee.

"CASSIN'S" SOLITARY VIREO (*Vireo solitarius cassinnii*)

	J	F	M	A	M	J	J	A	S	O	N	D	HABITAT	ELEVATIONS		
														N	T	W
WEST													OPW	3-7	F-10	
EAST													PW		6-10	

Uncommon transient below 3000', fairly common summer resident from 3000' to 6000', uncommon summer resident to 7500' and rare summer visitor or fall transient to treeline on west slope; uncommon transient below 8000' and rare summer visitor or fall transient to treeline east of crest.

In late April, an unhurried succession of short, cheerful phrases announces the Solitary Vireos' return. They favor dry, open forests where black or canyon oaks mingle with ponderosa pines, sugar pines, white firs and incense cedars. But they also nest along languid streams in shady groves of hardwoods, and, at higher elevations, among sequoias and red firs. Transients appear wherever there are trees.

Though one of our commoner birds, Solitary Vireos do not call attention to themselves. Their dress is simple, their manners demure, their throaty songs pleasing but not virtuosic. Yet of all our small passerines, only Western Wood-Pewees and Warbling Vireos are equally courageous in defense of nests and families. They attack jays, squirrels, Pygmy Owls and other predators, filling the woods with grating little war-crys. Rather then desert their young, they will usually suffer bodily removal from their nests.

In the vicinity of stables and campgrounds, Solitary Vireos are heavily parasitized by Brown-headed Cowbirds. Of six nests or family groups I found in Yosemite Valley in June, 1978, for example, all but one were parasitized.

Prior to departing for Mexican wintering haunts, Solitary Vireos say farewell in song (YNN 21:42). In late summer, when the woods are quiet and bereft of bird music, their voices have a poignancy that warns of winter but reminds of spring. Adios, little greenlets!

Extreme dates west: 4/7/31 Yosemite Valley (YM) - 10/16/81 2100' El Portal (JD).

Extreme dates above 8000': 6/17/46 8600' Tuolumne Meadows (PL) - 9/8/80 10,200' Hall Natural Area (DeSante MS).

Extreme dates east below 8000': 4/23/81 6800' Lee Vining (DG) - 6/18/80 8500' Log Cabin Mine Road, plumbeous?—KC); 8/8/84 6500' w. Mono Lake - 10/3/83 w. Mono Lake (DS).

Representative nesting localities: 4000' Yosemite Valley (GS 511-512); 4400' Tuolumne Grove road (RS); 4600' Ackerson Meadow (JW); (6200' Crane Flat—DG); 7500' near Merced Lake (GS 511).

Additional reference: YNN 9:48.

"PLUMBEOUS" SOLITARY VIREO (*Vireo solitarius plumbeous*)

Rare summer resident below 8000' east of crest.

In 1977, a pair of Plumbeous Solitary Vireos was discovered feeding young near the Inyo Craters (8200'—AB 31:1186)—the first confirmed nesting in the Sierra Nevada. In recent years, singing, territorial birds have also been found in dry, open stands of Jeffrey pine, pinyon pine and juniper west and east of the Mono Craters (approx. 7500'—AB 43:1365, 40:1253, ESt, GF) and in canyons circum Glass Mountain—DG,PM,DS), and Lee Vining Canyon (RS, ESt).

YELLOW-THROATED VIREO (*Vireo flavifrons*)

Extremely rare vagrant east of Sierran escarpment.

Record: 6500' w. Mono Lake 8/26/87 (ESt); accepted by California Bird Records Committee.

HUTTON'S VIREO (*Vireo huttoni*)

	J	F	M	A	M	J	J	A	S	O	N	D	HABITAT	ELEVATIONS N	T	W
WEST	■	■	■	■	■	■	■	■	■	■	■	■	OP	F-5		F-5
EAST																

Fairly common resident below 3500', rare resident to 5000' and rare late summer and fall visitor to 6000' on west slope.

Among the west slopes' evergreen oaks, repetitious whistles often betray the presence of Hutton's Vireos. While not particularly shy, these inconspicuous birds are more easily heard than seen as they hunt for bugs in interior live, canyon and black oaks, ponderosa pines and other trees. They favor moderately dense woodlands with shrubby understories.

Hutton's Vireos probably nest to 5000' in localized pockets of suitable habitat, as along the Tuolumne River above Hetch Hetchy (DG). In Yosemite Valley (4000'), where they regularly winter, territorial pairs have been found during March and April, but nesting has yet to be confirmed (EM 12, YNN 10:21, YM). In late summer and autumn, they drift above their nesting range, reaching the upper limit of large black oaks.

High elevation record: 6000' Chinquapin 10/15-16/81 (JD).
High elevation winter record: 4600' Ackerson Meadow 1/28/84 (JW).
Additional references: GS 513; YNN 23:41.

WARBLING VIREO (*Vireo gilvus*)

	J	F	M	A	M	J	J	A	S	O	N	D	HABITAT	ELEVATIONS		
														N	T	W
WEST										•			WPO	3-8	F-10	
EAST													WP	6-8	6-10	

Uncommon transient below 3000', locally uncommon summer resident from 2000' to 3000', common summer resident from 3000' to 7000', uncommon summer resident to 8500' and rare transient to treeline on west slope; common summer resident below 8500' and rare transient to treeline east of crest.

Warbling Vireos are one of our most ubiquitous birds. Like Western Wood-Pewees, they inhabit virtually every acre of mid-elevation forest throughout the region. From mid-spring through early summer, their simple, warbled song accompanies every woodland ramble. Yet their voice, while entirely pleasing, can be lost in the Sierra's rich avian chorus. Many a time, lulled by grosbeaks, tanagers, robins and the rest, I've failed to notice them, though they were singing incessantly. To one unattuned to their songs, they seem scarcer than they actually are.

Contrary to most accounts, Warbling Vireos are not restricted to deciduous trees (e.g., GM 389-390). They are partial, to be sure, to the cottonwoods, alders and aspens which line languid streams and gather about springs and seeps, and to the black oaks, maples and dogwoods which mingle with pines and firs in mid-elevation forests. But they also dwell in a variety of coniferous habitats, including pine and fir forests that lack deciduous trees entirely.

Nesting Warbling Vireos are, in sum, so catholic in their tastes that it's easiest to list the wooded habitats they avoid. All are on the arid or high side: foothill oak woodlands, subalpine lodgepole pine forests, eastside jeffrey pine forests and pinyon pine woodlands. In general, they favor moist conditions and moderate to dense cover. Transients mostly concentrate in riparian groves and along the wooded margins of moist meadows, but may appear wherever there are trees.

Like Solitary Vireos, Warblings are frequently parasitized by Brown-headed Cowbirds, perhaps more than any other Sierran bird. Both vireos have probably declined in the vicinity of stables, pack stations, campgrounds, grazed meadows and other places where cowbirds congregate (Verner and Rothstein 1986). For more discussion, see p. 318.

Extreme dates west slope, both Yosemite Valley (4000'): 4/7/31 (YM) - 9/22/28 (YM).

Extreme dates east of crest: 5/1/82 7600' Parker Creek (DG): - 10/3/82 6500' w. Mono Lake, 2 (DS); 10/15/84 6700' Lee Vining Creek (DG).

Extreme dates above 9000', both Hall Natural Area (10,200'): 6/2/77 - 9/24/79 (DeSante MS).

Representative nesting localities: (2200' El Portal—MR); 4000' Yosemite Valley (GS 508); 6200' Crane Flat (DG); 7200' near Merced Lake (YM); (8000' Siesta Lake—DG); 8500' Lundy Canyon (DG); 7400' Lee Vining Creek (DG); 6400' west shore Mono Lake (DG); 8500' ne. of Bodie Mountain (DG).

Additional references: EM 12; YNN 9:48; YNN 21:42.

RED-EYED VIREO (*Vireo olivaceus*)

Extremely rare vagrant east of Sierran escarpment.

Records: 6500' w. shore Mono Lake 6/9/91; 6900' Frazier Canyon, Glass Mountain 6/29/91 (AB 45:1159).

BLUE-EYED VIREO (Vireo gaineus)

First observed in Lee Vining 1/6/83. Common resident ever since.

Family EMBERIZIDAE: Emberizids

Avian taxonomists, ever seeking arrangements that better reflect evolutionary relationships, have recently lumped a number of families together as *emberizids*. This large, diverse family now includes the wood warblers, tanagers, blackbirds and orioles, New World grosbeaks and sparrows as subfamilies. The latter two groups, formerly considered part of the finch family (*Fringillidae*), are now thought to be more closely related to wood warblers, tanagers and the rest. All the *emberizids* are of New World origin, whereas the finches evolved in Eurasia.

Subfamily PARULINAE: Wood-Warblers

There be no brighter sign of spring than that of male warblers raising their voices in song from fresh vernal foliage. Yet despite their brilliant dress, these little birds are difficult to see as they flit through leaves and pine needles in search of sustenance. Because they prey primarily on caterpillars, grubs and other active insects, most leave the mountains to winter in subtropical Mexico.

Of our 31 species, 19 are eastern warblers that occur only as rare or extremely rare strays. Another three pass through as transients. The remaining nine are known to nest.

Most of our nesting warblers occur in two roles: (1) as breeders in species-specific forest habitats during late spring and early summer, and (2) as transients through mid-elevation montane meadows during mid- and late summer. Observations at Crane Flat (6200') exemplify the astonishing numbers of southward migrating warblers which congregate near such meadows during peak flights. At dawn on 8/30/70, for example, over 2,000 warblers were tallied in five minutes, 552 flitting through a single lodgepole pine. Of these warblers, 40 percent were Nashvilles, 30 percent were Hermits, 20 percent were Orange-crowneds, and the remainder were Black-throated Grays, MacGillivray's, Wilson's and Townsend's (AB 25:103). On 8/17/76 a spectacular aggregation appeared at the low elevation of 4000' following the passage of an unusual summer cold front (YM).

I have chosen to treat Audubon's separately from the now conspecific Myrtle Warbler, as the two are readily identifiable both by plumage and call note.

BLUE-WINGED WARBLER (*Vermivora pinus*)

Extremely rare vagrant east of Sierran escarpment.

Record: 6500' s. Bridgeport Lake Reservoir, male, 6/18/84 (AB 38:1059); accepted by California Bird Records Committee.

GOLDEN-WINGED WARBLER (*Vermivora chrysoptera*)

Extremely rare vagrant east of Sierran escarpment.

Record: 7000' Dechambeau Creek 8/16/87 (AB 42:132); accepted by California Bird Records Committee.

TENNESSEE WARBLER (*Vermivora peregrina*)

Extremely rare vagrant on west slope; irregularly rare spring vagrant (0-2/year) and extremely rare fall vagrant below 8000' east of crest.

Tennessee Warblers stray to riparian woodlands and thickets.

Record west slope: 7/3-5/83 4600' Ackerson Meadow, singing male, barely within Yosemite National Park (AB 37:1025).

Fall records east of crest: 9/2/79 approx. 7000' Crowley Lake (AB 34:198); 10/20/84 7200' Mammoth Creek (DG); 10/27/82 6800' Lee Vining (DG).

Extreme dates east excluding fall records, six records since 1980: 5/13-14/89 6400' Mono Lake County Park (AB 43:534) - 6/29/80 approx. 7500' Lee Vining Canyon (AB 34:928).

Additional reference: AB 26:807.

ORANGE-CROWNED WARBLER (*Vermivora celata*)

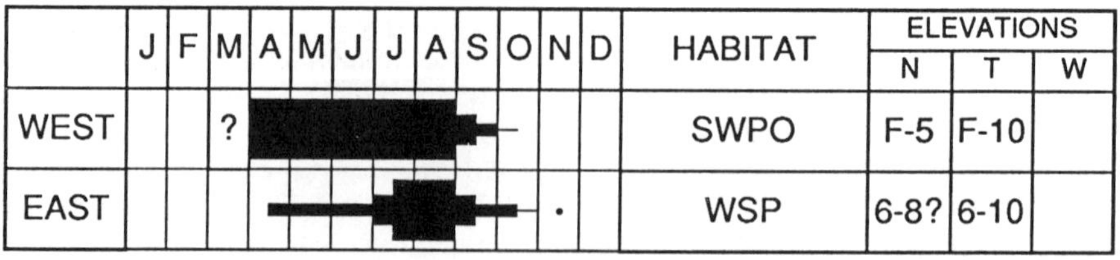

	J	F	M	A	M	J	J	A	S	O	N	D	HABITAT	ELEVATIONS		
														N	T	W
WEST			?										SWPO	F-5	F-10	
EAST											•		WSP	6-8?	6-10	

Common summer resident below 3500', uncommon summer resident to 5000' and common summer visitor and fall transient from 4000' to treeline on west slope; uncommon spring transient below 8000' and common summer visitor and fall transient to treeline east of crest—nesting status uncertain.

Orange-crowned Warblers, though one of the most numerous summer birds from mid-elevations to treeline, do not nest above 5000'. After fledging young, they forsake the foothills to follow spring upslope.

At lower elevations west of the crest, Orange-crowned Warblers are often the most numerous nesting bird. They nest in open, brushy woodlands of live and canyon oaks, digger pines and ponderosa pines as well as in dense, arborescent chaparral, usually on slopes or in ravines. They conceal their nests beneath dense shrubbery. Their stay corresponds to the blooming time of foothill flowers; they arrive about the time the oaks flower in April, and depart—after fledging young—before the Farewell-to-springs fade in June. During this period, the foothills are relatively moist, and insect food is abundant. With the advent of summer's heat and dryness, they begin to drift to higher elevations.

Small numbers of Orange-crowned Warblers' may nest east of the crest as well. In the lower reaches of Lundy, Lee Vining and other eastern Sierran canyons, singing birds have laid claim to willow thickets, but breeding has not been confirmed (AB 34:928; MM).

Because they nest so early in the year, post-breeding or juvenile Orange-crowned Warblers drift to higher elevations before most mountain birds have fledged young. By mid-June, the first mountaineers arrive in woodlands and meadows. By mid-July, they may outnumber all other birds in moist willow thickets. On 8/18-20/75, for instance, 66 were banded at Crane Flat (6200') in contrast to 18 Wilson's, 16 Nashvilles and eight MacGillivray's warblers (DDeS). They also range as high as any of their clan; while climbing Mt. Dana, I've enticed small flocks from willow thickets at 10,800', and they have reached 11,000' at nearby Mono Pass (AFN 10:409).

Though they favor thickets and meadows, Orange-crowned mountaineers forage in every terrestrial habitat. They flit among tall herbaceous vegetation, such as lupines, larkspurs and mulleins. They consort with other warblers in coniferous forests, oak woodlands and aspen groves, especially along the margins of meadows. I've seen them, for example, in timberline whitebark pines.

Not all Orange-crowned Warblers drift up from neighboring lowlands. In late August and September, a small proportion belong to the gray-headed race *V. c. celata*, which breeds across Alaska and Canada. These birds—and undoubtedly many others—utilize the Sierra as a migration route during their southward journeys.

Extreme dates: 3/29/83 6400' n. Mono Lake (DDeS) - 11/8/79 6500' Warford Spring (DG); (Orange-crowned Warblers may arrive in the western foothills by early March, as they do on the coast, but I have no records).

Extreme dates above 4000' on west slope: 6/5/78 (2) 6200' Crane Flat (SG) - 10/18/87 5000' Mather (DG).

Extreme dates above 8000': 6/11/81 10,000' Hall Natural Area (D&E) - 9/30/76 8600' Tuolumne Meadows (DG).

Representative nesting localities: (1300' Merced River Canyon—MR); (2000' Mariposa—DG); (2100' El Portal—DG); (4500' Alder Creek Trail near Wawona—DG).

Additional reference: AB 27:912.

NASHVILLE WARBLER (*Vermivora ruficapilla*)

	J	F	M	A	M	J	J	A	S	O	N	D	HABITAT	ELEVATIONS		
														N	T	W
WEST													OPWS	3-6	F-10	
EAST													WPS	6-8	6-10	

Common summer resident from 3000' to 5000', locally common summer resident to 6000', rare summer resident or visitor to 8500' and uncommon fall transient from foothills to treeline on west slope; rare summer resident and uncommon fall transient below 8000' and uncommon fall transient to treeline east of crest.

On the west slope, on dry, wooded slopes with shrubby understories, Nashville Warblers are plentiful nesting birds. Compared to Orange-crowneds, they breed in more forested habitats, usually at higher elevations. Both require shrubby undergrowth in which to hide their nests.

Nashville Warblers are partial to black oaks, canyon oaks, big-leaf maples and other deciduous trees, but also nest among ponderosa pines and white firs. Though they sing and forage high in the foliage, they conceal their nests beneath ceanothus, mountain misery, manzanita and other shrubs.

The upper limit of Nashville Warblers' west slope nesting range is not definitely known. Along the Tioga Road, Sallie Hejl has found singing males and family groups in red fir forests as high as 8300', but there are no positive records above the black oaks (approximately 6000').

East of the crest, Nashville Warblers' nesting status—like that of the closely related Virginia's—is likewise unclear. In spring, they and Hermits are the scarcest of transient western warblers. A few singing males, however, have summered as high as 9000' in eastern Sierran canyons (AB 34:928, AB 35:976, Auk 93:219-230, MM, RS). In Lee Vining Canyon, they have been seen carrying food (approx. 7500'—T&JH).

Like Orange-crowneds, Nashville Warblers drift upslope after fledging young at lower elevations, but in far fewer numbers. These mountaineering individuals frequent all types of wooded habitats, but concentrate in willow thickets and along the margins of moist meadows, where they consort with other passerines in loose flocks. Some are undoubtedly northerners migrating south through the Sierran cordillera.

Additional representative nesting localities: 4000' Yosemite Valley (GS 516); 4600' Ackerson Meadow (JW); (6000' Henness Ridge—DG); (6000' near top Nevada Fall—DG).

Extreme dates: 4000' Yosemite Valley 4/9/31 (YM) - 10,000' Hall Natural Area 9/22/75 (DeSante MS) and 7300' Dewey Point Ski Trail 9/22/85 (SH)

Additional references: EM 12; YNN 6:81; AFN 9:54.

VIRGINIA'S WARBLER (*Vermivora virginiae*)

Extremely rare transient on west slope; irregularly rare summer resident or transient below 8500' and extremely rare transient at higher elevations east of crest.

Of all our nesting warblers, Virginia's are the scarcest; they are not even found every year. Perhaps the population is impermanent, and is replenished every so often by young pioneers from the White Mountains and other ranges further east.

When they are found, Virginia's Warblers usually frequent open woodlands or riparian thickets. In Lee Vining Canyon, for example, at least three singing males, one carrying food, were observed in a woodland of pinyon pines and desert mahoganies on the north-facing side of a steep, lateral glacial moraine (7500'—June-August/75—MC). Singing males have also been heard above Green Lake (8500'—MM). Two canyons, Frazier and Kelty on the north slope of Glass Mountain were birded extensively in 1991. The observers, (PM, ESt, DS) report small numbers of Virginia's warblers and definite nesting (AB 45:1159).

Virginia's are so closely related to Nashville Warblers that some ornithologists consider them the same species. Since both apparently nest in the eastern Sierra, hybrids should be watched for. At least one of the birds observed near treeline in the Hall Natural Area may have been of hybrid origin (DeSante and Engstrom MS).

Records west slope: 4000' Yosemite Valley 7/31/81 (AB 36:215); 4000' Ackerson Meadow 8/6/83 (AB 38:244); 6200' Crane Flat, banded 8/25/74 (DDeS).

Records above 8500' east of crest, all Hall Natural Area: 10,300' 7/18/81, 9900' 7/31/86 and 10,000' 8/3-6/86 (DeSante MS).

Extreme dates, six records since 1975: Late June/75 Lee Vining Canyon (MC) - 9/20/85 6400' Mono Lake (DG).

Additional reference: AB 33:211.

NORTHERN PARULA (*Parula americana*)

Extremely rare vagrant on west slope; irregularly rare spring vagrant (0-2/year) below 8000' east of crest.

Northern Parulas, when they stray to our region, are partial to cottonwoods, willows and aspens. Many have been males in full, buzzy song.

Record west slope: 6/19/85 4000' Yosemite Valley (YM).

Extreme dates east, seven records since 1979: 5/24/85 6400' Mono Lake County Park (AB 39:347) - 7/3/78 approx. 7500' Lee Vining Canyon (KC).

YELLOW WARBLER (*Dendroica petechia*)

	J	F	M	A	M	J	J	A	S	O	N	D	HABITAT	ELEVATIONS		
														N	T	W
WEST													WPO	F-6		
EAST										•			W	6-8		

Common summer resident below 6500' on west slope and below 7500' east of crest; extremely rare in higher mountains.

The golden hues of Yellow Warblers blend with the light-colored, sun-filtered deciduous foliage in which they mostly dwell. No other warbler is as partial to the broad-leaved cottonwoods, willows and alders which line languid streams.

Yet, contrary to most accounts (e.g. GM 400), Yellow Warblers also nest in dry, montane chaparral with only scattered trees. They are numerous, for example, near Crane Flat Lookout (6400'), where pines, firs and oaks overlook dense carpets of ceanothus and manzanita. One associates this habitat, which often develops after a forest is burned or clearcut, with Fox Sparrows and Dusky Flycatchers, not Yellow Warblers. Yet, in the northern Sierra, these hydrophilic warblers have even colonized monocultural tracts of reseeded, six-foot pines (AB 25:904).

Unlike most migratory passerines, Yellow Warblers are extremely rare in the higher mountains; southward migrants must journey through or below their nesting range.

Records above 6500' on west slope or 8000' east of crest: 6/13/82 8600' Tuolumne Meadows (MR); Hall Natural Area—9900', singing male 6/22/79 and 10,200', late Aug./74 (AB 33:894, DeSante and Engstrom MS).

Extreme dates: 4000' Yosemite Valley 4/16/26 (YM) - 10/19/85 west shore Mono Lake (DG).

Representative nesting localities: (2100' El Portal—MR); 4000' Yosemite Valley (GS 522); 4600' Ackerson Meadow (JW); 6200' Little Yosemite Valley (YM); 6400' Crane Flat Lookout (MM, DG); 8000' Mammoth Lakes (C 41:251); 7400' Lee Vining Canyon (DG); 6800' Walker Creek (GS 522); 6400' Mono Lake County Park (DG).

Additional reference: YNN 21:42.

CHESTNUT-SIDED WARBLER (*Dendroica pensylvanica*)

Irregularly rare spring vagrant (0-2/year) and extremely rare fall vagrant below 8000' east of the Sierran escarpment.

Extreme dates east excluding fall records, five records since 1976: 6/13/80 7000' Dechambeau Creek (KC)- 6/25/76 7100' Convict Creek (AB 30:1001).

Fall records east of the crest: 8/19/79 7500' Lundy Canyon (DW, DG)- 8/21/89 6500' w.shore Mono Lake (AB 44:158).

MAGNOLIA WARBLER (*Dendroica magnolia*)

Extremely rare vagrant west and east of the crest.

Record west slope: 4000' Yosemite Valley 10/6/19 (GM 401).

Records east of crest: 6/15/91 6800'lower Walker Creek, singing male, (AB 45:1159); summer 1990 Rush and Parker Creeks (TB); 8000' Deadman Creek 10/11/87 (DG).

BLACK-THROATED BLUE WARBLER (*Dendroica caerulescens*)

Extremely rare vagrant east of crest.

Record: 7400' Lee Vining Canyon, male, 10/14/84 (DDeS, DG); 6700' Dechambeau Creek 11/1/87 (ESt).

"AUDUBON'S" YELLOW-RUMPED WARBLER (*Dendroica coronata auduboni*)

	J	F	M	A	M	J	J	A	S	O	N	D	HABITAT	ELEVATIONS		
														N	T	W
WEST													POWSG	4-10	F-10	F 4
EAST													PWSGMu	6-10	6-10	6-7

Common summer resident from 4000' to treeline, rare transient above treeline and uncommon winter resident below 4000' on west slope; common summer resident to treeline, rare transient above treeline and rare winter resident below 7000' east of crest.

Audubon's enjoy the broadest range of any Sierran warbler, nesting in a wide variety of coniferous forest habitats from 4000' to treeline. They dwell among stunted timberline pines and towering Sequoias, in dry, open woods and moist, shady forests, on steep canyon slopes and in level valleybottoms. The only conifers they shun are digger, knobcone and pinyon pines.

During migrations, Audubon's Warblers are even more widespread, ranging into every terrestrial habitat. On Mt. Dana, they mingle with Rosy Finches at 12,000'. At Mono Lake, they consort with pipits and shorebirds on muddy shores. They flit through chaparral and sagebrush scrub miles from trees, forage in marshes, meadows and grasslands, and snatch bugs from cliff walls and buildings. Flocks—sometimes numbering hundreds—forsake the conifers to dine in oaks, cottonwoods, willows, aspens, orchard trees and other hardwoods. Audubon's are the hardiest of warblers, arriving earliest in spring, departing latest in autumn, and sometimes weathering mountain winters. In early April, flocks materialize in woods, meadows and residential areas both west and east of the crest. Snow and sleet doesn't daunt these wee travellers. They roam the lower elevations in cheerful bands, waiting for winter to loosen its grip on the slopes above. Near treeline, they usually arrive in May, but this varies from year to year.

After the mild 1976 winter, for instance, they reached Tuolumne Meadows (8600') by 4/23, two weeks earlier than the year before (TH).

In autumn, Audubon's linger in the mountains a month or two longer than other warblers and most migratory passerines, even at high elevations. A vigorous autumn storm, however, can force large flocks to lower elevations. On 10/14/52, for instance, a storm brought "hordes" to Yosemite Valley (4000'); "every tree seemed to be filled with them" (AFN 7:35).

Resourceful personalities and varied diets enable Audubon's Warblers to brave wintry weather. They not only glean invertebrates from foliage like other warblers, but also pick them off the ground, nab them from the air, sponge from sapsucker drillings and, if times be lean, resort to berries and seeds. East of the crest, they may winter near hot springs. Hence they are able to weather storms and cold spells that would doom other warblers to starvation.

Representative nesting localities: 4000' Yosemite Valley (GS 528); 4600' Ackerson Meadow (JW); 6200' Crane Flat (DG); 7800' White Wolf (DG); 8600' Tuolumne Meadows (DG); 10,300' Hall Natural Area (DeSante MS); 7500' Lee Vining Canyon (DG); (9000' Glass Mountain—DG).

Extreme dates above 8000': 4/13/84 8900' Kerrick Meadow (YM) - 11/5/84 9700' Oneida Lake (DG).

"MYRTLE" YELLOW-RUMPED WARBLER
(*Dendroica coronata hooveri*)

Probably rare transient on west slope, but only three records; rare transient below 8000' east of crest.

I know of only three records for Myrtle Warblers on the west slope, but they are probably overlooked. To the east, they are rare transients below 8000' in the same habitats as Audubon's; they may sometimes winter, but have not been seen beyond the first of the year.

Records west slope: 4000' Yosemite Valley 3/16/81 (GSt) and 10/13/81, 3 (JD); 4600' Ackerson Meadow 4/25/87 (JW).

Extreme dates east: 3/21/81 6800' Lee Vining (DG) - 5/18/79 Lee Vining (DG); 10/14/77 6400' Mono Lake (DDeS) - 1/1/84 Mono Lake (AB 38:793).

BLACK-THROATED GRAY WARBLER
(*Dendroica nigrescens*)

	J	F	M	A	M	J	J	A	S	O	N	D	HABITAT	ELEVATIONS		
														N	T	W
WEST			•									•	OPSW	3-7	F-10	2
EAST													PSW	7-8	F-10	

Uncommon transient below 3000', common summer resident from 3000' to 5000', fairly common resident to 7000', rare fall transient to treeline and extremely rare winter visitor on west slope; rare transient below 8000' and extremely rare spring and rare fall transient to treeline east of crest, except on Cedar Hill (7000'-8000') and possibly elsewhere in southeastern and northern parts of Bodie Hills, where an uncommon summer resident.

More than other warblers, Black-throated Grays welcome heat and aridity. Their haunts are usually hot, especially on summer afternoons. Even their songs possess a somnolent quality that befits their sun-drenched homes.

On the west slope, Black-throated Gray Warblers are constant companions of canyon oaks. They also nest among black oaks, ponderosa pines, white firs and other trees, usually with understories of ceanothus, manzanita and mountain misery. In contrast to Hermit and Audubon's warblers, with which they sometimes dwell, they favor drier, more open groves and woodlands. Nor do they covet conifers. On the north side of Yosemite Valley (4200'), for instance, they nest in nearly pure groves of canyon oaks.

East of the Sierran escarpment, in parts of the Bodie Hills, Black-throated Gray Warblers nest in arid, open woodlands of Utah junipers and pinyon pines (JP, DG, AB 35:976). Junipers are apparently a crucial factor, for they shun pure stands of pinyons.

Transient Black-throated Gray Warblers, while still most numerous in oaks, range into virtually all wooded habitats. At higher elevations, they favor the wooded margins of meadows. Occasionally they stray into red fir forests and other densely wooded habitats. In the lodgepole pine forests at Peregoy Meadow (7000'), they have arrived as early as 6/20/85 (AB 39:960).

Compared to most warblers except Yellow-rumpeds and Orange-crowneds, Black-throated Grays arrive earlier in spring and linger, at least in small numbers, later in autumn. On the west slope, males are usually singing by mid-April.

Black-throated Gray Warblers are reluctant mountaineers, rarely straying to treeline. Of our regularly nesting warblers, only Yellows are scarcer at high elevations.

Spring record above 8000': 4/25/82 10,400' Hall Natural Area (DeSante and Engstrom MS).

Winter record: 2000' El Portal 12/22/79 (AB 34:670; LMcK)

Extreme dates west slope excluding winter record: 2100' El Portal 3/7/79 (MR); 4/1/84 4000' Yosemite Valley (JL) 10/16/81 Yosemite Valley and 4400' Foresta, 3 (JD); 11/16/90 Fish Camp (ESt).

Extreme dates east of crest: 4/30/83 6400' Mono Lake (DS) - 10/12/87 6800' Lee Vining (DG).

Extreme dates above 8000' excluding spring record: 7/17/81 8600' Tuolumne Meadows (MM) - 8/30/77 10,000' Hall Natural Area (DeSante and Engstrom MS)

Additional representative nesting localities: 3700' Hetch Hetchy (MM); 4000' Yosemite Valley (GS 531); 7100' Little Yosemite Valley (JL).

Additional references: EM 12; YNN 18:96; YNN 21:42.

TOWNSEND'S WARBLER (*Dendroica townsendi*)

	J	F	M	A	M	J	J	A	S	O	N	D	HABITAT	ELEVATIONS		
														N	T	W
WEST						•	•						POW		F-10	F-5
EAST				•			•						PW		6-10	

Rare spring transient below 8000', uncommon fall transient from 5000' to treeline and irregularly rare winter resident below 5000' on west slope; uncommon spring transient below 8000' and uncommon fall transient to treeline east of crest.

Townsend's Warblers pass through the Yosemite Sierra on migrations, but do not stop to nest. Like Audubon's Warblers, with which they often mingle, they visit all types of timber from foothill oaks to timberline whitebarks. They frequent hardwoods as well as conifers, but generally favor dense, shady forests. A few winter on the west slope, flocking with kinglets, nuthatches, chickadees and other small birds.

During the southward migration, Townsend's Warblers range to treeline until late August or early September, then linger at lower elevations into mid-October or rarely through the winter. At the Hall Natural Area (10,000'), they have been seen as late as 9/12/78 (DeSante MS); at Peregoy Meadow (7000'), as late as 10/14/80 (JD).

In early June, singing male Townsend's Warblers have been heard in Lee Vining Canyon (PM), at Mono Lake (6400'—AB 40:1253), near Sagehen Spring 8300'(HG), and near the top of Yosemite Falls (AFN 24:714). They are not known to nest closer than central Oregon.

High elevation record: 10,000' Hall Natural Area, many records (DeSante MS).

Extreme dates west slope: 7/17/81 8400' two miles e. of Siesta Lake (YM); 7/26/77 approx. 7000' near Crane Flat (SG) - 6/3/70 6900' near top of Yosemite Falls (AFN 24:714).

Extreme dates above 8000': 7/17/81 8400' two miles east of Siesta Lake (YM) - 9/12/78 10,000' Hall Natural Area (DeSante MS).

Extreme dates east of crest below 8000': 4/22/90 6400' Mono Lake County Park (JHu) - 6/15/91 6800' Lee Vining Canyon (PM); 9/23/84 6400' w. Mono Lake (SJ) - 10/15/85 6400' n. Mono Lake (DG).

Highest winter record: approximately 4700' above Wawona Campground 2/22/80 (JV).

Additional references: AFN 7:35, AB 28:544, YNN 17:41, YNN 32:11.

GRACE'S WARBLER (*Dendroica graciae*)

Extremely rare vagrant east of Sierran escarpment.

Record: 7200' Deer Springs, east of Glass Mountain 6/26/91, female (AB 45:1159); under review California Bird Record Committee.

HERMIT WARBLER (*Dendroica occidentalis*)

	J	F	M	A	M	J	J	A	S	O	N	D	HABITAT	ELEVATIONS		
														N	T	W
WEST													POW	4-8	F-10	
EAST				•					•				PW		6-10	

Rare spring transient below 4000', common summer resident from 4000' to 7000', uncommon summer resident to 8000' and uncommon fall transient to treeline on west slope; rare fall transient from 9000' to treeline on east slope; extremely rare transient below 9000' on east of Sierran escarpment.

Despite their brilliant dress, Hermit Warblers elude easy observation as they flit through the foliage of towering sugar pines, ponderosa pines, sequoias and white and red firs. But their variable songs—which can be confusingly similar to those of Black-throated Grays—betray their numbers. From the mixed oak-conifer forests through the red firs, they are the most plentiful nesting warbler.

Hermits and Black-throated Gray Warblers nest at the same elevations, but rarely in the same forests. Hermits choose wetter, shadier, conifer-dominated forests, Black-throated Grays drier, sunnier, oak-dominated ones. Climbing from a moist valley to a dry ridge, or crossing from a north to a south-facing slope, one often trades the Hermits' domain for that of their elegantly liveried cousins.

After fledging young, Hermit Warblers, like Orange-crowneds, Nashvilles and MacGillivray's, frequently drift to treeline. They mostly keep to coniferous habitats, flocking with other warblers along the margins of moist meadows.

East of the crest, except near treeline, Hermit Warblers are even scarcer than such "eastern vagrants" as Northern Parulas, Tennessee Warblers and American Redstarts.

High elevation record: 11,200' Red Slate Mountain 9/10/77 (DG).

Records below 9000' east of crest: 7500' Lee Vining Canyon 4/27/82 (DG); 8000' Lundy Canyon 8/6/87 (JD); 7600' Crestview 8/28/90 (ESt); 6400' Mono Lake 9/2/85 (DG); 7600' Yost Creek trailhead, June Lake Loop 9/14/90 (ESt).

Extreme dates: 4/16/30 4000' Yosemite Valley (YM) - 10/20/68 Yosemite Valley (AFN 23:104).

Extreme dates above 9000': 6/22-26/79 approx. 10,000' Hall Natural Area (AB 33:894; DeSante MS); 7/22/79 Hall Natural Area (DeSante MS) - 9/10/77 11,200' Red Slate Mountain (DG).

Representative nesting localities: 4000' Yosemite Valley (GS 532; YNN 21:42); 4400' Foresta (DG); 4600' Ackerson Meadow (JW); 6200' Crane Flat (DG); 7000' Peregoy Meadow (TB).

Additional references: EM 12, AB 36:215.

(HERMIT X TOWNSEND'S WARBLER)

The distinctive hybrids of Hermit and Townsend's warblers have been seen three times on the west slope.

Records: 6200' Crane Flat 6/?/74 (JW) and 8/25/75, banded (AB 30:123); 4000' Yosemite Valley 10/14/81 (JD).

BLACK-THROATED GREEN WARBLER (*Dendroica virens*)

Extremely rare vagrant east of Sierran escarpment.

Record: 6800' Lee Vining 10/31/87 (DG).

PRAIRIE WARBLER (*Dendroica discolor*)

Extremely rare vagrant east of crest.

Records: 6400' Mono Lake County Park 5/28/88 (AB 42:479); 8000' Lundy Canyon, immature 8/19/77 (AB 34:198); 7800' Mammoth Lakes 8/29/90 (AB 45:148); 10,600' Hall Natural Area 9/25/84 (DeSante and Engstrom MS).

PALM WARBLER (*Dendroica palmarum*)

Extremely rare vagrant east of crest.

Record: 10,000' Hall Natural Area 5/30/80 (AB 39:100, DeSante and Engstrom MS); (on the west slope, a bird thought to be this species was in Tuolumne Meadows on 10/7/74; though the date is plausible, the lack of substantiating details consigns this warbler—for now at least—to Yosemite's hypothetical list—YM).

BLACKPOLL WARBLER (*Dendroica striata*)

Extremely rare vagrant both west and east of crest.

Records: 4000' Yosemite Valley, male 4/28/80 (YM); 6400' Mono Lake County Park 9/11/81 (AB 36:215); 6500' Dechambeau Ranch 9/29/87 (PM); (also recorded just east of our region at Benton Hot Springs on 5/29-31/78—AB 32:1052).

CERULEAN WARBLER (*Dendroica cerulea*)

Extremely rare vagrant on west slope.

Record: 4100' Mirror Lake 10/12/81 (AB 36:215); accepted by California Bird Records Committee.

BLACK-AND-WHITE WARBLER (*Mniotilta varia*)

Extremely rare vagrant west slope; rare vagrant east of crest.

Curiously, most Black-and-White Warblers have been seen on the east side during June, and on the west side during September. In Lundy Canyon (approximately 8000'), two males were counter-singing on 6/18-20/81 (AB 35:976); and singing males were heard along Upper Owens River, lower Lee Vining Creek and lower Walker Creek

(ESt); but they are known to nest no closer than northeastern British Columbia. They frequent conifers as well as hardwoods.

Records west slope: 4000' Yosemite Valley 5/11/77 (YM), 9/18/64 (AFN 19:75) and 9/22-23/78 (YM); 9000' near Ten Lakes 9/12/59, foraging nuthatch-like on a lodgepole pine (AFN 14:69; RS).

Extreme dates and fall records east of crest: 5/20/89 6500' (AB 43:534)- 6/18/91 (AB 45:1159); 7/28/83- 8/25-27/87 6500' w. Mono Lake (DS, ESt); 10/12/87 6800' Lee Vining (DG).

Additional references: D 438; AB 35:860.

AMERICAN REDSTART (*Setophaga ruticilla*)

Irregularly rare spring and extremely rare fall transient below 8000' and extremely rare transient at higher elevations east of crest.

During June, in cottonwoods, aspens and willows east of the crest, a flash of color may betray an American Redstart. The presence of singing, adult males at June Lake boat dock (7600') (Bruce Gerow), in Lundy Canyon (approx. 8000'), Lee Vining Canyon (7400'), along the west shore of Mono Lake (6500') and in Lee Vining (6800'—MM, HG, DG) hints at the possibility of nesting. In eastern Oregon, they breed in aspen groves.

Extreme dates and fall records: 5/30/76 7000' Dechambeau Creek (MBRG) - 7/9/78 7500' Lee Vining Canyon (KC); 8/22/83 6400' Mono Lake (AB 38:241); 8/24/84 6500' (DS); 9/1/91 (PM); 9/16/84 (SJ) last three all w. shore Mono Lake.

Record above 8000': 9900' Hall Natural Area 8/27/81 (AB 36:215, DeSante and Engstrom MS).

Additional references: AB 28:105; AB 40:1253

PROTHONOTARY WARBLER (*Protonotaria citrea*)

Extremely rare vagrant east of crest.

Record: 6400' w. Mono Lake, male, 9/15/85 (KH); accepted by California Bird Records Committee.

OVENBIRD (*Seirus aurocapillus*)

Extremely rare vagrant both west and east of crest.

Record west slope: 4000' Yosemite Valley 6/31/84 (AB 38:1059)

Records east of crest, last two singing males: Dexter Canyon, Glass Mountain 6/12/91 (PM,DS); 7000' Dechambeau Creek 6/22/76 (BE, DG—the 6/6 date published in AB 30:1001 is an error); 6800' Lee Vining 6/24/83 (Michael Green).

NORTHERN WATERTHRUSH (*Seirus noveboracensis*)

Rare transient east of crest.

Records, first two singing males: 7200' Rush Creek by powerplant 6/17/88, 6/17-24/89, (AB 42:1338, AB 43:1365), and 6/20-25/90 (Bruce Gerow); 7500' Lee Vining Creek 6/10/83 (DG); 7600' Lundy Canyon 9/14/87 (Dianne Sierra and Chris Pattillo).

KENTUCKY WARBLER (*Oporornis formosus*)

Extremely rare vagrant east of crest.

Records: 8000' Mammoth Lakes, male killed by cat 6/15/84 (DG, specimen at California Academy of Sciences); 6500' w. Mono Lake 8/13/87 (DG— accepted by California Bird Records Committee).

MACGILLIVRAY'S WARBLER (*Oporornis tolmiei*)

	J	F	M	A	M	J	J	A	S	O	N	D	HABITAT	ELEVATIONS		
														N	T	W
WEST													WS	3-8	F-10	
EAST													WS	6-8	6-10	

Uncommon transient below 3000', fairly common summer resident from 3000' to 8500' and fairly common fall transient from 4000' to treeline on west slope; fairly common summer resident below 8000' and fairly common fall transient to treeline east of crest.

Of Sierran nesting warblers, MacGillivray's keep their lives best hidden. Only when singing or alarmed do they forsake low shrubbery or dense undergrowth.

During the nesting season, MacGillivray's Warblers skulk in moist, riparian thickets and the shrubby understories of humid forests. They dwell along languid streams, about seeps and springs, in or along the margins of meadows, and beneath red and white firs, sugar pines, sequoias, douglas firs and other conifers. They shun chaparral, however, unless it lies close to a stream or is shaded by trees. Among their favored shrubs are snowberry, thimbleberry, chokecherry, coffeeberry, snow brush, chinquapin, dogwood and willow.

MacGillivray's Warblers may occasionally nest to 10,000'. Males have been heard singing as high as Green Lake (9400'—MM) and in the Hall Natural Area (10,300') (DeSante MS). After fledging young at lower elevations, many drift to treeline, usually arriving in August.

During migration, MacGillivray's Warblers are more widespread, though still partial to dense cover. In spring, some visit chaparral and sagebrush scrub. During August, they join Orange-crowned Warblers, Wilson's Warblers and other southward migrants in the verdant willow thickets of montane meadows. They also forage in lupines, cow parsnip and other herbaceous greenery.

Representative nesting localities: 4000' Yosemite Valley (GS 357); 4600' Ackerson Meadow (JW); (6000' Henness Ridge—DG); (7800' Olmsted Point—DG); 8000' Lundy Canyon (MM, DG); 7500' Lee Vining Creek (DG); (6500' Rush Creek—DG); (8000' Glass Mountain—DG).

Extreme dates west: 4/23/21 4000' Yosemite Valley (YM) - 10/15/81 Yosemite Valley (AB 36:216).

Extreme dates east: 5/6/82 6400' west shore Mono Lake (BE) - 10/19/82 west shore Mono Lake (DG).

Extreme dates above 8500', both Hall Natural Area (10,300'): 6/30/81 - 9/27/80 (DeSante MS).

Additional references: C 18:124; EM 12; Wilson Bulletin 46: 251; YNN 9: 53; YNN 21:42.

COMMON YELLOWTHROAT (*Geothlypis trichas*)

	J	F	M	A	M	J	J	A	S	O	N	D	HABITAT	ELEVATIONS		
														N	T	W
WEST				•	•		•		—	—			MaGW		F-7	
EAST				—	■	—	—	—	■	—			MaGW	6-7?	6-7	

Extremely rare spring transient and summer visitor and rare fall transient below 7000' on west slope; extremely rare summer visitor or transient on east slope; fairly common spring transient, rare summer visitor and uncommon fall transient below 7000' east of Sierran escarpment.

Because they skulk in moist situations with low, dense cover, Common Yellowthroats are easily overlooked. They favor sedges, bulrushes, cattails and willow thickets, especially in or margining marshes, ponds, languid streams and wet meadows.

Common Yellowthroats may breed in the region, but I know of no positive records. East of the crest, Grinnell and Miller (1944) cite Mono Lake (6400') as a "nesting station," but do not give a source. Only once have I found a singing territorial male, but—alas—it never found a mate: lower Rush Creek (6500') 5/10-6/18/85.

At higher elevations and on the west slope, singing Common Yellowthroats have been found multiple times. In June, 1971, one was singing vociferously near Mirror Lake in Yosemite Valley (4200'—DDeS). On 6/17/84, at least five were harmonizing in Peregoy Meadow (7000')—an extraordinary number, especially at this elevation (TB). From 7/6-25/83, a lone bird sang incessantly near the Hall Natural Area (9700'—AB 36:892; DeSante and Engstrom MS). Other loners have been heard at 10,000' on Rock Creek (6/21/87—JP) and, just south of our region, at 10,200' at Honeymoon Lake (7/24/80--AB 34:928).

Additional spring and summer records west slope: 2100' El Portal 5/7/87 (DG); 4000' Yosemite Valley 4/29/33 (YM), 5/9/26 (YM) and 7/15/27 (EM 12).

Extreme dates: 4/5/78 6400' Mono Lake County Park (KC) - 10/31/86 6400' East Walker River (DS, SJ).

Extreme dates west slope excluding above records: 8/28/76 6200' Crane Flat (DG) - 4000' Yosemite Valley 10/21/28 (YM).

Hooded Warbler banded at Conway Ranch, November 3, 1981. Photograph by Michael R. Dressler.

HOODED WARBLER (*Wilsonia citrina*)

Extremely rare vagrant east of Sierran escarpment.

Records: 5/20-28/81 6800' male Lee Vining (AB 35:861); 5/28/87 6400' Mono Lake County Park (JW); 6/24/89 8000' Parker Creek male (AB 43:1365); 10/31-11/3/81 6900' male, banded Conway Ranch (AB 36:216—see photograph on following page).

WILSON'S WARBLER (*Wilsonia pusilla*)

	J	F	M	A	M	J	J	A	S	O	N	D	HABITAT	ELEVATIONS		
														N	T	W
WEST													WPG	4-10	F-10	
EAST													WPG	7-10	6-10	

Uncommon transient below 4000', uncommon summer resident from 4000' to treeline, common fall transient from 4000' to 8000' and fairly common fall transient to treeline on west slope; uncommon summer resident from 8000' to treeline, common transient below 8000' and fairly common fall transient to treeline east of crest.

Though nowhere common, Wilson's Warblers breed from 4000' to treeline. Only Audubon's share so wide an altitudinal nesting range, though different tastes in habitat. Unlike the conifer-loving Audubon's, Wilson's dwell in humid, deciduous trees and thickets near meadows, seeps, springs and languid streams. Though they range into lodgepole pines and other nearby conifers, they forage primarily in willows, alders, dogwoods and aspens.

While one of our scarcer nesting birds, Wilson Warbler's are common transients. Large flights pass east of the crest in early May, and through montane meadows in August. At times, these restless little birds flash like golden threads in every shrub and thicket.

Migrating Wilson's Warblers are more catholic in choice of habitat. In early May, transients appear almost everywhere, including sagebrush scrub and montane chaparral: 130 were seen in the vicinity of Mono Lake County Park May 23-24, 1989 (AB 43:534). In August, they congregate in moist montane meadows, foraging in willow thickets as well as lupines, cow parsnip and other herbaceous greenery. They also flock with other warblers in nearby conifers.

Representative nesting localities. 4000' Yosemite Valley (YM); 4600' Ackerson Meadow (JW); 5800' near Chinquapin (GS 542); 7200' Merced Lake (GS 542); 10,000' Hall Natural Area (JB, D&E); 10,000' above Tioga Lake (BS); 8500' Virginia Creek (C 41:251); (8500' Lundy Canyon—DG); 8000' June Lake (C 36:35).

Extreme dates west slope: 4/18/40 4000' Yosemite Valley - 9/23/86 4600' Ackerson Meadow (JW).

Extreme dates east of crest: 4/16/81 6400' Mono Lake (DW) - 9/28/87 w. Mono Lake, 2 (PM).

CANADA WARBLER (*Wilsonia canadensis*)

Extremely rare vagrant east of crest.

Record: 8600' Mammoth Lakes 6/21/86 (DSu); under review by California Bird Records Committee.

YELLOW-BREASTED CHAT (*Icteria virens*)

Extremely rare transient on west slope; irregularly rare transient and summer visitor below 7000' east of the Sierran escarpment.

Yellow-breasted Chats may nest sporadically in dense, moist willow thickets east of the Sierran escarpment. Along the west shore of Mono Lake (6400'), one or two singing birds were present in 1976, 1977 and 1983, but not in intervening or subsequent years (DW, DG, HG). While chats conventionally skulk in humid thickets, one at Benton Crossing (7000') was in sagebrush scrub (DP).

Extreme dates east: 4/20/80 Benton Crossing (DP) - 9/12/89 6500' w. shore Mono lake (PM).

Records west slope, all Yosemite Valley (4000'): 9/1/28 (YNN 15:16), 9/6/26 (EM 12), 9/22/35 (YNN 15:16) and 10/2/25 (EM 12).

Subfamily THRAUPINAE: Tanagers

SUMMER TANAGER (*Piranga rubra*)

Extremely rare vagrant east of crest.

Records: 6500' Mono Lake County Park, adult male 8/12/75 (MC); 6500' w. Mono Lake, female, 6/15/87 (Barry Sauppe).

WESTERN TANAGER (*Piranga ludoviciana*)

	J	F	M	A	M	J	J	A	S	O	N	D	HABITAT	ELEVATIONS		
														N	T	W
WEST													POW	0-0	[illegible] 10	
EAST													POW	6-8	6-10	

Uncommon transient below 3000', fairly common summer resident from 3000' to 7000', uncommon summer resident to 8000' and rare summer visitor and fall transient to treeline on west slope; fairly common summer resident below 8000', uncommon summer resident to 9000' and extremely rare spring transient and rare summer visitor and fall transient to treeline east of crest; uncommon transient below 8000' outside breeding range east of Sierran escarpment.

The deep blues of Steller's Jays, amber hues of Evening Grosbeaks and rosy reds of Cassin's Finches are resplendent, of course, but evolved under northern skies and sunsets. Western Tanagers add a touch of tropical splendor to the summer coniferous forests.

Western Tanagers favor open, coniferous forests with a mixture of different kinds of trees, though they also nest in hardwoods. On the west slope, they range from the oak-conifer belt to the upper limit of red firs, consorting with sugar pines, ponderosa pines, white and red firs, incense cedars and douglas firs. East of the crest, they dwell among jeffrey pines, white and red firs and western white pines. They are also at home among black oaks, canyon oaks, cottonwoods, aspens, willows, orchard trees and other hardwoods, though usually mixed with conifers. During the nesting season, they shun the lodgepole pine forests of higher elevations; except near streams, they avoid pinyon pines.

Because they sally after insects, Western Tanagers prefer open forests and the wooded margins of meadows, lakes, streams, openings and scrub. They also glean meals from foliage, or dine on the forest floor, in meadows or along the banks of lakes and streams. Wet or dry conditions make little difference; they nest along streams as well as in park-like woodlands miles from the nearest water.

During migrations, Western Tanagers visit all types of wooded habitat, including towns, isolated groves of trees, scrub and chaparral. In late summer, they are attracted by the ripening fruits of elderberry, dogwood, chokecherry, service berry and other shrubs and trees. Such fare, I suspect, tempts them to linger into September and rarely October—longer than most long-distance, tropical migrants.

Though amphibians are not usual predators, a bullfrog swallowed a Western Tanager at Mather (5200') on 8/25/59 (ABR).

High elevation record: 10,200' Hall Natural Area, many records (DeSante MS).

Extreme dates west slope: 4/24/23 4000' Yosemite Valley (YM) - 10/10/31 Yosemite Valley (YM); 10/11/53 2000' El Portal (AFN 8:40).

Extreme dates east of crest: 4/20/81 7000' Hilton Creek (DP) - 10/5/89 6800' Lee Vining (ESt).

Spring record and extreme dates above 9000': 5/29/81 10,200' Hall Natural Area (DeSante MS); 7/9/40 9000' Lewis Creek (YM) - 9/18/78 10,100' Hall Natural Area (DeSante MS).

Representative nesting localities: 4000' Yosemite Valley (GS 496); (4400' Foresta—DG); 4600' Ackerson Meadow (JW); 6200' Crane Flat (DG); (8000' Siesta Lake—DG); 8900' near Mammoth Lakes (MVZ); 7900' Lee Vining Canyon (DG); (7000' Mono Mills—DG); (8000' Glass Mountain—DG).

Subfamily CARDINALINAE: NEW WORLD FINCHES

Our five species evolved in the New World tropics, and are long-distance migrants to wintering areas in subtropical Mexico and Central America. Only Black-headed Grosbeaks and Lazuli Buntings regularly nest in our region; the others stray from the lowlands or the East.

ROSE-BREASTED GROSBEAK (*Pheucticus ludovidianus*)

Extremely rare vagrant on west slope; rare spring vagrant (0-3/year) and irregularly rare fall vagrant below 8000' east of crest.

When they stray to our region, Rose-breasted Grosbeaks frequent cottonwoods, willows and other deciduous trees. Most are seen during June.

Records west slope, both Yosemite Valley (4000'): 6/1/75 (AB 29:906) and 7/4/77 (YM).

Fall records east of crest: 8/8-10/83 7600' June Lake (DG); 8/15/72 approx. 8000' near Mammoth Lakes (AB 27:118);8/20/91 w. Mono Lake (DS); 9/5/70 6500' n. Mono Lake (AB 25:105); 9/11/81 n. Mono Lake (PM).

Extreme dates east of crest excluding fall records: 5/3/81 7000' Hilton Creek (DP) - 7/1/86 7000' Dechambeau Creek (JM).

Additional references: AB 35:977, AB 38:1059, AB 43:1365, AB 44:494.

BLACK-HEADED GROSBEAK (*Pheucticus melanocephalus*)

	J	F	M	A	M	J	J	A	S	O	N	D	HABITAT	ELEVATIONS		
														N	T	W
WEST													WOP	3-6	F-10	
EAST													WP	6-8	6-10	

Uncommon transient below 3000', common summer resident from 3000' to 5000', uncommon summer resident to 6000', rare summer visitor and fall transient to treeline and extremely rare winter visitor on west slope; uncommon summer resident below 8000' and rare summer visitor and fall transient to treeline east of crest.

By virtue of their far-carrying voice, colorful plumage and obliging habits, Black-headed Grosbeaks are among the most conspicuous summer inhabitants of the west slope's oak belt. In Yosemite Valley (4000'), for example, they impose themselves incessantly upon one's attention. Only Steller's Jays and American Robins are equally prominent, and they cannot match the grosbeaks' spring fever. From late April until early July, for hour after hour, the males celebrate the season in loud, joyful song, their ardor culminating in song-flights over trees and meadows.

Common to Black-headed Grosbeaks' varied nesting haunts are deciduous trees. They favor the cottonwoods, willows, aspens and other hardwoods that margin rivers and streams, but are plentiful in open oak-conifer forests and old orchards as well. At mid-elevations, they dwell among ponderosa pines, sugar pines, white firs, sequoias, incense cedars and other conifers, provided they are intermixed with black oaks, dogwoods and other hardwoods. They shun the shady interiors of dense, old-growth forests in favor of meadows, clearings, roads and other edge situations.

In mid-summer, Black-headed Grosbeaks move to shrubbier haunts in search of ripening berries. Dogwood, elderberry, bitter cherry and chokecherry are favorite restaurants.

Black-headed Grosbeaks forage in trees and shrubs as well as on the forest floor. Like most woodland birds, they occasionally nab insects on the wing. In campgrounds and picnic areas they descend from the trees to scavenge crumbs and other leftovers.

By mid-August, most Black-headed Grosbeaks have departed for Mexican wintering haunts. Males have lingered into October, however, and one has even wintered in Yosemite Valley (1/30-2/26/50—YM); this is the only Sierran winter record (YM).

High elevation record: 10,800' near Mt. Lyell 8/3/49 (YM).

Extreme dates and October records west slope: 4/9/30 Yosemite Valley (YM) - 9/20/17 Yosemite Valley (YM); 10/7/55 8000' near Porcupine Flat (YM); 10/11/56 5000' Big Oak Flat Road n. of Yosemite Valley (AFN 11:57).

Extreme dates east of crest: 4/21/79 6800' Lee Vining (DG) - 10/2/89 6800' Lee Vining (ESt).

Extreme dates above 7000' west slope and 8000' east of crest excluding October record: 6/22/85 7400' n. Harden Lake (AB 39:960) - 8/11/81 10,000' Hall Natural Area (DeSante MS).

Representative nesting localities: 4000' Yosemite Valley (GS 484); 4600' Ackerson Meadow (JW); 6000' top Nevada Fall (YM); 8000' Lundy Canyon (MM); 7700' Lee Vining Creek (AB 34:928); 6500' w. Mono Lake (Irene Timossi).

Additional references: AB 26:899, AB 33:894, AB 35:977, EM 11, YNN 21:43, YNN 29:47.

BLUE GROSBEAK (*Guiraca caerulea*)

Extremely rare transient and summer resident on west slope.

Records: 1700' Merced River, female incubating eggs, 7/1/41 (YNN 21:23); 2900' Buck's Meadow 5/15/83, immature male (AB 37:910); 4000' Yosemite Valley 4/29/48 and 8/8/40 (YNN 27:82).

LAZULI BUNTING (*Passerina amoena*)

	J	F	M	A	M	J	J	A	S	O	N	D	HABITAT	ELEVATIONS		
														N	T	W
WEST													WS	F-6	F-10	
EAST													WS	6-8	6-10	

Locally fairly common summer resident below 5000', uncommon summer resident to 6500', uncommon summer visitor and fall transient to 8000' and rare summer visitor and fall transient to treeline on west slope; locally fairly common summer resident below 7500' and rare summer visitor and fall transient to treeline east of crest.

Despite the males' dazzling dress, Lazuli Buntings are more easily heard than seen. They forage in shrubby or herbaceous cover, mounting nearby shrubs or trees to broadcast buzzy, warbler-like songs.

Though Lazuli Buntings are locally distributed, they nest in a variety of scrub and meadow habitats. At the dry end of the spectrum are chaparral-covered hillsides, as at 3000' to 4000' on the north side of the Merced River Canyon west of the crest, and at 7500' north of Dechambeau Creek to the east. At the wet extreme are streamside willows, wildrose, blackberry and other shrubbery. They also nest in meadows with high, dense herbaceous vegetation, such as cow parsnips and corn lilies. Common to all their haunts are dense thickets—either low shrubs or tall herbaceous growth—in which to hide nests. The cover is never continuous, but broken into patches interspersed with more open, grassier habitat.

Chaparral-nesting Lazuli Buntings favor a diversity of species. On the west slope, they dwell among mixtures of manzanita, buck brush, chamise and scrub oak; on the east slope, tobacco brush, snowberry, sagebrush and bitterbrush. They avoid the interiors of forests in favor of thickets, shrubbery and edge vegetation. In the arid ranges east of the Sierran escarpment, they are wedded to low thickets of willow, wildrose and other cover near streams and springs.

On the west slope, Lazuli Buntings may only nest at mid-elevations, such as Crane Flat (6200'), after dry winters; this deserves further study. Males have serenaded subalpine meadows at 10,000' (DeSante MS, DG), but there is no other evidence of nesting at such lofty elevations.

During migrations, Lazuli Buntings occur in a wider range of herbaceous and shrubby habitats, including residential yards. They often flock in small numbers; 25 at Badger Pass (7000') on 8/15/65 was an exceptionally large aggregation, especially at so high an altitude (DG).

Lazuli Buntings may have decreased in numbers in Yosemite Valley (4000'), where they were considered "fairly common" in the 1920s, but are now uncommon to rare. I know of no reason for such a decline.

High elevation record: 10,300' Hall Natural Area, many records.

Extreme dates west slope: 4/18/24 4000' Yosemite Valley (YM) - 9/24/83 4600' Ackerson Meadow (JW).

Extreme dates east of crest: 4/24/83 6400' Mono Lake (DS) - 10/1/76 n. Mono Lake (DG).

Extreme dates above 6500' west slope and 7500' east of crest: 6/17/79 9000' ridge w. Lee Vining (DG) - 9/13/79 10,300' Hall Natural Area (DeSante MS).

Representative nesting localities: (3700' above El Portal—DG); (4000' McCauley Ranch—DG); 4000' Yosemite Valley (EM 11, YM); 4600' Ackerson Meadow (JW); 6200' Crane Flat (AB 26:899, AB 27:912, DG); 7200' Lee Vining Canyon (MCh); 7100' Dechambeau Creek (DG); (6700' Lee Vining Creek—DG); (6500' w. Mono Lake—DG).

Additional references: AB 25:900, AB 33:894, GS 491.

INDIGO BUNTING (*Passerina cyanea*)

Irregularly rare transient east of Sierran escarpment.

Records: 6800' Lee Vining 5/4/80 (AB 34:813) and 7/7/86 (Bob Baez); 6500' near Mono Lake County Park, 5/29/89 (AB 43:534), 6/11/88, male, (AB 42:1338), 6/13/90, male, (PM); male singing 7/15/81 (DDeS); 7000' Dechambeau Creek 7/25/78 (DG); 6400' w. Mono Lake 6/13/90, female, (PM), 9/30/83 (DS, DG).

(LAZULI X INDIGO BUNTING)

A male Lazuli-Indigo Bunting hybrid was observed along the w. shore of Mono Lake on 6/17-19/84 (AB 38:1059).

Subfamily EMBERIZINAE: TOWHEES AND SPARROWS

Of 28 species, 17 nest in the region. Most forage for insects and seeds on or near the ground, using their conical bills to crack open seeds. At higher elevations, they leave before their dinner tables are buried in snow. Some winter in the western foothills or east of the Sierran escarpment, while others migrate to lowland California, the deserts or Mexico.

As "Mountain" and "Gambel's" White-crowned Sparrows are recognizable subspecies that occur in different roles, I treat them in separate accounts. Similarly, I discuss the "Oregon," "Slate-colored" and "Gray-headed" junco subspecies groups independently.

CALIFORNIA TOWHEE (*Pipilo crissalis*) (Green-tailed Towhee)

	J	F	M	A	M	J	J	A	S	O	N	D	HABITAT	ELEVATIONS		
														N	T	W
WEST										•		•	S	6-8	F-10	2
EAST										•	•	•	S	6-9	6-10	7-8

Extremely rare winter visitor and rare transient below 6000', rare summer resident from 6000' to 8000' and rare fall transient to treeline on west slope; common summer resident below 8500', uncommon summer resident to 9500', uncommon fall transient to treeline and extremely rare winter visitor east of crest.

Among the scented sagebrush east of the crest, the voices of California Towhees and Brewer's Sparrows dominate the avian chorus. During late spring and early summer, the towhees sing incessantly from the tops of shrubs as well as rocks, trees, fences and power poles. As the sun plays on their plumage, one may savor the greenish iridescence of their wings and tail as well as the brilliant orange of their headgear. They are not only cheerful songsters, but slick dressers as well.

On the west slope, California Towhees are far outnumbered by Fox Sparrows in montane chaparral, where they nest sparingly among manzanita, chinquapin, huckleberry oak and deer brush. East of the crest, they are many times more numerous, consorting with sagebrush, bitterbrush and, at higher elevations, tobacco brush, snowberry and desert mahogany. They favor a diversity of shrubs, shunning, for example, monotypical stands of sagebrush. They tolerate scattered pines or junipers, employing them for singing posts, but avoid woodlands and forests. Compared to Fox Sparrows, with which they often mingle in the mountainous parts of their range, they prefer sunnier haunts, somewhat smaller shrubs and fewer trees. Unlike Sage Thrashers, they are at home on steep slopes as well as level valley floors.

Late in the summer, when they are no longer singing, California Towhees become much less conspicuous. They skulk quietly in the scrub, flushing reluctantly with cat-like mews of complaint. A few drift to treeline, often hiding in moist willow thickets. During migrations, they visit riparian thickets as well as residential gardens.

High elevation record: 11,300' Shepherd Crest 8/1/38 (YM).

Winter record west slope: 2100' El Portal 12/28/80 (AB 35:737).

Winter records east of crest: 6800' near Lee Vining 12/12/79 (DG); 8000' near June Lake 12/8/76 (AB 31:372).

Extreme dates west slope excluding winter record: 4/29/33 4000' Yosemite Valley (YM) - 10/4/15 approx. 7800' near Glen Aulin (GS 484).

Extreme dates east of crest excluding winter records: 4/15/79 7500' Lee Vining Canyon (DG) - 11/10/90 Hot Creek (Geoff Geupel).

Representative nesting localities: 5000' Swamp Lake (YM); 6300' near Tamarack Flat (GS 483); (6400' road to Crane Flat lookout—MM, DG); (8000' near Siesta Lake—DG); 9500' Warren Fork (AB 34:928); 8000' Mammoth Meadow (DG); 8400' Bodie (DG); 7000' Convict Creek (C 41:253); 6500' South Tufa (DG).

Additional reference: EM 11.

RUFOUS-SIDED TOWHEE (*Pipilo erythrophthalmus*)

	J	F	M	A	M	J	J	A	S	O	N	D	HABITAT	ELEVATIONS		
														N	T	W
WEST													SWOP	F-6	F-10	F-5
EAST													SWP	6-7	6-10	6-7

Common resident below 3000', locally fairly common resident to 5000', uncommon summer resident to 6500', fairly common summer visitor or fall transient to 7000' and rare fall transient to treeline on west slope; uncommon resident below 7500' and rare fall transient to treeline on east slope; fairly common resident below 7500' and rare fall transient to treeline east of Sierran escarpment.

Rufous-sided Towhees belong to different subspecies west and east of the crest, which diverge in habitat and especially song. On the west slope, *P. e. falcinellus* usually nests in arid foothill chaparral, montane chaparral and the shrubby understories of open forests, dwelling in riparian thickets only in the foothills. East of the crest, *P. e. curtatus* and *P. e. montanus* are more closely tied to water, customarily nesting in the vicinity of willow-lined streams or seeps, but also in dry ravines and along the bases of rock outcrops.

Throughout their nesting range, Rufous-sided Towhees favor large, relatively dense shrubs or thickets with accumulations of leaf litter, in which they scratch for meals. Though they forage mostly on the ground, they ascend lofty trees to proclaim territorial claims, or to assess the situation when alarmed.

On the west slope, Rufous-sided Towhees consort with manzanitas, ceanothus, scrub oak and, in riparian areas, willows and blackberries. While they nest in unbroken chaparral, they also claim small patches of shrubbery in forest clearings and beneath open stands of ponderosa pines, black oaks, incense cedars and other trees. East of the crest, they nest in shrubby willows, Utah junipers and large sagebrush and bitterbrush, ranging into nearby sagebrush scrub and pinyon pine woodlands.

Breeding Rufous-sided Towhees, while scarce on the east slope of the Sierra, are relatively numerous in the Bodie Hills, the thickets around Mono Lake and other areas east of the escarpment.

They are most widespread during fall and winter, wandering throughout the pinyon pine belt and, less frequently, into open sagebrush scrub far from water.

In summer and early fall, Rufous-sided Towhees drift upslope to treeline. On the west slope, in September and early October, they may be fairly common as high as 7500'. They have been found in numbers, for example, all along the trail from the Big Oak Flat Road (4800') to the top of El Capitan (7600'—JL), and along the Tuolumne River from 4000' to Glen Aulin (7800'—SH).

To those familiar with the monotonous, junco-like trills of west slope Rufous-sided Towhees, the variable songs of east slope birds will sound like foreign tongues. They sometimes trill, but that is the exception. On the north shore of Mono Lake, for example, I've heard the same bird give emphatic, three note calls, "wut-zee' wut-zee' wut-zee'," for almost an hour, than shift to trills. I've heard of bilingual people, but bilingual birds?

High elevation record: 11,000' near Lake Catherine 9/26/27 (James Yurchenco).

Extreme dates above 6500' west slope and above 7500' east of crest: 8/4/82 and 8/4/87 10,300' Hall Natural Area (DeSante MS) - 10/31/76 8900' near Tuolumne Meadows (AB 31:221).

Representative nesting localities: 3500' above El Portal (DG); 4000' Yosemite Valley (GS 479); 5000' Swamp Lake (YM); (6300' Henness Ridge—DG); 6400' w. Mono Lake (DS); (7200' Cottonwood Canyon—DG).

Additional references: EM 11, GM 469-70, YNN 9:60, YNN 10:32.

BROWN TOWHEE (*Pipilo fuscus*)

	J	F	M	A	M	J	J	A	S	O	N	D	HABITAT	ELEVATIONS N	ELEVATIONS T	ELEVATIONS W
WEST	■	■	■	■	■	■	■	■	■	■	■	■	OS	F-4		F-4
EAST																

Common resident below 2500', locally uncommon resident to 4000' and extremely rare visitor in higher mountains on west slope.

Brown Towhees, like California Thrashers, are sedentary lowlanders. They are virtually unknown outside their nesting haunts on shrubby hillsides and flats.

While they shelter and nest in dense shrubbery, Brown Towhees forage in adjacent grassy habitats. They dwell in open woodlands, broken chaparral, riparian thickets and other situations where shrubbery edges on grasslands or meadows. They are also at home in shrubby residential yards, where they feed on lawns and in gardens. They shun continuous chaparral as well as meadows and grasslands lacking shrubby cover. Settlement and clearing has allowed them to colonize the oak-conifer belt, as in the com-

Cassin's Sparrow at South Tufa, Mono Lake, June 22, 1984. Photograph by Michael Wihler.

munity of Midpines (3000'—DG) and around isolated homesteads like McCauley Ranch (4000'—DG).

Records above 4000': approx. 4500' near Wawona 5/82 (YM); 6400' Mariposa Grove, summer/49 (YNN 29:48); 7800' White Wolf 9/13/86 (DG).

Additional representative nesting localities: (2000' Mariposa region—CL); (2100' El Portal—DG); (3300' above El Portal—GSt); (3700' Hetch Hetchy Valley—DG, YM).

CASSIN'S SPARROW (*Aimophila cassinii*)

Extremely rare summer visitor east of Sierran escarpment.

At least one singing male Cassin's Sparrow, and possibly two, skylarked above the rabbitbrush and greasewood at South Tufa, Mono Lake, from 6/17-28/84 (AB 38:1059, DG—accepted by California Bird Records Committee).

RUFOUS-CROWNED SPARROW (*Aimophila ruficeps*)

	J	F	M	A	M	J	J	A	S	O	N	D	HABITAT	ELEVATIONS		
														N	T	W
WEST													S	F-3		
EAST																

Locally uncommon resident below 2500' and extremely rare visitor at higher elevations on west slope.

Compared to most birds, Rufous-crowned Sparrows are fussier about habitat, and hence are locally distributed. They reside throughout the year on dry, sunny, predominantly grassy slopes with scattered small shrubs or rock outcroppings. They avoid continuous chaparral as well as woodlands.

Representative nesting locality: (2000' Miller Gulch—MR).

Records above 2500', both Yosemite Valley (4000'): 9/26/28 (YM) and 10/34/34 (YNN 14:25).

Additional reference: YNN 34:25.

AMERICAN TREE SPARROW (*Spizella arborea*)

Irregularly rare winter resident below 7000' east of Sierran escarpment.

Though one of our scarcest birds, American Tree Sparrows occasionally winter in low, shrubby willow and buffalo-berry thickets near Mono Lake (6400'), and probably elsewhere east of the Sierran escarpment. They also range into sagebrush scrub, usually in the vicinity of larger, denser shrubbery. Outside Mono Basin, three were near Crowley Lake Reservoir (6900') on 12/19/82 (AB 37:782, DG).

Peak count: 7, w. Mono Lake 1/1/84 (AB 38:793, AB 38:793).

Extreme dates, 8 records since 1976: 11/17/82 n. Mono Lake (DG) - 4/10/82 6500' Dechambeau Ponds (HG).

(Hypothetical record west slope: Yosemite Valley, 2, 1/23/69—YM—plausible date, but not details).

CHIPPING SPARROW (*Spizella passerina*)

	J	F	M	A	M	J	J	A	S	O	N	D	HABITAT	ELEVATIONS		
														N	T	W
WEST											•	•	OPGS	3-10	F-10	
EAST													PGS	6-10		

Uncommon transient below 3000', uncommon summer resident from 3000' to 5000', common summer resident to 9000' and irregularly rare to fairly common summer resident and fairly common fall transient to treeline on west slope; fairly common summer resident below 9000' and irregularly rare to fairly common summer resident and fairly common fall transient to treeline east of crest.

Chipping Sparrows and Dark-eyed Juncos share similar haunts as well as similar songs. Both dwell in forests, woodlands or the edges of meadows, where they scrounge for seeds and insects on the ground and in low, herbaceous vegetation. Chippings favor drier habitats, such as well-drained meadows and open forests with high sun penetration. Among jeffrey pines and desert mahoganies, the sparrows usually leave the juncos behind in wetter habitats. In dense, shady forests, the opposite is true.

While their haunts are varied, Chipping Sparrows invariably nest among trees or arborescent shrubs. Where the timber is dense, as in old-growth fir forests, they choose the margins of meadows or grassy openings. They also dwell in open forests and woodlands, provided there are sunny, dry openings between the trees. These openings may be bare or covered with grasses and forbs, but are never shrouded entirely with shrubs or lush meadow vegetation.

On the west slope, Chipping Sparrows nest among black oaks, incense cedars, white and red firs, ponderosa pines, sugar pines and western white pines. At higher elevations, they consort with lodgepole pines, following them to treeline in some years but not in others (DeSante MS). East of the crest, they also dwell among desert mahoganies and jeffrey pines, but usually shun pinyon pine woodlands.

During migration, Chipping Sparrows are more widespread, flocking in chaparral, sagebrush scrub and dry meadows outside their nesting haunts. In late summer, for example, I've encountered flocks of up to 100 individuals at Tuolumne Meadows (8600') and around Mono Lake (6400'). From mid-September through mid-October, they and White-crowned Sparrows replace California Towhees and Brewer's Sparrows in the sagebrush scrub; they are not evenly distributed, however, occurring here and there in sizable flocks.

High elevation record: 10,300' Hall Natural Area, many records (DeSante MS).

Extreme dates west slope, all Yosemite Valley (4000'): 4/7/24 (YM) - 10/29/28 (YM); 11/15/53 (AFN 8:40); 12/5/31 (YM).

Extreme dates east of crest: 3/30/86 6800' Lee Vining (DG) - 10/19/77 9700' Lee Vining Creek (DDeS).

Representative nesting localities: 4000' Yosemite Valley (YM, MVZ), 4600' Ackerson Meadow (JW); 6200' near Crane Flat (DG), 8600' Tuolumne Meadows (DG), 10,000' Hall Natural Area (DeSante MS), (8000' Lee Vining Canyon—DG), (7800' Williams Butte—DG), (8000' O'-Harrell Canyon—DG).

Additional references: D 307, GS 452, YNN 7:60.

BREWER'S SPARROW (*Spizella breweri*)

	J	F	M	A	M	J	J	A	S	O	N	D	HABITAT	ELEVATIONS		
														N	T	W
WEST				•	•	•		—	—				GS		4-10	
EAST				■	■	■	■	■	■				SG	6-9	6-10	

Extremely rare spring transient and rare fall transient (0-2/year) below treeline on west slope; common summer resident below 9000' and rare fall transient to treeline east of crest.

If one removes the breast spots, whisker marks, crown stripes and other flourishes which adorn other sparrows, one will have a reasonable picture of Brewer's. From a distance they are as plain as the sagebrush and bitterbrush in which they dwell. But they compensate for simple attire with sweet, high-pitched trills, endlessly varied in rhythm, pitch and timbre. Chipping Sparrows wear snazzier clothes, but their desert cousins outclass them as songsters.

Brewer's Sparrows, like California Towhees, are wedded to sagebrush and bitterbrush. On alkaline soils, as around Mono Lake, they also nest in rabbitbrush and greasewood. At high elevations in the Bodie Hills (ca. 9000'), they mingle with White-crowned Sparrows on moist slopes dominated by squaw currants. Unlike California Towhees, they shun arborescent desert mahoganies. On wind swept ridges, however, they dwell among hunched mahoganies, especially mixed with sagebrush, bitterbrush, tobacco brush, snowberry and other shrubs.

Brewer's Sparrows are mountaineers as well as valley dwellers. In favorable habitat, they follow sagebrush scrub to the crest of the range, as near Minaret Summit (9200'—DG). After fledging young, a few wander to treeline east of the crest.

High elevation record: 10,400' Granite Lake 8/23/81 (AB 36:216).

Spring records west slope: 7000' Peregoy Meadow, singing vociferously, 4/27/77 (RS; AB 31:1043) and 5/21/77 (AB 31:1043); 4000' Yosemite Valley 5/14/49 (YM); 6/6/79 4600' Hodgdon Meadow (MM).

Extreme dates west slope excluding spring records, eight records: 8/23/81 Granite Lake (AB 36:216) - 9/18/19 Yosemite Valley (GS 456).

Extreme dates above 9500', both Hall Natural Area (10,300'): 7/13/85 - 9/26/78 (DeSante MS).

Extreme dates east of crest: 4/13/86 7000' Long Valley (DG) - 9/28/83 6500' n. Mono Lake (HG).

Representative nesting localities: 6500' near Mono Lake (GS 456); 7000' Long Valley (DG); 8000' Mammoth Meadow (DG); 9200' Minaret Summit (DG); 9000' Bodie Mountain (DG).

Additional reference: C 20:18.

BLACK-CHINNED SPARROW (*Spizella atrogularis*)

Rare summer resident below 4000' on west slope; status east of crest uncertain, but probably irregularly rare summer resident below 7500'.

Black-chinneds are another sparrow with circumscribed nesting haunts. They nest on arid slopes grown to tall, moderately dense and diverse chaparral. On the west slope, they have been found above El Portal (approx. 3000') as well as near Hetch Hetchy Reservoir (3800'). East of the crest, they have appeared in or near Lundy Canyon (7500'-7900'). Sites on both slopes support a mixture of shrub species: buckbrush, manzanita, chamise and scrub oak on the west slope, tobacco brush, snowberry, sagebrush, and bitterbrush to the east.

Extreme dates west slope: 4/18/77 3800' near Hetch Hetchy Valley (MM) - 6/24/77 approx. 3000' above El Portal (MM); (they probably arrive earlier in spring and undoubtedly linger later into summer, but their habitat is seldom birded, and these are the earliest and latest dates I'm aware of).

Records east of crest: 7500' n. of Dechambeau Creek, at least four singing, 6/23-26/76 (DG, BE, DW); 7900' near Lundy Lake, two singing, 6/13/84 (AB 38:1060).

Additional reference: AB 36:1060.

VESPER SPARROW (*Pooecetes gramineus*)

	J	F	M	A	M	J	J	A	S	O	N	D	HABITAT	ELEVATIONS		
														N	T	W
WEST			•	•	•			—	—	—			G		F-10	
EAST				▬	▬	▬	▬	▬	▬				SG	6-9	6-10	

Extremely rare spring transient and rare fall transient below treeline on west slope; uncommon summer resident below 8000' and rare summer visitor or fall transient to treeline on east slope; uncommon summer resident below 9000' and uncommon fall transient to 10,000' east of Sierran escarpment.

Vespers are another sparrow of sagebrush scrub, but a pickier one than Brewer's. Not only must the shrubs be of no more than moderate height, they must also be interspersed with grassy cover, or margin dry, grassy meadows. They also shun steep slopes in favor of level or rolling terrain.

This predilection for grassy haunts is probably responsible for the Vesper Sparrow's decline in overgrazed habitats. In the 1920s, Grinnell and Storer considered them "common" in the vicinity of Mono, Walker and Silver lakes (GS 440), but this is no longer the case. In these and many other areas, years of heavy grazing, primarily by sheep, have depleted or eliminated grasses and forbs.

High elevation record: 10,500' Parker Pass 7/31/87 (MR).

Spring records west slope: 3/22/28 4000' Yosemite Valley (YM); 3/29/86, 2, 4400' Big Meadow (AB 40:521); 4/26/24 Yosemite Valley (DM 10); 3/29/87 and 5/9/81 4600' Ackerson Meadow (JW).

Extreme dates west slope excluding spring records: 8/24/54 8600' Tuolumne Meadows (AFN 9:54) - 10/16/81 Big Meadow (JD).

Extreme dates above 9000': 10,500' Parker Pass 7/31/87 (MR) - 9/24/79 10,200' Hall Natural Area (DeSante MS).

Extreme dates east of crest: 4/10/82 6500' Mono Lake County Park (BE) - 10/3/83 6500' w. Mono Lake (DS).

Representative nesting localities: (7000' Long Valley—DG); (7200' Lower Horse Meadow—DG); 8000' Bodie Hills (C 41:253); (9000' Bodie Mountain—DG).

Additional reference: AFN 8:40.

LARK SPARROW (*Chondestes grammacus*)

Rare winter and possibly year-round resident below 2000', rare spring transient and extremely rare summer visitor to 5000', rare fall transient to 7000' and extremely rare fall transient at higher elevations on west slope; rare transient below 7500' and extremely rare transient at higher elevations east of crest.

Lark Sparrows stray to meadows, grasslands, open scrub and other open habitats, usually with scattered trees. In past years, large numbers apparently wintered in the western foothills; approximately 300, for example, were tallied near El Portal (2100') on the 1953 Yosemite Christmas Bird Count (YNN 37:4), but they have not been seen at all since 1960.

Records above 7000' west slope and 7500' east of crest: 7800' White Wolf 9/16/80 (HF); 8600' Tuolumne Meadows 8/4/87 (JW) and 20, 9/20/39 (YM); 9,900 Hall Natural Area 9/23/79 (AB 34:199, DeSante and Engstrom MS); approx. 8000' Lundy Canyon 7/14/81 (DDeS); 8200' Kelty Meadows, Glass Mountain 9/13/90 (ESt).

Extreme dates above 2500' west slope: 4/9/27 4000' Yosemite Valley - 7/7/80 4600' Ackerson Meadow (JW); 8/11/73 6200' Crane Flat (YM) - 9/29/60 Yosemite Valley (ABR).

Extreme dates east of crest: 4/10/82 Mono Lake County Park (BE) - 6/3/82 6500' Dechambeau Ponds (HG); Lundy Canyon 7/14/81 (DDeS); 8/4/84 Mono Lake (SJ) - 9/23/79 Hall Natural Area (AB 34:199, DeSante and Engstrom MS); 12/10/90-1/1/91 7200' Tom's Place (CH).

Additional references: AFN 8:327, C 27:112, EM 10, GS 446, YNN 31:11.

BLACK-THROATED SPARROW (*Amphispiza bilineata*)

Extremely rare transient on west and east slopes; irregularly rare to uncommon summer resident below 7500' in valleys east of Sierran escarpment.

In general, Black-throated Sparrows prefer hotter, more desert-like habitats than those found in the region. As one travels east, however, and descends several thousand feet into the Benton, Hammil and Chalfant valleys, they become the most plentiful, and often the only, nesting bird on alluvial fans and rocky canyon slopes. But in certain summers, be it due to food shortages, population pressures, droughts or other factors, they invade the Mono Basin and undoubtedly other valleys east of the Sierran escarpment.

In 1984, for example, Black-throated Sparrows probably nested on Black Point (7000'—AB 38:1060), Negit Island (6500'—AB 38:1060) and at South Tufa (6400'—DG). They tend to choose more open haunts than Sage Sparrows, but sometimes breed in similarly dense sagebrush scrub.

Records in Sierra Nevada both west and east slope: 4600' Ackerson Meadow, 3, 8/25/87 (JW); 7000' Peregoy Meadow 5/16/70 (AFN 24:642); Hall Natural Area 10,100'—6/18/87 and 10,500'—found dead in snow 6/27/80 (D&E).

Extreme dates east of crest: 5/22/84 Negit Island (DS) - 8/28/84, 2, 6400' Paoha Island (SJ).

Additional reference: D 274.

SAGE SPARROW (*Amphispiza belli*)

	J	F	M	A	M	J	J	A	S	O	N	D	HABITAT	ELEVATIONS		
														N	T	W
WEST													S	F-3		F-3
EAST												•	S	6-8		7

Uncommon resident below 3500' and extremely rare transient at higher elevations on west slope; extremely rare transient on east slope; locally common summer resident and extremely rare winter resident below 8000' east of Sierran escarpment.

Both east and west of the crest, Sage Sparrows nest in dense, unbroken scrub, but inhabit disparate plant communities, differ in migratory proclivities and belong to separate subspecies. On the west slope, *A. b. belli* are year-round residents in continuous, dense chaparral, especially chamise. East of the crest, *A. b. nevadensis* or *A. b. canescens* are summer residents in sagebrush scrub, particularly sagebrush, bitterbrush and rabbitbrush, retreating to balmier climes in winter.

Around Mono Lake (6400'), Sage Sparrows are irregularly rare to fairly common, and do not nest in the same areas every year. Further east, as near Sagehen Summit (8000') and on Cedar Hill (7200'), they are much more numerous. I cannot explain this pattern.

Records above 3500' on west slope; 4000' Yosemite Valley 9/13/34 (YNN 13:95); 6400' Crane Flat Fire Lookout 9/4/73 (YM).

Record on east slope: 10,200' Hall Natural Area, (A. b. nevadensis), 7/12/79 (AB 33:894, DeSante and Engstrom MS).

Winter record east of crest: 7000' Long Valley, 3, 12/15/79 (AB 34:651, DG).

Extreme dates east slope excluding winter record: 3/16/80 6500' e. Mono Lake (DG) - 11/9/79 6500' Rush Creek (DG).

Representative nesting localities: 3300' above El Portal (GS 464, YNN 21:23); 8000' near June Lake (B 237:1007); 6400' South Tufa, feeding cowbird (DG); 6400' Negit Island (C 40:262); (7200' Cedar Hill—DG); (8000' e. Sagehen Summit—DG).

LARK BUNTING (*Calamospiza melanocorys*)

Extremely rare transient east of Sierran escarpment.

Records: 6800' Panum Crater, male, 6/28/81 (Sally Gaines); 6400' s. Mono Lake 9/4/83 (AB 38:245); 9/25/88, 2, (AB 43:165); 6400' e. Mono Lake 9/23/78 (KC); 6900' Crowley Lake Reservoir 9/24/87 (DWi) and 9/24/88 (AB 43:165).

SAVANNAH SPARROW (*Passerculus sandwichensis*)

	J	F	M	A	M	J	J	A	S	O	N	D	HABITAT	ELEVATIONS		
														N	T	W
WEST			•	•	SEE TEXT								G	9	F-10	
EAST													GMaMu	6-7	6-10	6

Uncommon summer resident at Tuolumne Meadows (8600') and extremely rare spring and rare fall transient below treeline elsewhere on west slope; common summer resident below 7500' and extremely rare summer visitor and rare fall transient to treeline and rare winter resident below 7000' east of crest.

Savannah Sparrows, which William Leon Dawson (1923) described as "detached bits of brown earth done up in dried grasses," are inquisitive denizens of boggy meadows, pastures and marshes. East of the Sierran escarpment, from spring through early summer, their buzzy, insect-like songs blend with the euphonious lays of blackbirds and the winnowing of snipe.

Despite their nondescript appearance, Savannah Sparrows are easily seen as they scrounge muddy shores for meals or perch on grasses, shrubs, rocks, fences and, at Mono Lake (6400'), tufa towers. As one slogs through their haunts, they flush from underfoot, hasten off in jerky flight and vanish into seas of herbaceous vegetation.

Savannah Sparrows breed in eastern Sierran canyonbottoms as well as in valleys east of the escarpment, concealing nests beneath bulrushes, sedges, grasses and tules several inches to several feet in height. Unlike Song Sparrows, they shun riparian thickets and arborescent shrubbery in general, though they employ small, scattered shrubs for singing and look-out posts. They usually shelter, and always nest, in herbaceous vegetation.

At Tuolumne Meadows (8600'), Savannah Sparrows were discovered nesting in 1985. At least five pairs returned in 1986 and 1987 (MR).

During migrations, Savannah Sparrows are partial to moist, meadowy habitats, but also stray into grasslands and the weedy margins of roads.

Spring records west slope: 4000' Yosemite Valley 3/20/32 (YM), 3/21/25 (YM) and 4/12/85, 4 (JD); 4600' Ackerson Meadow, 3, 3/31/80.

Summer record above 8000' east slope: 9800' Hall Natural Area 6/22/80 (DeSante MS).

Extreme dates west slope below 8000' excluding spring records: 7/15/85 4600' Ackerson Meadow - 11/13/83 4400' Big Meadow (JL).

Extreme dates above 8000' east of crest excluding spring record: 7/31/87 10,500' Parker Pass (MR) - 10/10/76 10,600' Isberg Pass (DG).

Additional representative nesting localities: (7400' Lee Vining Canyon—DG); (7200' Lower Horse Meadow—DG); 7000' Owens River (MVZ); 6400' Mono Lake (DG).

GRASSHOPPER SPARROW (*Ammodramus savannarum*)

Status uncertain; probably an irregularly rare summer resident below 5000' on west slope.

Grasshopper Sparrows were not reported in the region until 1984, when at least three singing, territorial males summered and probably bred in Ackerson Meadow (4600'—JW). They returned to the meadow in 1987 (JW, DG), and another was seen in Big Meadow (4400') on 6/15/85 (AB 39:960). Based on the adults' behavior, they nested at Ackerson Meadow in 1987 (JW, CL). Just west of the region, at Smith Creek (3200'), Grinnell and Storer found them in 1915, 1916 and 1920 (GS 443).

During most years, Grasshopper Sparrows probably breed in meadows and possibly grassy hillsides on the lower west slope, moving to meadows at higher elevations, such as Ackerson Meadow, during droughts. Foothill meadows are seldom birded, and these reclusive birds are easily overlooked.

Grasshopper Sparrows nest in dry grasslands and meadows where the vegetation is dense, diverse and relatively high. At Ackerson Meadow, for example, the herbaceous cover is two to four feet high, and consists of many different grasses and forbs. Except when singing, the birds stay well-concealed in herbaceous cover. Their dry, insect-like songs are often the only clue to their presence.

Extreme dates Ackerson Meadow: 6/12/87 (JW) - 9/2/84 (JW).

FOX SPARROW (*Passerella iliaca*)

	J	F	M	A	M	J	J	A	S	O	N	D	HABITAT	ELEVATIONS		
														N	T	W
WEST													SP	6-9	F-10	F-3
EAST											•	•	SP	6-9	6-10	7

Uncommon transient below 5500', common summer resident from 5500' to 9000', rare summer visitor and fall transient to treeline, uncommon winter resident below 4000' and extremely rare winter visitor at higher elevations on west slope; common summer resident below 8500', uncommon summer resident to 9500', rare summer visitor and fall transient to treeline and extremely rare winter visitor east of crest.

Of the avian denizens of montane chaparral, Fox Sparrows are the most numerous and vocal. From spring through mid-summer, their loud, melodious but variable songs ring from scrub-covered hillsides and the shrubby understories of open forests. A rustling of leaves often betrays their presence as they scatter the duff beneath dense bushes, picking out seeds and insects.

On the west slope, Fox Sparrows nest among chinquapin, snow bush, manzanita, ceanothus, choke and bitter cherries and huckleberry oak; to the east, tobacco brush, desert mahogany, snowberry and other shrubs. Less frequently, especially east of the crest, they also dwell in dense, shrubby willows near seeps and streams. Though plentiful in treeless scrub, they are not adverse to scattered or open stands of black oaks, ponderosa pines, jeffrey pines, western white pines, white firs and other trees, which they use for song and look-out posts. During the nesting season, they reside exclusively in the higher mountains, shunning foothill chaparral and sagebrush scrub.

During migrations, Fox Sparrows still favor shrubbery, but are more widespread. They visit riparian thickets, chaparral, sagebrush scrub and residential gardens. On the west slope, most winter in dense foothill chaparral.

Our breeding Fox Sparrows belong to different subspecies than those that visit during migration or winter. Even the west slope and east side breeding populations are divided into separate races, *P. i. megarhyncha* and *P. i. monoensis* respectively, though I can discern no difference in dress, songs or habitats. In the fall, after the breeding birds depart, their places are filled by races from as far north as Alaska (*unalaschcensis*, *insularis*, *sinuosa*, and probably others).

Most of the northern Fox Sparrow can be distinguished from the Sierran natives by plumage and call notes. The gray head and back of *megarhynchus* and *monoensis* contrast with their brown wings and tail. In most of the northern subspecies, the head and back are a uniform chocolate brown (see National Geographic Society *Field Guide*, p. 406). Moreover the "chip" notes of northern birds are lower-pitched and resemble those of waterthrushes or MacGillivray's Warblers, whereas those of Sierran birds resemble those of Brown Towhees.

On four occasions, reddish (fox-colored) Fox Sparrows, probably *P. i. altivagans*, have been seen east of the Sierran escarpment. They possess streaked crowns and upperparts, and look like different birds.

High elevation record: 10,300' Hall Natural Area, many records (DeSante MS).

Winter record above 4000' west slope: 2/2/87 6400' Crane Flat Lookout (YM).

Winter records east of Sierran escarpment: 12/30-31/77 6800' Lee Vining (AB 32:397); 12/31/83 approx. 7000' Mono Lake Christmas Bird Count (AB 37:760, DG)

Records of "fox-colored" subspecies: 4/26/91 7200' Mammoth Creek near Highway 395 (ESt); 11/6,9/90 7200' Tom's Place (CH); 11/13/85 6800' Lee Vining (DG) and 12/30-31/77 Lee Vining (AB 32:397).

Extreme dates between 5500' and 9200' (in breeding range) west slope: 4/19/26 6000' Chinquapin (YM) - 9/27/26 approx. 8000' Ostrander Lake Trail (YM).

Extreme dates above 9200' west slope and above 9500' east of crest, both Hall Natural Area (10,300'): 6/21/87; 7/2/79 - 10/14/77 (DeSante MS).

Representative nesting localities: 6000' Chinquapin (GS 475); 6300' Tamarack Flat (GS 475); 6400' Crane Flat Lookout (DG); 8000' Siesta Lake (DG); 8400' Olmsted Point (DG); 9200' near Tuolumne Meadow (MR); 9500' Warren Fork (AB 34:929); 9500' Blue Lake (AB 35:977); 8500' Virginia Creek (C 41:254); 7500' Lundy Canyon (DG); (9000' Bodie Mountain—DG).

SONG SPARROW (*Melospiza melodia*)

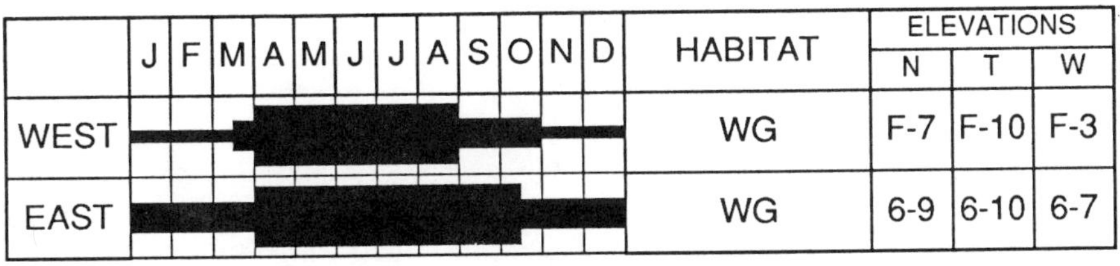

	J	F	M	A	M	J	J	A	S	O	N	D	HABITAT	ELEVATIONS		
														N	T	W
WEST													WG	F-7	F-10	F-3
EAST													WG	6-9	6-10	6-7

Common summer resident below 5000', uncommon summer resident to 7000', rare summer visitor or fall transient to treeline and uncommon winter resident below 2000' on west slope; common summer resident below 8000', uncommon summer resident to

9000', rare summer visitor or fall transient to treeline, fairly common winter resident below 7000' in Mono Basin and uncommon winter resident below 7500' elsewhere east of crest.

In wet meadows and along the margins of ponds, lakes and slow-moving streams, Song Sparrows are conspicuous denizens of dense, woody thickets. True to their names, they sing vociferously during spring and early summer, and again in early autumn. Their vigorous, cheerful lays are sometimes heard by night as well as day.

Compared to Lincoln's and Savannah sparrows, Songs favor woody rather than herbaceous vegetation, and larger shrubs. They usually conceal nests in dense willows, but also use azalea and dogwood. They desert cover, however, to forage on muddy banks and to sing from exposed, elevated perches.

During migration and winter, Song Sparrows still prefer riparian thickets, but wander into drier scrub, residential yards and tall, dense herbaceous vegetation. Unlike many sparrows, they rarely flock.

While Song Sparrows have increased on the west slope, the reasons are elusive. In Yosemite Valley (4000'), where they are prominent summer birds, they were first found nesting in 1939 (YNN 18:99, YM).

Song Sparrows belong to different races west and east of the crest (*M. m. fisherella* and *M. m. heermanni* respectively), though I can discern no great differences in plumage, song or habitat.

High elevation record: approx. 10,300' Hall Natural Area (DeSante MS).

Extreme dates above 2500' west slope, both Yosemite Valley (4000'): 3/20/40 (YM) - 10/16/80 (JD)

Extreme dates above 9000': 6/2/77 9800' Hall Natural Area (DeSante MS) - 9/25/15 9000' e. Tioga Pass (GS 469).

Additional representative nesting localities: (2000' Merced River—DG); (2000' Mariposa—CL); 4600' Ackerson Meadow (JW); 7000' Peregoy Meadow (AB 38:1060); (8000' Devils Postpile—DG); 9500' Blue Lake (AB 35:977); 7500' Lee Vining Canyon (DG); 6500' Mono Lake County Park (DG).

Additional references: C 41:254, GS 468.

LINCOLN'S SPARROW (*Melospiza lincolnii*)

	J	F	M	A	M	J	J	A	S	O	N	D	HABITAT	ELEVATIONS		
														N	T	W
WEST				?									GW	4-9	F-10	F-4
EAST													GW	8-10	6-10	6-7

Uncommon summer resident from 4000' to 6000', fairly common summer resident from 6000' to 8000', uncommon summer resident to 9000', uncommon summer visitor and fall transient to treeline and uncommon spring and fairly common fall transient and rare winter resident below 4000' on west slope; rare summer resident below treeline on east slope; uncommon spring transient below 7500', uncommon summer visitor or fall transient below treeline and rare winter resident below 7500' east of crest.

On the west slope, wherever shooting stars, camas and knotweed bloom in bright profusion, one may hear the Lincoln Sparrows' joyous, bubbling songs. They forage and nest in willows, corn lilies, sedges, grasses and other meadow plants. At nesting time, their haunts are often flooded by melting snow and overflowing streamlets.

Though more furtive than their Song Sparrow relatives, Lincoln's emerge from cover to sing or when alarmed. They choose exposed song and look-out posts on tall herbaceous vegetation, fallen logs and at middle heights in margining conifers.

East of the crest, nesting Lincoln's Sparrows are inexplicably scarce. They have been found at three localities: Valentine Ecological Reserve (8000'—AB 33:895, DG), Virginia Lakes —C 41:254), and Hall Natural Area (DDeS), the last two at exceptionally high elevations of 10,000' Why do they shun so many meadows with seemingly suitable conditions?

During migration, transient Lincoln's Sparrows, while partial to wet meadows, also visit riparian thickets, dense herbaceous vegetation and bushy residential areas.

High elevation record: approx. 10,600' Mt. Dana, 2, 9/2/83 (BE).

Extreme dates above 4500' west slope and above 7500' east of crest: 8000' Lee Vining Canyon 5/13/78 (KC) - 10/12/57 7000' Peregoy Meadow (AFN 12:56); (I suspect they arrive earlier at west slope nesting areas, such as Crane Flat, but do not have records).

Additional representative nesting localities: 4000' Yosemite Valley (GS 470, D 361); 4600' Ackerson Meadow (JW); 4600' Hodgdon Meadow (DG); 6200' Crane Flat (DG); 7800' White Wolf (DG); 8100' Porcupine Flat (GS 471); 8600' Tuolumne Meadows (MR).

Additional references: AB 33:895, AB 34:929, AB 37:911, AB 38:1060, EM 11, YNN 8:100.

SWAMP SPARROW (*Melospiza georgiana*)

Irregularly rare winter and spring visitor (0-2/year) below 7500' in Mono Basin and undoubtedly other valleys east of Sierran escarpment; extremely rare at treeline on east slope.

Swamp Sparrows, though one of our scarcest birds, occasionally winter around Mono Lake. They inhabit willow thickets, cattails and other dense, marsh vegetation in the vicinity of ponds, slow-moving streams, seeps and springs.

Record above 7500': 10,300' Hall Natural Area 10/23-24/77 (AB 32:255, DeSante and Engstrom MS).

Extreme dates, nine records since 1978: 10/29/86 6400' w. Mono Lake (SJ, DS) - 4/22/84 6500' Dechambeau Ponds, adult (DS, DG); 6/13/91 8600' McGee Meadows, Glass Mountain (also above 7500') (AB 45:1159-1160).

Additional references: AB 33:656, AB 34:652, AB 37:760, AB 38:793, AB 39:789.

WHITE-THROATED SPARROW (*Zonotrichia albicollis*)

Extremely rare transient and winter visitor on west slope; rare fall transient below 8000' east of crest.

When they stray to the region, White-throated Sparrows usually secrete themselves in moist brushy cover, often, but not invariably, in company with White-crowneds or Golden-crowneds. They are scarcer than Harris' Sparrows east of the crest.

Records west slope: approx. 2500' near Mariposa, winter/80 (CL); 2100' El Portal 10/15/87 (DG); 4000' Yosemite Valley, 2, 11/2-7/49 (YNN 28:147).

Extreme dates east of crest, both Lee Vining (6800'): 10/14/84 (DG) - 12/31/82 (AB 37:760, DG).

GOLDEN-CROWNED SPARROW (*Zonotrichia atricapilla*)

	J	F	M	A	M	J	J	A	S	O	N	D	HABITAT	ELEVATIONS		
														N	T	W
WEST							•						SWOP		F-10	F-4
EAST						•							SWP		6-10	

Common winter resident below 3000', uncommon winter resident to 4000', uncommon fall transient to 8000', rare fall transient to treeline and extremely rare summer visitor on west slope; rare spring transient and uncommon fall transient below 8000' and rare fall transient to treeline east of crest.

Golden-crowned Sparrows favor shadier haunts and larger, denser shrubbery than transient and wintering White-crowneds. On the lower west slope, for example, they winter in chaparral and brushy oak woodlands shunned by their White-crowned cousins. On the east slope and at higher elevations, they visit montane chaparral, large, shrubby willows and the brushy understories of woodlands and forests. They are rare in the sagebrush scrub east of the Sierran escarpment, preferring the denser, more diverse shrubbery of higher, steeper slopes.

High elevation record: 10,400' Hall Natural Area, many records (DeSante MS).

Summer record: 7/5/79 8600' Tuolumne Meadows (MR).

Extreme dates east of crest: 3/8/81 6800' Lee Vining (DG) - 4/25/86 7000' Hilton Creek (DP); 6/10/80 7000' Mammoth turnoff from U.S. 395 (AB 34:929); 9/22/78 10,400' Hall Natural Area (DeSante MS) - 1/2/80 6500' w. Mono Lake (DG).

Extreme dates above 4000' west slope and above 7500' east of crest: 9/21/79 7800' White Wolf (JW) - 11/11/56 7000' "in Yosemite" (ABR).

Extreme dates at or below 4000' west slope: ? (presumably late September or early October, but I have no dates) - 5/30/53 2100' El Portal (AFN 7:290).

Additional reference: EM 10.

"MOUNTAIN" WHITE-CROWNED SPARROW
(*Zonotrichia leucophrys oriantha*)

	J	F	M	A	M	J	J	A	S	O	N	D	HABITAT	ELEVATIONS		
														N	T	W
WEST													GWS	8-10		
EAST													GWS	8-10	6-10	

Common summer resident from 8500' to 11,000' on west slope—formerly nested in Yosemite Valley (4000'); common summer resident from 8500' to 11,000' and fairly common transient below 8500' east of crest.

If for nothing but song and habitat, one might fancy Mountain White-crowneds the finest of Sierran sparrows. From the meadows, streams and lakes which glorify the high country, their clear, plaintive lays greet the dawn, close the day and serenade the weary wanderer on moonlit nights. Of their songs, William Leon Dawson wrote (1923), "it has in it the sprightliness of springing heather, the bright, compelling cheer of sunshine battling with glaciers for imprisoned waters, and a little of the wistfulness of whispering pines."

In their Sierran nesting haunts, Mountain White-crowned Sparrows are wedded to meadows with low, dense willow thickets. For singing posts, look-outs and occasionally nest locations, they also avail themselves of small lodgepole or whitebark pines, sagebrush and large herbaceous plants, such as corn lilies.

To one familiar with their acadian Sierran haunts, it comes as a shock to find Mountain White-crowned Sparrows nesting in bleak, treeless settings east of the Sierran escarpment. Yet in the Bodie Hills, they are common denizens of moist meadows which often lack willows or trees entirely. In these settings, they sing and nest in the margining sagebrush and bitterbrush; in the ghost town of Bodie, they even serenade tourists from the decaying buildings. On the moist flanks of Bodie Mountain and Potato Peak (ca. 9000'), they nest among squaw currants, harmonizing with California Towhees and Brewer's Sparrows—a unique avian chorus.

Mountain White-crowned Sparrows have probably nested in even bleaker habitat on Paoha Island (D 321, C 40:262), but not in recent years. On the west slope, they formerly bred in Yosemite Valley at the exceptionally low elevation of 4000', but have not been found since the 1920s (D 321, EM 10, C 40:262).

Common to the Mountain White-crowneds' nesting haunts are damp, grass-covered ground, surface water and shrubs or small trees. They usually forage on damp ground in the vicinity of cover. During most years, they conceal nests under shrubbery or in thick, herbaceous vegetation. After heavy winters, however, when deep snow lingers into summer, they ensconce nests in shrubs and even small trees (Morton et al. 1972, Morton 1975).

During migrations, transient Mountain White-crowned Sparrows visit sagebrush scrub east of the Sierran escarpment, but are far outnumbered by *gambelii.*

Extreme dates: 4/13/80 6800' Lee Vining (DG) - 9/29/15 8600' Tuolummne Meadows (GS 449).

Earliest date above 8000': 4/30/76 8600' Tuolumne Meadows (YM).

Adult "Mountain" (left) and "Gambel's" (right) White-crowned Sparrows, courtesy Discovering Sierra Birds.

Extreme dates above 8500', both Tuolumne Meadows: 5/7/83 (YM) - 9/29/15 (GS 449).

Additional representative nesting localities: 8600' Tuolumne Meadows (GS 449, AFN 10:409); 9800' to 11,000' Hall Natural Area (DeSante MS); 8000' Mammoth Meadow (DG); 7000' Walker Creek (GS 449).

Additional reference: AFN 10:363.

"GAMBEL'S" WHITE-CROWNED SPARROW
(*Zonotrichia leucophrys gambelii*)

	J	F	M	A	M	J	J	A	S	O	N	D	HABITAT	ELEVATIONS		
														N	T	W
WEST													GSW		F-10	F-4
EAST													GSW		6-10	6-7

Common winter resident in Mariposa region (2000'—CL); rare winter resident below 4000', fairly common transient to 5000' and fairly common fall transient to treeline elsewhere on west slope; fairly common fall transient below treeline and common transient and rare winter resident below 7500' east of crest.

In mid-September, east of the Sierran escarpment, Gambel's White-crowned Sparrows replace California Towhees and Brewer's Sparrows in sagebrush scrub. Flocks of up to 100 individuals roam the sagebrush en route from Alaskan and northern Canadian breeding areas to balmier climes. Their numbers thin by November, and they rarely overwinter, though they winter by the thousands to the south in Owens Valley (4000'-

5000'). In April they return in scattered small flocks, but are not as plentiful as they were in fall.

In the high country, Gambel's White-crowned Sparrows appear in fall just as their nesting "mountain" cousins depart. They journey through lower elevations as well, wintering sparingly in the western foothills. During their travels, they visit a variety of open, brushy habitats, but shun forests, steep slopes and dense, continuous chaparral. Flocks forage in clearings, openings, meadows and residential yards, but never far from shrubs, thickets, wood piles, brush piles and other cover. They are fond of fleshy fruits, and even peck at overripe apples.

Extreme dates: 9/9/81 10,200' Hall Natural Area (DeSante MS) - 4/30/82 6400' Mono Lake (BE).

Additional references: Auk 90:83, EM 10, GS 449, YNN 10:40.

HARRIS' SPARROW (*Zonotrichia querula*)

Extremely rare transient on west and east slope; irregularly rare winter resident (0-2/year) below 7000' east of Sierran escarpment.

When they stray to the region, Harris' Sparrows favor the same brushy habitats as Gambel's White-crowneds.

Records west and east slopes: 4000' Yosemite Valley 12/1/34 (YNN 14:26); 9800' e. Tioga Pass 10/21/83 (Marty Morton).

Extreme dates east of crest: 12/8/76, 2, 6500' Bridgeport (DG) - 5/20/82 6800' Lee Vining, adult (DG, DB).

"OREGON" DARK-EYED JUNCO
(*Junco hyemalis thurberi* and other wintering subspecies)

	J	F	M	A	M	J	J	A	S	O	N	D	HABITAT	ELEVATIONS		
														N	T	W
WEST													POWG	3-10	F-10	F-4
EAST													PWG	7-10	6-10	6-8

Uncommon summer resident from 3000' to 4500', common summer resident to treeline, rare summer visitor above treeline, irregularly uncommon to common winter resident below 3000' and rare to fairly common winter resident to 4500' on west slope, sometimes lingering at higher elevations during mild years; common summer resident from 7500' to treeline and irregularly rare to common winter resident below 8000' east of crest.

During spring and summer, one cannot walk far through mixed conifer, fir or lodgepole pine forests without surprising a pair or two of Oregon Dark-eyed Juncos. From mid-elevations to treeline, they are conspicuous, ubiquitous and vocal woodland inhabitants.

Oregon Juncos' varied nesting haunts are usually dominated by pines or firs. Except for digger pines, knobcone pines, pinyon pines and junipers, they nest among every conifer. They also need shrubbery, downed timber, undercut banks or rocks in which to shelter and nest, and grasses and forbs in which to scrounge for seeds and insects. Hence they are partial to open forests, burns, and, in old-growth, the edges of meadows, streams, lakes, roads, campgrounds and other openings. They also nest in dense forests, however, provided there is herbaceous growth.

During migration and winter, Oregon Juncos are more widespread, ranging into oak woodlands, pinyon pine woodlands, residential areas and other habitats that are drier and sunnier than their nesting haunts. They still require trees or shrubs for cover, and open, grassy ground on which to forage. Their wintering numbers vary from year to year; tallies on the Yosemite Christmas Bird Count vary from 507 to 36; on the Mono Lake Christmas Bird Count from 210 to 35.

The return of Oregon Juncos to their mountain nesting haunts varies with altitude and snowpack. After the dry 1976 winter, for instance, they arrived at Tuolumne Meadows (8600') on April 5, a month earlier than the year before (TH).

Though Oregon Juncos forage on the ground, they sometimes mount lofty timber to declaim their territories. I've seen them singing from the tops of firs 150 feet in height.

High elevation record: 10,900' near Mt. Ritter 9/26/87 (James Yurchenco).

Extreme dates above 8000', all Tuolumne Meadows (8600'): 3/22/84 (YM); 4/5/76 (TH) - 11/10/82 (YM); 12/12/76—extremely light winter (YM).

Representative nesting localities: 4000' Yosemite Valley (GS 463); 6000' Chinquapin (GS 463); 6200' Crane Flat (DG); 7000' Peregoy Meadow (DG); 7200' Merced Lake (GS 463); 7800' White Wolf (ABR, DG); 8600' Tuolumne Meadows (MR); 9800'-10,600' Hall Natural Area (DeSante MS); 8900' Lake Mary (DG); 8500' Lundy Canyon (DG); (7500' O'Harrell Canyon—DG).

Additional references: YNN 16:4, YNN 18:23, YNN 20:12.

"SLATE-COLORED" DARK-EYED JUNCO
(*Junco hyemalis cismontanus* or *hyemalis*)

Rare winter resident below 5000' on west slope; rare winter resident below 8000' and extremely rare transient at higher elevations east of crest.

Slate-colored Juncos stray to the same habitats as wintering Oregons, with which they usually associate.

Records above 8000', both Hall Natural Area: 10,200'—10/11/77 and 10,000'—10/17/78 (DeSante and Engstrom MS).

Extreme dates excluding above records, both Yosemite Valley (4000'): 10/16/66 (AFN 21:76 - 4/9/27 (YM) and 4/9/86 (YM).

Additional references: AFN 8:269, GS 458, YNN 10:31.

"GRAY-HEADED" DARK-EYED JUNCO (*Junco hyemalis caniceps*)

Extremely rare winter visitor on west slope and east of Sierran escarpment.

Records west slope: 2100' El Portal 12/27/51 (YNN 31:11); 4000' Yosemite Valley 1/18/30 (YNN 10:30).

Records east of crest: 7000' Mammoth Creek 12/19/82 (AB 37:758, DG); 7200' Tom's Place 12/15/90 - 3/9/91 (AB 45: 318, AB 45:494).

MCCOWN'S LONGSPUR (*Calcarius mccownii*)

Extremely rare vagrant east of Sierran escarpment.

Record: 6400' South Tufa, 2, 4/17/83 (DG).

LAPLAND LONGSPUR (*Calcarius lapponicus*)

Extremely rare transient east of Sierran escarpment.

Records: 6400' South Tufa 10/14/85 (DG) and 10/30/79 (AB 34.199, DG); 6400' sw. Mono Lake 12/31/80 (AB 35:716, DG).

CHESTNUT-COLLARED LONGSPUR (*Calcarius ornatus*)

Extremely rare vagrant on west slope; irregularly rare winter resident (0-8/year) near Mono Lake (6400') and undoubtedly in other valleys east of Sierran escarpment.

Chestnut-collared Longspurs stray to dense, grassy meadows, sometimes in small flocks. They usually flush underfoot to vanish again in seas of grass. Most have been seen during autumn.

Peak count: 8, 6400' South Tufa 10/12-15/86 (AB 33:212).

Records west slope: 7800' White Wolf 9/21/87 (JW); 4600' Ackerson Meadow, 2, 9/24/87 (JW).

Extreme dates east of crest, eight records since 1978: 10/2/78 South Tufa (BE) - 4/17/82 s. of Dechambeau Ponds, 3 including male in breeding plumage (BE).

Additional references: AB 34:199, AB 35:716, AB 39:789.

Subfamily ICTERINAE: Blackbirds, Orioles and Allies

This diverse family includes birds that dwell in marshes, grasslands and forests. Some, like Brewer's Blackbirds, brave Sierran winters at lower elevations. Others, like Northern Orioles, migrate to the tropical climes of Mexico and Middle America. Of 12 species, six nest in our region.

As they are readily recognized subspecies, I treat the eastern "Baltimore" Northern Oriole separately from the western "Bullock's".

BOBOLINK (*Dolichonyx oryzivorus*)

Extremely rare vagrant on west slope and east of Sierran escarpment.

Record west slope: 4400' Big Meadow, male 5/19/79 (YM, George Peyton).

Records east of crest: 6400' Mono Lake 5/28/88 (AB 42:480), "flock" 9/?/01 (C 4:11); w. Mono Lake 9/30/82 (DG); Mono Lake County Park 6/20/88 (AB 42:1338), 10/18/86 (Gottlieb Dandliker); 6400' River Springs Lake, e. of Granite Mountain 6/14/91 (AB 45:1160).

RED-WINGED BLACKBIRD (*Agelaius phoeniceus*)

	J	F	M	A	M	J	J	A	S	O	N	D	HABITAT	ELEVATIONS		
														N	T	W
WEST													MaGMuWD	F-9		F-2
EAST													MaGMuMoWD	6-8		6-7

Uncommon summer resident below 3000', common summer resident to 5000', locally common summer resident to 7000', common summer resident at Tuolumne Meadows (8600'), extremely rare visitor elsewhere to treeline, rare winter visitor below 2500' and extremely rare winter visitor to 4000' on west slope; common summer resident below 8000', extremely rare visitor to treeline, fairly common winter resident at Mammoth Lakes dump (7000') and rare winter visitor below 7500' elsewhere east of crest.

From early spring through mid-summer, in marshes and boggy meadows, male Red-winged Blackbirds flash their flaming epaulets and gurgle musical challenges to the world at large. Their bravado is not show, for they mercilessly harry hawks, ravens and gulls who soar near nests and young.

Loose colonies of Red-winged Blackbirds conceal nests in dense cattails, sedges, bulrushes and shrubby willows. From breeding areas, they commute to stables, campgrounds and dumps to fill their bellies. They also forage in meadows and along the banks of lakes and streams.

At higher elevations on the west slope, Red-winged Blackbirds are localized in widely scattered pockets of suitable habitat. A colony of 20-30 individuals in a Tuolumne Meadows' cattail marsh (8600'), for example, is 1600' above the next highest site.

Long before most passerine migrants, Red-winged Blackbirds arrive in their nesting haunts. Most leave the mountains by early August. East of the Sierran escarpment, however, they linger into November, but trade marshy nesting haunts for dumps, stables and feeders. As many as 60 have overwintered at the Mammoth Lakes dump (AB 39:787, DG).

The west slope's Red-winged Blackbirds belong, not to the California subspecies *A. p. californicus*, but to the same race as eastside birds, *A. p. nevadensis* (GM 424). Apparently their forbears colonized from the east. Unlike the California race, *nevadensis* wear yellow bars on their red epaulets.

Records above 9000': 9800' Tioga Pass 6/19/77 (DG) and 10/8/78 (DG); 10,000' Mono Pass 7/15/85 (MR).

Winter record above 2500' west slope: 12/4-27/52 4000' Yosemite Valley (AFN 7:233, YNN 33:11).

Extreme dates above 4000' excluding winter record, all Yosemite Valley (4000'): 2/17/73 and 2/17/87 (YM) - 10/22/86 (YM).

Earliest date Tuolumne Meadows: 5/7/83 (YM).

Additional representative nesting localities: 4000' Yosemite Valley (GS 400, YM), 4400' Big Meadow (DG), 4600' Hodgdon Meadow (DG), 4600' Ackerson Meadow (JW), 5500' Tiltill Valley (DG), 6000' Lost Lake near Half Dome (TH), 7000' Jackass Meadow (SG), 8200' Lundy Canyon (MM), 7400' Lee Vining Canyon (DG), 7000' Long Valley (DG), 6400' Simons Spring (DG).

Additional reference: YNN 21:42.

WESTERN MEADOWLARK (*Sturnella neglecta*)

	J	F	M	A	M	J	J	A	S	O	N	D	HABITAT	ELEVATIONS		
														N	T	W
WEST													GWSOP	F-5	F-10	F-4
EAST												•	GWSP	6-7	F-10	7

Fairly common resident in Mariposa region (2000'); uncommon summer and rare winter resident below 4000', locally uncommon summer resident to 5000', extremely rare spring transient and rare summer visitor and fall transient to treeline elsewhere on west slope; fairly common summer and extremely rare winter visitor below 7000', common fall transient to 8000' and rare fall transient to treeline east of crest.

During the warmer months of the year, the rich, fluted voices of Western Meadowlarks rise from meadows, pastures and open, grassy sagebrush scrub, especially east of the Sierran escarpment. From the tops of shrubs, trees, fences and, at Mono Lake, tufa towers, these grassland minstrels air sweet melodies and keep watch for danger.

Though Western Meadowlarks favor the drier portions of large meadows, they also nest among sagebrush, rabbitbrush, greasewood and other shrubs. The spaces between the shrubs, however, must support enough grassy cover to conceal nests.

During late summer, small numbers of Western Meadowlarks drift upslope, lingering in meadows as high as treeline until the first autumn storms. On 7/27/36 one joined tourists on top of Half Dome (8800'—YNN 16:72).

For most of the year, Western Meadowlarks dwell on relatively level or gently rolling terrain. From late September through October, however, flocks materialize on steep, sagebrush-covered slopes east of the crest. They also visit small, forest-margined meadows and openings, and the grassy shoulders of roads.

On the west slope, Western Meadowlarks winter irregularly, but sometimes in sizable flocks. Thirty-five, for example, were in Big Meadow (4400') on 12/28/80 (LMcK). While eastside winters force them to balmier quarters, they return in time to sing at March snowstorms.

High elevation record: 11,000' above Parker Pass 10/10/32 (YM).

Winter records east of crest, first two Long Valley (7000'): 12/18/76 (AB 31:868) and 7, 12/19/81 (AB 36:745); 12/18/88 Mono Lake (AB 43:364).

Spring record at 8600': Tuolumne Meadows 4/?/80 (MR).

Extreme dates east of crest excluding winter records: 3/9/82 6400' South Tufa (BE) - 11/18/85 7000' w. Lee Vining (DG).

Extreme dates above 5000' west slope and above 8000' east of crest: 7/3/56 8600' Tuolumne Meadows (YM) - 11/13/54 7000' Peregoy Meadow (AFN 9:54).

Representative nesting localities: 4000' Yosemite Valley (EM 8, YM); 4600' Ackerson Meadow (JW); 7500' near Parker Creek (GS 410); 6400' near Mono Lake (GS 410); (7000' Long Valley—DG).

Additional references: AFN 8:40, AFN 10.408, AB 26:899.

YELLOW-HEADED BLACKBIRD (*Xanthocephalus xanthocephalus*)

	J	F	M	A	M	J	J	A	S	O	N	D	HABITAT	ELEVATIONS		
														N	T	W
WEST						•	•	•					G		4-5	?
EAST													MaMuMoG	6-7		

Rare spring transient at 4000' to 5000' and extremely rare spring transient and summer visitor at higher elevations on west slope; locally common summer resident below 7500' east of crest.

East of the Sierran escarpment, during spring and early summer, the caterwauling cries of Yellow-headed Blackbirds dominate the creaking, spluttering and honking marsh cacophony. Noisy colonies of "Bananaheads" nest in tall, dense cattails over standing water at least a few inches in depth. They forage on the muddy shores of lakes and ponds and in wet meadows and pastures.

During migration, Yellow-headed Blackbirds are more widespread, joining Red-winged and Brewer's blackbirds in fields and at residential feeders.

Grinnell and Storer cite a winter record from Yosemite Valley, but the details are conjectural; it was "said to have been killed...about January, 1917" (GS 399, GM 422).

Records above 5000' west slope: approx. 8000' "Yosemite" 5/16/70 (AB 24:641); 8600' Tuolumne Meadows 5/11/61 (YM), 5/23/73 (AB 27:817) and 6/22/77 (YM); 7000' Merced Lake Trail 7/6/76 (YM).

Summer record Yosemite Valley (4000'): 8/18/25 (YNN 29:50).

Extreme dates west slope excluding summer record, both Yosemite Valley: 4/7/67 (YM) - 6/9/77 (YM).

Extreme dates east of crest: 4/5/82 6400' se. Mono Lake (BE) - 9/29/83 6400' South Tufa (HG).

Representative nesting localities: 7600' June Lake (DG); 7000' Long Valley (D 1547); 6500' Dechambeau Ponds (DG); 6400' Simon's Spring (DG); 6500' Bridgeport Reservoir (DG).

Additional references: AFN 9:357, YNN 9:70, YNN 29:50.

RUSTY BLACKBIRD (*Euphagus carolinus*)

Extremely rare vagrant and winter visitor east of Sierran escarpment.

Records: 6400' Mono Lake 11/26-27/77 (AB 32:255) and 12/28/78 (AB 33:656); 7000' Hot Creek Fish Hatchery, 2, 12/31/83 (AB 38:792); (on the west slope, 5 Rusty Blackbirds were reported on the 1968 Yosemite Christmas Bird Count, but without substantiating details).

BREWER'S BLACKBIRD (*Euphagus cyanocephalus*)

	J	F	M	A	M	J	J	A	S	O	N	D	HABITAT	ELEVATIONS		
														N	T	W
WEST													GWD	F-9	F-10	F-4
EAST													GWD	6-8	6-10	6-7

Fairly common resident in Mariposa region (2000'); locally common summer resident below 8500', locally fairly common summer visitor to treeline, rare summer visitor above treeline and rare winter resident below 4000' on west slope; common summer resident below 8000', locally fairly common summer visitor to treeline, rare summer visitor above treeline, common winter resident at Mammoth dump (7000') and uncommon winter resident elsewhere below 7500' east of crest.

Brewer's Blackbirds have followed people into the Sierra. In Yosemite Valley (4000'), for instance, the nesting population increased from not more than six pairs in 1920 to "hundreds" 20 years later (YNN 13:33, YNN 19:12). Today there are large colonies ensconced in willows and cottonwoods along the Merced River, and they nest at least as high as Tuolumne Meadows (8600').

Compared to Red-wingeds, Brewer's Blackbirds are more widespread, tolerant of drier conditions and more partial to the company of humans. While they usually nest in the vicinity of meadows, ponds, lakes, streams or towns, they commute to stables, campgrounds, picnic areas, dumps and outdoor restaurants in search of food. They also forage in more natural habitats, such as meadows and the margins of lakes and streams.

Loose colonies usually secrete nests in dense-foliaged trees or tall shrubs, but, at Mono Lake (6400'), also use tufa towers. In west slope meadows, they often avail themselves of dense willows. During the summer, non-breeding Brewer's Blackbirds drift to and sometimes above treeline, usually in small flocks. It's surprising to encounter such prosaic backyard birds consorting with Mountain White-crowned Sparrows and Rosy Finches. Yet some favor the backcountry to the slovenly company of humans, flocking in meadows and along the margins of lakes and streams far from the nearest road or trail.

While a few overwinter, most Brewer's Blackbirds forsake the region for balmier climes. They linger in the higher mountains through September and at lower elevations, such as Yosemite Valley (4000'), through October. They return in mid- to late March, several weeks after Red-wingeds.

High elevation record: 11,200' flying over Lake Catherine Pass 9/26/87 (James Yurchenco); (in the southern Sierra, they have reached 12,500'—AB 28:946).

Extreme dates above 8000': 3/27/77 8400' Olmsted Point (YM); 4/6/77 8600' Tuolumne Meadows (YM) - 10/12/77 10,300' Hall Natural Area (DeSante MS).

Earliest date above 9000': 6/19/79 10,300' Hall Natural Area (DeSante MS).

Additional representative nesting localities: 4600' Ackerson Meadows (JW); 6200' Crane Flat (DG); 7800' White Wolf (DG); 8600' Tuolumne Meadows (MR); 7400' Lee Vining Canyon (DG); 6800' Lee Vining (DG).

Additional references: AFN 7:233, EM 8, GS 413, YNN 32:11.

GREAT-TAILED GRACKLE (*Quiscalus mexicanus*)

Extremely rare vagrant on west slope and east of Sierran escarpment.

Record west slope: 4000' Yosemite Valley, female, 5/13/86 (YM).
Record east of crest: 6800' Lee Vining, 2 males, 6/15-16/82 (DG).

COMMON GRACKLE (*Quiscalus quiscula*)

Extremely rare vagrant east of Sierran escarpment.

Record: 7000' McGee Creek, male at feeder, 4/12/87 (DP, DG AB 42:480); accepted by California Bird Records Committee.

(GRACKLE SPECIES)

Record: 6500' Mono Lake County Park 5/10-14/89 (AB 43:534)

BROWN-HEADED COWBIRD (*Molothrus ater*)

	J	F	M	A	M	J	J	A	S	O	N	D	HABITAT	ELEVATIONS		
														N	T	W
WEST			•										DGWPOMu	F-10		
EAST		•											DGWPOMu	6-10		

Locally common summer resident below 8500' and irregularly rare to uncommon summer resident to treeline on west slope; locally common summer resident below 8000' and irregularly rare to uncommon summer resident to treeline east of crest.

Brown-headed Cowbirds dine at stables, campgrounds, picnic areas and meadows, but search forests and thickets for foster parents to raise their young. Instead of rearing their own families, they abandon eggs in the nests of vireos, warblers, sparrows and other small songbirds, taking no further interest in the welfare of their progeny.

Brown-headed Cowbirds have followed humans, not only into the Sierra, but into most of California. Before 1900, they were virtually unknown in the state. Joseph Grinnell, in his 1915 *Distributional List of the Birds of California*, cites but a single record in the Pacific drainage. But with the advent of feedlots and irrigated agriculture, cowbirds arrived in droves. Flocks of up to 10,000 have been tallied in the Central Valley.

On the west slope, Brown-headed Cowbirds were first detected in Yosemite Valley (4000') during the spring of 1934. The following year they were observed at Crane Flat (6200') and Peregoy Meadow (7000'—YNN 13:94, YNN 18:96). Their subsequent spread and increase, however, is poorly documented. By 1956, "numbers" were present near Badger Pass (7000'—AFN 10:53). In 1961 they were "numerous" at White Wolf (7800') and Tuolumne Meadows (ABR), and had reached Tioga Pass (9800'—AFN 15:491).

East of the crest, Brown-headed Cowbirds likewise increased phenomenally. Through the 1930s, their numbers were so small that seasoned ornithologists failed to detect them. Tracy Storer, for example, searched for them in the Bridgeport Valley on 7/22/30, but failed to find a single bird (MVZ journal). In 1939, Rowley summarized several years of field work in the June Lake region: "I have not seen a single cowbird anywhere in the high country" (C 41:251). While their increase is undocumented, it undoubtedly paralleled that to the west.

Brown-headed Cowbirds arrive in mid- to late April, staging in large flocks in meadows and towns. I tallied 130, for example, in Lee Vining (6800') on 4/20/79. By early May, they invade the higher mountains in search of hosts.

On both slopes, Brown-headed Cowbirds are closely wedded to human habitations and livestock. Every horse corral and stable supports a summer flock, as do most campgrounds and bird feeders. They also forage in meadows and other open habitats, but rarely more than five miles from stables or other principal feeding centers. While they feed on the ground, they use willows, pines or other trees for roosting and singing.

Female Brown-headed Cowbirds range into virtually every terrestrial habitat in search of hosts' nests in which to lay eggs. They penetrate dense forests as well as chaparral and sagebrush scrub, but usually within several miles of stables, campgrounds or other foraging areas (Rothstein, Verner and Stevens 1984). Most adults leave by the end of July, but juveniles linger into September and rarely October.

The spread of Brown-headed Cowbirds has raised concern for some of their hosts, which raise cowbird young at the expense of some or all of their own broods. In lowland California, cowbird parasitism has almost certainly been a major factor in the precipitous decline of Willow Flycatchers, Bell's Vireos, Yellow Warblers and possibly other birds (Gaines 1974; Goldwasser, Gaines and Wilbur 1981). In our region, it "has apparently reduced densities of some species, especially Warbling Vireos," in areas of high cowbird density (Rothstein, Verner and Stevens 1980; Verner and Ritter 1983).

Parasite-host relationships, such as that between Brown-headed Cowbirds and the passerines it parasitizes, are usually detrimental only when the interacting populations have not had a common evolutionary history. Given such a history natural selection tends to moderate the impact of a parasite to a level bearable by its host, since the former is dependent on the latter for survival. In California, however, the spread of agriculture has "allowed the cowbird to penetrate into new regions where it has access to host populations that have had little or no ancestral experience through which to develop effective defenses against it" (Mayfield 1965).

It is all too easy, however, to vilify cowbirds. True they have tipped nature's balance to the detriment of native species. But let us not forget that we, through our use and abuse of the land, have allowed them to thrive and multiply. Without humans, there would be no cowbird "problem." The blame lies with us, not with them.

Peak counts: 40, 8600' Tuolumne Meadows stables 5/20/73 (YM); 20 4000' Curry Company stables, Yosemite Valley 7/4/78 (DG); 14, Park Service stables, Yosemite Valley 7/4/78 (DG).

Extreme dates west slope: 4000' Wawona 3/18/71 (YM); 4/18/77 6200' Crane Flat (MM) - 4000' Yosemite Valley 9/8/24 (YM).

Extreme dates east of crest: 6800' Lee Vining 2/23/86 (RS); Lee Vining 4/13/79 (DG) - 7000' Cain Ranch 10/30/86 (DS, SJ).

Representative breeding localities and hosts: 4000' Yosemite Valley, Warbling Vireo (DG), Solitary Vireo (YNN 18:96), Black-throated Gray Warbler (YNN 18:96), MacGillivray's Warbler (WB 46:104), Song Sparrow (DG) and Lincoln's Sparrow (DG); 4400' Foresta, Hermit Warbler (SG); 4600' Ackerson Meadow, Hermit Warbler (JW), 8600' Tuolumne Meadows, Yellow-rumped Warbler (DG); 9800' above Tioga Lake, Wilson's Warbler (BS); 10,100' Hall Natural Area, Yellow-rumped Warbler, Wilson's Warbler, White-crowned Sparrow and Dark-eyed Junco (DeSante MS); 9400' Virginia Lake, Ruby-crowned Kinglet (AFN 16:505); 9400' Lee Vining Canyon, Rosy Finch (SH); 8900' Lake Mary, Yellow-rumped Warbler and Dark-eyed Junco (DG); 8500' Virginia Creek, Wilson's Warbler (C 41:251); approx. 8000' Lundy Canyon, MacGillivray's Warbler, Song Sparrow and Dark-eyed Junco (DG); 8000' Mammoth Meadow, California Towhee (DG); 6400' South Tufa, Sage Sparrow (DG).

ORCHARD ORIOLE (*Icterus spurius*)

Extremely rare vagrant east of Sierran escarpment.

Record: 6500' near Mono Lake, adult male, 8/28/74 (AB 29:118).

HOODED ORIOLE (*Icterus cucullatus*)

Irregularly rare spring transient (0-2/year) below 7500' east of Sierran escarpment.

Hooded Orioles have strayed to deciduous trees in Lee Vining (6800'), along the west shore of Mono Lake (6500'), and Tom's Place (7200').

Extreme dates, both Lee Vining, seven records since 1980: 4/1/85 (AB 39:348) - 5/13/85 (DG).

Additional reference: AB 34:813.

"BULLOCK'S" NORTHERN ORIOLE (*Icterus galbula bullockii*)

	J	F	M	A	M	J	J	A	S	O	N	D	HABITAT	ELEVATIONS		
														N	T	W
WEST													WOS	F-4	F-6	
EAST													WS	6-8	6-10	

Common summer resident below 3000', uncommon resident to 4000', rare transient or summer visitor to 6500' and extremely rare transient at higher elevations on west slope; fairly common summer resident below 8000' and extremely rare transient at higher elevations east of crest.

In April, soon after oaks, cottonwoods, aspens and other deciduous hardwoods unfurl their leaves, noisy chattering announces the return of Northern Orioles from wintering haunts in Mexico and Central America. These tropical beauties favor live and blue oak woodlands and riparian forests. Females, which arrive a week or two after their mates, suspend elegant sack nests from the branches of large trees. Both sexes forage, not only in timber, but in humid shrubbery and lush meadows. During migration, they sometimes visit drier habitats, such as chaparral and sagebrush scrub.

Records above 6500' west slope and 8000' east of crest: 7000' Peregoy Meadow 7/25/71 (AB 25:900); 10,000'-10,300' Hall Natural Area 5/4/81, 5/9/81, 5/18/80, 7/22/81 and 8/6/81, all believed to be different birds (DeSante and Engstrom MS); 10,000' near Spillway Lake 7/14/85 (MR).

Extreme dates west slope: 3/18/71 4000' Wawona (YM); 4/1/76 2100' El Portal (YM) - 4000' Yosemite Valley 9/8/74 (YM).

Extreme dates east of crest: 4/2/81 6800' Lee Vining, in snowstorm (DG); 4/15/83 Lee Vining (DG) - 9/4/90 8000' Deadman Creek campground (ESt).

Additional reference: EM 8.

"BALTIMORE" NORTHERN ORIOLE (*Icterus galbula galbula*)

Extremely rare vagrant east of Sierran escarpment.

Record: 6900' Goat Ranch, male, 9/30/82 (DG).

Family FRINGILLIDAE: OLD-WORLD FINCHES

This family has recently become exclusive. Taxonomists now believe that sparrows, towhees, Black-headed Grosbeaks, Lazuli Buntings and other new world birds, despite their finch-like conical birds, are more closely related to warblers and tanagers than they are to nearctic, old world finches. Despite their similar names, for example, Black-headed Grosbeaks are distantly related to the nearctic Evening and Pine grosbeaks. Their similar bills are products of convergent evolution, not common ancestries.

The nearctic finches also differ from their new world look-alikes in migratory proclivities. Our 11 species, though prone to wanderings, are not migratory in the sense of predictable annual flights from one area to another. But their numbers and whereabouts, particularly in winter, tend to vary dramatically from year to year. During some winters, most subsist on buds and seeds within their nesting ranges, even at high elevations. In others, some desert the mountains to winter in the foothills or lowlands. Even in summer, many cannot be found in the same localities or even at the same elevations every year.

ROSY FINCH (*Leucosticte arctoa*)

	J	F	M	A	M	J	J	A	S	O	N	D	HABITAT	ELEVATIONS		
														N	T	W
WEST													CG	10+		10+
EAST													CG	10+		6-9

Extremely rare winter visitor below 8500', rare summer resident from 8500' to treeline and fairly common summer resident and irregularly rare winter visitor above treeline on west slope; rare summer resident from 8500' to treeline and fairly common summer resident above treeline on east slope; irregularly rare winter visitor above 9000' and locally fairly common winter resident below 9000' east of crest.

No peak is too high, too rugged or too exposed for Rosy Finches. To meet these feathered, confiding mountaineers in their breeding haunts, one must leave the timberline whitebarks far below. Among cirques and ridges, alpine lakes and meadows, sheer escarpments and eternal ice and snow, they pick insects from snowfields and harvest the seeds of alpine plants. They regularly visit the summits of the highest peaks, including Mt. Lyell (13,090'), the highest point in Yosemite.

Rosy Finches are hatched from nests concealed in crevices on fractured, vertical cliffs or among the large boulder fields below. They have also bred in abandoned mine shafts, the rock wall of a cabin and under a bridge on the Tioga Road (9400'). Near nesting sites are usually large snowfields that last well into summer, and alpine meadows or tundra vegetation. The adults undertake long foraging expeditions, employing their specialized cheek pouches to transport loads of insects and seeds to hungry nestlings. While they usually forage well above treeline, they occasionally descend into subalpine woodlands of whitebark and lodgepole pines, especially in spring and fall.

During the winter, most of our nesting birds, which belong to the subspecies *L. a. dawsoni*, move down the eastern slope of the Sierra or into the basin ranges and valleys immediately to the east. They winter in a relatively limited area to the east of the Sierran crest, never straying far into Nevada. During periods of mild weather, they venture back into alpine breeding grounds, foraging on slopes and ridges that blow free of snow. They gradually return to nesting areas between April and June (Miller 1987).

During winter, our Sierra Nevada Rosy Finches are joined by the much more migratory Hepburn race, *L. a. littoralis*, which may be distinguished by the more extensive gray on their faces (see National Geographic Society *Field Guide*, p. 438). Both races winter in sagebrush scrub and open pinyon pine woodlands, usually on slopes that are rocky and sparsely vegetated. They are attracted to road cuts, quarries and places where the ground has been disturbed. Near Bodie (approx. 9000'), they roost in vertical mine shafts; at McGee Creek (7000'), they regularly visit feeders (DP). They have reached both Negit and Paoha islands in Mono Lake (DW).

Wintering Rosy Finches often aggregate in tremendous flocks. On 3/31/80, for example, "an estimated 1,500 appeared in one swirling flock north of Conway Summit" (approx. 8000'); about 80 percent were *L. a. littoralis*, the rest *L. a. dawsoni* or the similar *L. a. tephrocotis*(AB 34:813).

Another subspecies, the Black Rosy Finch (*L. a. atrata*, has twice been recorded in the Bodie Hills.

Black Rosy Finch records: 8000' Bodie 1/15/04 (C 30:191); approx. 8000' n. of Conway Summit 3/31/80 (AB 34:813).

Record below 8500' west slope: 4000' Yosemite Valley 2/25/87 (YM).

Extreme dates below 8000' east of crest: 11/26/81 6500' South Tufa (TH) - 4/8/79 7000' w. Lee Vining, about 100 including several *littoralis* (DG).

Representative nesting localities: 8800' Half Dome (YM, YNN 18:112, JL); 9400' above Ostrander Lake (YM); 9900' Clouds Rest (YNN 3(12):4); 10,600' Gaylor Lake, nesting in mine shaft and cabin (YNN 16:46); 11,000' Mammoth Crest (D 162-165, Dixon 1936); 10,400-11,500' Hall Natural Area (DeSante MS).

Additional reference: AB 26:903.

PINE GROSBEAK (*Pinicola enucleator*)

	J	F	M	A	M	J	J	A	S	O	N	D	HABITAT	ELEVATIONS		
														N	T	W
WEST													PG	7-10		7-10
EAST													PG	8-10		8-10

Extremely rare visitor below 6000', rare resident from 6000' to 7000' and irregularly rare to fairly common resident from 7000' to treeline on west slope; irregularly rare to uncommon resident from 8000' to treeline on east slope.

Near the forested margins of meadows, streams and lakes, Pine Grosbeaks are sometimes so confiding one has no need for binoculars. Like Great Gray Owls and Black-backed Woodpeckers, these boreal finches have followed high mountains into sunny California. Sierran populations, relatively isolated from northern relatives since the last ice age, have evolved into an endemic subspecies, *P. e. californica*.

Pine Grosbeaks dwell in high elevation coniferous forests of lodgepole pines, whitebark pines, mountain hemlocks and, less frequently, red firs, almost invariably near meadows, streams or lakes. They forage in meadows as well as trees, and regularly visit mineralized springs, as at Soda Springs in Tuolumne Meadows (8600').

Though Pine Grosbeaks are resident, rarely descending below their breeding haunts, their numbers vary markedly. One year they abound throughout the lodgepole forests, the next become exceedingly scarce. These population cycles, which probably relate to food or weather, deserve further study.

Pine Grosbeaks are committed mountaineers, staying at high elevations throughout the year. I know of only two records below 6000', yet on one occasion they descended in numbers. From 5/17-26/55, "many hundreds" reached Yosemite Valley (4000') following "severe spring weather"; they had been "commoner than usual" in the Yosemite high country during the previous summer (AFN 9:357). A lone bird also reached Ackerson Meadow (4600') on 9/19/81 (JW).

Representative nesting localities: 7000' Peregoy Meadow (DG); 7600' near Smoky Jack, in red firs (SG); 8000' Siesta Lake (DS); 8600' Hart Lake (AB 40:522); 9900' Hall Natural Area (DeSante MS); approx. 9000' Mammoth Lakes (AFN 4:292).

Additional references: C 17:206, D 153, GS 419, YNN 4:68, YNN 4:88, YNN 19:62, YNN 21:23.

PURPLE FINCH (*Carpodacus purpureus*)

	J	F	M	A	M	J	J	A	S	O	N	D	HABITAT	ELEVATIONS		
														N	T	W
WEST													OPGD	3-8		F-5
EAST									•		•				7,10	

Common summer resident and irregularly rare to common winter resident from 3000' to 5000', fairly common summer resident to 7000', uncommon summer resident to 8000' and irregularly rare to common winter resident below 4000' on west slope; extremely rare transient east of crest.

Of the three *Carpodacus* finches, Purples prefer the shadiest, wettest haunts. They nest in oak-conifer and fir forests, never, as far as I know, straying above the firs into the lodgepole belt. At low elevations, they dwell among black oaks, ponderosa pines, sugar pines, incense cedars, douglas firs, sequoias and white firs; at mid-elevations, pure stands of red fir. They are not inveterate forest-dwellers, however, descending from trees to search meadows, clearings, scrub, roadsides and stables for buds, seeds and berries.

During winter, Purple Finches retreat from the higher parts of their range. In some years, they scatter over the foothills, waxing numerous in live and blue oak woodlands; in others, they remain in the higher mountains or desert the region almost entirely. Numbers on the Yosemite Christmas Bird Count, for example, have varied from 125 to 0.

Records east of crest: 10,200' Hall Natural Area 9/12/78 (AB 33:212, DeSante and Engstrom MS); 6800' Lee Vining 11/13/79 (AB 34:199).

Representative nesting localities: 4000' Yosemite Valley (YM); 4600' Ackerson Meadow (JW); (6200' Crane Flat—DG); approx. 8000', in burn, three miles w. of White Wolf (SG).

CASSIN'S FINCH (*Carpodacus cassinii*)

	J	F	M	A	M	J	J	A	S	O	N	D	HABITAT	ELEVATIONS		
														N	T	W
WEST													PGWD	5-10		F-4
EAST													PWGD	6-10		6-8

Locally fairly common summer resident from 4500' to 7500', common summer resident to treeline and irregularly rare winter resident below 4500' on west slope; common summer resident below treeline, irregularly rare to fairly common winter resident below 8500' and extremely rare winter visitor at higher elevations east of crest.

Cassin's are the mountain finch par excellence, following lodgepole pines nearly to treeline. In choice of habitat, they fall between Purples, which prefer wetter, shadier forests, and Houses, which dwell in drier, sunnier climes. Yet Cassin's nest with Purples at mid-elevations on the west slope, and rarely with Houses east of the Sierran escarpment.

In recent years we have come to realize that Cassin's as well as Purple finches nest together on the west slope at places like Ackerson Meadow (4600'), Hodgdon Meadow (4600') and probably Crane Flat (6200'). At these localities, I've been unable to discern consistent differences in the haunts of these closely related cousins. Both forage in the meadows as well as the margining forests, though I only see Purples in the deeper woods. Where do their niches diverge?

Above the fir forests and east of the crest, Cassin's Finches hold sole dominion. They cheerful songs ring through lodgepole pines, mountain hemlocks, whitebark pines and, especially east of the crest, aspen and cottonwood groves. These gregarious birds favor forests that edge on meadows, streams, lakes and shrub-covered slopes. At stables and pack stations, they scrounge grain with Brown-headed Cowbirds, Brewer's Blackbirds and Pine Siskins.

At the base of the eastern Sierran escarpment, in places like Lee Vining (6800'), Cassin's Finches sometimes meet the more desert-loving House Finch. Cassin's nest in cottonwoods and other large, shady trees, Houses in more open, shrubby habitats.

By mid-September, most Cassin's Finches have deserted the mountains. Most journey east across the Sierran crest into the Great Basin; on the west slope, they are exceedingly scarce in fall and winter. The majority probably winter in pinyon and pinyon-juniper woodlands east of the Sierran escarpment, though they also linger in other coniferous and hardwood habitats. In some winters, flocks are numerous in the Bodie Hills, the Glass Mountain region and, to a lesser extant, on the east slope of the Sierra; in others, they desert us entirely.

Winter record above 8500': 12/31/79 approx. 10,000' Hall Natural Area, 15 (DeSante MS).

Extreme dates above 8500' excluding winter record: 8600' Tuolumne Meadows 3/19/77 - 10/23/78 approx. 10,000' Hall Natural Area (DeSante MS).

Representative nesting localities: 4600' Ackerson Meadow (JW); 7000' Peregoy Meadow (GS 424); 7800' White Wolf (DG); 8600' Tuolumne Meadows (DG); 10,000' Hall Natural Area (D&F); 9000' near Mammoth Lakes (MVZ); 8600' near June Lake (C 40:9); 7400' Lee Vining Canyon (DG); 6800' Lee Vining (DG).

Additional references: D 201, YNN 10:32.

HOUSE FINCH (*Carpodacus mexicanus*)

	J	F	M	A	M	J	J	A	S	O	N	D	HABITAT	ELEVATIONS		
														N	T	W
WEST										•			SGB	2	F-5	
EAST			•										SGB	6	6-7	

Fairly common resident in Mariposa region (2000'); rare summer visitor below 5000' elsewhere on west slope; locally common summer visitor and fall transient below 8000' east of crest, uncommon summer visitor and fall transient to 9000' in Bodie Hills and extremely rare transient at higher elevations east of crest—nests near Mono Lake (6400'-6800').

House Finches nest in the Mariposa and Mono Lake regions, but, as far as I know, nowhere else in the region. These most desert-loving of finches range into treeless scrub and grasslands, but must have a source of water within their daily cruising radius.

At Mono Lake, House Finches nest in tufa groves as well as on the islands (GS 427, DW, DG). In mid-summer, their numbers are swelled by an influx of migrants. Flocks of hundreds roam the sagebrush in quest of seeds, materializing in pinyon woodlands and residential areas as well. On the north slopes of Bodie Mountain and Potato Peak, they climb to 9200' to feast on squaw currants (DG).

Records above 5000' west slope and 9200' east of crest: 7000' Peregoy Meadow 8/12/72 (AB 26:899); 9800' Hilton Lake 8/17/74 (AB 29:118); 10,300' Hall Natural Area 8/27/74 and 8/26/82 (DeSante and Engstrom MS; the report of eight and date of 8/24/74 published in AB 29:118 are incorrect).

Extreme dates west slope excluding Mariposa region, both Yosemite Valley (4000'): 5/12/43 (YM) - 10/10/31 (YM).

Extreme dates east of crest: 3/24/81 6400' Krakatoa Islet in Mono Lake (DW) - 11/8/79 6800' Lee Vining (DG); 11/29/81 Lee Vining (THa).

RED CROSSBILL (*Loxia curvirostra*)

	J	F	M	A	M	J	J	A	S	O	N	D	HABITAT	ELEVATIONS		
														N	T	W
WEST	▒	▒	▒	▒	▒	▒	▒	▒	▒	▒	▒	▒	POW	8-10		F-10
EAST	▒	▒	▒	▒	▒	▒	▒	▒	▒	▒	▒	▒	PW	8-10		6-10

Irregularly rare to fairly common year-round visitor from 3000' to treeline, apparently nesting only above 8000', and irregularly rare to fairly common winter resident below 3000' on west slope—most dependable at higher elevations; irregularly rare to fairly common resident below treeline east of crest.

Red Crossbills epitomize the enigmatic traits of the finch family. Their wanderings are as peculiar as their beaks. Flocks appear unpredictably, linger for days, weeks or months, then vanish. Nesting may occur at any time of year, including midwinter.

The key to loxian behavior is an appetite for pine nuts, particularly those of lodgepoles, but also whitebarks, jeffreys, ponderosas and pinyons. With their crossed mandibles, Red Crossbills pry apart the scales of closed cones, extracting the nuts with their tongues. This proteinaceous food not only nourishes adults, but nestlings as well. No other Sierran bird is so partial to a single source of sustenance.

But the pines are fickle. Some years cones are abundant, in others scarce or nonexistent. In lean times, Red Crossbills gypsy about the mountains in search of food, or forsake them entirely.

Red Crossbills breed when pine nuts are abundant, which may be almost any time of year. They may sometimes nest in midwinter, for they can use their crossed mandibles to harvest the nuts before warm weather opens the cones—an advantage over squirrels, nutcrackers and other competitors. At 10,000' in the Hall Natural Area, for example, they have been seen singing on New Year's Eve, and carrying nesting material in early March (AB 33:311, DeSante MS).

When food is scarce, Red Crossbills invade the lowlands, scrounging meals wherever they can. At such times, they are as apt to be seen in hardwoods as conifers. In the Mariposa region (2000'), for example, they sometimes winter in live and blue oak woodlands. East of the crest, they have appeared in cottonwoods at isolated ranches.

While they usually forage in trees, Red Crossbills also feed on the ground, searching cone and leaf litter for seeds. Like Pine Grosbeaks and Pine Siskins, they are attracted to mineralized water, as at Soda Springs in Tuolumne Meadows.

Additional representative nesting localities: 8100' Tenaya Lake (YNN 19:23); 8600' Tuolumne Meadows (YNN 19:60, C 50:44); 9000' Glass Mountain (DG).

Additional references: AFN 10:409, AB 26:903, GS 428; YNN 40:13.

Red Crossbill, courtesy of Discovering Sierra Birds.

PINE SISKIN (*Carduelis pinus*)

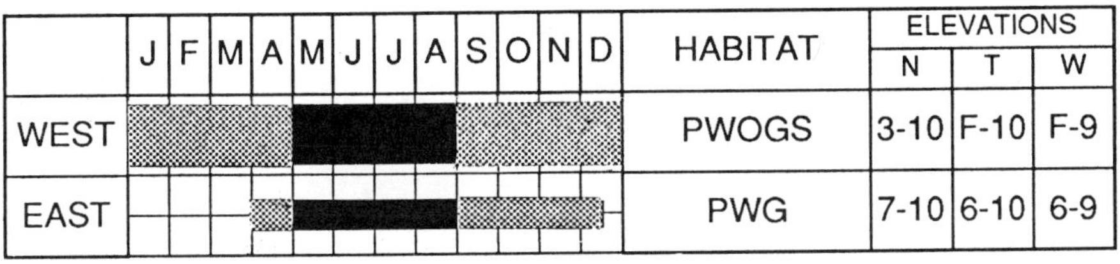

	J	F	M	A	M	J	J	A	S	O	N	D	HABITAT	ELEVATIONS		
														N	T	W
WEST													PWOGS	3-10	F-10	F-9
EAST													PWG	7-10	6-10	6-9

Irregularly rare to fairly common resident from 3000' to 7000', common summer resident and irregularly rare to fairly common winter resident to 9000', uncommon summer resident to treeline, rare summer visitor above treeline and irregularly rare to fairly common winter resident below 3000' on west slope; fairly common summer resident from 7000' to 9000', uncommon summer resident to treeline, rare summer visitor above treeline, irregularly rare to common transient below 7000' and rare winter visitor below 8000' east of crest.

Pine Siskins, like many of their family, are predictably unpredictable. Breeding as well as wintering populations vary in numbers and whereabouts from year to year.

True to their names, Pine Siskins usually nest in conifers. They breed from oak-conifer forests to treeline, consorting with every evergreen except digger pines, knobcone pines, pinyon pines and junipers. Nor are they restricted to conifers, dining in oaks, maples, aspens, cottonwoods, willows and other hardwoods as well. They also feed in meadows, clearings and on the forest floor, frequently scrounging at stables with Cassin's Finches, Brown-headed Cowbirds and Brewer's Blackbirds.

During fall and winter, Pine Siskins often trade coniferous forests for deciduous trees and thickets, meadows, grasslands, weedy fields and roadsides, scrub and chaparral, often associating with Lesser or American goldfinches in sizable flocks. East of the crest, they sometimes roam the sagebrush far from the nearest timber.

At higher elevations, Pine Siskins are particularly irregular in fall and winter. At Tuolumne Meadows (8600'), for example, they were "nearly as common as chickadees" during the dry 1976 winter, lacking entirely the year before (TH). The first heavy storms sometimes drive large flocks downslope. In some years, they desert the mountain entirely; numbers on the Yosemite Christmas Bird Count have varied from 192 to 0.

High elevation record: 12,000' Shepherd Crest 7/31/39 (YM).

Representative nesting localities: (4500' Alder Creek Trail—DG); (6200' Crane Flat—DG); (7800' White Wolf—DG); 8600' Tuolumne Meadows (GS 439); 10,000' Hall Natural Area (DeSante MS); 9000' near Mammoth Lakes (MVZ); 9000' Virginia Lakes (C 41:252); 8500' near June Lake (C 40:9); 7600' Dechambeau Creek (JB).

Additional references: C 41:252, D 184.

LESSER GOLDFINCH (*Carduelis psaltria*)

	J	F	M	A	M	J	J	A	S	O	N	D	HABITAT	ELEVATIONS		
														N	T	W
WEST													GOWS	F-5	F-10	F-3
EAST												•	GWS	6-7	6-10	

Fairly common summer resident and irregularly rare to fairly common winter resident below 3000', fairly common summer resident to 5000', irregularly rare to uncommon summer visitor to treeline and extremely rare winter visitor above 3000' on west slope; uncommon summer resident below 7500' and irregularly rare to uncommon summer visitor to treeline east of crest.

Though primarily foothill dwellers, Lesser Goldfinches nest to mid elevation in large meadows and open oak-conifer forests. They inhabit a variety of habitats with scattered trees or shrubbery, diverse herbaceous plant growth and streams, ponds, springs or other sources of fresh water within their daily cruising radius. While they nest and shelter in trees or shrubs, they forage on the ground and in herbaceous vegetation. At Ackerson Meadow (4600'), for example, flocks harvest seeds from grasses, composites and other meadow plants, concealing nests in adjacent shrubs and trees. They perch and sing from tall meadow vegetation, fences, rocks and trees.

Lesser Goldfinches also nest in live and blue oak woodlands, riparian woodlands, oak-conifer forests and other openly wooded habitats. During summer, small numbers follow spring upslope. Above the firs, they are irregular, reaching treeline in some years but not in others. In the southern Sierra, they have mountaineered to 12,000' (AB 35:977).

High elevation record: 10,300' Hall Natural Area, many records (DeSante MS).

Winter record at 4000': Yosemite Valley, 20, 2/26/75 (YM).

Extreme dates above 2500' west slope excluding winter record, all Yosemite Valley (4000'): 4/23/23 (YM) - 10/24/20 (YM); 11/28/72 (YM).

Extreme dates above 5000' west slope and above 8000' east of crest: 7/7/84 10,300' Hall Natural Area (DeSante MS) - 9/25/74 7000' Peregoy Meadow (AFN 9:54).

Extreme dates east of crest: 3/14/86 Lee Vining (DG) - 12/18-26/89 7200' Tom's Place (CH).

Representative nesting localities: 4000' Yosemite Valley (GS 437, EM 8); 4600' Ackerson Meadow (JW); 6800' Lee Vining (DG); 7500' O'Harrell Canyon (DG).

Additional references: AB 25:900, AB 26:899.

LAWRENCE'S GOLDFINCH (*Carduelis lawrencei*)

	J	F	M	A	M	J	J	A	S	O	N	D	HABITAT	ELEVATIONS		
														N	T	W
WEST													GOS	F-5		
EAST										•	•				6-7	

Irregularly rare to uncommon summer resident below 5000' and extremely rare visitor at higher elevations on west slope; extremely rare transient east of Sierran escarpment.

In dry meadows and open woodlands on the lower west slope, Lawrence's Goldfinches mingle with Lessers in similar habitats. At Ackerson Meadow (4600'), for example, I can discern no differences in the haunts of these cousins. The numbers of Lawrence's vary from year to year; they seem to be most numerous during droughts.

Records above 5000' on west slope: 6200' Crane Flat, 2, 8/16/75 (AB 30:124); 7000' McGurk Meadow 7/21/85 (AB 39:961).

Records east of crest: 6800' Lee Vining 10/13/84 (DG); 7200' Tom's Place 10/20/89 (AB 44:159); 6500' w. Mono Lake 11/8/81 (DG).

Extreme dates west slope: 5/11/80 4000' McCauley Ranch (YM) 10/1/86 4000' Yosemite Valley (YM).

Nesting locality: 4600' Ackerson Meadow (JW).

Additional references: AB 34:928; AB 38:957

AMERICAN GOLDFINCH (*Carduelis tristis*)

	J	F	M	A	M	J	J	A	S	O	N	D	HABITAT	ELEVATIONS		
														N	T	W
WEST		•											WG		F-5	
EAST													SW			6-7

Irregularly rare transient and summer visitor (0-2/year) and extremely rare winter visitor below 5000' and extremely rare summer visitor at higher elevations on west slope; fairly common fall transient, irregularly rare winter resident and extremely rare summer visitor below 7500' east of Sierran escarpment.

On the west slope, American Goldfinches are one of the scarcest birds. They favor willows, cottonwoods and other deciduous trees, but also dine in grasslands and meadows.

East of the crest, it's a different story. From mid-October through November, after summer birds have left, flocks of American Goldfinches materialize in sagebrush scrub and thickets of willow and buffalo-berry. On 11/29/85, for example, I tallied over 50 near the west shore of Mono Lake. They linger until driven south by snow, braving mild winters.

Winter record west slope: 2/10/65 4000' Yosemite Valley, "about" 30 (YM).

Record at 8600': Tuolumne Meadows 8/1/86 (MR).

Summer records east of crest: 6800' Lee Vining, adult male, 8/3/85 (DS); 6500' near Mono Lake 8/17/76 (DW).

Extreme dates west slope excluding winter record: 5/8/87 4600' Ackerson Meadow (JW) - 5/26/85 Ackerson Meadow (JW); 7/5/85 Ackerson Meadow (JW) - 10/16/81, 3, 4400' Foresta (JD).

Extreme dates east of crest excluding summer records: 9/10/84 Mono Lake (SJ) - 5/10/84 Mono Lake (DS).

Additional references: AB 34:199; AB 38:793.

EVENING GROSBEAK (*Coccothraustes vespertinus*)

	J	F	M	A	M	J	J	A	S	O	N	D	HABITAT	ELEVATIONS		
														N	T	W
WEST													OPWD	3-6	F-10	F-6
EAST													OPWD	7-8	6-10	6-8

Irregularly rare to common resident from 3000' to 6500', irregularly rare to uncommon visitor to 8500', irregularly rare summer visitor to treeline and irregularly rare to fairly common winter visitor below 3000' on west slope; irregularly rare to fairly common summer resident and irregularly rare to common transient or winter resident below 8500' and irregularly rare summer visitor to treeline east of crest.

Red Crossbills, Pine Grosbeaks, Evening Grosbeaks—they and their cousins are here one year, gone the next, presumably in response to food conditions, but who really knows? Of Evening Grosbeaks, James Dixon had this to say about their presence near June Lake (approx. 8000'): "If food conditions are right, they will stop and nest; usually from one to three pairs will be nesting in a small area...some years none will stop, and other years they will be quite common" (Bent 1968).

Evening Grosbeaks usually nest in forests with a diversity of trees, including oaks and other hardwoods as well as pines and firs. They forage on the ground as well as in the foliage, joining fellow finches in meadows and openings. I've seen them with Cassin's Finches, Pine Siskins, Brewer's Blackbirds and Brown-headed Cowbirds, for example, at the White Wolf stables (7800'), and with Lesser and Lawrence's goldfinches and Purple Finches in the McCauley Ranch corral (4000'). For some unfathomable reason, they are also attracted to potholed roads; I've seen them repeatedly, for example, on the road into Foresta (4400').

Outside the nesting season, flocks of Evening Grosbeaks materialize unpredictably wherever there are trees, both hardwoods and conifers. East of the crest, for example, they wander to groves of cottonwoods about remote ranches far from other trees. In Lee Vining (6800'), they appear in May to harvest samaras from non-native elms (DG). Their rambles are prompted, I suspect, by hungry bellies rather than migratory instincts.

While gregarious throughout the year, Evening Grosbeaks gather in especially large flocks in winter. On the west slope, for example, I tallied 300 or more wheeling in the firs above the snow-covered Crane Flat meadows (6200') on 12/24/73. East of the crest, flocks of up to 150 individuals spent the 1987 winter in jeffrey pine forests near Deadman Pass (8000'), where I had not seen any in the previous eight years.

Extreme dates above 8500' and high elevation records, all Hall Natural Area (to 10,300'): 5/3/81 - 7/23/81; 10/10/77 (DeSante MS).

Representative nesting localities: 4000' Yosemite Valley (EM 8, YM); 4600' Ackerson Meadow (DG); 6200' Crane Flat (DG); 7000'-9000' vicinity June Lake (C 36:35-36).

Additional references: AFN 7:35, AFN 7:234, AFN 11:58, AFN 18:533, GS 417, YNN 9:45, YNN 29:47.

Family PASSERIDAE: OLD WORLD SPARROWS

HOUSE SPARROW (*Passer domesticus*)

	J	F	M	A	M	J	J	A	S	O	N	D	HABITAT	ELEVATIONS		
														N	T	W
WEST													BD	F-4		F-4
EAST													BD	6-7		6-7

Introduced; locally common resident below 2500' and locally uncommon resident to 4000' on west slope; locally common resident below 7500' east of Sierran escarpment.

It's a shame to conclude our survey with these European exotics, but that's how the American Ornithologist's Union orders the list. Not that I don't admire the tenacity and hardiness of House Sparrows, which have followed our species into hot deserts as well as frigid mountains. In our region, they dwell about towns, farms, ranches and stables, usually nesting in holes and crannies in buildings. They scrounge seeds, crumbs and insects from streets, yards, gardens, stables, barnyards and outdoor restaurants. Occasionally they wander into other habitats, such as meadows and sagebrush scrub.

Representative nesting localities: 2000' Mariposa (CL); 2100' El Portal (SM); 4000' Yosemite Valley (AB 35:977); 6500' Bridgeport (DG); 6800' Lee Vining (DG); 7200' Silver Lake stables (DG); 7100' Hot Creek Fish Hatchery (DG).

HYPOTHETICALS

These species have been reported in the Yosemite Sierra, but without sufficient documentation.

YELLOW-BILLED LOON (*Gavia adamsii*)

A bird thought to be this species was on Grant Lake Reservoir (7100') on 12/8/76 (AB 31:367), but was rejected by the California Bird Records Committee.

WOOD STORK (*Mycteria americana*)

A Wood Stork was reported flying in a southwesterly direction over the canyon between Tenaya Lake and Olmstead Point (8200') on 6/13/77; "many people in group were excellent birders (Audubon Society trip) and had observed Wood Stork before...it was a positive identification" (YM). I've been unable to obtain further details. This species has been recorded in the Great Basin of Nevada and Utah (Ryser 1985), but not, to my knowledge, in the Sierra Nevada.

CALIFORNIA CONDOR (*Gymnogyps californianus*)

While there are no positive records, California Condors undoubtedly ranged into the region. On the west slope they have been seen 30 miles south at the San Joaquin Experimental Range as recently as 1950 (C 53:158). In the Tuolumne County foothills, they were last reported during the Gold Rush (Koford 1953); on the east slope, they were found in Owens Valley in 1893 (GM 95).

WILD TURKEY (*Meleagris gallopavo*)

The hunting fraternity has tried to introduce Wild Turkeys in many parts of California, including the western slope of the Sierra. Its current status in the region is uncertain, but it has been reported in recent years from Henness Ridge (5000'—YM) and Chinquapin (6000'—YM)

BLACK TURNSTONE (*Arenaria melanocephala*)

A Black Turnstone was reported on the Merced River between Merced Lake and Little Yosemite on 3/23/77, but there are no substantiating details (YM); at this elevation, this is an odd date for any shorebird.

WESTERN GULL (*Larus occidentalis*)

A Western Gull was reported on the west slope on Fletcher Lake on 7/29/36 (YNN 16:23). Though the description is convincing ("purplish pink feet, dark mantle almost like Black-backed Gull"), these maritime gulls virtually never stray inland. There are no other records from the Sierra Nevada.

RED-HEADED WOOPECKER (*Melanerpes erythrocephalus*)

For inexplicable reasons, Stebbins and Stebbins (1963) consider Red-headed Woodpeckers "infrequent" in Yosemite National Park. There is an undocumented report from the 1966 Yosemite Christmas Bird Count, but it—and other "Red-headeds"—were probably misidentified Red-breasted Sapsuckers.

THREE-TOED WOODPECKER (*Picoides tridactylus*)

Woodpeckers thought to be Three-toeds were observed near Tuolumne Meadows on 9/15/73 (YM) and in Cascade Valley (Fish Creek) on 7/16/80 (Bill Thompson); the latter is documented with a convincing description from an inexperienced observer. I would not expect so sedentary a species to wander so far from home, but almost anything is possible; the closest population dwells in the Cascade Mountains of southern Oregon.

KISKADEE FLYCATCHER (*Pitangus sulphuratus*)

I include this subtropical flycatcher because it is considered "infrequent" by Stebbins and Stebbins (1963). Why is anybody's guess.

GRAY JAY (*Perisoreus canadensis*)

Gray Jays have been reported near Wawona Point and at Tuolumne Meadows (YM), but without convincing details. Based on talking to the observer, I suspect the Tuolumne bird was a Northern Shrike. There are no positive records from the Sierra Nevada.

BLACK-CAPPED CHICKADEE (*Parus atricapillus*)

Black-capped Chickadees have been reported near Wawona and Tuolumne Meadows (YM), but are almost certainly misidentified Mountains. There are no positive records from the Sierra Nevada.

WOOD THRUSH (*Hylocichla mustelina*)

The distinctive song of a Wood Thrush was heard at the Mono Lake County Park on late May, 1976, but the bird could not be seen (RS).

PAINTED REDSTART (*Myioborus pictus*)

A Painted Redstart was reported in Yosemite Valley (4000') on 12/10/81, but without details (YM). Such a vivid bird, however, could scarcely be misidentified.

TRICOLORED BLACKBIRD (*Agelaius tricolor*)

A flock of 15 to 30 blackbirds believed to be Tricoloreds were "glimpsed" in Yosemite Vally in August, 1916 (C 20:11-19).

Afterward

"Bird and stream are inseperable, songful and wild, gentle and strong, the bird ever in danger in the midst of the stream's mad whirlpools, yet seemingly immortal. And so I might go on, writing words, words, words; but to what purpose? Go see him and love him, and through him as through a window look into nature's warm heart."

John Muir on the American Dipper, 1898

Literature Cited

Asay, Cristopher E. 1987. Habitat and productivity of Cooper's Hawks nesting in California. *Calif. Fish and Game* 73:80-87.

Asay, Christopher E. and William E. Davis. 1984. *Management of an endangered species in a national park: the Peregrine Falcon in Yosemite.* Cooperative National Park Research Studies Unit, Univ. Calif. Davis, Contribution #CPSU/UCD 019/6.

Bakker, Elna. 1971. *An Island Called California.* Univ. Calif. Press.

Beedy, Edward C. 1982. *Bird community structure in coniferous forests of Yosemite National Park, California.* Ph.D. thesis, Univ. Calif. Davis.

Beedy, Edward C. and Stephen L. Granholm. 1985. *Discovering Sierra Birds: Western Slope.* Yosemite Natural History Association and Sequoia Natural History Association.

Bellrose, Frank C. 1976. *Ducks, Geese and Swans of North America.* Stackpole Books.

Bent, Arthur C. 1948. *Life histories of North American nuthatches, wrens, thrashers and their allies.* Smithsonian Inst., U. S. Natl. Mus. Bull. 195.

Bent, Arthur C. and collabortors. 1968. *Life histories of North American cardinals, grosbeaks, buntings, towhees, finches, sparrows and allies, part one.* Smithsonian Inst., U. S. Natl. Mus. Bull. 237.

Chappell, Mark A., David L. Goldstein and David W. Winkler. 1984. Oxygen consumption, evaporative water loss and temperature regulation of California gull chicks in a desert rookery. *Physiol. Zool* 67:204-214.

Cooper, Scott D., David W. Winkler and Petra H. Lenz. 1984. The effect of grebe predation on a brine shrimp population. *Jour. Anim. Ecol.* 53:51-64.

Dawson, William Leon. 1923. *The birds of California.* South Moulton Co.

Denton, S. W. 1949. *Pages from a naturalist's diary.* V. Denton, ed. Alexander Printing Co., Boston, Mass.

DeSante, David F. MS. The subalpine and alpine avifauna of the central Sierra Nevada, with emphasis on the Hall Natural Area.

DeSante, David F. and F. Brett Engstrom. MS. Noteworthy bird records from the Hall Natural Area dn Tioga Pass region of the Sierra Nevada.

DeSante, David F. and Peter Pyle. 1986. *Distributional checklist of North American birds.* Artemisia Press.

Dixon, James B. 1936. Nesting of the Sierra Nevada Rosy Finch. *Condor* 38:3-8.

Emerson, W. O. 1893. Random bird notes from Merced Big Trees and Yosemite Valley. *Zoe* 4:176-182.

Gaines, David. 1974. A new look at the nesting riparian avifauna of the Sacramento Valley, California. *Western Birds* 5:61-80.

Gaines, David. 1977. *Birds of the Yosemite Sierra.* California Syllabus.

Gaines, David. 1981. *Mono Lake Guidebook.* Mono Lake Committee.

Garrett, Kimball and Jon Dunn. 1981. *Birds of Southern California: status and distribution.* Los Angeles Audubon Society.

Goldwasser, Sharon, David Gaines and Sanford R. Wilbur. 1980. The Least Bell's Vireo in California: a de facto endangered race. *Amer. Birds* 33:87-88.

Gould, Gordon I. 1974. Distribution of the Spotted Owl in California. *Western Birds* 8:131-146.

Granholm Stephen L. 1982. *Effects of surface fires on birds and their habitat associations in coniferous forests of the Sierra Nevada, California.* Ph.D. thesis, Univ. Calif. Davis.

Grinnell, J. 1911. Early summer birds in Yosemite Valley. *Sierra Club Bulletin* 8:118-124.

Grinnell, Joseph and Tracy I. Storer. 1921. Some birds of Yosemite National Park. In: Hall, Ansel F., *Handbook of Yosemite National Park*, G. P. Putnam's Sons, N.Y.

Grinnell, Joseph and Tracy I. Storer. 1924. *Animal life in the Yosemite.* Univ. Calif. Press.

Grinnell, Joseph and Alden H. Miller. 1944. *The Distribution of the Birds of California.* Cooper Ornith. Soc., Pacific Coast Avifauna 27.

Hejl, Sallie J. 1987. *Bird assemblages in true fir forests of the western Sierra Nevada.* Ph.D. thesis, N. Ariz. Univ.

Hoffmann, Ralph. 1927. Birds of the Pacific States. Houghton Mifflin Co., Boston.

Hurlbert, S. H., M. Lopez and J. O. Keith. 1984. Wilson's Phalarope in the Central Andes and its interaction with the Chilean Flamingo. *Rev. Chil. Hist. Nat.* 57:47-57.

Jehl, Joseph R. Jr. Biology of red-necked phalaropes at the western edge of the Great Basin in fall migration. *Great Basin Naturalist* 46:185-197.

Jehl, Joseph R. Jr., David E. Babb and Dennis M. Power. 1984. History of the California Gull colony at Mono Lake, California. *Colonial Waterbirds* 7:94-104.

Jehl, Joseph R. Jr. and Pamela K. Yochem. 1986. Movements of Eared Grebes indicated by banding recoveries. *J. Field Ornithol.* 57:208-212.

Jehl, Joseph R. Jr. 1985. Leucism in Eared Grebes in western North America. *Condor* 87:439-441.

Jehl, Daniel R. and Joseph R. Jehl Jr. 1981. A North American record of the Asiatic marbled murrelet (*Brachyramphus marmoratus perdix*). *American Birds* 35:911-912.

Johnson, Ned K. 1963. Biosystematics of sibling species of flycatchers in the Empidonax hammondii-oberholseri-wrightii complex. *Univ. Calif. Publ. Zool.* 66:423-238.

Johnson, Ned K. 1970. Fall migration and winter distribution of the Hammond Flycatcher. *Bird-Banding* 41:169-190.

Keeler, C. A. Bird life of Yosemite Park. *Sierra Club Bulletin* 6: 245-254.

Koford, Carl B. 1953. *The California Condor.* Dover Publications.

Linsdale, Jean M. 1932. Frequency of occurence of birds in Yosemite Valley, California. *Condor* 34:221-226.

Mahoney, Sheila A. and Joseph R. Jehl Jr. 1985. Avoidance of salt-loading by a diving bird at a hypersaline and alkaline lake: Eared Grebe. *Condor* 87:389-397.

Mahoney, Sheila A. and Joseph R. Jehl Jr. 1985. Adaptations of migratory shorebirds to highly saline and alkaline lakes: Wilson's Phalarope and American Avocet. *Condor* 87:520-527.

Mahoney, Sheila A. and Joseph R. Jehl Jr. 1985. Physiological ecology and salt loading of California Gulls at an alkaline, hypersaline lake. *Physiol. Zool.* 58:533-563.

Malliard, J. 1918. Early autumn birds in Yosemite Valley. *Condor* 20: 11-19.

Mayfield, H. 1965. The Brown-headed Cowbird with old and new hosts. *Living Bird* 9:13-28.

Michael, Charles and Enid. 1922. An adventure with a pair of Harlequin Ducks in Yosemite Valley. *Auk* 39:14-23.

Michael, Charles. 1927. Black Swifts nesting in Yosemite National Park. *Condor* 29: 89-97.

Michael, Enid. 1927. *A distributional list of Yosemite birds.* Yosemite Natural HIstory Association Bulletin No. 2

Miller, Jon. 1987. Breeding biology and nestling development of Rosy Finches and Water Pipits in the Sierra Nevada, California. Univ. Calif. Santa Cruz, Env. Field Program Publ. Natl. Hist.

Miller, Jon and Michael Green. MS. Distribution, status and origin of Water Pipits breeding in California.

Morton, Martin L., J. L. Horstmann and Janet M. Osborn. 1972. Reproductive cycle and nesting success of the Mountain White-crowned Sparrow in the central Sierra Nevada. *Condor* 74: 152-163.

Morton, Martin L. 1975. Adaptive strategies of *Zonotricia* breeding at high latitude or high altitude. *Proc. 16th Intern. Ornith. Congress.*

Muir, John. 1878. The humming-bird of California water-falls. *Scribner's Monthly* 15: 545-554. Reprinted in *Mountains of California.*

Muir, John. 1894. The Mountains of California.

Muir, John. 1898. Among the birds of Yosemite. *Atlantic Monthly* 82: 751-760. Reprinted in *Our National Parks*, 1901.

Munz, Philip A. and David D. Keck. 1970 *A California Flora.* Univ. Calif. Press.

National Geograhic Society. 1987. *Field Guide to North American Birds.*

Page, Gary W., Lynne E. Stenzel and Christine A. Ribic. 1985. Nest site selection and clutch predation in the snowy plover. *Auk* 102:347-353.

Page, Gary W., Lynne E. Stenzel, David W. Winkler and Christopher W. Swarth. 1983. Spacing out at Mono Lake: breeding success, nest density and predation in the snowy plover. *Auk* 100:13-24.

Page, Gary W. and Lynne E. Stenzel, eds. 1981. The breeding status of the snowy plover in California. *Western Birds* 12:1-40.

Patten, Duncan T., Chairman, Mono Basin Ecosystem Study Committee. 1987. The Mono Basin ecosystem: effects of changing lake level. National Academy Press.

Ryser, Fred A. Jr. *Birds of the Great Basin.* University of Nevada Press.

Rothstein, Stephen I., Jarred Verner and Ernest Stevens. 1980. Range expansion and diurnal changes in dispersion of the Brown-headed Cowbird in the Sierra Nevada. *Auk* 97: 253-267.

Rothstein, Stephen I., Jarred Verner and Ernest Stevens. 1984. Radio-tracking confirms a unique diurnal pattern of spatial occurrence in the parasitic Brown-headed Cowbird. *Ecology* 65: 77-88.

Schwan, T. G. and David W. Winkler. 1984. Ticks parasitizing humans and California Gulls at Mono Lake, California. In Griffiths, D. A. and C. E. Bowman, eds., *Acarology* VI, vol. 2, pp. 1193-1199. Ellis Horwood Ltd., Chichester, U.K.

Serena, Melody. 1982. The status and sitribution of the Willow Flycatcher in selected portions of the Sierra Nevada, 1982. *Calif. Dept. of Fish and Game Administrative Report* 82-5.

Shuford, David, Emilie Strauss and R. Hogan. 1984. Population size and breeding success of California Gulls at Mono Lake, California, in 1983. *Pt. Reyes Bird Observatory Contribution* 126.

Shuford, David, Paul Super and S. Johnston. 1985. Population size and breeding success of California Gulls at Mono Lake, California, in 1984. Pt. Reyes Bird Observatory Contribution 294.

Shuford, David. 1985. Reproductive succes and ecology of California Gulls at Mono Lake, California in 1985, with special reference to the Negit islets: an overview of three years of research. *Pt. Reyes Bird Observatory Contribution* 318.

Shuford, David. 1986. Population size and reproductive success of California Gulls at Mono Lake, California in 1986, with special reference to the Negit islets. *Point Reyes Bird Observatory Contribution* No. 347.

Stafford, Michael D. and Bradley E. Valentine. 1985. A preliminary report on the biology of the Willow Flycatcher in the central Sierra Nevada. Unpubl. report for Kings River Conservation District.

Stebbins, C. C. and R. C. Stebbins. 1963. *Birds of Yosemite National Park.* Yosemite Natural History Association.

Stine, Scott, David Gaines and Peter Vorster. 1981. Destruction of riparian habitat due to water diversions in the Mono Lake watershed. In: *California Riparian Ecosystems*, Univ. of Calif. Davis.

Storer, Robert W. and Joseph R. Jehl Jr. 1985. Moult patterns and moult migration in the Black-necked Grebe *Podiceps nigricollis.* Ornis Scandinavica 16:253-260.

Sumner, L. and John S. Dixon. 1953. *Birds and mammals of the Sierra Nevada.* University California Press.

Swarth, Christopher W. 1983. *Foraging ecology of snowy plovers and the distribution of their anthropod prey at Mono Lake, California.* Master's thesis, Calif. State Univ., Hayward.

Terres, John K. 1980. *The Audubon Society Encyclopedia of North American Birds.* Alfred A. Knopf.

Tomback, Diana F. 1978. Foraging strategies of the Clark's Nutcracker. *Living Bird* 16: 123-161.

Tomback, Diana F. 1982. Dispersal of whitebark pine seed by Clark's Nutcrackers: a mutualism hypothesis. *Jour. Animal Ecol.* 51.

Verner, Jarred and L. V. Ritter. 1983. Current status of the Brown-headed Cowbird in the Sierra National Forest. *Auk* 100: 355-368.

Widmann, O. 1904. Yosemite Valley birds. *Auk* 21: 66-73.

Winkler, David W. and W. David Shuford. 1988. Changes in the numbers and location of California Gull nesting at Mono Lake, California in the period 1863-1986. *Colonial Waterbirds*, in press.

Winkler, David W., Christine P. Weigen, Brett Engstrom and Eliot Burch. 1977. *An ecological study of Mono Lake, California.* Univ. Calif. Davis, Inst. of Ecol. Publ. No. 12.

Winkler, David W. 1983. *Ecological and behavioral determinants of clutch size: the California gull in the Great Basin.* Ph.D. dissertation, Univ. of Calif., Berkeley.

Winkler, David W. 1985. Factors determining a clutch size reduction in California Gulls: A multi-hypothesis approach. *Evolution* 39:667-677.

Weeden, Norman F. 1986. *A Sierra Nevada FLora.* Wilderness Press.

Winter, Jon. 1974. The distribution of the Flammulated Owl in California. *Western Birds* 5:25-44.

Index

Species accounts are boldfaced.